Essentials of Business Law

Fifth Edition

Joseph G. Bonnice, Ph.D.
Manhattan College
Riverdale, New York

Anthony L. Liuzzo, Ph.D., J.D.
Wilkes University
Wilkes-Barre, Pennsylvania

McGraw-Hill Glencoe

New York, New York   Columbus, Ohio   Chicago, Illinois   Peoria, Illinois   Woodland Hills, California

Photo Credits:
Michael Agllono/ImageState 433; Ed Brock/Corbis 359; Duomo/Corbis 451;
Walter Hodges/Corbis 397; Index Stock 177; Mary Kate Denny/PhotoEdit 151;
Rob Lewine/Corbisstockmarket 107; Rob Lewine/Corbisstockmarket 79, 333;
Dennis MacDonald/PhotoEdit 49; Jose L. Pelaez/Corbisstockmarket 1;
PhotoDisc/Getty Images 400; PhotoEdit 254, 285; Elke Selzle/Getty Images 295;
S. Shipman/Getty Images 205; V.C.L./Paul Viant/Getty Images 212;
David Young Wolff/PhotoEdit 300; David Young-Wolff/PhotoEdit 194

McGraw Hill Glencoe

The McGraw·Hill Companies

Copyright © 2003 by Glencoe/McGraw-Hill, a division of the McGraw-Hill Companies. All rights reserved. Except as permitted under the United States Copyright Act, no part of this publication may be reproduced or distributed in any form or by any means, or stored in a database or retrieval system, without prior written permission of the publisher, Glencoe/McGraw-Hill.

Printed in the United States of America.

Send all inquiries to:
Glencoe/McGraw-Hill
21600 Oxnard Street, Suite 500
Woodland Hills, California 91367

ISBN: 0-07-830505-5

2 3 4 5 6 7 8 9   DOW/DOW   09 8 7 6 5 4 3

Contents

Preface ... iv

PART I
Introduction to the Law ... 1

Chapter 1 Our System of Law ... 2
Chapter 2 Ethics and the Law ... 18
Chapter 3 Criminal Law ... 32
Chapter 4 Tort Law ... 46
Chapter 5 Administrative Law ... 64

PART II
Contracts ... 79

Chapter 6 Introduction to Contracts ... 80
Chapter 7 Offer, Acceptance, and Mutual Agreement ... 97
Chapter 8 Consideration ... 118
Chapter 9 Competent Parties ... 131
Chapter 10 Legal Purpose of Contracts ... 144
Chapter 11 Form of Contracts ... 159
Chapter 12 Operation of Contracts ... 173
Chapter 13 Discharge of Contracts ... 187

PART III
Sales, Agency, and Consumer Protection ... 205

Chapter 14 Transfer of Title ... 206
Chapter 15 Sales ... 223
Chapter 16 Agency and Employment ... 243
Chapter 17 Warranties and Product Liability ... 263
Chapter 18 Professional Responsibility ... 280

PART IV
Property ... 295

Chapter 19 Real and Personal Property ... 296
Chapter 20 Bailments ... 315
Chapter 21 Landlord-Tenant Relations ... 329
Chapter 22 Wills, Intestacy, and Trusts ... 344

PART V
Commercial Paper ... 359

Chapter 23 Introduction to Commercial Paper ... 360
Chapter 24 Transfer and Discharge of Commercial Paper ... 379

PART VI
Business and Technology ... 397

Chapter 25 Computer Privacy and Speech ... 398
Chapter 26 Conducting Business in Cyberspace ... 416

PART VII
International Business and the Environment ... 433

Chapter 27 International Business Law ... 434
Chapter 28 Business and the Environment ... 450

Glossary ... G-1
Index ... I-1

PREFACE

WELCOME TO *Essentials of Business Law*

The new, fifth edition of the *Essentials of Business Law* program is the most practical, most current, and only concise, broad-based introduction to the dynamic field of business law. It continues to offer you and your students all of the benefits that have made it such a popular book in the past. Traditional areas of law, such as contracts, as well as current and emerging areas, such as e-commerce, are covered in short, informative chapters written to capture the essence of each topic. The program has been developed not as a comprehensive study of the field, but as a basic overview of the concepts and principles that are essential to understanding business law.

THE STUDENT EDITION

The student edition of *Essentials of Business Law* retains all of the strengths of past editions, but has been revised and enhanced to cover the latest developments in the legal field. Students will discover a wealth of information and learning opportunities that will give them a clear understanding of business law topics. They will also be able to identify, explain, and apply the principles of business law in their daily lives and in the larger world in which they live.

New and Revised Content

The fifth edition of *Essentials of Business Law* includes newly revised and updated content that adds currency to the discussion in each chapter, and it ensures that your students are made aware of the latest developments in the law. The new edition also offers expanded coverage of current or emerging areas in the business law field, including e-commerce, environmental, and international law. As a result, *Essentials of Business Law* offers you and your students coverage of essential topics that many larger, more expensive book programs miss entirely.

New Presentation and Design

The fifth edition includes many new and exciting features that add interest and relevance to the study of business law.

- A ***direct and lucid style,*** and an ***organized presentation,*** make the text easy to use and understand.
- An abundance of ***detailed examples*** illustrate the law at work in realistic scenarios.
- A ***new, attractive design*** sparks visual interest in legal topics, and makes using the book and learning business law easier than ever.
- ***New illustrations*** elucidate difficult legal concepts. Captions ask students questions that help develop important critical thinking skills.

New Learning and Assessment Tools

The program's expanded pedagogy, with its emphasis on ease of use and assessment, offers you and your students a wealth of opportunities for learning, studying, and assessing progress throughout the course.

- ***Legal Terms*** are listed at the beginning of each chapter, as well as in the margins where they occur in the text. Students' understanding of the legal terms is tested in the Matching Legal Terms exercises in the Chapter Assessments.
- ***Performance Objectives*** are identified at the beginning of each chapter and in the margins where they are satisfied in the text. Each performance objective also has a corresponding answer or explanation in the Chapter Summary.
- ***Chapter Summaries*** highlight the key legal concepts in each chapter. You can use these features to summarize a classroom lesson, while students can use them to study and prepare for exams.
- ***Chapter Assessments*** include a wide array of assessment tools. Matching legal terms, true/false quizzes, discussion questions, critical thinking exercises, case questions and

analyses, and legal research are all covered in each chapter assessment.

- ***New case studies,*** both in the chapters and chapter assessments, provide a real-world context in which students can recognize, analyze, and apply the principles of law.
- ***Ethics*** have been integrated into the text. Ethical questions (and dilemmas) are presented in a way that requires students to consider whether a law is just or unjust, and to think about how the law affects the ways people live and do business with each other.
- ***Teamwork activities*** foster a sense of camaraderie, remind students that business is in essence a social enterprise, and encourage students to work together to solve problems.
- ***Technology-based exercises*** familiarize students with technology resources like the Internet and asks them to use technology as a way of researching and solving problems.
- ***Writing exercises*** help develop students' communication skills and are involved throughout the Chapter Assessments.

THE INSTRUCTOR MANUAL AND KEY

The *Instructor Manual and Key* has been significantly expanded to include a variety of teaching tools that make it simple for you to organize your classroom discussions, effectively communicate the important business law concepts in each chapter, and assess your students' grasp of the material.

New, Easy-to-Use Teaching Aids

Each chapter in the new *Instructor Manual and Key* offers an abundance of features that will help you to successfully teach a course using *Essentials of Business Law.* These teaching aids allow you to quickly and easily prepare your lesson plans and ensure that your presentations cover all of the important topics in each chapter.

Legal Terms and Performance Objectives

The Legal Terms and Performance Objectives from the student edition are included in the *Instructor Manual and Key.* You can use them to focus on the key terms and concepts in each chapter and to ensure that your students can demonstrate all of the skills required by the objectives.

Lecture Outlines Organized in a clear, concise structure, the Lecture Outlines map the presentation of every chapter. You can use these outlines to prepare your lesson plans, organize class discussion, and ensure that you cover each chapter's most important topics.

Teaching Tips The *Instructor Manual and Key* contains several tips that offer helpful, creative suggestions for teaching the important legal concepts in each chapter of the book. The teaching tips also indicate how you might best use the Transparency Masters and other components of the *Essentials of Business Law* program.

New, Enriched Assessment Opportunities

The new *Instructor Manual and Key* includes an array of tools to help you prepare your students for exams and to assess and challenge their understanding of the course material.

Chapter Assessment Answers The *Instructor Manual and Key* includes answers to all of the Chapter Assessments in the student edition. You can use these answers to measure your students' success in completing the Chapter Assessments. Students can also use these answers to study and to prepare for exams.

Chapter Tests Easy-to-use, two-page exams, and corresponding key, are provided so that you can assess your students' understanding of each chapter in the book. These tests assess students' grasp of key legal terms and principles; their critical thinking skills; and their ability to analyze real and hypothetical cases, identify the laws involved, and render a decision. Short-answer and essay questions are also included to develop and assess students' writing abilities.

Internet Activities The *Instructor Manual and Key* includes an Internet exercise for every chapter in the student edition. You can assign these activities to develop your students' understanding of technology and the law, and to encourage them to use technology, such as the Internet, to research and solve legal problems.

MULTIMEDIA RESOURCES

The new *Essentials of Business Law* program includes two multimedia resources: PageOut®, which you can use to build and manage online courses, and Transparency Masters, which you can use to create illustrative material to enhance important legal ideas in the textbook.

PageOut Distance Learning Tool

PageOut is McGraw-Hill's custom course Web site development tool. With PageOut, you can

- build online courses, for which your students can self-register
- easily add your own content
- post announcements
- upload files
- create quizzes
- build a syllabus
- host discussions
- maintain a grade book

You can learn more about PageOut by visiting the PageOut Web site at www.pageout.net.

The *Essentials of Business Law* PageOut template is available for customized use from the McGraw-Hill PageOut library of templates. To access the *Essentials of Business Law* template or create your own course Web site with PageOut, you need a connection to the Internet, and a login and password for registration. You can obtain the login and password for the PageOut site from your publisher's representative.

Transparency Masters

The new *Essentials of Business Law* program includes several Transparency Masters, located in the *Instructor Manual and Key*. Formal contracts, bills of sale, promissory notes, and check indorsements are some of the business law topics represented by the Transparency Masters. These masters can be used as visual enhancements during classroom presentations, end-of-part reviews, or as handouts to help students to learn or study. Suggestions about how and where each master can best be used in the program are provided in the Teaching Tips in the *Instructor Manual and Key*.

ACKNOWLEDGEMENTS

We would like to thank the reviewers who have contributed their time and ideas to the development of the fifth edition. Our sincere appreciation to the following:

Betty Alexander
Coordinator of Business and
Computer Programs
Tidewater Tech
Norfolk, Virginia

Leon Bean, J.D.
Law Instructor
International Business College
El Paso, Texas
University of Phoenix
Santa Teresa, New Mexico

Nancy Feather, J.D.
Instructor
Pittsburgh Technical Institute
Oakdale, Pennsylvania

Jan Johnson
Evening Education Supervisor
Career College of
Northern Nevada
Reno, Nevada

Kim Rugon
Business Instructor
LTC-Sidney N. Collier
Technical College
New Orleans, Louisiana

Jessie Schwartz
Director / Dean / Instructor
Drake Business School
Staten Island, New York

Debra K. Wicks, Ph.D., J.D.
Instructor
ICM School of Business
Pittsburgh, Pennsylvania

Our authors would also like to extend special thanks to the following: Gloria Frey, educator, creative writer, and editor, contributed her enormous talents to making this edition a significant improvement over previous editions. Ann Marie Feldmeth typed, edited and reviewed all of the text material, helping to make the transition from the fourth edition to the fifth edition a seamless one.

PART I

INTRODUCTION TO THE LAW

CHAPTER 1	Our System of Law
CHAPTER 2	Ethics and the Law
CHAPTER 3	Criminal Law
CHAPTER 4	Tort Law
CHAPTER 5	Administrative Law

CHAPTER 1

OUR SYSTEM OF LAW

PERFORMANCE OBJECTIVES

After studying this chapter and completing the assessments, you will be able to:

1. Provide an example of how law affects (a) your personal or social life, and (b) business or business operations.

2. Identify the principle origins of law in the United States.

3. Identify the sources of law in our legal system.

4. Cite and describe the major classifications of law.

5. Distinguish moral obligations from legal obligations.

6. Describe the structure of our federal and state court systems.

7. Distinguish between trial courts and appellate courts.

LEGAL TERMS

plaintiff
defendant
express powers
implied powers
judicial review
stare decisis
common law
precedent
case law
statutory law
ordinance
administrative law
Uniform Commercial Code (UCC)
jurisdiction

THE LAW IN OUR WORLD

When students in their twenties were asked to say the first thing that came to mind when they heard the word *law,* responses included "cops and robbers," "courtroom," "narcs," "drug raid," "legislators," "speed limit," and "traffic violation." Without doubt, the impressions that most people have of the law are influenced, not so much by actual experience, but by the way the law is portrayed on television and in movies. Sometimes the picture is distorted. Justice always seems to triumph, the "good guys" usually win, and the "bad guys" are ultimately caught and punished. It's a view that society wishes were true.

Unfortunately, movies and television programs provide the only picture many people get of the law. In real life, the administration of justice can be a lot less exciting than is often portrayed. There are areas of the law that do not hinge on clear-cut "right" or "wrong" answers, but on an ill-defined middle ground. Still, justice and law are hallmarks of a free society in today's world.

The fact of the matter is that our system of law functions largely outside the spotlight of public attention. Every business day, in every city, town, and community in this country, courts are in session, juries are being selected, and attorneys are busy seeking favorable decisions for their clients, who might be either a *plaintiff* (someone who brings suit against another) or a *defendant* (someone against whom a suit is brought or who is charged with a violation of the law).

Although the ordinary applications of law are not quite as exciting as a television drama, it is important to understand certain essential legal principles because they affect both your business and your personal life. No one person can possibly know the entire body of law. Even learned judges and lawyers tend to specialize in certain fields of law. The average person should, however, strive to understand some of the general principles of law, how to avoid common problems and pitfalls, and when to seek professional help.

The law presented in this text deals primarily with the general principles of law and their applications to business. Some chapters focus on personal applications of the law, however, and others treat ethical aspects of personal and business behavior.

plaintiff The party who begins a lawsuit by filing a complaint in the appropriate court.

defendant The party against whom a lawsuit is brought and from whom recovery is sought.

APPLICATIONS OF LAW

The effects of law are felt throughout society. Indeed, some aspects of the law apply to all persons, institutions, and organizations.

OBJECTIVE 1(a)

Provide an example of how law affects your personal or social life.

Personal Applications of Law

Imagine, for a moment, how the law affects just one day in your life. The alarm clock that awakens you in the morning is set to a time that is regulated by a law establishing standard time zones. Various federal and state laws regulate the purity and wholesomeness of your breakfast foods. The clothing you wear is labeled in compliance with governmental regulations. Your right to drive a car is regulated by state laws, and speed limits and other traffic laws are often the responsibility of state or local officials. You know that no one else may occupy your home while you are away at school or work because the law protects your property rights. The safety and freedom you enjoy are possible because you live in a nation of order—and that order is a result of laws passed for the benefit of the people and the protection of their rights.

OBJECTIVE 1(b)

Provide an example of how law affects business or business operations.

Business Applications of Law

Every business must comply with many federal, state, and local laws that are primarily aimed at regulating business activity. A firm that wishes to establish a business in a particular community may find that there are laws that prohibit such activities. For example, local zoning ordinances might prohibit the operation of a noisy factory in a residential area. State and federal laws prohibit or regulate the operation of certain businesses that may pollute the environment. Still other laws require that businesses provide safe working conditions for employees or demand that only qualified persons perform certain jobs. State laws, for instance, require that barbers and pharmacists pass examinations or be licensed.

Government Applications of Law

Legislatures at all levels of government pass many laws that apply only to businesses and individuals, but some laws apply specifically to governments. For example, the federal government may pass a law that provides funding for building highways or for low-income housing. The same law may require that states, counties, or municipalities maintain them.

ORIGINS OF LAW

OBJECTIVE 2

Identify the principle origins of law in the United States.

The ever-changing body of law that affects all persons in our country has arisen from a number of sources. As a result, laws sometimes conflict with one another. The ways in which these conflicts are resolved will be discussed in this chapter.

Constitutional Law

In our country, the principles and ideals that protect individual liberty and freedom are incorporated in the Constitution of the United States (the federal Constitution). This historic document gives the federal government certain reasonable powers, and at the same time, clearly limits the use of those powers. In addition, each state has a constitution of its own that gives certain powers to the various levels of government within that state. Like the federal Constitution, state constitutions provide safeguards for the rights of individuals within that particular state.

Constitutional Powers In the United States, the federal Constitution and state constitutions confer two types of powers on the governments of which they are a part:

- *Express powers* are powers that are specifically stated. For example, the federal Constitution grants the federal government the explicit power to raise an army and to assess taxes.
- *Implied powers* are powers that have arisen as a result of an interpretation of the express powers by the courts. For example, the U.S. Constitution gives Congress the implied power to create an agency to explore outer space—something not even imagined by the people who wrote the federal Constitution.

Constitutional Amendments Although the drafters of the federal Constitution were men of vision, they could not, of course, foresee the changing needs of our country and its people in the years that were to follow. The Constitution has been amended or changed 26 times, and it will probably continue to be amended. Each Constitutional amendment must be proposed by a two-thirds vote of Congress and ratified or approved by the legislatures of three-fourths of our 50 states.

Judicial Review Courts have the power to determine whether laws enacted by legislatures or decisions made by lower courts violate the provisions of the Constitution. If a court decides that a law is contrary to the Constitution, the law can be declared unconstitutional and, therefore, invalid. The process of deciding whether a law is contrary to the Constitution is known as *judicial review.*

Common Law

After the Revolutionary War, one of the most difficult tasks faced by our newly independent nation was to establish a system of law. Because the original states were formerly English colonies, it is not

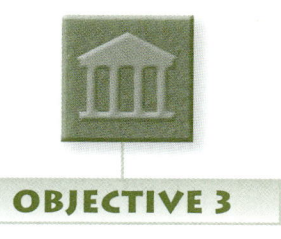

OBJECTIVE 3

Identify the sources of law in our legal system.

express powers Powers that are explicitly stated; for example, in the U.S. Constitution.

implied powers Powers that arise as a result of an interpretation of the express powers by the courts.

judicial review The process by which a court determines the constitutionality of various legislative statutes, administrative regulations, and executive actions.

Our System of Law   CHAPTER 1

surprising that the new states adopted the system of laws that had been used in England for hundreds of years—that is, relying on previous legal decisions when similar disputes arose. This practice of relying on previous decisions is known as *stare decisis,* which means, "to stand on decided cases." The English system is known as the *common law* and still influences legal decisions in the United States today.

stare decisis The practice of relying on previous decisions in which similar disputes arose.

common law The body of recorded decisions that courts refer to and rely upon when making later legal decisions.

precedent A model case that a court can follow when facing a similar situation.

Precedent

A *precedent* is a court decision on which later courts rely in similar cases. In some instances, a court may be influenced by precedent; in other cases, it may not. Whether a court follows a precedent depends on the court that has ruled on the case and whether the previous case was decided by the highest court in the same state. Decisions made by the U.S. Supreme Court, for example, must be followed by other courts.

Court decisions are recorded in writing so that lawyers and judges can refer to them in preparing or hearing a case. These decisions are published in books called reporters. Each case decision is identified by a citation, which includes the names of the parties involved followed by the volume number, the name of the reporter, and the beginning page number of the case. For example, in the case of *Milkovich v. News-Herald,* 473 N.E.2d 1191, the case is reported in volume 473 of the *Northeastern Reporter, Second Series,* and begins on page 1191.

Case Law

Sometimes a statute or a common law precedent may be difficult to apply to certain cases, or as time passes, may take on different meaning. An existing statute or an accepted precedent may be based on outmoded standards of justice. In these cases, a court may disregard earlier interpretations of a statute or a principle of common law, or it may interpret them differently. The court's decisions in these cases influence later cases because they also become precedents that may be followed in similar cases. The effects of these decisions have been called *case law.*

case law The effects of court decisions that involve the same or similar facts.

Statutory Law

Both federal and state constitutions are general statements of the powers of governments and the rights of individuals. The specific applications of powers and rights are provided for in laws enacted by federal, state, and local governments. Each state constitution provides for a legislature that represents the people and that has the power to enact laws so long as they do not conflict with either the federal or the state constitution. The laws passed by Congress and by state legislatures are called statutes, and the field of law that deals with these statutes is known as *statutory law.* A law that is passed by a local government, such as city councils, is often called an *ordinance.*

Not only do statutes provide the specific applications of the powers and rights in the constitutions, they also allow governments to respond to particular circumstances. For example, when the federal and state constitutions were written, television was not even a dream, much less a matter to be regulated. Yet shortly after television was developed, various state legislatures passed statutes that prohibited the installation of television receivers in the front-seat area of automobiles.

statutory law The field of law involving statutes, which are laws passed by Congress or by state legislatures.

ordinance A law that is passed by a local government, such as a city council.

Administrative Law

Protection of the rights and freedom of individuals and organizations is well established by the federal Constitution and the state constitutions, by statutory law, and by common law. Still, today's complex society and system of justice present special needs that require laws that include their own administrative machinery. Sometimes when a federal, state, or local legislative body enacts a law, it sets up an organization to establish rules and to enforce them. *Administrative law* is the body of rules, regulations, and decisions created by administrative agencies.

administrative law The body of rules, regulations, and decisions created by administrative agencies.

The practice of establishing specialized administrative agencies has several advantages. For example, it relieves the police and the courts from having to establish and enforce regulations that are often highly technical. Administrative agencies include federal agencies such as the National Labor Relations Board, state agencies such as public service commissions, and local agencies such as boards of health. These agencies have in common the authority to establish rules that have the force of law and to maintain "courts" that are often called appeal boards. The "trials" are often called hearings. Because administrative law has become such an important part of our legal system, an entire chapter will be devoted to covering this topic.

UNIFORM COMMERCIAL CODE

When the United States was primarily a farming nation and there was relatively little commerce between states, it did not matter that the state constitutions and statutes differed from state to state. As interstate trade increased, however, so did the problems caused by the conflict in business laws among the different states. For example, a business person knowing the laws of his or her state had little difficulty

Uniform Commercial Code (UCC) A set of laws that govern various commercial transactions that is designed to bring uniformity to the laws of the states.

so long as customers were all from the same state. But when business was conducted with customers in many states, she or he had to know the laws in all of them.

To solve this problem, the **Uniform Commercial Code (UCC)** was prepared in 1952 by the National Conference of Commissioners on Uniform State Laws. The UCC is a set of laws governing various commercial transactions that is designed to bring uniformity to the laws of the states. Over a period of 15 years, 49 states have adopted the UCC as part of their state law. Not every state has adopted the entire UCC, and state courts often have differing interpretations of their UCC sections. Louisiana, having been a French territory and therefore greatly influenced by French civil law, has adopted only parts of the Code. Because the UCC is so widely accepted, this book is based on it.

Classification of Laws

OBJECTIVE 4

Cite and describe the major classifications of law.

The various laws, regardless of origin, can be grouped into several broad classifications, each of which represents a legal specialty. Frequently a lawyer will specialize in one of these areas.

- *Constitutional law* is the study of the federal Constitution, its interpretation by the federal courts, and its relationship to existing laws.
- *Civil law* is the study of the rights and obligations of individuals and includes the law of property, the law of contracts, and the law of torts.
- *Criminal law* is concerned with acts against society (criminal acts) and the regulation of criminal activity.
- *Administrative law* is concerned with the conduct of governmental administrative agencies and their regulations. Examples are tax laws and laws dealing with transportation and trade.
- *International Law* is concerned with the conduct of nations in their relations with other nations.

Moral Law

OBJECTIVE 5

Distinguish moral obligations from legal obligations.

Since earliest times, people have recognized that they are to a certain extent responsible for one another and have obligations to one another beyond those required by the law. For example, a person who sees someone drowning has a moral obligation to try to save him or her, and a person who hears someone screaming for help in the night has a moral duty to at least call the police. Such obligations are based on moral law—that is, the "law" concerned with the unenforceable obligations that people have to one another. Many legal obligations are based on moral obligations, but not all moral obligations are legally enforceable; a person's conscience is often the only means of enforcement.

THE OPERATION OF OUR SYSTEM OF LAW

Some of our laws came from sources that were not originally concerned with human freedom. However, most legal scholars feel that today's laws provide adequate protection of the rights of the individual. But the mere existence of laws is not enough. There must be a means of administering the law to protect the rights of individuals and businesses and to curtail the activities of wrongdoers. In this country, courts and governmental agencies have been established to administer the law.

A SYSTEM OF COURTS

The federal and state constitutions and the entire body of written law would be of little value to individuals and businesses if there were no provision for enforcing the law. Police alone cannot fulfill this function. The federal and state constitutions provide for the establishment of a system of courts that ensures citizens' rights and enforces federal and state statutes.

Court Jurisdiction

The authority of a court, as granted by a constitution or legislative act, is known as the court's *jurisdiction.* A court may be limited in its powers to certain kinds of cases or to certain geographical areas. A court has original jurisdiction if it is authorized to hear and decide a case when it is first presented. If a court has the power to review the decisions of another court, it has appellate jurisdiction (that is, the authority to hear appeals).

Courts that are given the power to hear only certain kinds of cases have special jurisdiction. Examples are family courts, traffic courts, and tax courts.

jurisdiction The authority of a court, as granted by a constitution or legislative act, to hear and decide cases.

Federal Courts

The U.S. Constitution provides for a federal court system: "The judicial power of the United States, shall be vested in one Supreme Court, and in such inferior courts as the Congress may from time to time ordain and establish."

OBJECTIVE 6

Describe the structure of our federal and state court systems.

The court system that has developed has various levels. The U.S. Supreme Court in the United States is the highest court in the federal system. It serves as the court of original jurisdiction for certain kinds of cases, such as those in which a state is one of the parties. The Supreme Court rules on the constitutionality of laws by hearing selected cases that test those laws. The Supreme Court also hears appeals from the highest state courts. However, the court actually hears only a small percentage of appeals because it has no legal obligation to review decisions of lower courts, except in very limited cases.

The federal district courts have original jurisdiction in cases involving federal statutes, and in cases in which the parties are citizens of different states and the amount involved is greater than $75,000. Every state has at least one federal district court.

Most appeals from the district courts go to one of the 13 circuit courts of appeals. The decisions of the circuit courts are usually final, although further appeal to the U.S. Supreme Court is possible. Appeals of the decisions of federal administrative agencies, such as the Federal Trade Commission (FTC), are also made to the U.S. Circuit Courts of Appeals.

The federal court system also includes specialized courts that hear only certain kinds of cases. Two of these specialized courts are the U.S. Tax Court and the U.S. Claims Court.

State Courts

State court systems vary, but there are certain basic similarities in all state court systems. All states have general trial courts, which are courts of original jurisdiction that are authorized to hear cases not otherwise restricted to specialized courts. General trial courts handle nearly every important dispute involving contracts, criminal law, and cor- porations. Trial courts in a state may be large municipal courts, with such specialized areas of jurisdiction as traffic violations, juvenile conduct, and domestic relations, or they may be small justice-of-the-peace courts called magistrate courts, established to hear certain minor violations of law.

If one of the parties in a case feels that he or she did not have a fair trial in the court of original jurisdiction, he or she can, with the aid of an attorney, seek an appeal in a state appellate court, which hears appeals from the trial courts. The names of appellate courts vary in different states. Beyond the courts of appeals are higher-level courts, often called supreme courts, which make final determinations on

OBJECTIVE 7

Distinguish between trial courts and appellate courts.

matters of law. In some less populous states, which have no intermediate court of appeals, the state supreme court also serves as a court of appeals.

Many communities have special courts to handle small or minor cases. Where these courts exist, there is usually a limit, ranging from $1,000 to $15,000, on the amount of the claim. Because there is a limit on the amount of money that can be involved, these courts are often called small claims courts. The proceedings are typically informal, and the parties involved are usually allowed to appear without lawyers to represent them.

CHAPTER SUMMARY

1. Examples of how the law affects a person's personal and social life can be seen everywhere from the foods eaten, the medicines used, the goods purchased, to the clothing worn. Examples of how the law affects business can be seen in zoning ordinances, regulation of environmental pollution, and licensing laws.

2. The origins of law in the United States are the Constitution, common law, statutory law, and administrative law.

3. The various sources of U.S. law include the common law of England, which embodies the concept of *stare decisis,* case law, statutory law, and administrative law.

4. Law in the United States is typically classified as constitutional law, civil law, criminal law, administrative law, and international law.

5. Moral law is concerned with the unenforceable obligations that people have to one another; legal obligations are those required by enacted statutes and other laws.

6. The structure of the federal and state court systems includes courts of original jurisdiction (federal district courts and state courts) and appeals courts (federal circuit courts of appeals, the U.S. Supreme Court, and state appellate courts).

7. Trial courts are courts of original jurisdiction. Appellate courts allow a party, with the aid of an attorney, to have the application of law to their case reconsidered by a higher court.

Chapter 1 Assessment

MATCHING LEGAL TERMS

Match each of the following definitions with the correct term in the list below. Write the letter of your choice in the answer column.

- a. administrative law
- b. appellate court
- c. civil law
- d. common law
- e. criminal law
- f. defendants
- g. express powers
- h. implied powers
- i. original jurisdiction
- j. plaintiffs
- k. precedents
- l. statutory law
- m. *stare decisis*
- n. trial court
- o. Uniform Commercial Code (UCC)

1. Governmental powers that are specifically stated in a constitution. **1.** g
2. The portion of the law based on the decisions of the old English courts. **2.** d
3. A judicial body that has original jurisdiction in cases involving state law. **3.** N
4. Court decisions that later courts tend to follow. **4.** K
5. Those who bring suit against others. **5.** J
6. A judicial body empowered by law to review the findings of a lower judicial body. **6.** B
7. The practice of a court to follow previous decisions. **7.** M
8. The category of law concerned with acts against society. **8.** E
9. The authorization of a judicial body to hear certain types of cases when they are first brought to court. **9.** I
10. The legal specialty concerned with the rights and obligations of individuals. **10.** C
11. A group of laws dealing with business transactions in a consistent manner that has been adopted by most of the states. **11.** O
12. The legal specialty concerned with the relationship between businesses or individuals and government agencies. **12.** A
13. The branch of the law concerned with the laws passed by Congress and by state legislatures. **13.** L
14. Governmental powers that the courts have found in constitutions through interpretation and inference. **14.** H
15. Those against whom a suit is brought or who are charged with a violation of the law. **15.** F

Chapter 1 Assessment

MULTIPLE-CHOICE QUIZ

Select the answer that best completes each of the following statements. Write the letter of your choice in the answer column.

16. In the United States, the principles and ideals guarding our individual liberty and freedom are presented in **(a)** judicial decisions; **(b)** the U.S. Constitution; **(c)** the common law.   16. B

17. Amendments to the federal Constitution require approval, or ratification, by **(a)** three-fourths of the states; **(b)** a general election; **(c)** a majority vote by Congress.   17. A

18. The power of a court to determine whether laws enacted by legislatures or decisions made by lower courts violate the constitution is **(a)** judicial skepticism; **(b)** constitutional review; **(c)** judicial review.   18. C

19. Statutes are laws passed by **(a)** state and federal legislatures; **(b)** the Supreme Court; **(c)** old English courts.   19. A

20. Laws enacted by local governments, such as a city council, are often called **(a)** statutes; **(b)** ordinances; **(c)** declarations.   20. B

21. The kind of law that results when a court disregards an existing statute, an accepted precedent, or a principle of common law, or interprets them differently, with the result that a new precedent is established, is known as **(a)** precedent law; **(b)** law of court review; **(c)** case law.   21. C

22. The purpose of the Uniform Commercial Code is to provide **(a)** uniform laws for all states to regulate business transactions in all states; **(b)** regulations to be followed in the sale of uniforms; **(c)** laws to regulate international business transactions.   22. A

23. Unenforceable obligations that people have to one another are considered to be an aspect of **(a)** moral law; **(b)** the law merchant; **(c)** the law of unenforceable promises.   23. A

24. The authority of a court, as granted by a constitution or legislative act, is known as the court's **(a)** mandate; **(b)** jurisdiction; **(c)** territory.   24. B

25. If a court has the power to review the decisions of another court, it has **(a)** appellate jurisdiction; **(b)** original jurisdiction; **(c)** overrule authority.   25. A

26. Juvenile courts, the U.S. Tax Court, and domestic relations courts are known as **(a)** specialized courts; **(b)** justice courts; **(c)** courts of original jurisdiction.   26. A

27. The court that has original jurisdiction in cases involving federal statutes, and in cases when the parties are citizens of different states, is known as **(a)** federal district court; **(b)** circuit court of appeals; **(c)** U.S. Supreme Court.   27. A

28. Normally appeals from federal district courts are initially heard by **(a)** the U.S. Supreme Court; **(b)** circuit courts of appeals; **(c)** state supreme courts.   28. B

Chapter 1 Assessment

29. Special courts set up to handle small or minor cases, often with a limit on the amount of the claim, are known as **(a)** circuit courts; **(b)** district courts; **(c)** small claims courts.

29. C

30. State courts that have original jurisdiction for cases not otherwise directed to a specialized court are **(a)** trial courts; **(b)** circuit courts of appeals; **(c)** district courts.

30. A

DISCUSSION QUESTIONS

Answer the following questions and discuss them in class.

31. Explain how law affects **(a)** your personal or social life, and **(b)** business or business operations.

32. Identify the principle origins of law in the United States.

33. Cite and describe the major classifications of law.

34. Can common law and statutory law operate side by side? What are the advantages of each?

Chapter 1 Assessment

THINKING CRITICALLY ABOUT THE LAW

Answer the following questions, which require you to think critically about the legal principles that you learned in this chapter.

35. Business Applications of Law Consider the numerous laws that affect businesses and evaluate the regulatory climate in which they operate. Does it seem that there are too many regulations, or too few? Explain your answer.

_____
_____
_____

36. Government Regulation of Governments Various levels of government enact laws that affect other levels of government. Explain the reason for such seemingly inefficient interrelationships and offer an opinion of whether there might be other ways to achieve the same objectives.

_____
_____
_____

37. *Stare Decisis* The legal concept of *stare decisis,* which means "to stand on decided cases," is an important factor in our system of law. Is it possible that previous cases, or precedents, do not always embody the exact same issues, concepts, and present day circumstances as the current case to which the earlier one is applied and by which the current one is judged? What would you suggest as an alternative to the use of precedents?

_____
_____
_____

38. A Question of Ethics Normally, there are no prosecutions for "padding" an expense account, yet it is considered unethical. Should such activity be prosecuted more forcefully? Why or why not?

_____
_____
_____

CASE QUESTIONS

Study each of the following cases. Then answer the questions that follow by writing *Yes* or *No* in the answer column.

39. Precedent Ferguson was arrested for possession of marijuana in a state where it was illegal. He argued at his trial that the highest court in a neighboring state had ruled a similar law invalid, which would be a binding precedent.

    a. Is Ferguson correct in his belief?   **a.** _____

Chapter 1 Assessment

    b. Can a state's highest court rule a state law invalid?   **b.** _____

    c. Does a precedent in one state affect the law in another?   **c.** _____

40. Jurisdiction A television station broadcast insulting remarks about a local official. The official had the broadcaster charged under a state statute that prohibited making defamatory remarks on public airwaves. The broadcaster argued that the statute was in conflict with the Constitution's guaranty of free speech. The public official countered that the statute was legal and enforceable.

    a. Can states enact laws that limit free speech?   **a.** _____

    b. Can defamatory remarks be made illegal?   **b.** _____

    c. Can a state statute be in conflict with the U.S. Constitution?   **c.** _____

41. Jurisdiction Phipps became involved in a case of mistaken identity. A local merchant falsely accused him, in front of people who knew him, of shoplifting. Phipps was charged but not convicted. Angry and embarrassed, yet not wanting to spend money for an attorney, he acted as his own attorney and sued the merchant for false arrest in small claims court.

    a. Can Phipps act as his own attorney?   **a.** _____

    b. Does small claims court have jurisdiction in this case?   **b.** _____

    c. Is there a dollar limit on the kind of case that can be brought to small claims court?   **c.** _____

CASE ANALYSIS

Study each of the following cases carefully. Then briefly state the principle of law and your decision.

42. Interpretation of Statute Muscarello illegally sold marijuana, which he transported in a small truck. Police discovered a handgun in the locked glove compartment of the truck. A provision in the firearms chapter of the federal law demands a five-year required prison term for persons who use or carry a firearm during or related to trafficking in drugs. Muscarello claimed that because the gun was in the locked glove compartment of the truck it did not fall within the description of the word *carries* as used in the statute and that he was not subject to the required five-year prison term. *Did Muscarello violate the firearms chapter of the criminal code?* [*Muscarello v. United States,* 118 S.Ct. 1911 (U.S. Sup. Ct. 1998).]

Principle of law:

_____

_____

Decision:

_____

_____

Chapter 1 Assessment

43. Contract Essentials Evelyn and Joseph Carabetta had been married in a religious ceremony, although they failed to obtain a marriage license, and thereafter lived together as husband and wife. They raised four children, all of whose birth certificates listed Joseph Carabetta as their father. At no time did either party ever deny that they were married. In an action to dissolve the marriage, Evelyn Carabetta claimed that the lack of a marriage license made the marriage void. *Does the lack of a marriage license make the marriage void?* [*Carabetta v. Carabetta,* 438 A.2d 109 (Connecticut).]

Principle of law:

Decision:

LEGAL RESEARCH

Complete the following activities. Then share your findings with the class.

44. Working in Teams In teams of three or four, interview the owners or managers of small businesses to determine the levels of laws—federal, state, or local—to which the firm is subject. Further, ask the interviewee to provide examples.

45. Using Technology Using the Internet and search engines, investigate the operation of small claims courts in your community or one nearby. Determine the kinds of cases typically heard and the limit in dollars involved in cases that these courts are authorized to hear.

CHAPTER 2

ETHICS AND THE LAW

PERFORMANCE OBJECTIVES

After studying this chapter and completing the assessments, you will be able to:

1. Distinguish among ethics, morals, and values.
2. Cite several influences on group and individual values.
3. Discuss the similarities and differences between law and ethics.
4. Provide examples of responses to the growing awareness of ethics by business firms, educational institutions, governments, and trade and professional associations.
5. Provide reasons for social actions taken by corporations.
6. Discuss corporate codes of ethics.
7. Explain "whistleblowing."

LEGAL TERMS

ethics
morals
values
culture
subculture
code of ethics
whistleblower

ETHICS IN OUR WORLD

It is difficult to read a daily newspaper or watch TV without seeing some reference to ethics—or the lack of them. Such accounts may refer to the latest government purchasing scandal, the wrongful use of insider information for personal gain, or a violation of consumers' interests and rights.

EXAMPLE 2.1

> In 2002, top executives of a multi-million dollar energy company, Enron Corp., and its outside accounting firm, Arthur Andersen LLP, were alleged to have engaged in unethical and illegal behavior involving questionable accounting practices, fraud, deception, insider trading, and attempting to influence politicians, and the media. According to widespread media coverage, executives who knew the firm was headed for bankruptcy were quietly selling their shares of stock while encouraging employees to hold and even buy additional shares. Employees' investments in Enron's plummeting stock suffered enormous losses, as did their pension funds similarly invested. It was charged that such financial skullduggery could only have happened with the complicity of Enron's outside accounting firm.

The fact that the Enron and Arthur Andersen case dominated the media and resulted in numerous congressional investigations showed the widespread concern with ethical behavior in business. Examples could also be found in other professions and in government. In addition, entirely new applications and demands for ethical behavior continue to surface. Environmental ethics, for example, is a growing field as citizens voice their concerns about the pollution of our natural habitat by businesses. Demands for additional government regulation are frequently heard.

The development of technology has introduced a burgeoning array of ethical questions. Advances in genetics, cloning technologies, and the use of stem cells in medical science, for example, have raised ethical dilemmas unheard of even a decade earlier. Ethical issues involving Internet and computer technology have also prompted people to consider ethical issues such as privacy and free speech on the Internet.

The development of global markets has also presented today's business professionals with ethical predicaments, as they have to cope with different ethical standards in other countries and cultures. Is it ethical for an American company to do business with a company in an undemocratic country? If an American firm wants to operate a chain of

OBJECTIVE 1

Distinguish among ethics, morals, and values.

ethics The philosophical study of what is right and wrong, good and bad.

morals Beliefs about behavior as judged by society.

values Beliefs or standards considered worthwhile, and from which a society derives its moral rules.

OBJECTIVE 2

Cite several influences on group and individual values.

culture The set of shared attitudes, values, goals, and practices that characterize a social, racial, religious, or corporate group.

subculture An ethnic, economic, regional, religious, or social group with attitudes or behavior that distinguish it from others within a larger culture.

stores in Saudi Arabia, should it offer the same kinds of consumer protection to Saudi consumers as it does to American consumers? These kinds of ethical issues are essential to business law.

It is evident then, that we need to reexamine our ethics and to clarify the distinction between what is ethical versus what is legal.

WHAT IS ETHICS

Both ethics and morals are concerned with standards of right and wrong. *Ethics* is a philosophical approach to examining what is right and wrong, good and bad. *Morals* are concerned with behavior as it's judged by society. Ethical theories and moral standards are derived from *values*—that is, beliefs or standards considered worthwhile. Clearly, all are important to creating a just and orderly society.

SOURCES OF GROUP AND INDIVIDUAL VALUES

There are group values and individual values, both influenced by religions, traditions, and customs. An individual's values are significantly influenced by the values held by the groups to which he or she belongs.

There are numerous influences on the development of group and individual values. Of utmost importance are the values held by a *culture*—those of a nation or an ethnic group. The American culture, for example, holds that such characteristics as freedom, individualism, family life, fair play, hard work, and honesty are important.

On the other hand, the values held by a *subculture* (for example, employees of a corporation, or a department within a company) may differ from those of the larger culture.

THE RELATIONSHIPS BETWEEN LAW AND ETHICS

Legal mandates are imposed on individuals or groups by authorities or governments. Ethical considerations, on the other hand, generally spring from within individuals or organizations. However, ethical ideas have been the foundation of much of the legislation enacted by federal, state, and local governments. Consider the role of ethics in the laws that protect consumers against misleading advertising, deceptive labeling, and price fixing. These laws are clearly based on ethical considerations. Court decisions, too, are frequently influenced by ethics as judges and juries examine the facts of a case and form beliefs about the parties and issues involved.

A distinction between law and ethics is that legal mandates are usually more precise. The law requires individuals and organizations to behave in specified ways, requiring or prohibiting certain acts. Ethical issues may be multifaceted.

> **EXAMPLE 2.2**
>
> The Burger Bonanza fast-food chain was faced with the legal requirement of paying its employees a specified minimum wage. It could have simply fulfilled that requirement. However, the management decided, based on ethical considerations, to increase the pay of their workers beyond the mandated wage, feeling the required minimum was inadequate. While this decision might be commendable from an ethical standpoint, however, it could involve several other ethical issues as well—the cost of the extra pay might result in higher prices for consumers or reduced earnings for shareholders.

OBJECTIVE 3

Discuss the similarities and differences between law and ethics.

Responses to Ethical Issues

The growing awareness of the importance of ethics is evident in the responses of businesses, educational institutions, governments, and trade and professional associations.

Responses of Business Firms

There is increasing concern about ethics in the business world. Some of this concern is undoubtedly the result of enlightened self-interest, as when corporate executives say that ethical practices are simply good business. For example, by voluntarily paying their workers more than the legally required minimum wage, Burger Bonanza may also attract scarce workers in a tight labor market. Executives may also be interested in ethical practices because of the favorable publicity it gives to their firm. Corporations may also be concerned with the possible legal consequences of unethical behavior. Businesses concerned with ethics usually focus on their corporate responsibility and the development of codes of conduct.

OBJECTIVE 4

Provide examples of responses to the growing awareness of ethics by business firms, educational institutions, governments, and trade and professional associations.

Corporate Responsibility The actions of corporations that are intended to demonstrate their wish to behave responsibly take many forms and are conducted under the banner of corporate responsibility. In some cases, the corporation will "adopt" a nearby school and provide equipment and expert personnel to teach particular skills. In other cases, the firm might construct a park, donate funds to the local symphony orchestra, or provide scholarships to a university. In some instances, these actions are little more than thinly veiled public

OBJECTIVE 5

Provide reasons for social actions taken by corporations.

Ethics and the Law   CHAPTER 2   21

relations efforts to enhance the image of the corporation. In other cases, corporate actions reflect a moral and ethical concern with social problems and a sincere effort to improve society.

Critics of corporate social action, however, question whether it is appropriate to commit corporate resources to socially desirable goals. It might be better, they suggest, to maximize earnings for shareholders, who could then use the higher earnings to advance society if they so desire. It is interesting to note that in many states, charitable contributions by corporations are legal, while political contributions are not.

Codes of Ethics Despite a few glaring lapses, many companies today understand the need to maintain ethical standards in their dealings with customers, suppliers, and employees. Some firms or industries establish a ***code of ethics,*** sometimes called a "credo," which establishes the principles of ethical behavior expected of its personnel in various situations. For example, a firm or industry may place a dollar limit on the value of gifts that may be accepted from suppliers doing business with the firm. A code makes clear that the company expects its personnel to recognize the ethical dimensions of corporate policies and actions.

code of ethics A set of rules that a company or other group adopts to express principles of ethical behavior that are expected of its personnel.

OBJECTIVE 6

Discuss corporate codes of ethics.

> **EXAMPLE 2.3**
>
> Johnson & Johnson was confronted with a crisis when people in the Chicago area began dying of cyanide poisoning after taking the firm's Tylenol® capsules. Although no connection between the poison and Tylenol was established, Johnson & Johnson recalled the product at great cost. James Burke, Chairman, said that the established ethics credo was invaluable during this crisis because everyone in the firm knew what the standard of ethics required of them, and allowed personnel at various levels to make the necessary decisions quickly.

While the areas covered in ethical codes vary from one firm or industry to another, a general list of topics typically covered includes the following:

- fundamental honesty and adherence to the law
- product safety and quality
- health and safety in the workplace
- possible conflicts of interest
- employment practices
- fairness in selling and marketing practices
- financial reporting
- supplier relationships
- pricing, billing, and contracting

- trading in securities and using insider information
- payments to obtain business

Responses of Educational Institutions

Educational institutions have responded to the increased need to examine ethics by adding courses, workshops, and programs. They have also expanded the study of ethics in existing courses. Typically topics include fairness in hiring, employment, and promotions; ethical issues in multinational business; ethical issues arising from technology; economic justice; and environmental ethics and ecology.

Responses of Governments

Governments endeavor to protect consumers and the environment, and to influence the ethical behavior of business firms in various ways. For example, governments enact legislation to ensure fair labor practices and to enforce existing statutes. The Federal Sentencing Guidelines, for example, provide an inducement for corporations to act more ethically. Legislators reasoned that if firms integrate ethics into their corporate structure, employees will be less likely to break the law for the company's benefit, and that companies that have taken positive steps to integrate ethics should not be penalized as harshly as those that have not. The Guidelines are a response to the public's desire to hold companies to a higher standard and to impose on white-collar criminals heavier penalties than previously imposed.

Even the operation of government itself is monitored and regulated. The U.S. Office of Government Ethics, for example, is concerned with the following topics: conflicting financial interests, misuse of position, financial disclosure, impartiality in performing official duties, and other areas of concern. On an international level, federal and state governments require that U.S. firms perform ethically in global markets. For example, the Foreign Corrupt Practices Act prohibits American firms from bribing foreign officials. In addition, diplomatic activities aim to protect American firms from corrupt practices in other countries (see Chapter 28).

Responses of Trade and Professional Associations

Trade associations develop guidelines for ethical business practices for their diverse memberships. For example, The Direct Marketing Association (DMA) provides self-regulatory standards of conduct for some of the following activities: telephone marketing, sweepstakes, fund raising, marketing to children, and collecting and marketing data.

WAYS TO ENSURE ETHICAL PRACTICES

Despite the efforts of the aforementioned groups—businesses, governments, and trade and professional associations—unethical practices persist. Such behavior frequently results in unfavorable public relations, loss of consumer good will, and poor employee morale. Legal prosecution and penalties may not correct all unethical practices. Sometimes the driving force for reform may be the individual whistleblower.

Whistleblowing

Our language has a number of derogatory words to describe people who disclose information about wrongdoing. Terms such as "stool pigeon," "stoolie," "fink," "informer," "rat," and "tattle-tale" suggest that our society does not regard such behavior highly. But in spite of society's disdain for informers, certain individuals have been so outraged by what they consider unethical behavior that they have risked widespread condemnation and loss of their jobs to reveal information about the activity. These people are usually termed "whistleblowers."

Typically, a ***whistleblower*** is a person who reveals to a government authority, to the media, or to upper-management confidential information concerning corporate conduct that he or she believes is illegal or unethical. The information may have come to him or her in the course of employment or in other ways. Authorities may respond by prosecuting the company. The media may also publicize the wrongdoing, which can be equally damaging to a firm.

The whistleblower, too, may be confronted with an ethical dilemma. Often the choice is between revealing information—resulting in adverse effects to the firm and that may cause many coworkers to lose their jobs—or remaining silent.

It is not surprising that retaliation is frequently the result of speaking out. The whistleblower is often regarded as an outcast to the organization or to peers. The federal government and many states have statutes that protect whistleblowers from retaliation. Still, with the possible exception of certain individuals who may have a personal grudge, the usual motivation behind whistleblowing is the outrage to a person's sense of ethics.

Integrating Ethics into Business and Government

In the abstract, there is agreement that business should be conducted in ways that will not harm the consumer or the environment. What is the most effective way to achieve this result? A corporation may

---

OBJECTIVE 7

Explain "whistleblowing."

whistleblower An employee that discloses to the government, media, or upper-management that the company is involved in wrongful or illegal activities.

indeed adhere to the highest ethical practices, but a new CEO or board of directors may discontinue those practices if profits suffer or for other reasons. Further government regulation could ensure compliance with ethical standards, but such an arrangement might require a costly and oppressive bureaucracy. The ideal method is for responsible individuals and watchdog groups to encourage corporations and governments to accept mutually agreeable ethical practices.

CHAPTER SUMMARY

1. Ethics is a philosophical approach, examining theories of what is good or bad. Morals are concerned with behavior as judged by society. Values are beliefs or standards considered worthwhile.

2. Individual and group values are influenced by religion, tradition, and customs.

3. Legal mandates are imposed on individuals or groups by authorities or governments. In contrast, ethical considerations generally spring from within individuals or organizations. However, ethical beliefs are the foundation of many of our laws.

4. Business firms respond to ethical concerns by acts of corporate responsibility and by creating codes of ethics. Educational institutions offer courses and workshops. Governments try to protect consumers and the environment and to ensure ethical behavior of business firms, and of the government itself. Trade and professional associations develop guidelines for their members.

5. Corporate actions such as sponsoring a park may show ethical concern and responsible behavior. It may also be effective public relations.

6. Corporate codes of ethics vary from one firm or industry to another. Topics typically include: fundamental honesty, financial integrity, employment practices, and product safety.

7. Whistleblowing is the exposing of an unethical situation to an authority or to the media.

Chapter 2 Assessment

MATCHING LEGAL TERMS

Match each of the following definitions with the correct term in the list below. Write the letter of your choice in the answer column.

- **a.** code of ethics
- **b.** culture
- **c.** ethics
- **d.** morals
- **e.** subculture
- **f.** values
- **g.** whistleblower

1. A philosophical approach to examining what is good or bad.
2. An examination of what is good or bad concerned with behavior as judged by society.
3. The beliefs or standards considered worthwhile by an orderly society.
4. The sum total of all the learned beliefs, values, and customs that serve to regulate the behavior of members of a particular society.
5. A smaller group within a culture.
6. A document that sets down a firm's principles of the ethical behavior expected of its employees.
7. A person who reveals confidential information concerning some wrongdoing or unethical behavior.

1. _____
2. _____
3. _____
4. _____
5. _____
6. _____
7. _____

TRUE/FALSE QUIZ

Indicate whether each of the following statements is true or false by writing *T* or *F* in the answer column.

8. Unethical behavior has not been a problem in society until recent times.
9. Generally, what is unethical is also illegal.
10. The term *values* relates to the price of merchandise on sale.
11. Personal values can vary from one individual to another.
12. People tend to behave in accordance with accepted principles of what is right and wrong that govern the conduct of their group and that reflect the values of the group.
13. Public disclosure of a firm's unethical practices can affect other companies as well.
14. A whistleblower is one who calls attention to illegal or unethical behavior.
15. A corporate code of ethics might be called a set of guidelines for the ethical behavior expected of employees.
16. *Corporate culture* is the expression used to describe the values and standards of acceptable behavior in a corporation.

8. _____
9. _____
10. _____
11. _____
12. _____
13. _____
14. _____
15. _____
16. _____

26   PART 1   Introduction to the Law

Chapter 2 Assessment

17. The corporate culture may either foster or discourage moral action on the part of its management and workers.

17. _____

18. "Moral standards" includes theories holding that a society has certain common, objective, consistent standards that forbid certain behavior as wrong and hold that other behavior is right.

18. _____

? DISCUSSION QUESTIONS

Answer the following questions and discuss them in class.

19. Describe the motivation behind the behavior of the executives and personnel at the Enron and Andersen companies described in the text.

20. Identify some typical issues for people who are ethically concerned with the environment.

21. Discuss and provide examples of values that are highly regarded in our society.

22. Suggest several unfavorable consequences facing a business firm that consistently engages in unethical practices.

23. Discuss the relationship between ethics and the law.

24. Discuss several responses by businesses to ethical issues.

Ethics and the Law   CHAPTER 2   27

Chapter 2 Assessment

THINKING CRITICALLY ABOUT THE LAW

Answer the following questions, which require you to think critically about the legal principles that you learned in this chapter.

25. **Whistleblowing** A person who blows the whistle on some unethical practice in a firm, is often treated as an outcast by his or her coworkers. Why does this occur? Does this mean that the coworkers are less ethical?

26. **Codes of Ethics** A number of firms accused of unethical behavior has established codes of ethics or "credos" and formal employee orientation programs. It might seem that these efforts had little influence on the practices of the firm. Critique the practice of establishing codes of ethics and suggest ways that their use could be made more effective.

27. **Corporate Responsibility** Critics of corporate social action question whether it is appropriate to commit corporate resources to socially desirable goals. It might be better, they suggest, to maximize earnings for shareholders, who could then use the higher earnings to advance society if they so desire. Critique the arguments of those who advocate direct corporate action to achieve social goals versus the views of those who oppose such action.

28. **Responses of Governments to Ethical Issues** Analyze and critique some current activities of government relating to ethics in business.

29. **A Question of Ethics** The corporate culture exerts a major influence on the ethical behavior of every employee and executive in the firm. Since it is recognized that management largely determines the corporate culture, recommend steps management might take to establish a culture that will instill reasonable standards of ethical behavior for everyone in the firm.

Chapter 2 Assessment

CASE QUESTIONS

Study each case below and answer the questions that follow by writing *Yes* or *No* in the answer column.

30. Whistleblowing Dilemma Ayer, an engineer with product development responsibilities, was confronted with an ethical dilemma. He knew that a product being manufactured by the firm was unsafe for consumer use as a result of cost cutting. He also believed that if he complained to management or to a government body concerned with product safety, he would probably be fired.

    a. If Ayer did nothing, would he still be making an ethical decision?   **a.** _____

    b. If Ayer did nothing because he was concerned that if he complained and manufacturing was suspended, many workers would lose their jobs, would he be making an ethical decision?   **b.** _____

    c. Ayer considered blowing the whistle on the firm by releasing information to the newspapers and television networks. Is it likely that such action would have any effect on the firm or on Ayer?   **c.** _____

31. Illegal Activity Perkins intended to sell his two-year-old car through an advertisement in the local newspaper. Since the car had more than 80,000 miles on it, Perkins reasoned that a buyer would be more willing to buy it if he turned back the odometer to 30,000 miles. The car still looked quite new, and Perkins needed the money the sale would bring.

    a. Would turning back the odometer be an ethical action?   **a.** _____

    b. If Perkins did not turn back the odometer and the car could not be sold for as high a price, and if his family suffered as a result, would Perkins be justified in turning back the odometer to benefit his family?   **b.** _____

32. Ethical Decisions Lackowitz, a college student, was concerned about a final examination. During previous examinations in the same course, he had seen other students cheat and get good grades. If he failed the course, he would have to repeat it and pay the additional tuition. Also, if he had to repeat the course, his graduation would be delayed one semester, as would his entry into the full-time job market. The financial considerations were of great concern to him.

    a. Would Lackowitz be justified in cheating on the examination?   **a.** _____

    b. Could a decision by Lackowitz to inform the instructor about the cheating that he had seen on previous examinations represent an ethical decision?   **b.** _____

Chapter 2 Assessment

CASE ANALYSIS

Study each of the following cases carefully and then briefly state the principles of law and your decision.

33. Deception In March 1977, Joe Siwek took his new Oldsmobile Delta 88 to his dealer for minor repairs. While the car was in the dealer's repair shop, the dealer informed Siwek that the car was equipped with a Chevrolet engine. The standard engine for a 1977 Oldsmobile Delta 88 was a 231-cubic-inch V-6 manufactured by the Buick division of General Motors. Before the introduction of the 1977 models, the manufacturer determined that there would not be enough engines built to equip all the Oldsmobile Delta 88's manufactured. For this reason, it was decided to install Chevrolet engines in some Oldsmobile cars without disclosing the practice to the buyers. Siwek complained to the Illinois attorney general, who filed a class-action suit against General Motors charging that it deceived consumers by not informing them of the engine switch.

Principle of law:

_____

_____

Decision:

_____

_____

34. Ethical Responsibility Greenway Markets expected to remodel three stores. They intended to install new checkout counters that would read the Universal Product Code (UPC) on each item of merchandise by using a laser-beam reader connected to a computer. While there were a number of advantages to the new system, a major cost saving would be in eliminating the need to put price stickers on each item of merchandise. The management of the market was concerned that it would be a hardship for consumers to have to wait until checkout time to find out how much each item cost. One manager pointed out that the price was already on the shelf near the merchandise, and that it was costly to provide the price on the merchandise as well. Someone else pointed out that the shelf price tags were often inaccurate, and that the firm had an ethical responsibility to help the buyer make the best purchasing decisions.

Principle of law:

_____

_____

Decision:

_____

_____

35. Ethical Violation Stotts was employed as a technician in the engineering department of Raytron Corporation. All the engineers on staff were required to sign agreements that they would not accept employment with another company in the industry within three years of leaving Raytron. Technicians, who had limited access to company secrets, were not required to sign such agreements. After working at Raytron for about two years, Stotts realized that he was deeply involved in development and had access to the same data as the engineers

PART 1 Introduction to the Law

Chapter 2 Assessment

did. Stotts actively sought a position with Raytron's primary competitor, and was hired by Watani Engineering. Because he did not have an engineering degree, he assumed that he had been hired because of his knowledge of Raytron's trade secrets. Did Stotts violate legal or ethical dictates?

Principle of law:

_____
_____

Decision:

_____
_____

LEGAL RESEARCH

Complete the following activities. Then share your findings with the class.

36. Working in Teams One of the important functions of corporate executives is to develop and implement ethical policies for their companies. In groups of four or five, imagine that you are the executives of a major corporation charged with developing a corporate code of ethics. What are some of the issues you would want to address? Create a list and share them with the class.

_____
_____
_____
_____
_____
_____
_____
_____

37. Using Technology Using the Internet and search engines, find news about businesses that are currently facing actual or potential charges of ethical indiscretions. Record your findings and share them with the class.

_____
_____
_____
_____
_____
_____
_____
_____

CHAPTER 3

CRIMINAL LAW

PERFORMANCE OBJECTIVES

After studying this chapter and completing the assessments, you will be able to:

1. Distinguish between crimes and torts.
2. Identify the three major classifications of crimes.
3. Discuss several common crimes of particular concern to businesses and employees.
4. Explain what is meant by the expression *white-collar crime*.

LEGAL TERMS

crime
tort
treason
felony
misdemeanor
arson
larceny
bribery
false pretenses
forgery
perjury
embezzlement
extortion

CRIME

The law assures each person certain rights and assigns each person certain duties. As you recall from Chapter 1, the law enforcement authorities of federal, state, and local governments enforce specific laws, called statutes, that are designed to protect the public at large. A violation of a specific statute is a ***crime.*** A private wrong that causes injury to another person's physical well-being, property, or reputation is called a ***tort.***

It is important to note that a certain action can be both a crime and a tort. For example, a person who operates an automobile recklessly or negligently and causes injury to another, or damages his or her property, has committed both the crime of reckless driving and the tort of negligence. The reckless driver can be prosecuted by the appropriate law enforcement authorities for the crime and can also be sued for the tort in a civil court by the person whose property was damaged or who was injured. Chapter 4 is devoted to torts and how they may relate to both your personal and business life.

While statutory law determines what is and what is not a crime, many statutes reflect legal principles derived from common law. What makes a particular act, or failure to act, a crime? Why is a certain act, or failure to act, a crime in one state and not in another? Why is a certain act, or failure to act, a crime one day and not the next? These questions can all be answered by one statement: An act, or failure to act, is a crime because the governing statutes say it is. Of course, a high degree of uniformity has emerged among the states, so it is uncommon for a particular act being legal in one state and illegal in another. Also, legislatures try to reflect the public interest and enact legislation that makes an act a crime if there is sufficient demand.

In other instances, also reflecting changing public sentiments, legislatures and courts may decide that a particular act previously considered a crime should no longer be viewed as a violation of the law. For example, laws concerning abortion, homosexuality, and drug abuse have been modified considerably in recent years. Similarly, a legislature may repeal legislation, thereby making an act legal when it previously had been a crime.

OBJECTIVE 1

Distinguish between crimes and torts.

crime An offense against the public at large punishable by the official governing body of a nation or state.

tort A private wrong that injures another person's physical well-being, property, or reputation.

OBJECTIVE 2

Identify the three major classifications of crimes.

treason The levying of war against the United States, or the giving of aid and comfort to the nation's enemies.

felony A crime punishable by death or by imprisonment in a federal or state prison for a term exceeding one year.

misdemeanor A less serious crime that is generally punishable by a prison sentence of not more than one year.

CLASSIFICATION OF CRIMES

Crimes are classified into the following three groups according to the seriousness of the offense:

- Treason
- Felonies
- Misdemeanors

Federal law and the laws of the states determine the classification and largely specify the punishment.

Treason

Treason is a major crime defined by the U.S. Constitution as follows: "Treason against the United States shall consist only in levying War against them, or in adhering to their Enemies, giving them Aid and Comfort."

Felony

A *felony* is a serious crime against society, such as murder, arson, larceny, bribery, and embezzlement. It may be punished by execution, by a prison sentence of more than a year, and/or by a fine.

> **EXAMPLE 3.1**
>
> Flogg was an employee of a firm that manufactured expensive electronic equipment. A truckload of the equipment was held at the shipping dock because of a delay and was going to be left there over a three-day weekend. Flogg stole the truck and its contents, intending to drive to another state, sell the equipment, and fly to another country before the theft was discovered. Unfortunately for him, he was caught 75 miles away and ultimately charged with grand larceny, a felony.

Misdemeanor

A *misdemeanor* is a less serious offense than a felony. It is usually punished by a fine and/or imprisonment for no more than one year. Examples of misdemeanors are certain traffic offenses, thefts of small amounts of money, illegal picketing, using illegal measuring devices, and other relatively minor infractions of statutes.

> **EXAMPLE 3.2**
>
> Centerport had a local ordinance that prohibited door-to-door sales without a permit. Dowe began calling on homeowners in the town,

> without obtaining the permit, trying to sell home repairs. When a resident objected, the local police issued Dowe a citation—similar to a traffic ticket—that required him to appear in court, pay a fine, and avoid similar actions until the permit was issued.

CRIMES IN THE BUSINESS WORLD

Many people associate crime with criminals and gangsters as they are portrayed on television and in the movies. However, crimes are not always committed in the sensational style of blazing guns and wild car chases. Often the site of a business crime is the well-appointed office of a corporate executive, or his or her private club, or a nearby bar where employees meet after work.

OBJECTIVE 3

Discuss several common crimes of particular concern to businesses and employees.

White-Collar Crime

Originally, white-collar crime related only to nonviolent crimes against businesses, usually committed by their own employees. The most common white-collar crime was the theft of an employer's funds by employees with access to such funds (called embezzlement). In recent years, however, this unofficial category of illegal activity has been applied to nonviolent crimes committed *by* business firms as well as *against* business firms. In this newer, broader application, white-collar crime covers a wide range of crimes, including embezzlement, stock swindles, frauds against insurance companies, credit card frauds, income tax invasion, computer fraud and theft of computer programs, agreements to fix prices, stock trading based on nonpublic information, and others. As a result, the expression *white-collar crime* is used to describe various crimes that typically do not involve force or violence committed by and against businesses.

OBJECTIVE 4

Explain what is meant by the expression *white-collar crime*.

Depending on its seriousness, a white-collar crime can be either a felony or a misdemeanor and can violate federal or state law.

EXAMPLE 3.3

> Updike, the chief executive officer of TransAmerica Airlines, knew that Air America intended to purchase all outstanding shares of TransAmerica at a higher price than its current market value. Using his inside information, Updike bought as much stock in TransAmerica as he could afford and resold it to Air America at a huge profit. If discovered, Updike could be charged with the white-collar crime of insider trading.

Criminal Law   CHAPTER 3   35

arson The willful or malicious act of causing the burning of another's property.

Arson

The crime of **arson** is the willful or malicious burning of a house or building belonging to another person. Some states have broadened the definition of arson to include the burning of a house by its owner and the destruction of property by other means, such as by explosion. Aside from the few mentally unbalanced persons who start fires for irrational reasons, most instances of arson are profit-related acts. When the motivation is profit, the arsonist is usually trying to collect money from an insurance company for a building that he or she owns. Most states have statutes that provide for the punishment of persons who burn their own property with the aim of collecting insurance money. Such statutes establish a special category of crime, *burning to defraud*. To combat these practices, the insurance industry has developed sophisticated investigation techniques and has an impressive record of assisting in successful prosecutions.

Larceny

larceny The act of taking and carrying away the personal property of another without the right to do so.

Larceny is a broad term that includes most forms of theft—that is, robbery, hijacking, embezzlement, and shoplifting. Larceny is often classified as *petty* (small) or *grand* (large). It is important to distinguish among the various types of larceny. *Robbery* is defined as the taking of property in the possession of another person against that person's will and under threat of bodily harm—as in the case of a holdup. *Burglary* is illegal entry for the purpose of committing a crime. *Hijacking* is stealing from a vehicle in transit or stealing the vehicle itself. *Shoplifting* is stealing merchandise from a retail store.

Bribery

bribery The act of offering, giving, receiving, or soliciting something of value to influence official action or the discharge of a public duty.

The crime of **bribery** consists of giving or taking money or property of value with the intent of influencing someone (usually a public official) in the performance of his or her duty. Some states have enacted laws that also make it a crime to bribe someone other than a public official, such as a purchasing agent employed by a business firm. Both the giver of the bribe and the receiver can be charged with bribery.

> **EXAMPLE 3.4**
> Rodriguez was employed as a secretary at Balasen Corporation. She had access to enormous amounts of confidential information, including sales projections and product development plans. Turner, an executive with a competing firm, initially came to know Rodriguez socially and after a short time recognized the value of the personal contact. An agreement resulted whereby Rodriguez turned over to Turner photo-

copies of many confidential documents in exchange for a cash sum. Both parties could be charged with bribery.

False Pretenses

The expression *false pretenses* describes a broad category of crimes that involve activities intended to deceive others or to obtain goods by making false claims. A number of federal and state statutes govern activities that might be considered false pretenses.

false pretenses A broad category of crimes that involves activities intended to deceive others or to obtain goods by making false claims.

EXAMPLE 3.5

Rollings operated a small catering and take-out food service. He could see that his business was headed for failure unless he installed additional equipment to increase productivity. For this project he needed a bank loan, but he was afraid that he did not have enough assets to qualify. As a result, when he applied for the loan, he claimed that he owned certain equipment that he was actually renting from a restaurant supply company.

A person who makes false statements to a bank for the purpose of obtaining a loan could be prosecuted under the appropriate statute. In Example 3.5, there were no actual "goods," but the bank had extended credit and the credit could be considered a "good."

Forgery

The crime of *forgery* consists of wrongfully making or altering the writings of another with the intent to defraud. Forgery could include falsifying a signature on a check or the indorsement (the signature on the reverse side of the check). The act of signing another person's name to a credit card charge slip without permission is also considered forgery. The common practice of a secretary signing a boss's name to letters, however, could hardly be considered forgery because she signs the letters with the authorization of her boss and with the his or her implied consent.

forgery The false making or alteration of a writing with the intent to defraud.

Perjury

The crime of *perjury* consists of intentionally giving false oral or written statements under oath in a judicial proceeding after having sworn to tell the truth. In some cases, giving false information on a government form is also considered perjury.

perjury The crime of intentionally giving false oral or written statements under oath in a judicial proceeding after having sworn to tell the truth.

EXAMPLE 3.6

Danvers, a former government official, was called to testify before a Congressional committee regarding his activities after leaving

Criminal Law CHAPTER 3

government service that might have been in violation of the law. Under oath, he intentionally lied about the extent of these activities. Investigation revealed the untruths in his testimony, and he was charged with and convicted of perjury.

Embezzlement

embezzlement The wrongful taking of money or other property that has been entrusted to a person as a part of his or her job.

The crime of *embezzlement* may be defined as the wrongful taking of money or other property that has been entrusted to a person as a part of his or her employment. Some jobs, such as accountant, cashier, and bank teller, generally provide more opportunity for embezzlement than other jobs in which the employee has little contact with money. The growing use of computers in business had led to some ingenious schemes for embezzling.

EXAMPLE 3.7

Folsom was employed as a computer programmer at the headquarters of a bank. He secretly programmed the computer so that interest earned on depositors' accounts would be split; only part of the payment would go to the depositor's account, while a small amount would be placed in an account that Folsom had set up to receive the payments. When he was caught, Folsom was charged with embezzlement.

Extortion

extortion The act of taking or demanding money or other property from someone by using force, threats of force, or economic harm.

The crime of *extortion* is the act of taking or demanding money or other property from someone by using force, threats of force, or economic harm. The difference between extortion and bribery is that both parties to bribery are willing participants, whereas in extortion one person is willing and the other is unwilling.

Other Business-Related Crimes

The number of crimes that involve businesses continue to grow as changes in business practices and technology offer new opportunities for wrongdoers to benefit from illegal or questionable activities.

Credit Card Fraud Credit cards provide cardholders with many conveniences. However, certain individuals have seized the opportunity for illegal gain by using stolen or counterfeit credit cards. The practice of altering credit card charge slips, and that of obtaining credit card numbers under false pretenses to use in making counterfeit cards, continue to plague banks, credit card issuers, and consumers.

Insider Trading In several celebrated cases of the late 1980s, people were convicted and imprisoned for having violated federal laws by using information that is not available to the general public for their own financial gain. Typically, someone who had information that, when it was made public, would probably influence the price of certain companies' stocks, used this information to profit from increases in the price of the stocks. This illegal activity, of using information not available to the general public for personal gain, is considered a "manipulative and deceptive practice," and has come to be popularly referred to *insider trading*. (Trading by officials of a company in the stock of the firm is also called insider trading, but as long as it is reported, is not illegal.)

The nonpublic information may have come from various sources. In some cases, individuals had advance access to newspaper and magazine articles that, once published, would probably affect the price of a company's stock. The people who gained the advanced information speculated in the stock of the firm discussed in the news item.

In other cases, top officials of a company, knowing of some development that would affect the price of the firm's stock, gave the information to friends or relatives, who then speculated in the company's stock. These officials used friends or relatives because federal law requires high officials to report their trading in the stock of the company with which they are associated.

CHAPTER SUMMARY

1. A violation of a specific statute is a crime. A tort is private wrong that causes injury to another person's physical well-being, property, or reputation.

2. The three classifications of crimes, based upon their perceived seriousness, are **(a)** treason, **(b)** felonies, and **(c)** misdemeanors.

3. Many crimes are particularly important to business and employees, including the following: arson, larceny, robbery, burglary, hijacking, shoplifting, bribery, false pretenses, forgery, perjury, embezzlement, extortion, credit card fraud, and inside trading.

4. The expression *white-collar crime* is used to describe various crimes committed by or against businesses that typically do not involve force or violence. Depending on its seriousness, a white-collar crime can be either a felony or a misdemeanor, and can violate federal or state law.

Chapter 3 Assessment

MATCHING LEGAL TERMS

Match each of the following numbered with the correct term in the list below. Write the letter of your choice in the answer column.

- **a.** arson
- **b.** bribery
- **c.** burglary
- **d.** extortion
- **e.** felony
- **f.** forgery
- **g.** misdemeanor
- **h.** perjury
- **i.** robbery
- **j.** white-collar crime

1. A classification of serious crimes such as murder or arson.   **1.** _____
2. A classification of less serious crimes such as certain traffic offenses.   **2.** _____
3. An act of willful or malicious burning of a house or building.   **3.** _____
4. The giving or taking of money or property with the intent of influencing, or being influenced, in the performance of an official duty.   **4.** _____
5. Wrongfully making or altering the writing of another with the intent to defraud.   **5.** _____
6. The taking of someone's property against that person's will under threat of bodily harm.   **6.** _____
7. An unofficial category of crime that generally does not involve force or violence.   **7.** _____
8. Breaking into and entering another person's property in the night with the intent of committing a felony or stealing property of value.   **8.** _____
9. Taking or demanding money or other property from someone and using force or threats of force or economic harm.   **9.** _____
10. Making false oral or written statements under oath.   **10.** _____

TRUE/FALSE QUIZ

Indicate whether each of the following statements is true or false by writing *T* or *F* in the answer column.

11. The purpose of criminal law is to compensate injured parties for their losses.   **11.** _____
12. If a person's reckless driving results in an automobile accident, he or she can be charged with both a tort and a crime.   **12.** _____
13. Treason is a major crime against the federal government consisting of levying war or giving aid and comfort to an enemy.   **13.** _____
14. White-collar crime, as distinguished from other types of crime, generally does not involve force or violence.   **14.** _____
15. Burning to defraud is a special category of crime committed by persons who burn their own property with the intention of collecting insurance money.   **15.** _____

Chapter 3 Assessment

16. Larceny is a broad term that includes most forms of theft. 16. _____

17. Shoplifting is the term that describes the theft of money by employees, such as accountants or cashiers, who steal money from retail stores. 17. _____

18. The theft of goods from a vehicle in transit is known as hijacking. 18. _____

19. In all states, the crime of bribery is limited to giving or taking money or property to influence a public official. 19. _____

20. The legal term that covers such activities as obtaining goods and other benefits by the use of misleading statements and deception is false pretenses. 20. _____

21. The crime of perjury is limited to the false swearing under oath before a judge in a federal court. 21. _____

22. When employees with access to a firm's money, such as accountants, cashiers, and bank tellers, wrongfully divert funds to themselves or to others, they are usually charged with burglary. 22. _____

23. It is always illegal for an executive of a firm to buy or sell the stock of the firm. 23. _____

24. A person who profits from the sale of stock as a result of using nonpublic information can be charged with violations of federal law. 24. _____

25. The difference between extortion and bribery is that, in extortion, both parties are willing participants in the crime. 25. _____

DISCUSSION QUESTIONS

Answer the following questions and discuss them in class.

26. What is the difference between a tort and a crime?

_____
_____
_____

27. What are the three major classifications of crimes?

_____
_____
_____

28. What are some crimes that are particularly applicable to business?

_____
_____
_____

Criminal Law CHAPTER 3 41

Chapter 3 Assessment

29. What are some acts that were previously considered a crime but are no longer viewed as a violation of the law?

30. What are some typical misdemeanors common to most jurisdictions?

31. What are some common examples of white-collar crime?

THINKING CRITICALLY ABOUT THE LAW

Answer the following questions, which require you to think critically about the legal principles that you learned in this chapter.

32. White-Collar Crimes Why do some highly paid business executives engage in illegal practices such as insider trading? What would you recommend to reduce the incidence of such practices?

33. Burning to Defraud What would be the effect on the insurance business and the economy generally, if there were no "burning to defraud" statutes?

34. Embezzlement How has using computers in business increased or reduced the incidence of embezzlement?

35. Extortion What is the difference between extortion and bribery?

Chapter 3 Assessment

36. False Pretenses What is the intent of someone who is said to engage in activities called "false pretenses"?

37. A Question of Ethics Do you think that a U. S. citizen that disagrees with U.S. foreign policy against one of its enemies should be charged with treason for donating money to that enemy's war efforts against the United States? Why or why not?

CASE QUESTIONS

Study each case below and answer the questions that follow by writing *Yes* or *No* in the answer column.

38. Arson Williamson owned and operated a restaurant, Plum Pudding, and had a difficult time competing with Green Apple Snak Shoppe, located across the street. It seemed that whenever Plum Pudding offered a new special price on a particular meal, its competitor met the price and offered some other inducement as well. As a last desperate effort to remain in business, Williamson hired a "torch" to set fire to the Green Apple. Just as the hired criminal had finished his work, he was apprehended by an off-duty police officer. The hired "torch" admitted his guilt and implicated Williamson.

  a. Would Williamson be charged with arson? a. _____
  b. Would the hired "torch" be charged with arson? b. _____
  c. Is it likely that Green Apple's insurance would pay for the damage? c. _____
  d. Is this an example of the crime of extortion? d. _____

39. False Pretenses Zaks, the owner of a hairstyling salon, Locks Unlimited, applied for a bank loan to buy new hair dryers and other equipment she felt were needed to attract new customers. To enhance her chances of getting the loan, she told the bank that she owned considerable equipment and furniture, although most of the equipment and furnishings in the shop were actually rented.

  a. If Zaks' deception were discovered, is it likely that she could be charged with false pretenses? a. _____
  b. If the bank accepted the false statements at face value, did the bank perform responsibly? b. _____
  c. Could Zaks be charged with extortion? c. _____
  d. Could the banker be charged with bribery? d. _____

40. Bribery Gelfis owned and operated Welltech, a janitorial service company that provided services to a number of city and state agencies. Eager to expand his firm and increase his profits, he approached Biondi, the director of purchasing for a state agency, and offered to sell Biondi stock in Welltech at a greatly reduced price. It was clear to both Gelfis and Biondi that Biondi would be expected to award the janitorial services contract to Welltech.

Criminal Law   CHAPTER 3   43

Chapter 3 Assessment

a. If the arrangement were completed, could Gelfis be charged with bribery?

b. Could Gelfis be charged with grand larceny?

c. Could Gelfis be charged with extortion?

a. _____

b. _____

c. _____

CASE ANALYSIS

Study each of the following cases carefully and then briefly state the principle of law and your decision.

41. Larceny, Credit Card Fraud, False Pretenses Buckley, a worker in a restaurant, stole a credit card from the coat of its owner with the intention of using it to charge goods. He purchased some merchandise at a retail store and paid for them by presenting the credit card to the salesperson and signing the name of the person whose name appeared on the card. *Was Buckley guilty of a crime?* [*Buckley v. Indiana,* 322 N.E.2d 113 (Indiana).]

Principle of law:

Decision:

42. Price Fixing Gorden Tameny had worked for 15 years for Atlantic Richfield Company (ARCO) and had risen to the position of retail sales representative. While he never had a formal contract of employment, his duties included managing relations between ARCO and various independent dealers in his territory. ARCO and some of its agents had been manipulating the retail gasoline prices of ARCO dealers. Those violations of federal and state antitrust laws had resulted in an agreement between ARCO and the courts under which ARCO and its agents agreed to stop those activities. In spite of this agreement, ARCO continued to pressure Tameny to threaten and persuade dealers to cut their gasoline prices to a point at or below the level specified by ARCO. Tameny refused, and was subsequently fired for alleged incompetence and unsatisfactory performance. On appeal, the Supreme Court of California was asked to decide: (1) whether an employer's authority over employees included the right to demand that an employee commit a criminal act; (2) whether an employer may force compliance by discharging an employee who refuses to do so; and (3) whether an employee may bring a tort action for wrongful discharge. *Will Tameny be successful in his action claiming wrongful discharge?* [*Tameny v. Atlantic Richfield Co.,* 610 P.2d 1330 (California).]

Principle of law:

Decision:

Chapter 3 Assessment

43. Insider Trading Franken, president of Monarch Pharmaceuticals Incorporated, was one of only three persons who knew that one of the firm's experimental drugs had just been approved by the federal government. The drug had been found to cure several serious diseases. As soon as news of the approval became public, Franken reasoned, the price of the firm's stock would increase substantially. He arranged with a friend to buy thousands of shares of the company's stock, hoping to sell at a profit after the price increased as a result of the good news. *Can Franken be prosecuted for his actions?*

Principle of law:
_____
_____

Decision:
_____
_____

LEGAL RESEARCH

Complete the following activities. Then share your findings with the class.

44. Working in Teams Small and medium-sized businesses are often concerned with crimes that could affect the firm. In teams of three or four, interview one or several business owners/managers and ask them to briefly describe the kinds of crimes they are concerned about and the steps they take to minimize the risk of crime.

_____
_____
_____
_____
_____
_____
_____

45. Using Technology Using the Internet and search engines, investigate common internal business crimes committed by employees.

_____
_____
_____
_____
_____
_____
_____

CHAPTER 4

TORT LAW

PERFORMANCE OBJECTIVES

After studying this chapter and completing the assessments, you will be able to:

1. Describe five common torts and how they might involve businesses.
2. Compare contributory negligence with comparative negligence.
3. Explain the legal concept of liability and provide examples.
4. Explain vicarious liability and provide examples.
5. Explain strict liability and provide examples.

LEGAL TERMS

tort
defamation
libel
slander
nuisance
conversion
negligence
vicarious negligence
contributory negligence
comparative negligence
liable
vicarious liability
strict liability

THE NATURE OF TORTS

Chapter 1 defined a crime as a violation of the rights of society as a whole, whether an individual is the victim of the crime or there is no identifiable wronged party. A *tort,* in contrast to a crime, is a violation of the rights of an identifiable individual or business that has been wronged either intentionally or by negligence. For example, when the crime of larceny has been committed and the victim can be identified, then both a crime has been committed and the victim of the larceny has suffered the tort of conversion. The law of torts does not deal with duties imposed by contract, but is concerned only with the violation of private rights.

THE LAW OF TORTS

Whether acting as an individual or as an employee of another person, a person has a responsibility to consider the rights of others. The common torts discussed in this chapter all have some direct or indirect bearing on an individual's personal life and on how he or she performs his or her job.

DEFAMATION

Defamation is the harming of a person's reputation and good name by the communication of a false statement. For an act to be considered defamation, it is necessary to show that the statement was made in such a way that others hear or read it. To call someone a thief to the person's face may be an insult, but it is not defamation. A defamatory statement usually holds a person up to hatred, ridicule, or contempt, or lowers a person's esteem, respect, or social position. Defamation also involves some suggestion of disgrace, and it tends to generate negative feelings about the person who suffers the defamation. The charge of defamation has been separated into two torts: libel and slander.

LIBEL AND SLANDER

Generally, *libel* is the spreading of damaging statements in written form, including pictures, cartoons, and effigies (likenesses). Defamation on radio and television is also considered libel.

Slander is the spreading of damaging words or ideas about a person, directly or indirectly, in all other forms not considered libel. Of

OBJECTIVE 1

Describe five common torts and how they might involve businesses.

tort A violation of the rights of an identifiable individual or business that has been wronged either intentionally or by negligence.

defamation The harming of a person's reputation and good name by the communication of a false statement.

libel The spreading of damaging statements in written form, including pictures, cartoons, and effigies.

slander The spreading of damaging words or ideas about a person, directly or indirectly, in all other forms not considered libel.

course, the most common form of slander involves spoken words, but slander can also be committed by means of gestures and actions.

Characteristics of Libel

Although many libel cases involve defamatory statements published in books, newspapers, and magazines, the possibility of libel also exists in business and personal letters, memos, and catalogs. The libel need not be direct. Subtle suggestion or implication is enough to bring about legal charges. For example, there have been cases in which the use of quotation marks has been interpreted as giving a libelous meaning to otherwise harmless words.

> **EXAMPLE 4.1**
>
> Roscoe, a manager, wrote a memo to his boss explaining the absence of one of his female employees. The memo included the words, "and I tried to contact the fellow who used to be a 'friend' of hers."

By placing the quotation marks around the word *friend,* Roscoe suggested that the fellow he referred to was really not a friend, but a lover. The important point in this case is that it is not so much the exact wording of the statement that matters, but rather how others—including a jury—might reasonably interpret the statement.

Example 4.1, which is based on an actual case, may not seem very damaging given today's more liberal standards of social behavior, but the same principle can apply to other situations. Suppose that a supervisor had written a memo stating, "I don't know what became of the laptop computer, but you might want to check with Fred Chaffee; he has been known to 'borrow' things before."

Another example of how a statement might be interpreted as damaging a person's reputation is illustrated in the following case, in which no statement was made, but the implication was damaging nevertheless.

> **EXAMPLE 4.2**
>
> The First National County Bank noticed shortages of money and asked its employees to submit to lie detector tests. One employee, Baxter, was unable to pass the test, and the bonding company refused to renew her bond (a form of insurance that protects a firm from losses due to employee dishonesty). The local newspaper learned of the problems at the bank and interviewed the president, who mentioned that some employees were no longer working because the insurance company would not issue bonds for them. When the newspaper printed the story, Baxter sued the bank, charging libel.

Although the newspaper account did not mention Baxter by name, she charged that people who knew her and knew that she was no longer working at the bank would assume that she had been involved in the shortages of money.

Most cases of libel are not quite as unusual as those previously described. Many problems simply involve thoughtless written remarks or unfounded gossip. Other problems concern common occurences, such as obtaining references from past employers.

In recent years, the threat of a libel suit by former employees who are unhappy with the references given by the former employer has gotten so serious that many firms refuse to respond to any inquiry about former workers—even those who have good records.

Characteristics of Slander

Slander is the term that describes almost all defamation that cannot be classified as libel. Slander includes spoken words, gestures, actions, and even omissions. Most cases of slander involve thoughtless statements that reflect on another person's good name and reputation. Because oral statements, unless recorded, cannot be reproduced as evidence, some people tend to speak carelessly about others without realizing that anyone hearing a slanderous statement can be called upon later to testify to having heard it.

Photo 4.1

Slander

The First Amendment does not protect defamatory speech such as slander. *What are some of the reasons why slander is not protected by the Constitution?*

The tort of slander does not require a directly defamatory statement. Gestures and actions can sometimes be equally damaging. Consider Example 4.3, in which no defamatory words were spoken.

> **EXAMPLE 4.3**
>
> Mason entered a variety store, examined various articles of merchandise, and then left. The store manager, Conant, suspecting that Mason had stolen something, followed her into the street, and in full view of several bystanders, he ordered her to stop. He then searched her and examined her handbag. Finding nothing, he released her and returned to the store. Mason believed that Conant had, by his actions and gestures, falsely accused her of being a thief. She brought suit for damages to her reputation, charging slander.

Although the store manager did not actually call the customer a thief, he implied as much by his actions. Cautious business persons, given a similar situation, would quietly ask the shopper to return to the store and submit to a search in the privacy of the manager's office. Obviously, the seriousness of a slanderous statement is influenced by the number of people who hear it. Many people are careful to avoid making such statements publicly before large groups. However, making a defamatory statement to even one person can still provide the basis for legal action.

Trade Libel

In conducting business, a firm and its owners have the right to remain free from false and malicious statements by others that may cause a loss or damage to the reputation of the firm, the owners, the products produced, or the merchandise carried or manufactured by the firm. The tort of *trade libel* is similar to traditional defamation but deals with an individual's title to property, or to the quality or conduct of a business.

> **EXAMPLE 4.4**
>
> Philo told several suppliers that his competitor, Willit, was about to file for bankruptcy and go out of business. The statements were without foundation because Willit's business was prosperous and there was no likelihood of a bankruptcy. Because such an untrue statement could damage his business, Willit could sue Philo, charging trade libel.

Humor and Slander

It might seem that a quick apology and a "sorry, just kidding" might be enough to avoid some charges of slander. Not so! Consider the following case, in which the subject of a seemingly harmless remark did not think it was funny.

> **EXAMPLE 4.5**
> Radio Station WKMF was sued as a result of its broadcast of a listener call-in program that invited listeners to nominate a person or a business for the title of "dodo of the day." A listener, who identified herself only as "Bonnie," called to nominate her insurance agent, Lawrence Faro, as the "dodo of the day." She claimed that after she consulted him about a damaged windshield, he advised her to throw a brick through her windshield to make the claim large enough that the insurance company would pay it. Faro denied knowing a customer named Bonnie and sued the radio station for defamation.

DEFENSES TO DEFAMATION

There are two common defenses to charges of defamation: (1) truth, and (2) privilege. If a defamatory statement can be proved to be true, the person who claims that he or she was defamed cannot recover damages. If the person accused of defamation had a special privilege in making the defamatory statement, such as an attorney in a court proceeding who accuses a witness of lying, then the defamed person cannot recover damages. However, a person should still be careful because it is often expensive to go to court to prove the truth of a statement. The expense can be avoided by being cautious in the first place.

NUISANCE

An unlawful interference with the enjoyment of life or property constitutes a *nuisance.* The law gives everyone the right to enjoy his or her land without unreasonable interference from others. A person who acts in a way that denies this right to a specific person or persons has created a *private nuisance.* A *public nuisance,* by comparison, affects the community or the general public. Creating a nuisance does not mean taking another's property—only detracting from the enjoyment of it. A person can be charged with creating a private nuisance by causing loud noises, foul odors, or bright lights. A nuisance may even be created by diverting a stream.

nuisance An unlawful interference with the enjoyment of life or property.

> **EXAMPLE 4.6**
> Springs Manufacturing Company had operated a small factory in the town of Burlingame for many years and was regarded as a responsible firm that created no problem for the community. It even employed 30

> townspeople. In an effort to expand the company's business, management decided to begin making a line of goods that required a noisy stamping process. The families in the immediate area complained about the noise. Management took the position that the noise was the price the community had to pay for the economic benefits of having the plant located there.

Example 4.6 illustrates the tort of nuisance. It also illustrates the tough choices people must sometimes make between seeking relief from a nuisance and having to do without some offsetting benefit. The law recognizes that when people live together in a society such as ours, not all people can have their own way. The benefits to one person must be balanced against the inconvenience to another.

CONVERSION

The law gives each person the right to own and use personal property without interference from others. When this right is denied or abridged by another, the wrongdoer is said to have committed the tort of *conversion.* This tort can involve a wrongful taking, a wrongful detention, or an illegal assumption of ownership. Conversion may involve removal, damage, destruction, or unauthorized use. A shoplifter commits the crime of larceny as well as the tort of conversion.

A suit charging a person with conversion provides the victim with the means of collecting money damages from someone who steals personal property. It is one thing to have a dishonest employee arrested, found guilty of the crime of larceny, and punished, but a criminal action does not replace the stolen goods or money. A tort action for conversion is one way to help replace the money or property.

conversion The wrongful exercise of dominion and control over another's personal property.

EXAMPLE 4.7
> Clemente stole Dowtin's car. While it was in Clemente's possession, the car was destroyed. Dowtin had no insurance on his car because he had intended to sell it. The only way he could recover the cost of the car would be to sue Clemente, charging him with conversion.

NEGLIGENCE

The tort of *negligence* is the failure to exercise necessary care to protect others from unreasonable risk of harm. The number of lawsuits charging negligence has grown tremendously in recent years, in part

negligence The failure to exercise necessary care to protect others from unreasonable risk of harm.

because news accounts of large jury awards have encouraged others to sue. Also, there seems to have developed an attitude that when a person experiences misfortune, someone else must pay.

Lawsuits have charged professionals such as doctors, dentists, nurses, lawyers, and accountants with malpractice (a term that is used in cases of the negligence of professionals). Homeowners have been sued for negligence for injuries that have occurred on their property. Corporations have been sued for negligent design or for manufacturing products that cause injury. Schools have been sued for failing to educate students properly, and municipalities have been sued for negligently designing roads that have contributed to accidents. And, of course, automobile drivers are sued in great numbers for negligent operation of an automobile.

To avoid legal action either as an individual or as an employee, each person must exercise great care and good judgment to avoid causing injury to others. Even so, all the good judgment and care will not prevent all accidents. It is also important to carry adequate insurance coverage for protection against the financial losses that can result from being adjudged liable for the tort of negligence.

EXAMPLE 4.8

> Jensen, employed as a truck driver, was driving a new light truck at 40 miles per hour on a mild day when a tire blew out. As a result, his truck collided with another vehicle and caused both extensive damage to the other vehicle and injury to the driver.

While it is difficult to predict how a jury would decide this case, most reasonable persons would say that Jensen was not negligent. But suppose that Jensen was driving at 70 miles per hour, the tires were worn, the day (and pavement) was hot, and the truck was heavily loaded. In that case, most people would say that Jensen was negligent. It is not just a particular act that constitutes negligence, but also the circumstances that surround it.

Unavoidable Accident

In theory, all accidents are avoidable. Jensen, the truck driver, could have avoided the accident by simply not driving the truck at all—or by not getting out of bed that morning. But the concept of unavoidable accident is intended to focus attention on whether an accident could have been avoided if the person alleged to be responsible had acted reasonably.

The "Reasonable Person"

The law provides certain ways by which juries can determine if a person has acted negligently. One of these ways is the doctrine of the "reasonable person of ordinary prudence," a fictitious person who is assumed to have the judgment and skill one would expect from a person with the strengths and limitations of the person whose behavior is being judged. While there is no standard reasonable person, a jury is asked to determine how the mythical person would have behaved under the same or similar circumstances. Obviously, one reason the law uses an imaginary person is to prevent jurors from judging a defendant in terms of how they themselves would have behaved.

Kinds of Negligence

The legal concept of negligence is not quite so simple as deciding if the driver of an automobile was driving negligently. Many cases are far more complex, particularly when the law must decide if one or more third parties can also be held responsible for the negligence.

Vicarious Negligence The term *vicarious,* as used in the law, means essentially the same as when it is used generally, that is, to describe an act performed by one person as a substitute for another. **Vicarious negligence,** therefore, means charging a negligent act of one person to another.

vicarious negligence
Charging a negligent act of one person to another.

> **EXAMPLE 4.9**
>
> Christensen rented a house from Hoover. After a few months, a dispute developed about the amount of rent owed. Hoover obtained a court order to recover possession of the house. Because Christensen was out of town at this time, Hoover hired a local moving and storage company to remove and store the renter's possessions. After Christensen paid the rent owed, Hoover told the storage company to release Christensen's possessions. Unfortunately, some items were damaged and others were missing. Christensen sued, and after the first trial in favor of Hoover, the Colorado State Supreme Court held that Hoover was responsible for the loss that occurred while the goods were in the hands of the moving company.

In many cases that involve the negligence of an employee, the employer is held responsible provided the employee was performing the tasks he or she was hired to do. (The practical reason is that the employer usually has the money or insurance to settle the suit. There is little to gain from a judgment against an employee who does not have the financial resources to pay the damages.)

Contributory Negligence The previous paragraphs described the concept of negligence. The idea of **contributory negligence** is not an accusation but rather a defense by someone who is charged with negligence. In effect, a person says, "Sure, maybe I was negligent, but you were too and contributed to your own injuries." Perhaps a better term for this principle would be *contributory fault.* In many cases, the injured party could not sue successfully because he or she was partly responsible, even in a minor way. Note the case in Example 4.10, involving Alvis and Ribar, in which the trial court rejected Alvis' suit because of his contributory negligence.

Comparative Negligence In recent years, many legislatures and courts have applied the idea of **comparative negligence.** Under this doctrine, the injured party bringing the lawsuit is not prevented from recovering damages even if he or she was partly at fault. The jury determines how much the plaintiff was at fault and reduces the verdict by that amount. If the plaintiff was found to be 10 percent negligent, he or she would get an award 10 percent less than the full damages as determined by the jury.

OBJECTIVE 2

Compare contributory negligence with comparative negligence.

contributory negligence A legal defense that involves the failure of an injured party to be careful enough to ensure personal safety.

comparative negligence A form of negligence that requires the court to assign damages according to the degree of fault of each party.

EXAMPLE 4.10

Alvis had been injured while riding in a car driven by Ribar. The car had crashed into a metal barrel anchoring an intersection stop sign at the site of some highway construction. Alvis sued Ribar, the county, and a contractor. The suit was dismissed in the trial court because of contributory negligence; apparently there was some evidence of carelessness on Alvis' part as well. But when the appeal reached the Supreme Court of Illinois, it saw injustice in denying any damage to Alvis simply because he had contributed to his injuries. The Supreme Court sent the case back to the trial court to let a jury decide the extent to which Alvis had contributed to the accident and to proportion damages accordingly.

LIABILITY

When a person has been judged to be responsible for a loss, he or she is said to be ***liable*** (not to be confused with *libel,* covered earlier). In most lawsuits, the court must decide if the defendant is liable for the damages as charged. In some instances, the law shields certain persons. In other instances, liability is automatically assumed.

It would be easy to say that all liability results from negligence and all negligence creates liability, but this is not the case. Sometimes a person is liable even though no negligence has been proved.

OBJECTIVE 3

Explain the concept of liability and provide examples.

liable Being judged legally responsible.

OBJECTIVE 4

Explain vicarious liability and provide examples.

vicarious liability The concept of laying responsibility or blame upon one person for the actions of another.

OBJECTIVE 5

Explain strict liability and provide examples.

strict liability The doctrine under which people may be liable for injuries to others whether or not they have been negligent or committed an intentional tort.

Vicarious Liability

In some cases, the law holds persons liable for the acts of others, such as when an employer is held responsible for the acts of employees, or a general contractor is held responsible for acts of a subcontractor. The expression for this shifting of responsibility is *vicarious liability,* and it is related to vicarious negligence, discussed earlier.

Strict Liability

Certain events cause death or injury to others even when no negligence exists. Under a doctrine known as *strict liability,* people may be liable for injuries to others regardless of whether they have done something wrong. Examples include damage caused by inherently dangerous activities, events, or animals, and might involve domestic pets, fire, water, explosives, or dangerous chemicals.

> **EXAMPLE 4.11**
>
> The Crocker Construction Company was building a highway and found it necessary to use explosives to blast away some rock formations. Employees of the firm were well trained and careful in their work. In spite of the care, however, some rock fragments damaged a nearby house. The owner of the house sued the construction company for the damages. Crocker raised the defense that the homeowner could not show negligence on the part of the company. Judgment was entered for the homeowner because under the doctrine of strict liability, it was not necessary to show negligence, only that the damage occurred.

The broad range of injuries suffered by employees on the job is another example of strict liability. Workers' compensation laws limit the amount employees may recover from their employers for most injuries, but the employer and the firm's insurance company cannot avoid payment by claiming that the employee contributed to his or her own injury or assumed the risks of the job.

In recent years, the doctrine of strict liability has also been applied to cases involving injury or death caused by manufactured products, such as machinery—even if the injured person misused the product. Some courts believe that the manufacturer of the product is in a better position than the injured person to absorb the costs of paying for the loss suffered because the manufacturer's insurance company will actually pay the loss and the manufacturer can pass along the cost of insurance to all users of the product.

A purchaser who is injured by a product has a cause of action by merely demonstrating that (1) the product was defective, (2) the defect was the cause of the injury, and (3) the defect caused the product to be unreasonably dangerous. Strict liability has been recognized and applied in at least two-thirds of the states in this country.

Proponents of strict liability claim that eliminating the need to prove negligence on the part of the manufacturer will encourage manufacturers and sellers to be more concerned with producing safer products. Others argue that the application of strict liability will inhibit the development of new products because of the fear of product liability lawsuits and the high cost of product liability insurance.

CHAPTER SUMMARY

1. Common torts, and examples of how businesses may be involved, include the following: libel, slander, nuisance, conversion, and negligence.

2. Contributory negligence is a defense by someone who is charged with negligence. Essentially, the defendant says, "Maybe I was negligent, but you were, too, and contributed to your own injuries." Recently, many legislatures and courts have applied the idea of comparative negligence. Under this doctrine, the injured party is not prevented from recovering damages if he or she was partly at fault. The jury determines the extent to which the plaintiff was negligent and reduces the verdict by that amount.

3. The legal concept of liability involves judging a party legally responsible for a loss or wrong. Examples include being found guilty of any of the torts mentioned in this chapter, including defamation, nuisance, conversion, or negligence.

4. Various liability occurs when the law holds a party responsible for the acts of others. Examples include when an employer is held responsible for actions of an employee, or a general contractor is held responsible for acts of a subcontractor.

5. Strict liability occurs when the law holds a party responsible for death or injury to others even when no negligence exists. Examples include damage caused by inherently dangerous activities, events, or animals, and might involve domestic pets, fire, water, blasting, or dangerous chemicals.

Chapter 4 Assessment

MATCHING LEGAL TERMS

Match each of the following numbered definitions with the correct term in the list below. Write the letter of your choice in the answer column.

- **a.** conversion
- **b.** contributory negligence
- **c.** defamation
- **d.** liability
- **e.** libel
- **f.** negligence
- **g.** nuisance
- **h.** slander
- **i.** tort
- **j.** vicarious liability

1. A broad category of violations of the rights of individuals.
2. False written or spoken statements that harm a person's reputation.
3. Actions that unreasonably deny someone the enjoyment of his or her land.
4. False written statements that harm a person's reputation or good name.
5. Actions that physically remove or destroy the personal property of others.
6. False spoken statements or actions that damage a person's reputation or good name.
7. Carelessness that results in injury to another person or his or her property.
8. The state or condition of being responsible for wrong or injury.
9. The shifting of responsibility from one person to another.
10. A concept that states that one person contributed to his or her own injuries.

1. _____
2. _____
3. _____
4. _____
5. _____
6. _____
7. _____
8. _____
9. _____
10. _____

TRUE/FALSE QUIZ

Indicate whether each of the following statements is true or false by writing *T* or *F* in the answer column.

11. A tort is a violation of the rights of a particular person.
12. Tort law is concerned with compensation for losses suffered by injured parties.
13. Defamation includes both libel and slander.
14. The tort of libel is concerned with injury to a person's reputation caused by false statements that are used in testimony in court.
15. A person who defames a person by exhibiting an insulting drawing in a public place could be charged with libel.
16. The tort of slander is concerned with injury to a person's reputation caused by false statements that are spoken.
17. Two defenses to charges of defamation are truth and privilege.

11. _____
12. _____
13. _____
14. _____
15. _____
16. _____
17. _____

Chapter 4 Assessment

18. The tort of nuisance does not entail taking another's property, only detracting from their enjoyment of it.

18. _____

19. Liability is the state of being responsible.

19. _____

20. The tort of conversion is concerned with acts that deny a person the possession of their property.

20. _____

21. The tort of negligence is a form of carelessness.

21. _____

22. Vicarious liability means that one person can be held responsible for the negligent acts of another.

22. _____

23. Another, perhaps better, name for the concept of contributory negligence might be contributory fault.

23. _____

24. The "reasonable person" doctrine is concerned with the appeal to a jury to assume how a person would behave under the best conditions.

24. _____

25. Under the doctrine of comparative negligence, juries attempt to determine how much in percent terms the plaintiff was at fault and then reduce the verdict by that amount.

25. _____

DISCUSSION QUESTIONS

Answer the following questions and discuss them in class.

26. Identify several common torts and explain how they might be committed in a business environment.
_____
_____
_____

27. Explain the legal concept of liability and provide examples.
_____
_____
_____

28. Compare contributory negligence with comparative negligence and provide examples of each.
_____
_____
_____

29. Explain vicarious liability and provide an example.
_____
_____
_____

Chapter 4 Assessment

30. Explain strict liability and provide an example.

THINKING CRITICALLY ABOUT THE LAW

Answer the following questions, which require you to think critically about the legal principles that you learned in this chapter.

31. Defamation Why is it that public figures find it difficult to successfully sue a publication for libel, whereas private persons have a better chance? Should public figures be required to accept libelous accusations as the price of fame?

32. Trade Libel The law protects businesses against defamatory statements or writings just as it does for individuals. Should there be a different standard for businesses that would permit a firm to attack a competitor?

33. Private Nuisance The law gives the right to enjoy a person's land without unreasonable interference from others. If a person plays loud music on his property and his neighbor charges him with creating a public nuisance, where does the music player's constitutional right to free expression end, and where does the neighbor's right to be free of a private nuisance begin? How would a court decide?

34. A Question of Ethics Do you believe it is unethical to exaggerate the extent of injuries suffered in an automobile accident resulting from another driver's negligent driving in an effort to increase the amount of a financial settlement that will be paid by an insurance company?

Chapter 4 Assessment

CASE QUESTIONS

Study each case below. Then answer the questions that follow by writing *Yes* or *No* in the answer column.

35. **Nuisance** The Sock 'n' Rock Music Store was located in a small shopping mall. In an effort to attract additional customers, the manager of the store installed an outdoor loudspeaker and played rock music at high volume. Nearby stores in the shopping mall objected, claiming that the loud music drove their customers away.

    a. Does Sock 'n' Rock have the right to use the rented property as it pleases? a. _____

    b. Do the other stores in the mall have a basis for suit, charging private or public nuisance? b. _____

    c. Do the other stores in the mall have a basis for suit, charging conversion? c. _____

    d. Would a court order preventing the loud music seem to be a good remedy? d. _____

36. **Negligence** Leffingwell engaged the Bartwell Tree Removal Service to cut down and remove a diseased tree from her property. When the work began, it was a calm day. As the work progressed, however, a high wind arose and blew a portion of the tree onto a neighbor's car, causing considerable damage. The neighbor brought suit against Bartwell, charging negligence.

    a. Does it seem likely that the accident could have been prevented? a. _____

    b. Could the owner of the car be charged with negligence for parking his car in a place where it could be damaged by the falling tree? b. _____

    c. Would the neighbor have a sound basis on which to sue for damages? c. _____

    d. Do the circumstances seem to support a defense Bartwell might make claiming an unavoidable accident? d. _____

37. **Conversion** Pratt, a stock-car racing driver, had entered a race to be held several months later. Two days before the race, he left his racing car at a shop to have some last-minute adjustments made. When Pratt went to pick up the car before the race, the shop owner refused to release it until Pratt paid for work that had been done two years earlier on another car. Pratt could not raise the money in time and was unable to participate in the race. As a result he had to forfeit the $75 fee he had paid to enter.

    a. Does it seem that the repair shop acted responsibly? a. _____

    b. Could Pratt bring suit, charging conversion? b. _____

    c. Could Pratt bring suit against the repair shop to recover his $75 entry fee? c. _____

    d. Could Pratt have the shop owner arrested for larceny? d. _____

Tort Law   CHAPTER 4

Chapter 4 Assessment

CASE ANALYSIS

Study each of the following cases carefully and then briefly state the principle of law and your decision.

38. Defamation At a special meeting, the board of directors of Family Federal Savings & Loan Association asked Newton, its president, manager, and director, to resign. He did so. Shortly thereafter, a reporter for the *Oregon Statesman* talked about Newton's resignation with one of the directors. The very next day, the paper published an article that stated: "The board of directors of the six-branch Family Federal Savings & Loan Association has forced Thomas Newton out of his position as the Association's president, charging that he is 'administratively incapable.'" Newton thereupon sued the Association and its individual directors for defamation. When a jury awarded him damages, the directors appealed on the grounds that the quoted language was not capable of a defamatory meaning. *Will the directors succeed in overturning the judgment?* [*Newton v. Family FS&L Association,* 616 P.2d 1213 (Oregon).]

Principle of law:

Decision:

39. Conversion Rensch left two diamond rings for cleaning at Riddle's Mall in Rapid City, South Dakota. Riddle's was advertising free ring cleaning to the public. When Rensch returned for the rings, he found that a clerk had mistakenly given them to another customer. They were never recovered, and Rensch ultimately sued Riddle. *What tort was involved in this case, and is it likely that the court will find for Rensch?* [*Rensch v. Riddles's Diamonds of Rapid City,* 393 N.W.2d 269 S.D. (South Dakota).]

Principle of law:

Decision:

40. Trade Libel Robin Williams, famous entertainer and comedian, gave a performance at a San Francisco nightclub, The Great American Music Hall. As part of his comedy routine, he disparaged a particular brand of wine, Rege, by suggesting that it would be a great success if it were directed toward a particular minority group. The discussion of the wine also included certain obscene and vulgar expressions. It seemed that the Rege wine was the target of Williams' jokes. Video and audiotapes were made of the performance and were distributed by the recording company, Polygram Records. Rege brought suit, claiming trade libel. *What would be the probable outcome of this suit? Did the fact that the alleged libel took place during a comedy routine alter the case?* [*Polygram Records v. Superior Court,* 11 Med.L. Rptr. 2364 (California).]

Chapter 4 Assessment

Principle of law:

_____

_____

Decision:

_____

_____

41. Defamation, Slander Fortrell, an aide in a child-care center, was particularly concerned about the behavior of a certain child who frequently fought with and teased other children at the center. LaRena, the mother of one of the children who had been a victim of the troublesome child, was at the center one day, and Fortrell explained that the behavior of the problem child was caused by his mother, Yung, who was herself unbalanced and unfit to have custody of the child. What Fortrell did not know was that LaRena was a friend of Yung and reported he conversation to her. Yung sued Fortrell, charging defamation. *Will Yung succeed in a defamation suit?*

Principle of law:

_____

_____

Decision:

_____

_____

LEGAL RESEARCH

Complete the following activities. Then share your findings with the class.

42. Working in Teams In teams of three or four, interview several property/casualty insurance agents or claims adjusters (as distinguished from life or health insurance personnel) to learn more about claims filed against small businesses for negligence, or other torts. Ask what steps or measures might have been taken to avoid the commission of the tort.

_____

_____

_____

43. Using Technology Using the Internet and search engines, investigate one or several torts discussed in the chapter, concentrate particularly on negligence.

_____

_____

_____

Tort Law   CHAPTER 4

CHAPTER 5

ADMINISTRATIVE LAW

PERFORMANCE OBJECTIVES

After studying this chapter and completing the assessments, you will be able to:

1. Identify the chief reasons for forming administrative agencies.
2. Describe, by using examples, the operation of a typical administrative agency.
3. Explain the similarities and differences between administrative agencies and governments.
4. Discuss current criticism of administrative agencies.

LEGAL TERMS

administrative agency
legislative branch
executive branch
judicial branch
administrative hearing

Administrative Agencies

Administrative agencies were introduced in Chapter 1, where the point was made that they affect nearly every individual, business, and organization in the country. Just as we are governed by common law, statutory law, and case law (discussed in Chapter 2), businesses and individuals must also conform to administrative rules or be subject to penalties if they do not. An ***administrative agency*** is a governmental body responsible for the control and supervision of a particular activity or area of public interest. Our society is extraordinarily complex, and no legislature can pass laws specific or specialized enough to ensure that all objectives are achieved under all circumstances.

Legislatures lack the time and expertise to make the necessary rules to govern the operations of complex areas of our social and economic life, such as energy, taxation, transportation, environmental pollution, and communication. Neither do legislatures have the time or expertise to supervise the many details of these complex areas on a daily basis. As a result, legislatures delegate these responsibilities to administrative agencies, or regulators.

When a legislature passes a particular law, it often stresses general objectives and guidelines. At the same time, it may create an administrative agency to establish specific rules to be followed by those affected by the law. When the agency is established, the legislature usually specifies the purpose and the powers of the agency, and the actions the agency may take in carrying out the intentions of the law. Administrative agencies have various names, including boards, commissions, and departments. In many respects, administrative agencies are like governments within a government because they combine all three governmental functions—legislative, executive, and judicial.

Administrative agencies exist at the federal, state, and local levels of government:

- Typical federal agencies include the Consumer Product Safety Commission, Equal Employment Opportunity Commission, Environmental Protection Agency, Federal Communications Commission, Federal Trade Commission, Internal Revenue Service, Nuclear Regulatory Commission, Occupational Safety and Health Administration, and Securities and Exchange Commission.

administrative agency
A governmental body responsible for the control and supervision of a particular activity or area of public interest.

OBJECTIVE 1

Identify the chief reasons for forming administrative agencies.

Administrative Law CHAPTER 5

- Typical state agencies include the Alcoholic Beverage Control Board, Department of Insurance, Public Service Commission, and Workers' Compensation Board.
- Typical local agencies are the Board of Education, Board of Health, Consumer Protection Agency, and Department of Weights and Measures.

Organization of Governments

To appreciate the similarity of administrative agencies and governments, it will be valuable to review the traditional constitutional governments that operate at the federal, state, and local levels.

Each level of government has three branches: legislative, executive, and judicial. Each branch has specific duties and powers. The organization of administrative agencies often resembles the organization of governments.

Legislative Branch of Government

legislative branch The branch of a government body that consists of elected representatives who have the responsibility for passing laws that represent the will of the people.

The *legislative branch* at all levels of government consists of elected representatives who have the responsibility for passing laws that represent the will of the people.

At the federal level, there are two houses of Congress: the House of Representatives and the Senate. At the state level, the legislative branch is often called the general assembly; like the federal Congress, it consists of two houses (except in Nebraska). At the local level, the legislative branch is often called a city council or given a similar name.

Executive Branch of Government

executive branch The branch of a government body that consists of an elected executive, including his or her appointed staff.

The *executive branch* at all levels of government sees that all enacted legislation is enforced. At the federal level, the executive branch is headed by the President. At the state level, the executive is the governor, and at the local level the executive is the mayor, county executive, or someone with a similar title.

Judicial Branch of Government

judicial branch The branch of a government body that determines if there have been violations of the law and interprets the law if there are questions about what the law means in particular situations.

The *judicial branch* of government determines if there have been violations of the law. It also interprets the law if there are questions about what the law means in particular situations.

At the federal level, there are district courts, appeals courts, and the U.S. Supreme Court. Each state also has several levels of courts—trial courts, appeals courts, and a supreme court. At the local level, there are municipal courts, justices of the peace, and magistrate courts.

PART 1 Introduction to the Law

Functions of Administrative Agencies

Administrative agencies have been created for a variety of purposes and to fulfill diverse functions. These functions include regulating conduct, fulfilling government requirements, dispersing benefits, and providing goods and services, among others.

Regulating Conduct

Often an agency regulates such economic matters as price, entry into a particular geographical area, or entry into a particular kind of business.

> **EXAMPLE 5.1**
>
> Yamoto decided to start his own insurance agency. He learned that before he could enter this kind of business, he would have to pass an examination to test his knowledge of insurance and related law and be licensed by the state insurance department. State insurance regulations require insurance agents to be licensed to make sure that persons in this position are competent to perform their duties and to serve the people who rely on them.

Fulfilling Government Requirements

Administrative agencies exist at all levels of government, for example, to collect taxes and to raise revenues through various licensing laws. At the federal level, one of these agencies is the Internal Revenue Service (IRS), which collects taxes needed to operate the federal government.

Disbursing Benefits

A number of governmental agencies distribute subsidies and benefits of various kinds to farmers, recipients of public assistance, students, the unemployed, and the elderly.

Providing Goods and Services

Although the United States is largely a capitalist country in which the private sector provides most of the goods and services needed by the people, certain essential services cannot be efficiently provided by the private sector. Governments at all levels provide goods and services, such as electricity, water, hospital care, and public housing.

How and Why An Administrative Agency is Formed

For purposes of illustration, suppose that the consumers in a mythical, medium-sized city called Legis have been having problems with local

OBJECTIVE 2

Describe, by using examples, the operation of a typical administrative agency.

Administrative Law   CHAPTER 5

businesses. Merchants are cheating customers, scales in stores are inaccurate, businesses that promise certain services don't actually provide them, advertising is often false and misleading, and auto shops overcharge and perform poor-quality work. In short, consumers in the imaginary city of Legis are really having trouble coping with the abuses of the businesses in their community.

As might be expected, many consumers have complained to their elected representatives on the city council. When the need for a change became apparent, the city council decided to pass a consumer protection law. The law required that all businesses in the city of Legis be licensed and also stated that it would be unlawful for businesses to engage in "false advertising, deception, or the employment of unqualified workers to perform auto repair work."

Now let us examine a few aspects of the Legis consumer protection law. The law as passed does not define just what will be considered deceptive. For example, would a furniture store's newspaper advertisement be deceptive if it announced a Presidents' Day sale but failed to mention that the sale would be in effect at their downtown store only and not at their branch stores? Would the advertisement be deceptive if it failed to mention that quantities of certain items were significantly limited? The city council cannot legislate answers to these questions and many more like them. If it tried, it would be tied up for months or years because the legislators have neither the time nor the expertise to cope with these kinds of problems.

The city council knew that the goals of the consumer protection law would not be met by merely licensing businesses unless someone developed answers to such specific questions. Consequently, the law also established a consumer protection agency. The new agency would be headed by a director with the authority to (1) hire experts in various fields to clarify and enforce the law, and to assist in the formulation of agency rules or regulations; (2) license businesses operating in the city; and (3) establish rules that businesses would have to follow to keep their licenses. In addition to establishing the Consumer Protection Agency (CPA), the law required that all businesses would have to be licensed to operate within the city of Legis.

After the law had been passed, the mayor, with the approval of the city council, hired Sally Savus, a qualified consumer affairs person, to be the head of the CPA. Of course, the CPA—like any government entity—needs money to operate. So the city council appropriated a certain amount of money that the CPA could use to hire the necessary people, rent office space, pay telephone bills, and so on. The director, Ms. Savus, hired experts to develop rules and regulations governing advertising, auto repair shops, and other kinds of businesses. Unfortunately, people do not always obey rules and laws simply because they have been enacted. There must be some authority to ensure that people will obey the rules. For this reason, Ms. Savus also hired a group of inspectors to check the accuracy of scales, others to check the truthfulness of newspaper advertising, and so on.

Carrying the example a bit further, suppose that an inspector from the CPA finds that a scale in a supermarket is inaccurate and customers are being overcharged. The inspector notifies the store manager of the condition, but the manager, knowing that the inspector does not have the power of a police officer, points to the door and says, "Get lost." What happens next? The inspector might report back to the CPA director, informing her that the scale in the store is inaccurate and in violation of one of the rules established by the CPA. The director would probably send a letter to the merchant ordering him to appear at a hearing to answer the inspector's complaint. An *administrative hearing* conducted by an administrative agency is in some respects like an informal court trial, but without a jury. If the merchant refuses, his or her license can be revoked. The CPA director would then notify the regular court prosecutor that the business is operating without the required license—a violation of the law that established the agency. The court could then order the business closed.

administrative hearing
A trial-like judicial proceeding, without a jury, in which an administrative agency rules on matters of the law that the agency is charged with enforcing.

SIMILARITIES BETWEEN ADMINISTRATIVE AGENCIES AND GOVERNMENTS

Earlier in this chapter, we reviewed the three branches of federal, state, and local government—that is, the executive, legislative, and judicial branches. We pointed out that administrative agencies often carry out all three functions. Let us go back to the city of Legis and look at the CPA to see the similarities between governments and administrative agencies.

Executive Function

The executive function of the CPA is performed by the CPA director, Ms. Savus, together with her staff of experts, inspectors, and others. The executive function of the CPA includes the day-to-day operation of the agency and the establishment of general policies and objectives.

Legislative Function

The rules and regulations established by the CPA resemble the laws passed by a legislature and have the force of law. This is the legislative function of the administrative agency.

OBJECTIVE 3

Explain the similarities and differences between administrative agencies and governments.

Judicial Function

The activity of the CPA in holding hearings and requiring compliance with the decisions of the CPA made as a result of the hearings has an effect similar to the decisions made in a regular court of law. This activity is the judicial function of the administrative agency.

DIFFERENCES BETWEEN ADMINISTRATIVE AGENCIES AND GOVERNMENTS

While administrative agencies are very much like the three levels of government—federal, state, and local—they also differ in some important respects.

Executive Function

At all three levels of government, the voter has the opportunity to vote the executive into and out of office. Voters elect the President, a governor, and a mayor. Usually, however, voters do not elect the administrator of a regulatory agency. For the most part, the voter has little control over the activities of an administrative agency.

There are two general patterns in the executive organization of an administrative agency. In some agencies, the executive is appointed by and serves at the discretion of the elected executive of the government—the President or the governor—subject to approval by the legislature. At the federal level, examples include the people who head the Department of Transportation, the Department of the Interior, and the Department of Commerce. These executives can be removed from office without cause. In other cases, Congress has created agencies outside the executive branch that are headed by groups or individuals, such as boards or commissions appointed by Congress. Such boards or commissions carry out the executive function of the agency. After they are appointed to their multiyear terms, they may not be removed by the President without cause. Examples include members of the Federal Trade Commission (FTC) and the Securities and Exchange Commission (SEC).

Legislative Function

At one time there was heated debate about whether a legislature could delegate legislative functions to an administrative agency—thereby delegating authority that some people felt should remain with the legislature. This issue was resolved, and the notion of administrative agencies functioning in a law-making role is now widely accepted.

Rules and regulations are established by the agency, and not by elected representatives. Again, the voter does not have direct control over the legislative function of the administrative agency. Administrators are usually appointed by the executive with the advice and consent of the legislature. This practice gives the public, through its legislatures, at least some indirect control over the operation of administrative agencies. After administrators have been approved, however, it is generally difficult to remove them. Suppose the people do not like the way the agency is being run. In this case, they can do little except bring pressure on the executive or legislative branch to change the agency or to remove the administrator.

Judicial Function

The hearings conducted by an administrative agency do not provide for a jury, and the procedures are not as formal as in the case of a regular court hearing. Moreover, unlike the judge in a court trial, the "judge" at an administrative agency hearing is not entirely impartial because he or she is determining whether a person or firm has complied with the agency's own rules rather than with statutes enacted by the legislature. There was early debate over whether a legislature could delegate to an administrative agency the authority to function as judge in certain matters. This question was largely settled in the case of *Crowell v. Benson,* 285 U.S.22 (1932), in which the Supreme Court decided that an administrative agency does have such authority.

The determinations reached at a hearing conducted by an administrative agency can be appealed through the regular court system. As a practical matter, the courts seldom reverse the decisions of the agency unless it can be shown that the agency had clearly abused its authority.

To determine whether an administrative agency has abused its authority, the courts are guided by the statutes that established the agency and by the constitutions of the United States and the various states.

CRITICISM OF ADMINISTRATIVE AGENCIES

A number of critics allege that certain administrative agencies have been "captured" by the enterprises they were created to regulate. Because of the economic benefits or burdens that administrative agencies can bestow on a firm or an industry, those regulated have a powerful incentive to secure favorable rulings. In many cases, the need for specialized expertise in a given area can usually come only from the

OBJECTIVE 4

Discuss current criticism of administrative agencies.

industry being regulated. The insurance industry, for example, is highly complex, and many of the people who have the expertise needed to perform as effective regulators are, or have been, employed by the industry. Some have suggested that the heads of administrative agencies be elected by popular vote, as some insurance commissioners are. However, this change would not mean that these individuals could not be influenced as time passes, or that they would not use the position to further their own political or economic ambitions.

CHAPTER SUMMARY

1. Legislatures do not have the time and expertise to make the necessary rules to govern the operations of complex areas of our social and economic life. Legislatures also lack the time or expertise to supervise the many details of these complex areas on a day-to-day basis. Consequently, legislatures delegate these responsibilities to administrative agencies.

2. A typical administrative agency is a consumer protection agency, which licenses firms, formulates agency regulations, and clarifies and enforces the laws.

3. *Similarities:* Each level of government has three branches: legislative, executive, and judicial. Each branch has specific duties and powers. The organization of administrative agencies often resembles the organization of governments.
Differences: At all three levels of government, the voter has the opportunity to vote the executive into and out of office. Usually, however, voters do not elect the administrator of a regulatory agency. For the most part, voters have little control over the activities of an administrative agency.

4. Critics allege that administrative agencies are too closely aligned with the enterprises they were created to regulate. In many cases, the need for specialized expertise in a given area can come only from the industry being regulated. Some have suggested that the heads of administrative agencies be elected by popular vote.

Chapter 5 Assessment

MATCHING LEGAL TERMS

Match each of the following definitions with the correct term in the list below. Write the letter of your choice in the answer column.

    a. administrative agency   **c.** hearing   **e.** executive branch
    b. executive agency   **d.** legislative branch   **f.** judicial branch

1. A branch of government headed by the President, a governor, or a mayor.   1. _____
2. A branch of government with responsibility for enacting legislation.   2. _____
3. An organization that has executive, legislative, and judicial functions.   3. _____
4. A branch of government with responsibility for deciding cases brought before it.   4. _____
5. An activity conducted by an administrative agency to receive complaints and to make decisions as to the guilt or innocence of parties charged.   5. _____

TRUE/FALSE QUIZ

Indicate whether each of the following statements is true or false by writing *T* or *F* in the answer column.

6. Each level of government usually has three branches: executive, legislative, and judicial.   6. _____
7. The executive at all levels of government is usually elected by the voters.   7. _____
8. The heads of administrative agencies at all levels of government are appointed only by the executive branch.   8. _____
9. The executive branch of government sees that all enacted legislation is enforced.   9. _____
10. The judicial branch of government determines if there have been violations of the law.   10. _____
11. There is little similarity between government and the operation of administrative agencies.   11. _____
12. The hearings conducted by administrative agencies customarily include trial by jury.   12. _____
13. Administrative agencies enforce only laws enacted by legislatures.   13. _____
14. The only purpose of administrative agencies is to regulate business firms.   14. _____

Chapter 5 Assessment

15. There is no recourse from the decisions made at an administrative agency hearing.

15. _____

16. Once an administrator has been appointed, it is generally difficult to remove him or her from office.

16. _____

17. Administrative agencies are found at local, state, and federal levels of government.

17. _____

18. In most cases, the individual voter has direct control over administrative agencies.

18. _____

19. The courts often reverse the decisions of administrative agencies.

19. _____

20. Administrative agencies have various names, including boards, commissions, and departments.

20. _____

DISCUSSION QUESTIONS

Answer the following questions and discuss them in class.

21. Explain the similarities and differences between administrative agencies and governments.

22. Describe, using examples, the operation of a typical administrative agency.

23. Name at least three administrative agencies at each level of government—federal, state, and local.

24. Discuss current criticism of administrative agencies.

25. Explain why legislatures establish regulatory agencies.

74   PART 1   Introduction to the Law

Chapter 5 Assessment

THINKING CRITICALLY ABOUT THE LAW

Answer the following questions, which require you to think critically about the legal principles that you learned in this chapter.

26. Operation of Administrative Agencies Compare and contrast the operation of a government body with the operation of an administrative agency.

27. Judicial Function of an Administrative Agency Compare the procedure followed by an individual appearing as a defendant in a court of law with the procedure followed by an individual charged with a violation of a regulation appearing at a hearing of an administrative agency.

28. Criticism of Administrative Agencies Discuss some aspect of current criticism of administrative agencies and evaluate the validity of these views.

29. Impact of Administrative Agencies Individuals as well as businesses are affected by actions of administrative agencies in different ways. Select a particular agency and discuss how the agency affects individuals and businesses.

30. A Question of Ethics Analyze and discuss what recourse is available to citizens who determine that an executive of an administrative agency is behaving unethically.

Administrative Law   CHAPTER 5   75

Chapter 5 Assessment

CASE QUESTIONS

Study each case below and answer the questions that follow by writing *Yes* or *No* in the answer column.

31. **Government Regulations** For three years, Patterson operated a small restaurant and enjoyed a growing business. His customers were pleased with the food and service. One day an inspector from the city Board of Health visited the restaurant to inspect the sanitary conditions in the kitchen. The inspector informed Patterson that he would have to install a tile floor to replace the wooden one in the kitchen, because the wooden floor permitted the growth of disease-carrying insects and was, therefore, a health hazard.

   a. Does the Board of Health have the authority to force Patterson to make the alteration? a. _____

   b. Can Patterson appeal the order to a regular court with jurisdiction in the city? b. _____

   c. Can the Board of Health close the restaurant if Patterson refuses to comply with the order? c. _____

   d. Does it appear that the Board of Health is acting in the interest of the people of the community? d. _____

32. **Government Permits** Billings lived in a community that required a building permit before any major alterations could be made to a residential property. Billings refused to obtain the permit and proceeded to build a garage on her property.

   a. Can the city agency responsible for enforcing the law issue an order to stop the construction? a. _____

   b. Does it seem likely that the legislation requiring a building permit was intended to prevent construction? b. _____

   c. Does it seem likely that an appeal to a regular court would be successful? c. _____

   d. If Billings constructed the garage on her property without obtaining the permit, but met all the requirements of the appropriate building codes in her city, would the administrative agency require that it be torn down? d. _____

33. **Federal Regulations** Technology Unlimited employed 100 workers, operated one small factory, and manufactured special measuring devices that were sold throughout the world to the aircraft industry.

   a. Would federal regulatory agencies have control over any of the operations of Technology Unlimited? a. _____

   b. Would state regulatory agencies have control over any of the operations of Technology Unlimited? b. _____

   c. Would regulatory agencies in other countries in which the firm sold its products have control over any of the operations of Technology Unlimited? c. _____

   d. Would local regulatory agencies have control over any of the operations of Technology Unlimited? d. _____

Chapter 5 Assessment

CASE ANALYSIS

Study each of the following cases carefully and then briefly state the principle of law and your decision.

34. State Agencies The law in a particular state provided that the commissioner of insurance had the authority to approve or disapprove the rates charged consumers for automobile insurance. The managers of a particular insurance company felt that the services they provided their policyholders were superior to those offered by other companies and that they should be allowed to charge higher rates than those approved by the commissioner for all companies licensed to sell insurance in the state. At a hearing held in response to the company's request for permission to charge the higher rates, the commissioner considered the request. *Does it appear likely that the decisions of the state insurance commissioner will be binding on the company?*

Principle of law:

Decision:

35. State Authority An inspector from the Department of Weights and Measures in a particular city made a routine examination of the gasoline pumps at a service station to check their accuracy. The inspector found that one pump delivered only 4.5 gallons when the meter showed 5 gallons. The inspector sealed the pump and issued a summons ordering the station owner to report to a hearing the following day that would be conducted by the commissioner of the department of weights and measures. The operator of the service station claimed that the commissioner lacked authority to compel him to appear at the hearing. *Does the commissioner have the authority to regulate the operation of the service station?*

Principle of law:

Decision:

36. Local Agencies English was an employee of the City of Long Beach, California. His fitness to perform his duties was brought into question by an administrative agency of the city, which customarily held hearings at which such decisions were made. English was not notified of the meeting at which it was decided that he was unfit to continue his employment. He appealed the decision on the grounds that he was not present at the hearing and that the commission had acted improperly. *Does it appear that the administrative agency acted properly in making a decision affecting a person's employment without his being present?* [*English v. City of Long Beach,* 217 P.2d 22 (California).]

Administrative Law   CHAPTER 5   77

Chapter 5 Assessment

Principle of law:

_____

_____

Decision:

_____

_____

37. Government Codes The New York City charter authorizes the Board of Health to adopt a health code and to take other appropriate steps to ensure the health of the citizens of the city. The charter states that the code "shall have the force and effect of law." The board took action in 1964 to provide for the fluoridation of the public water supply. Paduano objected to the plan and brought suit to prevent the water treatment, claiming that the action was discriminatory because it benefited only children and the dental health of children could be achieved in other ways. *Is it likely that Paduano would succeed in his action?* [*Paduano v. City of New York*, 257 N.Y.S. 2d 531 (New York).]

Principle of law:

_____

_____

Decision:

_____

_____

LEGAL RESEARCH

Complete the following activities. Then share your findings with the class.

38. Working in Teams Working in teams of three or four, interview officials or supervisors of a department or agency of municipal government—the Department of Weights and Measures, Board of Health, or the like. Topics that might be included in the interview could range from the purposes of the agency, how the agency's performance is evaluated, and by whom? Report your findings to the class.

_____

_____

_____

39. Using Technology Using the Internet and search engines, locate the Web site of one of the administrative agencies that affect the lives of individuals and businesses in the community. Identify the kinds of services provided to the community.

_____

_____

_____

PART II

CONTRACTS

CHAPTER 6	Introduction to Contracts
CHAPTER 7	Offer, Acceptance, and Mutual Agreement
CHAPTER 8	Consideration
CHAPTER 9	Competent Parties
CHAPTER 10	Legal Purpose of Contracts
CHAPTER 11	Form of Contracts
CHAPTER 12	Operation of Contracts
CHAPTER 13	Discharge of Contracts

6
INTRODUCTION TO CONTRACTS

PERFORMANCE OBJECTIVES

After studying this chapter and completing the assessments, you will be able to:

1. Distinguish between agreements and contracts.

2. Identify the six elements of an enforceable contract.

3. Distinguish between oral and written, implied and express, simple and formal, and entire and divisible contracts.

4. Distinguish between executed and executory contracts, and among valid, void, and voidable contracts.

LEGAL TERMS

contract
offer
acceptance
mutual agreement
consideration
competence
legality of purpose
proper form
express contract
implied contract
valid contract
void contract
voidable contract

THE NATURE OF A CONTRACT

A *contract* is a legally enforceable agreement that is created when two or more competent parties agree to perform, or to avoid performing, certain acts that they have a legal right to do and that meet certain legal requirements. The Uniform Commercial Code (UCC) defines a contract as "the total legal obligation which results from the parties' agreement as affected by the Code or any other applicable rules of law" [UCC 1-201(11)].

This chapter introduces the six elements of a contract. Later chapters will examine each of these elements in greater detail. The enforceability of contracts is also discussed in this chapter.

contract A legally enforceable agreement that is created when two or more competent parties agree to perform, or to avoid performing, certain acts that they have a legal right to do and that meet certain legal requirements.

AGREEMENTS THAT RESULT IN CONTRACTS

All contracts are agreements, but not all agreements are contracts. The reason is that agreements often deal with personal or social matters that cannot be enforced by law. If an agreement imposes a legal obligation, an enforceable contract results. If an agreement imposes only a social or moral obligation, however, it is not a contract and is not legally enforceable.

OBJECTIVE 1

Distinguish between agreements and contracts.

> **EXAMPLE 6.1**
>
> Allen, an executive secretary, agreed to meet Yung, a college friend from the firm's accounting department, at noon to share a ride to a company training seminar. Allen failed to keep the appointment, and Yung, who waited an hour for her, missed the seminar. She had no legal course of action against Allen because the agreement was based on a social, rather than legal, relationship.

PURPOSES OF A CONTRACT

Contracts may be created for any number of reasons. They may relate, for example, to the sale of merchandise or services, to employment, or to the transfer of ownership of land (real estate) or personal property such as a sailboat. A contract may also be extended and revised as needed to reflect the wishes of the parties. An engineer, for example, might enter into a contract with an assistant, who might agree to provide research help. Later, the two might broaden the contract to form a partnership; and finally, they might extend their contractual relationship to actually manufacturing and selling the products they develop.

OBJECTIVE 2

Identify the six elements of an enforceable contract.

offer A proposal made by one party (the offeror) to another person (the offeree) that indicates a willingness to enter into a contract.

acceptance An indication made by the offeree that he or she agrees to be bound by the terms of the offer.

mutual agreement The state of mind that exists between an offeror and an offeree when a valid offer has been accepted, and the parties know what the terms are and have agreed to be bound by them. Mutual agreement is also known as "a meeting of the minds."

consideration The promise to give up something of value that a party to a contract has a legal right to keep, or to do something that the party is not otherwise legally required to do.

competence Being mentally capable of understanding the terms of a contract.

legality of purpose The requirement that the intent of a contract be legal for the contract to be enforceable.

ELEMENTS OF AN ENFORCEABLE CONTRACT

To be legally enforceable, a contract must contain six elements: (1) offer and acceptance, (2) mutual agreement, (3) consideration, (4) competent parties, (5) legal purpose, and (6) proper form. If one of these elements is missing, the courts will usually refuse to enforce the contract. Each of these elements will be discussed in this chapter.

Offer and Acceptance

An *offer* is a proposal made by one party, the offeror, to another party, the offeree, that indicates a willingness to enter into a contract. An *acceptance* is an indication made by the offeree that he or she agrees to be bound by the terms of the offer.

Mutual Agreement

The parties to a contract must have a clear understanding of what they are undertaking. The contract must show *mutual agreement,* that is, a meeting of the minds.

Consideration

In most cases, each party to a contract must promise either to give up something of value that he or she has a legal right to keep or to do something that he or she is not otherwise legally required to do. This exchange of promises is called *consideration.* If only one party promises something, such as paying a certain amount of money, and the other party promises nothing, then the agreement lacks consideration. Exceptions to the general rule will be discussed in Chapter 7.

Competent Parties

The parties to a contract must have *competence,* that is, be capable of understanding what they are doing. They must be of legal age and normal mentality. The functioning of a party's mind must not be impaired by injury, mental disease, or the influence of drugs or alcohol.

Legality of Purpose

The intent of a contract must not violate the law. It must have *legality of purpose.* The courts will not enforce a contract to do something that is against the law.

Proper Form

Certain contracts, such as those involving $500 or more, or those that cannot be fulfilled within a year, must be in writing to be enforceable. Other kinds of contracts must not only be in writing but must also follow a prescribed form. These requirements for contracts are known as *proper form.*

These essential elements of a contract will be discussed in more detail in later chapters. At this point, it is necessary only to remember that an agreement, to be legally enforceable, must contain these six elements.

proper form The requirement that the form of a contract be correct for the terms of the contract to be enforceable.

> **EXAMPLE 6.2**
>
> Rossetti offered to sell his grand piano to Bray for $1,200. Bray agreed to buy it at that price, and the two parties put their agreement in writing. Both Rossetti and Bray were legally competent to enter into a contract. They came to a mutual agreement about the terms of the transaction. Rossetti promised to give up his grand piano in return for Bray's promise to pay $1,200 for it. This was the consideration given by Rossetti and by Bray. Because the agreement involved more than $500, the proper form was a written contract. And, of course, the sale of a grand piano was perfectly legal. Because the agreement contained the six elements, a legally enforceable contract resulted.

Kinds of Contracts

Contracts may be classified in several ways, depending on the manner in which they are created, expressed, or performed. Thus, a contract may be either oral or written; it may be express or implied; it may be formal or simple; it may be entire or divisible.

Oral Contracts

Most contracts in business and in private life are simple, unwritten agreements that result from conversation between the parties involved. Even a telephone conversation can result in an enforceable oral contract. An *oral contract* is one that is not in writing nor signed by the parties. That is, it is a real contract created entirely by the conversation of the parties. A person who discusses the terms of a purchase with a salesperson, pays cash for it, and takes the item with him or her is making an oral contract. A person makes many such contracts in a day, and yet each of these simple transactions contains all the elements of a contract.

OBJECTIVE 3

Distinguish between oral and written, implied and express, simple and formal, and entire and divisible contracts.

Written Contracts

A *written contract* is one that is reduced to writing in a permanent form. Although an oral contract may be just as binding as a written contract, it is advisable to put a contract in writing if the transaction is important or complicated, if the contract involves a large amount of money, or if the contract will extend over a long period of time. Thus, a contact calling for the construction of a building, the installation of expensive machinery, or the payment of a large sum of money for household furnishings should be in writing to protect the parties involved and to prevent a later disagreement over the terms.

The law does not specify any particular form or language to be used. It is sufficient that the parties clearly express themselves in understandable language. A written contract can be simply a handwritten note, a printed statement, a typewritten letter, or any other memorandum containing the terms of the agreement, as long as it is signed by the party or parties who wish to be bound by the agreement. Some important agreements are not even called contracts although in fact they are; they may be called simply a "Memorandum of Agreement" or other such name.

> **EXAMPLE 6.3**
>
> Ward, an editor with a publishing company, had frequent dealings with Michalski, an author with whom the company had a binding contract. During the course of working together on a book manuscript, a number of agreements concerning matters that were not covered in the existing contract were made during personal meetings and telephone conversations. Wishing to strengthen the existing contract and make it more specific, Ward sent Michalski a letter that began, "The purpose of this letter is to reduce to writing the substance of our several discussions in which you agreed to. . . . " At this point, the letter confirmed all the points that needed clarification. The letter concluded with, ". . . if the above reflects our agreements, please sign and date one copy of this letter in the place indicated and return one copy to me at your earliest convenience. The extra copy of the letter is for your files." At the bottom of the page, there was the following: "Accepted and agreed to: _____, Date: _____."

The purpose of this simple business letter was to reduce the possibilities of later disagreement. In the event of a dispute involving an oral contract, the parties must depend on circumstances, or on the testimony of witnesses, to determine the rights of the parties. The problem, of course, is that memories fade, personal conversations cannot be filed and produced as evidence, and even witnesses cannot be relied on to recall exactly what was said. With a written contract, these particular problems never arise.

Express Contracts

A contract that explicitly states the agreement of the parties, either orally or in writing, is called an *express contract.* The term is used to distinguish such contracts from others in which the meaning or the intention of the parties is inferred from their actions.

express contract A contract that explicitly states the agreement of the parties, either orally or in writing.

Implied Contracts

Certain business and personal transactions are neither oral nor written, but are nevertheless legally binding. The terms of these agreements are understood from the conduct of the parties, the customs of the trade, or the conditions or circumstances rather than from oral or written words. A transaction of this kind is considered an *implied contract.* Thus, an implied contract results when a customer asks a merchant to deliver an article to his or her home with no mention of payment. The buyer implies that he or she will pay the market price of the article when it is delivered or when the bill is presented.

implied contract A contract that does not explicitly state the agreement of the parties, but in which the terms of the agreement can be inferred from the conduct of the parties, the customs of the trade, or the circumstances.

EXAMPLE 6.4

> Levy entered a retail computer store, ordered a word processing program, and left instructions that it was to be delivered to his office. The price of the program, when payment was to be made, and the exact time of delivery were not discussed. This is an implied contract. Several implied agreements are involved: (1) that the market price of the software will be paid; (2) that payment will be made on delivery or when it is customary to make payment, depending on the usual relationship of the merchant and the customer or the customs of the business; and (3) that delivery will be made within a reasonable time.

An implied contract results when a person accepts goods or services that cannot reasonably be considered a gift. A person who stands idly by while another confers an unrequested benefit implies a promise to pay a reasonable amount for the benefit. Such a promise of payment, however, is not implied if goods were delivered or the services were rendered during the absence of, and without the knowledge of, the recipient.

Formal Contracts

A *formal contract,* or specialty contract, is a written contract under seal. The seal on a formal contract may consist of simply the word *Seal* or *L.S.,* (which means *locus sigilli,* the place of the seal), a scroll, a wafer, or an impression on the paper. Today, only a few types of contracts, such as bonds, mortgages, and deeds conveying title to real estate, are required to have a seal. Many states have stopped using the seal entirely.

Simple Contracts

A contract that is not formal, whether it is written, oral, or implied, is called a *simple contract.* That is, a simple contract is an informal contract made without seal—even though the subject matter of the contract is extremely complex and may involve large amounts of money.

The laws of a certain state require that every real estate mortgage be in writing and under seal. A mortgage bond was made in this state on the prescribed form by a homeowner who printed the letters *L.S.* opposite the signature and thereby fulfilled the legal requirement that the mortgage bond be under seal. A seal may consist of any design adopted for that purpose.

Entire Contracts

An *entire contract,* or indivisible contract, has two or more parts. Each part is dependent on the others for satisfactory performance. Such a contract must be completely performed. The law of sales specifically states that "unless otherwise agreed, all goods called for by a contract for sale must be tendered [offered] in a single delivery and payment is due only on such tender" [UCC 2-307].

> **EXAMPLE 6.5**
>
> DeWitt Real Estate had planned to move into new offices and ordered 20 new desks and accompanying chairs from Belmont Office Supply. On the delivery date, Belmont delivered only the desks and explained that the manufacturer of the chairs had been experiencing labor difficulties. Belmont, however, demanded immediate payment for the desks. The order for the desks and chairs is an entire contract because these items are usually ordered in sets and the desks are of little use without the chairs. DeWitt Real Estate is not required to pay for the desks until the chairs are delivered.

Divisible Contracts

A *divisible contract* is one that consists of two or more parts, each part being independent of the others. In the case of a contract for the sale of goods, a party to such a contract must be paid upon request for any part of the contract performed as agreed, even though the entire contract is not performed. The law of sales provides that "where the circumstances give either party to a contract for sale the right to make or demand delivery in lots, the price, if it can be apportioned, may be demanded for each lot" [UCC 2-307].

> **EXAMPLE 6.6**
>
> Schiff, a dealer in playground equipment, placed an order with Play and Grow Company for five playground swings and three slides. Play and Grow delivered the swings, but because of a shortage of materials, could not deliver the slides until three months later. Schiff must accept and pay for the swings, even though the slides were not sent with the swings, because the swings can be used without the slides (unlike the previous case, in which the chairs were needed to use the desks).

STATUS OF CONTRACTS

Contracts frequently have a long life. At any particular time, a contract may be completed, in the process of completion, or awaiting the first act of the parties to execute its terms.

Executory Contracts

An *executory contract* is one in which some future act or obligation remains to be performed under its terms. A contract is completely executory if no part of it has been performed. It is partly executory if some provisions have been performed and some have yet to be performed. If an article is ordered and delivered but not paid for, for example, the contract is completed on the part of the seller but executory on the part of the buyer.

> **EXAMPLE 6.7**
>
> Tran signed an agreement with the Epsilon Technology Company for the installation of an office computer network. The computers were installed, but because of a shortage of the new models of laser printers covered by the contract, the printers were not installed. The part of the contract dealing with the computers and connecting cables was completed, but the part concerned with the printers was still executory.

Executed Contracts

A contract in which the terms of the agreement have been fully performed by both parties is an *executed contract*. An executed contract is not really a contract at all. It is more a record of an agreement that has been completed in all respects by all the parties.

OBJECTIVE 4

Distinguish between executed and executory contracts, and among valid, void, and voidable contracts.

ENFORCEABILITY OF CONTRACTS

It is important to determine whether a contract is valid, void, or voidable, because not all contracts can be enforced.

Valid Contracts

The vast majority of contracts entered into in any business day are valid. A ***valid contract*** is an agreement resulting in an obligation that is legally enforceable. They meet all the requirements of a contract because all six essential elements are present.

valid contract An agreement resulting in an obligation that is legally enforceable.

> **EXAMPLE 6.8**
>
> Gorbea, the owner of a computer supply company, agreed in writing with the Diaz Sign Company to pay $800 to have a specific sign erected on her property within 30 days. The Diaz Sign Company constructed and installed the sign. All the essentials of a legal contract are present in this case.

Offer and Acceptance Gorbea offered Diaz Sign Company $800 to erect a specific sign within 30 days. Diaz Sign Company indicated its acceptance of the offer by signing the contract.

Mutual Agreement There was no confusion regarding the amount, the specifications, or the time limits for completion of the transaction.

Consideration Gorbea promised to pay $800, and the Diaz Sign Company promised to build and install the sign.

Competent Parties Gorbea and the Diaz Sign Company are competent to enter into a legal contract.

Legality of Purpose The sale and installation of the sign is a legal act. There are no indications of violations of local codes or ordinances.

Proper Form The contract concerned the sale of a sign for an amount over $500, and it was in written form.

Now, consider the six elements again. If Gorbea offered Diaz Sign Company $800, and Diaz said it would charge $900, then there would be no acceptance of the offer. If Gorbea thought she was getting a revolving electric sign and Diaz Sign Company thought she wanted a simple electrically lighted sign, there would not be mutual agreement. If Gorbea did not agree to pay for the sign, consideration would be lacking. If Gorbea were a minor, she would not have been a competent party. If local zoning regulations prohibited the kind of sign Gorbea wanted, the contract would not have been for a legal purpose. The UCC requires that contracts for the sale of goods for $500 or more be in writing. If the agreement were not in writing, it would not be enforceable because it would lack the proper form.

Void Contracts

An agreement that lacks one or more of the essential elements of a contract is a ***void contract*** from the beginning. That is, it is not a true contract at all and is therefore unenforceable.

void contract A contract that is not enforceable from the beginning because it lacks one of the requirements of a valid contract.

> **EXAMPLE 6.9**
>
> Philmore operated a manufacturing firm and entered into an agreement with an illegal enterprise that brought illegal aliens into the country to work in his factory. When the first truckload of immigrants arrived, Philmore realized that they were unable to follow directions because of their inability to speak English. Philmore refused to pay, but the enterprise wanted its money. Neither Philmore nor the enterprise would have access to any legal remedy because their agreement violated federal immigration laws and was void from the beginning. It lacked an essential element of a contract: legality of purpose.

Voidable Contracts

An agreement that may be rejected by one of the parties for a legally acceptable reason is a ***voidable contract.*** Such a contract is valid and enforceable until or unless it is rejected by the party who has the right to withdraw. Thus, in a contract between a minor and an adult, the adult must perform his or her part of the agreement unless the minor decides to withdraw from the contract.

voidable contract An agreement that can be rejected by one of the parties for a legally acceptable reason.

> **EXAMPLE 6.10**
>
> Braun, a minor, agreed with Main Street Used Cars to buy a certain car. The car company must perform as agreed, but Braun, who is not legally a competent party, can withdraw from the contract.

Suppose that Braun was an adult and she had agreed to buy a certain car if it were repainted blue. Because of an error, however, it was repainted green. Braun can withdraw from the contract because the seller failed to perform according to the terms of the contract. The contract is voidable, at Braun's option. If the color green is not acceptable to Braun, she can withdraw from the contract, insist that the car be painted blue, or accept the car as is but with some settlement, such as a lower price than she originally agreed to pay.

Introduction to Contracts CHAPTER 6

CHAPTER SUMMARY

1 A contract is a legally enforceable agreement. All contracts are agreements, but not all agreements are contracts. In some cases, agreements are of a social nature and are not enforceable by law.

2 The six elements of an enforceable contract are (1) offer and acceptance, (2) mutual agreement, (3) consideration, (4) competent parties, (5) legal purpose, and (6) proper form.

3 An oral contract is one that is a legally enforceable contract created entirely by the conversation of the parties. A written contract is one that is reduced to writing in a permanent form.

Express contracts specifically state the agreement of the parties, either orally or in writing. Implied contracts are agreements the terms of which are inferred from the conduct of the parties, the customs of the trade, or from the circumstances.

A formal contract is a written contract under seal. A simple contract is an informal contract made without seal—even though the subject matter of the contract is extremely complex.

An entire contract has two or more parts, each dependent on the others for satisfactory performance. A divisible contract is one that consists of two or more parts, each part being independent of the others.

4 An executory contract is one in which some future act or obligation remains to be performed under its terms. An executed contract is one in which the terms of the agreement have been fully performed by both parties.

Valid contracts are agreements resulting in obligations that are legally enforceable. Void contracts are agreements that lack one or more of the essential elements of a contract. Voidable contracts are agreements that may be rejected by one of the parties for a legally acceptable reason.

Chapter 6 Assessment

MATCHING LEGAL TERMS

Match each of the following definitions with the correct term in the list below. Write the letter of your choice in the answer column.

- **a.** competent party
- **b.** consideration
- **c.** divisible contract
- **d.** entire contract
- **e.** executed contract
- **f.** executory contract
- **g.** express contract
- **h.** formal contract
- **i.** implied contract
- **j.** legality of purpose
- **k.** mutual agreement
- **l.** oral contract
- **m.** proper form
- **n.** voidable contract
- **o.** void contract

1. A "meeting of the minds" regarding the rights and obligations of the parties to a contract. 1. _____
2. A person who is of legal age and normal mentality. 2. _____
3. The promises exchanged by parties to a contract. 3. _____
4. A contract that is created entirely through conversation of the parties involved. 4. _____
5. A contract that is understood from the acts or conduct of the parties. 5. _____
6. A written contract that bears a seal. 6. _____
7. A contract with several unrelated parts, each of which can stand alone. 7. _____
8. The requirement that a contract cannot violate the law. 8. _____
9. A contract with several related parts, each dependent on the other parts for satisfactory performance. 9. _____
10. A contract that's meaning is not determined by the conduct of the parties. 10. _____
11. A contract that has not yet been completed by both parties. 11. _____
12. A contract that allows the disabled party to withdraw. 12. _____
13. A contract that has been fully completed by both parties. 13. _____
14. A contract that lacks an essential element and hence was never legally a contract. 14. _____
15. A requirement for contracts for the sale of goods for $500 or more. 15. _____

TRUE/FALSE QUIZ

Indicate whether each of the following statements is true or false by writing *T* or *F* in the answer column.

16. All agreements between two competent parties are contracts. 16. _____
17. Written contracts must be handwritten to be legally enforceable. 17. _____
18. Implied contracts are those dealing only with personal transactions. 18. _____
19. Entire contracts are those composed of several related parts. 19. _____

Chapter 6 Assessment

20. To be legally enforceable, contracts must be in writing.   **20.** _____

21. Contracts need not be stated in legal language.   **21.** _____

22. Implied contracts are neither oral nor written.   **22.** _____

23. The terms of express contracts are specifically stated.   **23.** _____

24. A contract is considered executed as soon as all parties have performed all parts of it.   **24.** _____

25. In a contract between a minor and an adult, the adult must perform his or her part of the agreement unless or until the minor decides to withdraw.   **25.** _____

DISCUSSION QUESTIONS

Answer the following questions and discuss them in class.

26. Parties to a contract must have a clear understanding of what they are undertaking—a meeting of the minds. Provide an example of two parties who have reached such a clear understanding.

_____
_____
_____

27. Provide an example of a contracting party offering consideration by doing something that he or she is not legally required to do.

_____
_____
_____

28. The law requires that the parties be competent to enter into a contract. Give an example of a party who lacks competence.

_____
_____
_____

29. The law requires that the purpose of a contract be legal. Provide an example of a contract that would not be enforceable because it lacks legality of purpose.

_____
_____
_____

30. Provide an example of an agreement that would need to be in writing to be enforceable.

_____
_____
_____

Chapter 6 Assessment

THINKING CRITICALLY ABOUT THE LAW

Answer the following questions, which require you to think critically about the legal principles that you learned in this chapter.

31. Competent Parties The law allows a minor to withdraw from a contract simply because he or she is a minor, whereas the other party is bound if the minor wishes to carry out the contract. Do you think the law is fair in such instances? Why or why not?

32. Implied Contracts Certain business and personal transactions are neither oral nor written, but are nevertheless legally binding. The terms of these agreements are understood from the actions or conduct of the parties, from the customs of the trade, or from the conditions or circumstances rather than from oral or written words. Do you think implied contracts should be enforceable? Explain your answer.

33. Legality of Purpose Some activities that are neither crimes nor torts are made illegal by state or federal statutes and are unenforceable. Examples are wagering agreements or lending money at high rates of interest (usury). Do you believe legislatures should interfere with the free will of contracting parties? Why or why not?

34. Proper Form The law for many years has required certain kinds of contracts, such as those involving $500 or more, must be in writing to be enforceable. Should the amount of $500 be increased to reflect the effects of inflation? Explain your answer.

35. A Question of Ethics Do you think it is unethical for an underage person, who appears to be older, to enter into a contract with another person who in good faith expects the underage party to fulfill the terms of the contract? Why or why not?

Introduction to Contracts   CHAPTER 6

Chapter 6 Assessment

CASE QUESTIONS

Study each of the following cases and indicate whether the contract is executed, executory, or neither, and whether it is valid, voidable, or void, by placing an *X* in the space provided.

36. Status of Contract Knoll and Kalichuk signed an agreement for the sale of Knoll's sailboat. The agreement was complete in all respects, including the provision of time and place of delivery, sale price, and accessories included. On the date agreed for the exchange of payment and delivery of the boat, Knoll informed Kalichuk that he had changed his mind and decided not to sell.

   a. Executed _____   Executory _____   Neither _____

   b. Valid _____   Voidable _____   Void _____

37. Status of Contract Arslantian, a suburban homeowner who was involved in a major landscaping project, offered to pay Manley, a county employee, 50 percent of the market price for certain shrubbery belonging to the County Parks Commission, if Manley would deliver it to a meeting place in a shopping mall.

   a. Executed _____   Executory _____   Neither _____

   b. Valid _____   Voidable _____   Void _____

Study the case below and answer the questions that follow by writing *Yes* or *No* in the answer column, or by writing other answers.

38. Elements of Contract Fiscus, age 23, entered into an oral contract with Badger, a 30-year-old bricklayer, for the construction of a backyard barbecue for a fee of $300. The work was completed in two weeks, as agreed.

   a. Is there an offer and an acceptance? _____

   b. Is this a valid contract? _____

   c. Are the parties competent? _____

   d. Name the parties. _____

   e. Is the purpose of the contract legal? _____

   f. What is the purpose? _____

   g. Is there consideration present? _____

   h. What is the consideration? _____

   i. Is there mutual understanding? _____

   j. Explain the purpose of the contract. _____

   _____

Chapter 6 Assessment

CASE ANALYSIS

Study each of the following cases carefully and then briefly state the principle of law and your decision.

39. Elements of Contract Esposito hired Excel Construction Company to repair a porch roof for $625 while she was out of town on vacation. All terms of the agreement were specified in a written contract, but the agreement failed to specify whether it was the front or rear porch that needed repair. When Esposito returned, she discovered that Excel had repaired the rear porch roof. She refused to pay, claiming that she wanted the front porch roof repaired. *Were all essential elements of a contract present, and will Esposito be required to pay for the work that was done?*

Principle of law:

_____

_____

Decision:

_____

_____

40. Consideration William Storey, Sr., promised his nephew, William Storey II, that he would pay him $5,000 if he avoided drinking, using tobacco, swearing, and playing cards or billiards for money until he became 21 years old. The nephew agreed to the offer and kept his part of the bargain. At the age of 21, he wrote to his uncle and asked for the $5,000. The uncle acknowledged the promise, praised his nephew for keeping his part of the bargain, but did not pay the money at that time. A short time later, the uncle died. The executor of his estate refused to pay the nephew, claiming that the contract was invalid due to the lack of consideration. *Was the nephew's promise to avoid drinking, using tobacco, swearing, and playing cards or billiards for money until he became 21 legal consideration?* [*Hamer v. Sidway*, 27 N.E.256 (New York).]

Principle of law:

_____

_____

Decision:

_____

_____

41. Proper Form Hodge, a 54-year-old employee of a bank, discussed his job and future with Tilley, President of Evans Financial Corporation and his employer. They agreed orally on a number of matters, including job title and location. After eight months on the new job, Tilley became dissatisfied with Hodge's work and discharged him. Hodge immediately sued, claiming that the oral agreement provided for employment until he retired at age 65. *Does the length of time needed to fulfill the contract have a bearing on the enforceability of the contract?* [*Hodge v. Evans Financial Corp.*, 778 F.2d 794 (District of Columbia).]

Principle of law:

_____

_____

Introduction to Contracts **CHAPTER 6** 95

Chapter 6 Assessment

Decision:

___

42. Divisable or Entire Contract Grogan, a marketing consultant, was hired by Kreger Bottling Company to conduct market research into the taste preferences of consumers in a major city. Before he concluded the project, he was asked to take on the additional task of analyzing the appeal of various shapes of bottles that Kreger was considering for a new line of soft drinks. When the taste test was finished, but before the second project was completed, Grogan submitted his bill for the taste test. Kreger refused to pay until the bottle test was completed. *Does Grogan have a basis for demanding payment for the portion of the work done?*

Principle of law:

___

Decision:

___

LEGAL RESEARCH

Complete the following activities. Then share your findings with the class.

43. Working in Teams In teams of three or four, interview several small businesses to learn some of the steps that business persons routinely follow to avoid problems involving contracts.

___

44. Using Technology Using the Internet and search engines, locate the Web site of one of several legal databases to expand your depth of knowledge of the legal terms related to the kinds of contracts described in the chapter.

___

CHAPTER 7

OFFER, ACCEPTANCE, AND MUTUAL AGREEMENT

PERFORMANCE OBJECTIVES

After studying this chapter and completing the assessments, you will be able to:

1. Explain and provide examples of the three requirements of a valid offer.

2. Distinguish between a call for bids and an offer.

3. Evaluate, in given situations, whether an advertisement would be considered an invitation to trade or a valid offer.

4. Explain and provide examples of the two requirements for a valid acceptance.

5. Identify the three ways in which an offer may be terminated.

6. List seven ways in which a lack of a meeting of the minds may interfere with the legal enforcement of agreements.

LEGAL TERMS

invitation to trade
counteroffer
termination by lapse of time
revocation
rejection
fraud
puffery
misrepresentation
mistake
undue influence
duress
contract of adhesion
unconscionable contract

REACHING MUTUAL AGREEMENT

In Chapter 6, the six requirements of an enforceable contract were discussed. One of these elements is offer and acceptance, which results in mutual agreement, another element of an enforceable contract.

Various aspects of offers and acceptances are discussed in this chapter. Potential problems with achieving a meeting of the minds, as well as different ways in which an offer can be terminated, are also discussed.

CHARACTERISTICS OF A VALID OFFER

For an offer to be valid, it must be (1) definite and certain; (2) communicated to the offeree; and (3) made with a serious intention that the offeror will be bound by it.

OBJECTIVE 1

Explain and provide examples of the three requirements of a valid offer.

An Offer Must Be Definite and Certain

To be definite and certain, an offer should specify all the terms and conditions of the contract. Later disagreement can be avoided if the offer is made as specific as possible. Under the Uniform Commercial Code (UCC), however, the omission of one or more essential terms does not necessarily make an offer invalid provided that the contract contains sufficient information to suggest that the parties intended to enter into a contract [UCC 2-204].

According to the UCC, uncertainty does not necessarily invalidate a contract. When an offer of sale does not specify a price, it will be assumed that the parties intended "a reasonable price at the time set for delivery" [UCC 2-305]. Moreover, uncertainty regarding place of delivery, time for shipment, and time for payment do not always invalidate a contract [UCC 2-308, 309, 310]. Of course, a court resolution to a dispute that arises from uncertainty about contract terms is a difficult way to do business. As a general rule, if an offer is to be definite and certain, it should cover the same points as a good newspaper story—who, what, when, where, and how much.

An Offer Must Be Communicated

An offeror can make the offer known to the offeree in various ways. The usual means of communication are generally used, including oral communication (in person, by telephone, television, or radio), and written communication (letters, telegrams, fax, computer transmission, and other written forms). Making an offer and having it accepted is such a common event in today's business world that people in business usually use a printed purchase order on which the terms of the offer are shown. Purchase orders are usually considered offers to buy. The buyer is the offeror and the seller is the offeree; communication may also be implied by the actions of the parties.

> **EXAMPLE 7.1**
>
> Ellenby, an executive secretary, went into Metro Stationery, where she and her employer frequently purchased office supplies. She selected a box of ballpoint pens and a box of computer floppy disks and showed them to the owner, who was busy with another customer at the time. The owner nodded and smiled, and the secretary left the store. By her action, she made an implied offer. The store owner, by his conduct, had implied that he had accepted the offer and that he would add the charges for her purchases to her employer's account.

An Offer Must Intend an Enforceable Obligation

Offers made in anger or jest, or those made under severe emotional strain, are obviously not made with the intent of entering into a valid, enforceable agreement. In these cases, there is no meeting of the minds, and as a result, no valid offer. The lack of serious intent must, however, be apparent to a reasonable person.

> **EXAMPLE 7.2**
>
> Clayton, a retired executive, was outraged at the amount of a repair bill for his one-year-old car, which was worth about $12,000. He screamed that repair bills were costing him more than the car was worth. He said, "I'll sell this bucket of bolts to anyone for $500." One of the mechanics present quickly offered Clayton five $100 bills. It is doubtful that the mechanic could force the sale because there was a lack of serious intent.

BIDS, ADVERTISING, AND PUBLIC OFFERS

The requirement of offer and acceptance is usually fairly straightforward in contracts involving two or a few parties. However, the issue gets complicated when there is little or no direct contact between the parties, as in the case of bidding, advertising, and public offers.

Bids and Estimates

A call for a bid or estimate for materials to be furnished or work to be done is not considered an offer, but rather a request for an offer or an invitation to negotiate that can be accepted or rejected by the person

OBJECTIVE 2

Distinguish between a call for bids and an offer.

calling for the bid. Such an announcement or solicitation is often called a *request for proposal,* or RFP. Many cities and states that wish to enter into a contract with private firms or individuals for the performance of work or the purchase of goods or services require that the lowest bid be accepted. The main purpose of such a regulation is to ensure that the purchaser gets the most economical price and to prevent dishonesty in the form of bribery and kickbacks.

> **EXAMPLE 7.3**
>
> The Board of Education of a particular city decided to incorporate a new computer course in its vocational program. Because the course was highly specialized, it was felt that experts would be needed to prepare the new curriculum. Requests for proposals were sent to experts in computer education, and an announcement was published in publications that normally reach specialists in that field.

Note that, in Example 7.3, if the Board of Education's call for bids was considered an offer, and the bids were considered acceptances, then a valid contract would result when the first bid was submitted. Instead, the call for bids or proposals was regarded as a solicitation of offers, and thus the proposals submitted were deemed offers.

Advertising

An advertisement, such as those that appear every day on television and in newspapers and magazines, is generally regarded as an ***invitation to trade,*** or an invitation to make an offer, rather than a valid offer, because it does not contain sufficient words of commitment to sell. Sometimes goods are advertised in a newspaper at an incorrect price. Generally, if the mistake is obvious to a reasonable person, the store need not honor the price. Otherwise, they must. These rules follow the consumer protection laws in most states. In this case, the merchant, even when the mistake is not his or her fault, may decide to sell the goods as advertised even though doing so may not profitable. The reason is usually that the merchant believes it is a good business decision to sell at the advertised price to retain public goodwill. Goodwill is worth more than whatever the merchant would gain by enforcing his or her legal rights. If the error is the fault of the newspaper, the merchant will expect some adjustment.

If, however, an advertisement contains a positive promise and a positive statement of what the advertiser expects in return, the courts will usually hold that the advertisement is an offer. This is especially true if the word *offer* is used in the advertisement.

OBJECTIVE 3

Evaluate, in given situations, whether an advertisement would be considered an invitation to trade or a valid offer.

invitation to trade An announcement published for the purpose of creating interest and attracting a response by many people. It is not considered a valid offer because it does not contain sufficient words of commitment to sell.

> **EXAMPLE 7.4**
>
> Surplus Store ran an advertisement in a newspaper that said, "SATURDAY 9 A.M. 2 BRAND NEW PASTEL MINK 3-SKIN SCARFS SELLING FOR $800. OUT THEY GO SATURDAY. EACH $200. 1 BLACK LAPIN STOLE, BEAUTIFUL, WORTH $300, $1.00 FIRST COME, FIRST SERVED." Lefkowitz was the first to arrive on Saturday and demanded the lapin stole for $1.00. Surplus Store refused to sell it to him because of a "house rule" that the offer was intended for women only. Lefkowitz sued and was awarded $299. The court held that the words, "*First come, first served,*" created a promise that is ordinarily lacking in advertisements.

Public Offers

When an advertisement offers a reward for information that might lead to the arrest of a criminal or for the return of a lost article, it is regarded as a general offer to the public at large. Acceptance of a *public offer* by anyone, as indicated by the performance of the act, results in an enforceable contract.

> **EXAMPLE 7.5**
>
> Jamison lost an expensive pedigreed dog while at a shopping mall. He placed an advertisement in the *Daily Journal,* offering a $200 reward for the dog's return. This offer is valid, even though it is directed to thousands of readers, only one of whom could accept it.

The number of persons reached by an advertisement has no bearing on the validity of the offer. The purpose of such an advertisement is to reach a person of unknown identity with whom a valid contract can be made.

Characteristics of a Valid Acceptance

The valid acceptance of an offer must be (1) communicated to the offeror, and (2) unconditional.

Acceptance Must Be Communicated

The usual forms of communication, such as telephone, letter, telegram, e-mail, and others, may be used in accepting an offer unless the offer specifies a certain form of communication, such as "Reply by registered mail," "Reply by return mail," or "Reply by e-mail." E-mail has the advantages of being as fast as a telephone and constituting a written record like a letter. The UCC states: "An offer to make a contract shall be construed as inviting acceptance in any manner and by any medium reasonable under the circumstances" [UCC 2-206].

OBJECTIVE 4

Explain and provide examples of the two requirements for a valid acceptance.

If an offer is sent to an offeree by e-mail or by letter, requesting acceptance by e-mail, and the offeree accepts the offer by letter, the acceptance becomes valid at the time it is received by the offeror. If the medium of acceptance is the same as that used by the offeror or specified in the offer, it becomes effective when it is sent. Thus, an acceptance by letter becomes effective when the letter is mailed, if the offer came by letter or it specified that acceptances must be made by letter. However, many written offers stipulate that the acceptance will not take effect until it has been received at the office of the offeror. When offers and acceptances use the mail, it is understood to mean the U.S. Postal Service—not the mail services of FedEx, UPS, or e-mail. The general rule is that an acceptance becomes binding when the parties so intend.

In general, a person cannot be compelled to speak or to write to avoid a binding agreement, and is under no obligation to reply to an offer. However, silence may indicate assent to an offer when both parties agree beforehand that it is to be the means of acceptance.

> **EXAMPLE 7.6**
>
> In a letter to Westerly Dry Cleaners, Central Solvent, a regular supplier, offered to sell a newly formulated cleaning solvent and stated that they would consider the offer accepted if Westerly did not respond within ten days. Westerly did not respond, and the solvent was shipped. Central billed Westerly for the solvent and shipping charges. Westerly refused to pay and demanded that the solvent be removed from the premises. Central claimed that Westerly's silence indicated acceptance of the offer. A court would hold that Westerly's silence cannot be considered an acceptance because Central cannot force the firm to speak.

However, suppose that Westerly and Central had previously agreed that Westerly's failure to turn down Central's written offer for the sale of goods would result in a valid, enforceable contract. Then both parties would have agreed that silence was to be the manner of acceptance. The UCC provides that a "contract for the sale of goods may be made in any manner sufficient to show agreement, including conduct by both parties which recognizes the existence of such a contract" [UCC 2-204].

Acceptance Must Be Unconditional

A ***counteroffer***—that is, a conditional, or qualified, acceptance of an offer—is generally interpreted as a rejection and is not binding on the parties.

counteroffer A response to an offer in which the terms and conditions of the original offer are changed.

> **EXAMPLE 7.7**
> Churchill, the owner of an apple orchard, signed a contract in February to sell the land to Czek, but reserved the right to recover the apples when they ripened in the fall. Czek signed the contract, but crossed out the words that pertained to the recovery of the apples. In this case, there was no contract because Czek did not accept Churchill's offer and his act of crossing out the words made it a counteroffer.

The general rule of contract provides that the acceptance of an offer must be the same as the offer, and that if there are any differences between the offer and the acceptance, the acceptance is regarded as a rejection of the offer. The UCC changes this rule and states that, between merchants, "a definite and reasonable expression of acceptance or a written confirmation which is sent within a reasonable time operates as an acceptance even though it states terms additional to or different from those offered or agreed upon, unless acceptance is expressly made conditional on assent to the additional or different terms" [UCC 2-207].

The UCC also provides that "additional or different terms are to be construed as proposals for addition to the contract, and between merchants, become part of the contract unless the offer expressly limits acceptance to the terms of the offer, or they materially alter it; or notice of objection to them is given within a reasonable time after they are received" [UCC 2-207].

> **EXAMPLE 7.8**
> Wayfar Printers ordered a drum of printing ink from Bartlett & Co. On their order, Wayfar stated that delivery must be made by June 1. When the Bartlett Company accepted the order, they included the statement, "impossible to ship before June 15." The acknowledgment also stated that "if these terms are not acceptable, buyer must notify the seller at once." Wayfar did not complain about the later delivery date. It was held that Bartlett's acceptance was valid even though it stated terms different from those offered. Because the code states that the different terms become a part of the contract unless they materially alter it, disagreements can easily result as to whether such different terms are material. (In the law, *material* means important.)

TERMINATION OF AN OFFER

Offers are terminated by: (1) lapse of time, (2) revocation, or (3) rejection.

OBJECTIVE 5

Identify the three ways in which an offer may be terminated.

Termination by Lapse of Time

When the offeree fails to accept an offer within the time specified, the opportunity to form a contract ends because of a ***termination by lapse of time.*** When no definite time for acceptance is stated in an offer, it terminates after a reasonable time has passed. What is considered a reasonable time will vary with the circumstances.

termination by lapse of time When an opportunity to form a contract ends because the offeree fails to accept an offer within the time specified.

> **EXAMPLE 7.9**
>
> In the early spring, Wilkerson, a wholesaler of sporting goods, offered several gross of a popular brand of tennis racquet at a specified price to Sportique Stores. Three months later, the store accepted the offer and demanded delivery. Obviously, an offer to sell seasonal goods, such as tennis racquets, has a short life and must be accepted long before the passage of three months.

Termination by Revocation

An offer that has been neither accepted nor rejected by the offeree can be revoked, or withdrawn, by the offeror. The offeror may communicate the ***revocation*** to the offeree in either spoken or written words. The Uniform Commercial Code provides, however, that any written offer by a merchant to buy or sell goods that says that offer will be held open for a stated time cannot be revoked during the time stated, or if no time is stated, until a reasonable time has passed. An offer that includes specific time limits expires automatically when the time is up, unless the offeror chooses to extend the offer [UCC 2-309].

revocation The calling back of offer by the offeror before an offer has been accepted or rejected.

Termination by Rejection

A direct, unqualified ***rejection,*** terminates an offer. The offer, once rejected by the offeree, cannot be revived or made into a counteroffer once the communication of the rejection has been received by the offeror. If the offeror acknowledges the rejection but restates the offer, the offeree still has the opportunity to accept, or reject, or make a counteroffer.

rejection The express or implied refusal by an offeree to accept an offer.

> **EXAMPLE 7.10**
>
> Kenna (offeror) offered to sell his antique car to Fishkin (offeree) for $20,000. Fishkin sent a note to Kenna saying, "You know how much I'd like to buy the car, but I simply cannot afford it at this time." Kenna acknowledged Fishkin's rejection of the offer by saying, "I received your note rejecting my offer, but if you want to think about it for another

> month or two, I'll keep the offer open." By his acknowledgment of Fishkin's rejection and restatement of the offer, Kenna has allowed Fishkin an opportunity to make another, later offer.

Just as a qualified acknowledgment of the rejection of an offer serves to keep an offer alive, a qualified rejection may have a similar effect. Suppose that, in Example 7.10, Fishkin had said, "Although I'd like to buy your car, I'm pretty sure I won't accept your offer; but I'd like to think about it for a week." The qualified rejection was, in fact, not a rejection at all.

Defective Agreements

Genuineness, or reality, of agreement is present in a contract when there is a true meeting of the minds of the parties. If there is any misunderstanding or if any force or deception is used by either party to obtain the necessary agreement of the other party, the contract may be voided, or disaffirmed at the choice of the injured party. A voidable contract results if agreement of either party is obtained by fraud, misrepresentation, mistake, undue influence, duress, or if the contract is unconscionable. These terms will be explained in this chapter.

Fraud

Fraud is the intentional misstatement, or nondisclosure of a *material* (essential) *fact* made by one party with the hope of influencing the other party. It does not matter how the fraud is committed. It may be by spoken or written words or by acts or conduct. For the injured party to claim fraud, he or she must prove that the statement or act:

1. was a misstatement of a material fact
2. was made with knowledge of its falsity or with reckless disregard of its truth
3. was made with the intention of enticing the other party enter into an agreement
4. was relied on by the injured party
5. resulted in loss to the injured party

EXAMPLE 7.11

> Eppers had decided to buy a personal computer and went to Micro New Age Computer Store. Donaldson, the owner of the store, quickly sensed that Eppers did not know much about computers and was

OBJECTIVE 6

List seven ways in which a lack of a meeting of the minds may interfere with the legal enforcement of agreements.

fraud The intentional misstatement, or nondisclosure of a material (essential) fact made by one party with the hope of influencing the other party.

> concerned that any computer he bought would have sufficient memory to handle most available word-processing software. In response to Eppers' questions about the memory of a particular model, Donaldson assured him that the model would accommodate any software on the market and any likely to be developed in the foreseeable future. Eppers, relying on Donaldson's assurances, bought a compatible model with 256K memory. (Computer memory of 256K is inadequate for many popular software programs.)

Now, reexamine the case:

1. Was there a misstatement of a material fact? Yes, computer memory is a vital part of such equipment.
2. Was the misstatement made intentionally or recklessly? Yes, Donaldson should reasonably have known that the 256K memory was inadequate for many programs.
3. Was the misstatement made with intent to deceive Eppers? Yes, Donaldson knew that the memory was important to Eppers.
4. Did Eppers rely on Donaldson's statements and act on them? Yes, Eppers bought the computer that Donaldson recommended.
5. Did Eppers suffer a loss as a result of his reliance on the false statements? Yes, he would have to add memory at added cost to use the computer as he had intended.

It is important to recognize the difference between a fraudulent statement and a salesperson's ***puffery,*** which is considered a mere expression of opinion. Most salespersons use persuasive statements in an effort to induce a prospective purchaser to buy. In Example 7.11, Donaldson used other statements, such as: "This machine is the best buy in town," and "This computer is as good as 'Big Blue,' but why pay for their initials?" In the eyes of the law, these statements are merely "dealer's talk" and are not considered misrepresentations of material facts. Puffing refers to generalities, whereas misrepresentation falsifies specifics and is often directed toward the five senses (e.g., it looks great, it sounds great, etc.).

Intentional concealment (deliberately hiding important information) of material facts or information is as fraudulent as making false statements. Suppose that, in Example 7.11, Donaldson didn't comment on the adequacy of the computer memory, but knew from Eppers' comments that he intended to use it with a particular brand of software and Donaldson knew, or should have known, that a computer with 256K memory was not adequate. Because Eppers relied on Donaldson's information, Donaldson was guilty of intentional concealment.

puffery A general expression of opinion, typically in a sales context, that is used to persuade a prospective purchaser to buy. It does not constitute a misrepresentation of material fact.

Misrepresentation

Misrepresentation is a misstatement of a material fact that results in inducing another to enter into an agreement to his or her injury. When the misstatement is made knowingly, it is called *intentional misrepresentation* and is, in reality, fraud. When the misrepresentation is unintentional, it is termed *innocent misrepresentation.*

There is an important distinction between fraud and innocent misrepresentation, because the remedy is different. An injured party who can successfully prove fraud (intentional misrepresentation) may have the contract canceled and bring suit for damages. If the party can prove only innocent misrepresentation, the contract can be canceled, but the injured party cannot sue for damages.

misrepresentation A misstatement of material fact that results in inducing another to enter into an agreement to his or her injury.

EXAMPLE 7.12

Arnold hired Blue Water Pool Company to build a swimming pool in his backyard. It was only after construction had begun that Arnold learned from a neighbor that local zoning ordinances prohibited backyard swimming pools in the community. The salesperson for Blue Water admitted his misrepresentation but claimed that he had been thinking

Photo 7.1

Puffery

The law allows for a certain amount of "sales talk" that is not considered fraudulent. *Can you think of some examples of puffery and the situations in which it occurs?*

Offer, Acceptance, and Mutual Agreement — CHAPTER 7

about another community where no prohibitions existed. Arnold may void the contract, but he may not seek damages, because Blue Water's misrepresentation was innocent.

Mistake

In the eyes of the law, a ***mistake*** is a belief that is not in accord with the facts. Mistakes relating to contracts may be concerned with the nature of the subject matter or the quality of the subject matter. Obviously, not every erroneous idea or notion is a mistake, and the law makes it clear that the mistaken belief must concern an existing fact and not a belief about what might happen in the future. Court decisions involving mistakes are often complex, and the courts attempt to determine whether the mistake was "unilateral," that is, made by only one party, or whether the mistake was "mutual," that is, made by both parties. For a contract to be dissolved because of a mistake, the law usually requires that both parties be a part of the misunderstanding. That is, the mistake must be mutual.

mistake A belief that is not in accord with the facts.

EXAMPLE 7.13

Chin, a collector of rare paintings, offered to sell a particular Picasso drawing (catalog number 1401) to Kovacs for $4,000. When it came time to exchange the drawing for the money, it was obvious that Kovacs was expecting a different Picasso (catalog number 1410) and not the catalog number 1401 that Chin had expected to sell. Chin also was surprised, because he thought Kovacs wanted to buy catalog number 1401. The contract can be canceled by either party: This was a mutual mistake.

Undue Influence

Sometimes a person has the power to control the actions of another because of a special or confidential relationship to that person. Such relationships are sometimes found between employer an employee, physician or nurse and patient, teacher and student, attorney and client, and so on. When someone uses this power improperly to his or her personal advantage, ***undue influence*** is said to exist. A contract resulting from the use of undue influence is voidable at the option of the party wrongfully influenced.

undue influence The improper use of excessive pressure by the dominant member of a confidential relationship to convince the weaker party to enter a contract that greatly benefits the dominant party.

EXAMPLE 7.14

Hsu, a professor of electrical engineering, was working with a foreign student, Placido, on a new ceramic compound in the field of superconductivity. Hsu encouraged his student to continue his research and said that he would undertake to secure the patent on the new compound in both names. Placido was suspicious about the arrangement suggested by Hsu, but recognized Hsu's influence over him. After the patent was issued, Placido realized that it was his work and inventiveness that had resulted in the new compound—and not that of his professor. In this case, the court would likely find that the relationship between professor and student resulted in undue influence.

Duress

Duress is the act of applying unlawful or improper pressure or influence to a person to gain his or her agreement to a contract. Such pressure can take the form of a threat of bodily harm to an individual or to his or her family, or the threat of serious loss or damage to his or her property. When threats are used to force someone to enter into a contract, the agreement may be dissolved by the injured party.

duress The act of applying unlawful or improper pressure or influence to a person to gain his or her agreement to a contract.

EXAMPLE 7.15

Brent, the owner of a small trucking company, called on Goodwin, president of Goodwin Manufacturing Company, to sell his company's trucking services. As they concluded their conversation, Brent indicated that it would be a good idea to let Brent's company handle Goodwin's trucking needs because other companies, which did not use Brent's service, usually experienced unexpected fires. Brent's message was clearly a threat, and Goodwin agreed to sign the contract for trucking services. The contract could be rescinded because of the duress applied by Brent.

Contracts of Adhesion

A contract that involves parties who have unequal bargaining power is known as a ***contract of adhesion.*** These take-it-or-leave-it contracts are quite common and are normally enforceable. But when enforcement of an otherwise legal contract will result in a significant hardship to one of the parties, courts have sometimes considered such agreements to be so unfair as to be unenforceable.

The inequality of bargaining power can show up in contracts that are prepared by one party and simply presented to the other without the opportunity for meaningful negotiation, such as insurance policies or the disclaimers printed on checkroom and luggage receipts. Also, some contracts have become so routine that one of the parties may not even realize that he or she has entered into a contract—an example would be checkroom and luggage receipts, tickets to a parking garage, or a theater.

contract of adhesion A contract drawn by one party that must be accepted as is on a take-it-or-leave-it basis

unconscionable contract
A contract that is so one-sided that it is oppressive and gives unfair advantage to one of the parties.

Unconscionable Contracts

For hundreds of years, courts have been unwilling to enforce a shockingly unfair contract. A contract that is regarded as shockingly unjust or unfair is called an *unconscionable contract.* In recent years, however, the UCC has made such contracts even less likely to be enforced. The Code states: "If the court as a matter of law finds the contract or any clause of the contract to have been unconscionable at the time it was made, the court may refuse to enforce the contract, or it may enforce the remainder of the contract without the unconscionable clause, or it may so limit the application of any unconscionable clause as to avoid any unconscionable result" [UCC 2-302].

When the Uniform Commercial Code was written, it was intended that the unconscionable clause would apply only to sales of goods. In recent years, however, virtually the only successful use of unconscionability under the Code has been made by consumers in various kinds of contracts involving such acts as making home improvements, opening a checking account, leasing a gasoline station, and leasing an apartment. For example, the UCC has been cited to cancel contracts in which one party has written agreements in such a way as to take clearly unfair advantage of another party who lacked familiarity with the English language.

> **EXAMPLE 7.16**
>
> The sales representative for Frostifresh Corporation sold a freezer to Reynoso, who spoke little English. The salesman neither translated nor explained the contract, but told Reynoso that the freezer would cost nothing because he would receive a bonus of $25 for each sale made to his friends. The total price of the freezer, made with periodic payments, would have been more than $1,100. The cash price would have been $900, and the wholesale price to the company was $348. The court ruled that the contract was unconscionable and awarded the company a reasonable profit, service and finance charges, and its own cost of $348.

CHAPTER SUMMARY

1. For an offer to be valid, it must be **(a)** definite and certain, **(b)** communicated to the offeree, and **(c)** made with a serious intention that the offeror will be bound by it. One example would be a salesperson offering a potential buyer an item in a

store, putting the terms of sale in clear writing, and signing the document before handing it to the potential buyer for his or her consideration.

2 A call for bids or estimates is not considered an offer, but rather a request for an offer or an invitation to negotiate that can be accepted or rejected by the person calling for the bid.

3 To determine whether an advertisement is an invitation to trade or a valid offer, carefully examine whether the wording in the advertisement contains a sufficient words to demonstrate a commitment to sell. If it contains a positive promise and a positive statement of what the advertiser expects in return, the courts will usually hold that the advertisement is an offer.

4 A valid acceptance of an offer must be **(a)** communicated to the offeror, and **(b)** unconditional. An example would be when a buyer tells a seller that she will accept his offer of $1 for the newspaper.

5 An offer can be terminated by **(a)** lapse of time, **(b)** revocation, or **(c)** rejection.

6 Seven ways in which a lack of a meeting of the minds may interfere with the legal enforcement of agreements include cases involving **(a)** fraud, **(b)** misrepresentation, **(c)** mistake, **(d)** undue influence, **(e)** duress, **(f)** contracts of adhesion, and **(g)** unconscionable contracts.

Chapter 7 Assessment

MATCHING LEGAL TERMS

Match each of the following definitions with the correct term in the list below. Write the letter of your choice in the answer column.

- **a.** acceptance
- **b.** contract of adhesion
- **c.** counteroffer
- **d.** duress
- **e.** innocent misrepresentation
- **f.** fraud
- **g.** intentional concealment agreement
- **h.** invitation to trade
- **i.** lapse of time
- **j.** mutual
- **k.** offeree
- **l.** offeror
- **m.** public offer
- **n.** revocation
- **o.** unconscionable
- **p.** undue influence

1. A new and different response to an offer.   **1.** ____
2. A contract regarded as shockingly unfair and unjust.   **2.** ____
3. Agreement to a proposal or an offer.   **3.** ____
4. Domination of a person's will by force or by threat of force or injury.   **4.** ____
5. The prevailing legal view of a newspaper advertisement.   **5.** ____
6. Recall, by the offeror, of an offer that has never been accepted by the offeree.   **6.** ____
7. A contract characterized by unequal bargaining power of the parties.   **7.** ____
8. The party to whom an offer is made.   **8.** ____
9. A "meeting of the minds."   **9.** ____
10. The reason for termination of an offer that has not been accepted by the offeree within the time limits specified.   **10.** ____
11. An offer to large groups of people, only one of whom can accept.   **11.** ____
12. The person who makes an offer.   **12.** ____
13. Intentional misrepresentation of a material fact.   **13.** ____
14. Withholding material facts from a contracting party.   **14.** ____
15. The power to control the actions of another that results from a special or confidential relationship.   **15.** ____
16. Unintentional misstatements of material facts.   **16.** ____

TRUE/FALSE QUIZ

Indicate whether each of the following statements is true or false by writing *T* or *F* in the answer column.

17. For an offer to be valid, it must be definite and certain.   **17.** ____
18. The person who makes a proposal to enter into a contract is the offeror.   **18.** ____

Chapter 7 Assessment

19. For an acceptance to be valid, it must be communicated to the offeror. 19. _____

20. Requests for proposals and announcements asking for bids or estimates are usually considered legally binding offers. 20. _____

21. The distinction between fraud and innocent misrepresentation is important because the remedies available to an injured party are different. 21. _____

22. A newspaper advertisement of goods for sale is usually considered an invitation to trade. 22. _____

23. For a contract to be dissolved because of a mistake, the law usually requires that both parties be a part of the misunderstanding. That is, the mistake must be mutual. 23. _____

24. A contract of adhesion is characterized by unequal bargaining power of the parties. 24. _____

25. If a person knowingly makes a false statement of a material fact in a contract intending the other party rely on it and the other party does so, the person can be charged with puffing. 25. _____

26. A contract considered shockingly unjust or unfair is an unconscionable contract. 26. _____

DISCUSSION QUESTIONS

Answer the following questions and discuss them in class.

27. What are some circumstances that can lead to uncertainty in offers and acceptances and how can they be avoided?

_____
_____
_____

28. What are some advantages of having a written offer and acceptance over spoken ones?

_____
_____
_____

29. Why might a specific time be crucial to transactions that involve offers and acceptances?

_____
_____
_____

30. When a definite time for acceptance has not been set, when does the acceptance time terminate?

_____
_____
_____

Offer, Acceptance, and Mutual Agreement   CHAPTER 7

Chapter 7 Assessment

31. Persuasive statements based on a sales person's opinion are referred to as puffery. Provide examples of sales situations in which you think puffery is commonly used.

32. What are some examples of undue influence?

THINKING CRITICALLY ABOUT THE LAW

Answer the following the questions, which require you to think critically about the legal principles that you learned in this chapter.

33. Offers Why are newspaper advertisements not considered valid offers?

34. Acceptance Describe the circumstances under which silence on the part of an offeree would be a valid acceptance. Does this seem reasonable and fair?

35. Counteroffer Why does the law interpret a counteroffer, that is, a conditional, or qualified, acceptance of an offer, as a rejection and not binding on the parties?

36. Termination of an Offer If an offer is rejected, should the offeree have the right to negotiate before the offer is considered terminated? Explain your answer.

PART 2 Contracts

Chapter 7 Assessment

37. A Question of Ethics Is the failure to disclose material facts or information to a prospective buyer, fair and ethical? Why or why not?

_____

_____

_____

CASE QUESTIONS

Study each case below and answer the questions that follow by writing *Yes* or *No* in the answer column.

38. Definite and Certain Offer Neto learned that Quan, his neighbor, intended to sell his power boat. Neto left a note in Quan's mailbox stating that he wanted to buy the boat and he would pay a "fair price." A few days later, Quan sold the boat to someone else for a higher price than Neto would have been willing to pay.

   a. Does Neto have a legal course of action against Quan?   a. _____

   b. Is there anything illegal about this case?   b. _____

   c. Can Quan safely ignore Neto's offer because it lacked certainty and definiteness?   c. _____

   d. If Neto had specified a price he was willing to pay, would Quan have been obligated to accept it?   d. _____

39. Intentional Concealment Gortino, while trying to sell his house to Stein, was asked if he had ever seen or suspected termites in the house. Gortino replied that he had not, and that the house was sound. Several months after Stein had purchased the house, she learned from neighbors that Gortino had paid for soil treatment to eliminate termites.

   a. Can the contract for sale be cancelled because of fraud?   a. _____

   b. Was there a misrepresentation of a material fact?   b. _____

   c. Did Stein suffer a loss as a result of Gortino's actions?   c. _____

   d. Can Stein sue for damages?   d. _____

40. Voidable Contract Gallagher Restaurant Supply was in the business of leasing equipment to small restaurants. Quezada, the operator of a small diner, leased a coffee-making machine from Gallagher. It was only after the contract had been signed that Quezada learned that similar lease agreements with other restaurants were far less costly. Also, the agreement between the parties provided for an accelerated payment of the entire balance if Quezada failed to perform any condition of the lease, "no matter how trivial the condition may be." In addition, Gallagher would be entitled to take back the coffeemaker and collect a 20 percent penalty.

   a. Is this an example of a contract signed under duress?   a. _____

   b. Is it likely that a court would enforce this contract?   b. _____

   c. Is this an example of a void contract?   c. _____

   d. Is this an example of a voidable contract?   d. _____

Chapter 7 Assessment

CASE ANALYSIS

Study each of the following cases carefully and then briefly state the principle of law and your decision.

41. Mutual Mistake Brooking agreed to sell a tract of land to Dover Pool & Racquet Club, Inc., on which Dover planned to build a swim and tennis club. Neither party to the contract knew that just before the contract was signed, the local zoning board of the town in which the land was located published a notice of public hearings on a proposal to amend the zoning in a way that would have prevented Dover from using the land as it had planned to do. *Will this contract be enforced?* [*Dover Pool & Racquet Club, Inc. v. Brooking,* 322 N.E.2d 168 (Massachusetts).]

Principle of law:

_____

_____

Decision:

_____

_____

42. Contract of Adhesion Weaver, a high school dropout, leased a gas station from American Oil Company and signed a standard agreement prepared by the oil company's lawyers. The lease (contract) contained a clause in fine print that provided that the oil company would not be liable for any injury occurring on the premises regardless of fault. No one representing the oil company called Weaver's attention to the clause or explained it to him. In addition, the lease provided that Weaver would have to pay American Oil for any loss or damages, even if they resulted from the oil company's negligence. An employee of the oil company spilled gasoline on Weaver and his assistant, causing them to be burned and injured. The oil company brought an action seeking to be relieved of liability for the injury and to have Weaver held liable for any damages to the assistant. *Will the contract provision for Weaver being held liable be enforced?* [*Weaver v. American Oil Co.,* 276 N.E.2d 144 (Indiana).]

Principle of law:

_____

_____

Decision:

_____

_____

43. Misrepresentation Malina, the owner of an old, multistory factory building, offered to lease the building to Larson, a manufacturer. Larson wanted to know whether the construction of the floors was strong enough to support the heavy machinery he planned to install. Malina assured him that the floors would support any machinery brought into the building. After the lease was signed, Larson's engineer studied the construction and reported that the floors would hold only half of the machinery that Larson planned to install. *Is Larson bound by the lease?*

PART 2   Contracts

Chapter 7 Assessment

Principle of law:
_____
_____

Decision:
_____
_____

44. **Valid Offer** Sanderson Mart ran an advertisement in the *Daily Tribune* that stated, "Special offer to our customers—3/8-inch Electric Hand Drills, Saturday only—$14.99, only 100 in stock, while they last! Be here when we open for the bargain of the year!" Cruz arrived at the store at 8:00 A.M., when the store opened. The salesperson refused to sell him an electric drill, claiming that they had only two in stock and those were already set aside for another customer—and besides, the advertisement was not really a binding offer. *Would Sanderson be required to sell the electric drill for the advertised price?*

Principle of law:
_____
_____

Decision:
_____
_____

LEGAL RESEARCH

Complete the following activities. Then share your findings with the class.

45. **Working in Teams** In teams of three or four, interview a local retailer and ask him or her how, when planning and writing advertising copy, he or she avoids wording that might cause a reader to regard the ad as a definite offer, instead of simply an advertisement.
_____
_____
_____

46. **Using Technology** Use the Internet and search engines to investigate unconscionable contracts. Then with additional research, find examples of existing legislation in several jurisdictions that concern such contracts. Share your findings with the class.
_____
_____
_____

Offer, Acceptance, and Mutual Agreement **CHAPTER 7**

CHAPTER 8

CONSIDERATION

PERFORMANCE OBJECTIVES

After studying this chapter and completing the assessments, you will be able to:

1. Explain the three essential characteristics of valid consideration, and provide an example of an agreement having these characteristics.

2. Describe the position generally held by the courts on the issue of adequacy of consideration.

3. Distinguish between valid consideration based on (a) a promise for a promise, (b) a promise of forbearance, and (c) a pledge or subscription.

4. Define a general release, and based on a given illustration, write one to cover a typical situation.

5. Identify four kinds of agreements that lack consideration.

LEGAL TERMS

forbearance
promisor
promisee
pledge
general release
barren promise
preexisting duty
gratuitous promise
moral consideration
past consideration

The Nature of Consideration

Consideration was defined in Chapter 6 as the promises exchanged by the parties to a contract, either to give up something of value they have a legal right to keep—such as money or property—or to do something they are not otherwise legally required to do—such as performing a service or refraining from action. The promise to refrain from doing something that a party has a legal right to do, or the promise of inaction, is known as ***forbearance.***

Consideration in a contact may be more than just the promises exchanged by the parties, but the actual benefit gained and the detriment suffered by them. A party who makes a promise, the ***promisor,*** may make a promise to pay a sum of money to another party, the ***promisee,*** for the performance of a certain act.

In Example 8.1, the consideration is the money promised by the promisor and the performance of the act promised by the promisee.

forbearance The promise to refrain from doing something that a party has a legal right to do.

promisor In the making of a contract, the party who makes a promise.

promisee In the making of a contract, the party to whom a promise is made.

EXAMPLE 8.1

Stein promised to pay his nephew $1,000 on his twenty-second birthday if he refrained from smoking and gambling until he graduated from Northern State College.

This contract is legal and illustrates the promise of forbearance as consideration. Although it seems unlikely that Stein would break his promise or that the nephew would bring suit to collect, it is possible. For example, if Stein were to die before the nephew's birthday, the executors of his estate might not wish to pay and the nephew might then want to sue to collect.

Characteristics of Valid Consideration

There are three essential characteristics of valid consideration: (1) legality, (2) adequacy, and (3) the possibility of performance.

Legality of Consideration

If the contract in Example 8.1 required the nephew to obey all traffic laws, it would not be enforceable because the nephew is legally required to obey the laws anyway. Also, a valid contract cannot exist if the consideration is a promise to perform an illegal act or to avoid performing an act that is required.

OBJECTIVE 1

Explain the three essential characteristics of valid consideration, and provide an example of an agreement having these characteristics.

Consideration   CHAPTER 8   119

OBJECTIVE 2

Describe the position generally held by the courts on the issue of adequacy of consideration.

Adequacy of Consideration

Traditionally, the courts generally made no attempt to judge whether the exchange of promises in a contract was fair—that is, whether there was adequacy of consideration. The law assumed that, as long as no undue pressure was used, the parties were free to reject a proposed unfair contract. In recent times, however, society has recognized some of the problems associated with contractual relationships in which the unrestricted bargaining power of one party gives that party an unfair advantage when dealing with those who lack the economic power or the education to enter into contracts on an equal footing.

In an attempt to level the playing field, many consumer protection statutes have been passed, and the notions of unconscionable contracts (contracts that are shockingly unfair and unjust) and contracts of adhesion (contracts in which the parties have unequal bargaining power) have been more widely applied.

Possibility of Performance

A legally enforceable contract cannot be based on a promise that is impossible to fulfill. However, a party who promises to do something that is merely difficult to perform, or poses unforeseen expenses, is still bound by the terms of the contract.

KINDS OF VALID CONSIDERATION

Consideration required in an enforceable contract can take various forms: exchange of promises, forbearance, and pledges or subscriptions.

OBJECTIVE 3

Distinguish between valid consideration based on (a) a promise for a promise, (b) a promise of forbearance, and (c) a pledge or subscription.

A Promise for a Promise

As indicated earlier in this chapter, the most common form of valid consideration is the promise of money by one party for the promise of an act by another. The Stein case discussed earlier is a good example. It should be noted that the mere promise to act is usually deemed valid consideration. Whether the promise is actually carried out is another matter, having to do with the execution of the contract terms, and specifically, with the issue of performance by the parties. The law provides certain remedies to a wronged party when there is partial performance or nonperformance of a promised act. (This topic will be discussed in Chapter 13.) A promise of an act by one party in exchange for the promise of an act by another is also considered valid consideration. The exchange of money is not an absolute requirement.

Promises of Forbearance

Valid consideration is not necessarily either the performance of an act or the payment of money. One party to a contract may, for a variety of reasons, wish to exchange his or her promise to pay money for a promise of inaction from the other party. Many contracts in which part of the consideration is forbearance involve agreements not to compete. In Example 8.2 that part of the consideration is a promise not to act.

> **EXAMPLE 8.2**
>
> Kim agreed to purchase a fruit and vegetable business from Rosen for a certain price if Rosen promised to refrain from opening another fruit and vegetable business in the same town for three years. In this case, the consideration was Kim's promise to pay the agreed selling price for both Rosen's business and her promise of inaction, or forbearance. Rosen's consideration was her promise to (1) transfer the business to Kim, and (2) avoid opening a similar business in the same town for three years.

Pledges or Subscriptions

Churches and temples, hospitals, colleges, cultural institutions, charitable institutions, and other groups frequently raise money by asking for a ***pledge,*** or subscription (a promise to donate money). Are these pledges enforceable? What is the consideration? What benefit is gained by the person making the pledge? Because these pledges are usually for some worthy cause, the courts have generally held that they are enforceable. Some have held that the consideration given by the charitable institution is the promise to use the money for the purpose for which it was donated. Other courts have held that the consideration is the promises of all the other parties who have subscribed to the same fund. Still other courts hold that if the charitable institution has made commitments to spend the money as a result of relying on the promises, the subscriptions are enforceable. As a practical matter, few charitable organizations sue because doing so would affect their future ability to raise contributions.

pledge A promise to donate money to a church, hospital, charity, or other organization.

CONSIDERATION AND THE UNIFORM COMMERCIAL CODE

In some cases that involve contracts to sell goods, the Uniform Commercial Code dispenses with the requirements for consideration in certain contracts that involve any of the following:

- A merchant's written firm offer that provides that the contract is irrevocable
- A written discharge of a claim for an alleged breach of contract
- Modifications of existing contracts [UCC 2-209].

EXAMPLE 8.3

> Sullivan and Baker agreed that Sullivan would sell 5,000 imported shirts to Baker at a certain price and be delivered by May 15. Sullivan learned that he would be unable to meet the delivery date because of transportation delays. He contacted Baker, who agreed to an extension of the time of delivery. Later, Baker had a change of heart and demanded that the goods be delivered by the original date. Under the UCC, Baker is bound by the agreed modification even though Sullivan gave no additional consideration for the extension of the delivery date.

GENERAL RELEASE

Statutes in many states have permitted a person who has a claim against another to give up, or release, his or her claim without an exchange of consideration by making a written statement to that effect. The UCC provides that "any claim or right arising out of an alleged breach can be discharged in whole or in part without consideration by a written waiver or renunciation signed and delivered by the aggrieved party" [UCC 1-107]. Such a written agreement is called a ***general release.***

A general release may be regarded as valid consideration if the parties so intend. In such cases, the general release would be viewed as forbearance.

AGREEMENTS THAT LACK CONSIDERATION

Certain agreements are not enforceable because they lack consideration.

Barren Promises

A promise to do something that one is already required to do either by law or by contract represents no additional sacrifice, and as a result, is not valid consideration. A promise to pay an existing debt, to obey the law, or a similar promise is called a ***barren promise;*** the obligation to perform acts already required is known as a ***preexisting duty.***

OBJECTIVE 4

Define a general release, and based on a given illustration, write one to cover a typical situation.

general release A written agreement in which an aggrieved party can discharge in whole or in part a claim resulting from an alleged breach of contract.

OBJECTIVE 5

Identify four kinds of agreements that lack consideration.

barren promise A promise to pay an existing debt, to obey the law, or a similar promise of something already owed.

preexisting duty An obligation that a party is already bound to by law or by some other agreement. The party may not use this as consideration in a new contract.

EXAMPLE 8.4

> The First State Bank was robbed of more than $30,000 by three armed men. The local bankers' association advertised a reward of $5,000 for the arrest and conviction of each bank robber. In time, all three robbers were convicted. Claims to the reward were made by a number of people, including employees of the bank and the police officers who arrested the robbers. The court ruled that neither the bank employees nor the police were able to collect the reward because they had a pre-existing duty to aid in the capture of the criminals. Another police officer, from another county, who had no duty to assist in this case, was allowed to collect the reward.

Gratuitous Promises

A person who makes a promise without requiring some benefit in return has made a *gratuitous promise.* Agreements based on such one-sided promises are not generally enforceable. A promise to give a gift is a gratuitous promise, that is, one that is made without receiving anything in return. Because there is no consideration, the promise is not enforceable. Once a promised gift is presented or delivered, however, the transfer of ownership is complete and consideration is not required.

gratuitous promise A promise that does not require some benefit in return.

Agreements Supported by Moral Consideration

A person is not legally bound to do what he or she may feel bound to do because of love, friendship, honor, sympathy, conscience, or some other *moral consideration.* Some courts, however, will justify the enforcement of some contracts, even though there is no consideration, by stating that there was "moral consideration." A better explanation is that the enforcement of certain contracts is socially beneficial.

moral consideration Something that a person is not legally bound to do, but that he or she may feel bound to do because of love, friendship, honor, sympathy, conscience, or other reason.

EXAMPLE 8.5

> Gerber, the owner of Nail Style, a fingernail styling salon, had many financial obligations to suppliers, as well as to the landlord of the building where the salon was located. When the firm failed and Gerber declared bankruptcy, she was relieved of her obligations to pay her creditors. Gerber made a gratuitous promise, based on her own values, to pay the now-forgiven debts from her future earnings. Most courts would agree that the promise is enforceable, even though there was no consideration.

Agreements Supported by Past Consideration

Past consideration is a promise to repay someone for a benefit after it has been received. Such a promise is generally not valid consideration

past consideration A promise to repay someone for a benefit after it has been received.

and is considered a gratuitous promise, except in cases such as we described in the discussion of moral consideration.

> **EXAMPLE 8.8**
>
> George Welt promised his brother Frank that he would give him a round-trip ticket to Paris if Frank graduated from a particular college. Frank graduated as agreed, and George gave him the plane ticket. When Frank realized how much the ticket had cost, he offered to pay George one-half of the round-trip fare. If, however, Frank changed his mind and decided not to keep his promise, he could not be held to it because his promise was based on past consideration.

CHAPTER SUMMARY

1 The three essential characteristics of valid consideration are (**a**) legality, (**b**) adequacy, and (**c**) the possibility of performance.

2 Historically, the courts would not evaluate the adequacy of consideration. More recently, many consumer protection statutes have been passed, and the notions of unconscionable contracts and contracts of adhesion have been more widely applied.

3 Consideration can be based on a promise being exchanged for another promise. It can also be based on one party's promise not to do something they have a legal right to do (forbearance). A third kind of valid consideration is a pledge, or subscription (a promise to make a donation).

4 A general release occurs when a claim or right arising out of an alleged breach of contract is discharged in whole or in part without consideration by a written waiver or renunciation signed and delivered by the aggrieved party.

5 Four kinds of agreements that lack consideration are (**a**) barren promises, (**b**) gratuitous promises, (**c**) agreements supported by moral consideration, and (**d**) agreements supported by past consideration.

Chapter 8 Assessment

MATCHING LEGAL TERMS

Match each of the following definitions with the correct term in the list below. Write the letter of your choice in the answer column.

- **a.** barren promise
- **b.** consideration
- **c.** forbearance
- **d.** gratuitous promise
- **e.** general release
- **f.** moral consideration
- **g.** past consideration
- **h.** pledge for subscription
- **i.** preexisting duty
- **j.** promise

1. The benefit received and the detriment suffered by parties to a contract. **1.** _____
2. A demand of the conscience based on love, friendship, honor, or sympathy. **2.** _____
3. A promise to do what one is already required to do. **3.** _____
4. An offer to confer a benefit on someone without requiring a sacrifice in return. **4.** _____
5. An enforceable promise to contribute to a charitable organization. **5.** _____
6. An obligation to perform actions that are already required. **6.** _____
7. An offer to pay for a benefit that has already been received. **7.** _____
8. The act of refraining from exercising a legal right. **8.** _____
9. A written agreement to give up a claim or settle a debt for less than the agreed amount. **9.** _____
10. The party to an agreement who receives a promise. **10.** _____

TRUE/FALSE QUIZ

Indicate whether each of the following statements is true or false by writing *T* or *F* in the answer column.

11. Consideration is one of the required elements of a valid contract. **11.** _____
12. The courts generally do not rule on the adequacy of consideration. **12.** _____
13. A promise of inaction, or forbearance, can be valid consideration. **13.** _____
14. Pledges and subscriptions are not legally enforceable because of the lack of consideration. **14.** _____
15. A contract in which consideration is based on a promise that is impossible to fulfill cannot be enforced. **15.** _____
16. Preexisting duty refers to existing debts that must be paid. **16.** _____
17. An offer to pay for a benefit after it has been received is enforceable. **17.** _____

Chapter 8 Assessment

18. An agreement based on a gratuitous promise is enforceable if the purpose of the agreement is legal. 18. _____

19. A general release allows for the discharge of a debt because it is viewed as forbearance, a form of consideration. 19. _____

20. No contract is enforceable without consideration. 20. _____

21. Courts sometimes enforce a contract that lacks consideration because it is socially beneficial. 21. _____

22. The Uniform Commercial Code states that additional consideration is always required in the modification of an existing contract. 22. _____

23. A contract performed because "it is the right thing to do" is an example of forbearance consideration. 23. _____

24. Past consideration is a promise to repay someone for a benefit after it has been received. 24. _____

25. A promise to do something that one is already required to do either by law by contract contains valid consideration. 25. _____

DISCUSSION QUESTIONS

Answer the following questions and discuss them in class.

26. Explain how forbearance can satisfy the requirements of consideration.

27. Explain the three characteristics of a valid consideration, and provide an example of an agreement having these characteristics.

28. Describe the position generally held by the courts on the matter of adequacy of consideration.

29. Identify four kinds of agreements that lack consideration.

Chapter 8 Assessment

30. Why do courts usually not rule on the adequacy of consideration?

_____
_____
_____

31. In some contractual relationships, the bargaining power of one party gives that party an unfair advantage when dealing with another who might lack the economic power or the education to enter into contracts on an equal footing. What has the law done in an attempt to level the playing field in such cases?

_____
_____
_____

THINKING CRITICALLY ABOUT THE LAW

Answer the following questions, which require you to think critically about the legal principles that you learned in this chapter.

32. Forms of Consideration Critique the various exchanges of promises that are legally regarded as acceptable consideration. Your analysis should concentrate on whether each type of consideration facilitates or hinders the execution of a contract.

_____
_____
_____
_____

33. Invalid Consideration A promise to commit an illegal act is not valid consideration. Describe a promise to commit an illegal act that would not likely be legally acceptable.

_____
_____
_____
_____

34. Consideration—A Promise for a Promise The most common form of valid consideration is the promise of money by one party for the promise of an act by another. Why is a mere promise deemed adequate in the eyes of the law when consideration bases on completed actions might result in fewer disputes?

_____
_____
_____
_____

Chapter 8 Assessment

35. Consideration—Forbearance Valid consideration is not necessarily either the performance of an act or the payment of money. One party to a contract may, for a variety of reasons, wish to exchange his or her promise to pay money for a promise of inaction from the other party. Because promises of inaction are often difficult to verify, should promises of forbearance be legally acceptable? Why or why not?

_____
_____
_____
_____

36. A Question of Ethics Agreements between parties of unequal bargaining power are known as contracts of adhesion. For example, an apartment house owner presented a tenant with a lease renewal that contained additional and burdensome provisions. The tenant, finding it difficult to move, was forced to accept the lease in spite of the hardship. Beyond the legal aspects of a contract of adhesion, what are the ethical dimensions to consider in this example?

_____
_____
_____
_____

CASE QUESTIONS

Study each case below and answer the questions that follow by writing *Yes* or *No* in the answer column.

37. Adequacy of Consideration Duggan inherited some nondescript furniture, including an old desk, which he sold to Andersen for $50. A short time later, he learned that the desk was an antique worth about $500. Duggan brought suit to recover $450, the difference between the sale price and what the desk was really worth.

   a. Will Duggan succeed in this suit?   **a.** _____

   b. Is the contract between Duggan and Andersen unconscionable?   **b.** _____

   c. Is the contract void because of the inadequacy of consideration?   **c.** _____

38. Forbearance Helfrich, in a bar brawl, broke Grady's arm. Grady brought suit against Helfrich for damages. Before the case came to trial, Helfrich offered to give Grady a $500, 30-day notice in full settlement of all claims he had against Helfrich. When the note was due, Helfrich refused to pay, claiming that there was no exchange of benefits and no consideration.

   a. Is Helfrich correct in his claim that consideration was lacking?   **a.** _____

   b. Could Grady's action in dropping the suit be regarded as consideration?   **b.** _____

   c. Is forbearance a form of consideration?   **c.** _____

Chapter 8 Assessment

39. Acceptable Consideration Alfieri, a hunting enthusiast, frequently shot birds in his own and his neighbor's backyard in violation of a city ordinance that prohibited guns being discharged within the city limits. The neighbor offered to pay Alfieri $100 if he would refrain from shooting birds for one year. At the end of the year, the neighbor refused to pay, claiming that there was no consideration.

  a. Will Alfieri succeed in collecting the $100? a. _____

  b. Is there consideration present in this agreement? b. _____

  c. Is a barren promise acceptable consideration? c. _____

CASE ANALYSIS

Study each of the following cases carefully and then briefly state the principle of law and your decision.

40. Unconscionable Contract Jackson, a widow who was desperate for money, sold land to her brother, Seymour for $275. Later, Seymour found valuable timber on the land and sold some of it for $2,353. When Jackson realized that the property was worth much more than she had thought when she sold it, she offered to return the sales price, with interest, but Seymour refused. Jackson sued, claiming fraud—that her brother, on whom she relied for the management of her affairs, had misrepresented the value of the land. The initial court decision favored Seymour, and the decision was appealed. *Is it likely that the court will invalidate the sale of the property?* [*Jackson v. Seymour,* 71 S.E.2d 181 (Virginia).]

Principle of law:

_____

_____

Decision:

_____

_____

41. Specificity of Consideration Forrer was an employee of Sears for many years. He eventually left because of health problems and began operating a farm. Sears persuaded Forrer to return to work on a part-time basis, and about one month later promised permanent employment if Forrer gave up the farm and returned to work full-time. Forrer did so, but four months later he was discharged without cause. Forrer sued for damages, lost the case in the trial court, and appealed. *Will Forrer be successful in his complaint against Sears? What consideration did Forrer and Sears promise?* [*Forrer v. Sears, Roebuck & Co.,* 153 N.W.2d 587 (Wisconsin).]

Principle of law:

_____

_____

Decision:

_____

_____

Chapter 8 Assessment

42. Consideration The Spring Well Drilling Company entered into a contract with Towne Construction Company to drill a well to supply water on a particular piece of property where Towne was building a house. Spring Well offered no guarantee that water would, in fact, be produced. The drilling proceeded, but no water flowed. Towne refused to pay on the grounds that there was a failure of consideration. Spring Well sued to collect the agreed fee. *Will Spring Well succeed in the suit?*

Principle of law:

_____
_____

Decision:

_____
_____

43. Validity of Consideration Maitland, a fund raiser for Arbor College, solicited contributions for the college's building program. Hamill Manufacturing pledged a contribution to the program. When the company did not pay, Maitland sued. Hamill claimed there was no consideration. *Will Maitland be successful in the suit?*

Principle of law:

_____
_____

Decision:

_____
_____

LEGAL RESEARCH

Complete the following activities. Then share your findings with the class.

44. Working in Teams In teams of three or four, interview officials of religious organizations, hospitals, colleges, cultural and charitable institutions, or any group that raises money by asking for pledges or subscriptions (a promise to donate money). What is the rate of success collecting on these pledges? Have the officials ever attempted to enforce collection by legal means?

_____
_____
_____

45. Using Technology Using the Internet and search engines, investigate the existing laws relating to unconscionable contracts. Do you believe these laws offer sufficient protection? Why or why not?

_____
_____
_____

PART 2   Contracts

CHAPTER 9

COMPETENT PARTIES

PERFORMANCE OBJECTIVES

After studying this chapter and completing the assessments, you will be able to:

1. Explain the age of majority and how it affects the legal status of minors.
2. Weigh the legal effects of ratification of a minor's contract.
3. Describe the operation of the law as it relates to a minor's torts and crimes.
4. Assess the legal status of contracts made by intoxicated persons.

LEGAL TERMS

competent party
contractual capacity
minor
age of majority
necessaries
disaffirmance
ratified
emancipation
abandonment
incompetent

OBJECTIVE 1

Explain the age of majority and how it affects the legal status of minors.

competent party A person of legal age and at least normal mentality who is considered by law to be capable of understanding the meaning of a contract and is permitted to enter into a valid contract.

contractual capacity The ability to make a valid contract

minor A person who has not yet reached the age of majority.

age of majority The age at which a person is legally recognized as an adult and bound by the terms of their contracts.

necessaries Goods and services that are essential to a minor's health and welfare.

disaffirmance In contract law, to indicate by a statement or act an intent not to live up to the terms of a contract.

THE CAPACITY TO CONTRACT

Parties to a contract must be competent, both as to age and mentality. A *competent party* is a person of legal age and at least normal mentality who is considered by law to be capable of understanding the meaning of a contract. A competent party is said to have *contractual capacity,* that is, the ability to make a valid contract.

A person who has not yet reached the age of majority is a *minor,* or an infant, in the eyes of the law. Minors, insane persons, and intoxicated persons are usually considered incompetent and lacking in contractual capacity. As a result, they cannot make legally binding contracts, although they are not denied the opportunity to benefit from their legal rights. The responsibility of determining whether a person is competent to contract rests on everyone who enters into a contract.

MINORS' CONTRACTS

The law has always tried to protect young people from adults who might try to take advantage of them. Until individuals reach what is known as legal age, or the *age of majority,* they are not legally required to carry out most of their contracts because such contracts are voidable, as discussed in Chapter 5. The legal age of majority varies from state to state. In some states it is 18, and in others it is 19 or 21.

Exactly when does a person reach the age of majority? An interesting example of the common law is seen in the legal determination of exactly when a person ceases to be a minor. A person's legal birthday is 12:01 A.M. of the day before his or her actual birthday. Thus, a person who will celebrate his or her eighteenth birthday on April 26, for example, in a state where the age of majority is 18, becomes an adult—and legally competent—at 12:01 A.M. on April 25.

Avoidance of Minors' Contracts

In contracts between a minor and a competent person, except for contracts for *necessaries,* (such as food, shelter, and medical care) only the minor has the privilege of *disaffirmance,* or avoidance of the contract. The other party is bound if the minor wishes to carry out the contract.

EXAMPLE 9.1

Blevins, an automobile dealer who is not a minor, agreed to sell Alvarez, a minor, a used car for $1,000. Before the car was delivered, Blevins received a higher offer from another person and attempted to cancel the contract with Alvarez on the grounds that the buyer was a

132   PART 2   Contracts

minor. The law permits Alvarez to cancel, or disaffirm, the contract, but not Blevins, who is considered a competent party.

Ratification and Disaffirmance of Minors' Contracts

The right of a minor to avoid a contract depends on whether the contract is executory or executed. In most cases, if the contract has not yet been performed (an executory contract), the minor may disaffirm it if he or she wishes. However, once the minor reaches legal age, the contract must be either *ratified,* (that is, agreed to) or disaffirmed within a reasonable time. A contract involving a minor can be ratified by an act that shows that the minor party intends to live up to the terms of the contract. If a reasonable period of time passes after a minor reaches legal age and he or she has said nothing about disaffirming the contract, it is considered ratified in the eyes of the law. In this sense, silence or inaction is the basis for a voidable contract becoming a valid, enforceable contract through ratification.

An individual may disaffirm a contract, that is, state his or her intention to honor a contract that was made before reaching legal age. Disaffirmance may be done before reaching legal age or within a reasonable time after reaching adulthood. The exact time will vary depending on the nature of the contract and current legislation. Disaffirmance, like ratification, may be implied by the acts of the person who has reached legal age and wishes to disaffirm. Disaffirmance might, for example, be implied by failing to make an installment payment. A written or oral disaffirmance would have a similar effect.

When a contract is ratified, the entire contract must be ratified, not merely a part of it. Suppose that a contract involved personal property and had already been performed (an executed contract) before the minor reached legal age. Then, in many states, the minor could either return the property or money received or demand the return of the money or property at any time (either before reaching majority or within a reasonable time afterwards). In some states, the minor may avoid the contract even if he or she falsely represented himself or herself as being of age. The minor may then, however, be subject to criminal prosecution on the charge of fraud as well as civil liability (damages) for the tort of deceit.

EXAMPLE 9.2

Gibbon, age 17, sold her pickup truck to Deng for $800. Shortly after completing the transaction, Gibbon realized that, in her eagerness to sell her truck, she had priced it considerably below market value. She then demanded the return of her truck and offered to refund the $800

OBJECTIVE 2

Weigh the legal effects of ratification of a minor's contract.

ratified An approval of a contract made by a minor after reaching maturity.

> purchase price to Deng. A court would permit Gibbon to disaffirm the contract and get back her truck if she returned the $800 to Deng.

If, however, the situation were reversed—that is, Deng, the adult, had sold the truck to Gibbon, the minor, and wanted to cancel the sale—he could not do so if Gibbon were unwilling to cancel the contract.

Minors' Enforceable Contracts

The law that protects minors from their contractual commitments is not intended to deny them the opportunity to enter into contracts for necessaries that are not provided by their parents or a guardian. Of course, the nature of the contract must bear some relationship to the minor's individual needs and to her or his social and financial status. As a result of a minor's *emancipation,* he or she assumes the rights and obligations of a person of legal age. Emancipation could occur through marriage or through voluntary separation of a minor from parents or guardians to assume adult responsibilities. Emancipated minors are liable for necessaries purchased for themselves or supplied to a spouse, just as if they were adults.

The law regards actions on the part of the minor that result in emancipation as *abandonment,* that is, a surrender of the special protection given to them by the law.

emancipation In contract law, the condition that exists when minors are no longer under the control of their parents and are responsible for their contracts.

abandonment In contract law, the condition that exists when a minor has left home and given up all rights to parental support.

> **EXAMPLE 9.3**
>
> Eakins was 17 years old and married. A doctor sued him to recover the cost of medical care and surgery provided to Eakins' wife, who had neither medical insurance nor an income of her own. The court would hold that Eakins was responsible for the necessaries the doctor provided to his wife.

If a merchant brings suit to collect payment for merchandise furnished to a minor, the merchant must show that the articles of merchandise are necessaries and that the minor did not already have an adequate supply.

> **EXAMPLE 9.4**
>
> Pineapple Plantation Clothing Store brought suit to recover the cost of clothing sold to Bautista, who was a minor and had refused to pay for the clothing. Bautista already had an ample wardrobe. The store could not recover the cost of the goods because Bautista already had an adequate supply; therefore the purchases from Pineapple were not necessaries, even though Pineapple had no way of knowing this fact.

With the passing years and the growing independence of young people, the courts have recognized that in many instances minors need relatively little protection from the consequences of their youthful decisions. In some cases, the courts have held that contracts made by minors who are nearly adults or that deal with a business are enforceable contracts.

However, a minor is liable only for the reasonable value of necessaries purchased by him or her. If the contract price is more than the sum that the minor should have been charged, he or she can be held responsible only for the lower amount. If the minor has already paid the amount called for in the contract, he or she can recover the amount that was overcharged.

EXAMPLE 9.5

For several years, a druggist charged Zarb, a minor, $50 for medication that she needed each month for a chronic disease. The price was three times the price normally charged other purchasers. In this case, a court would enable Zarb to recover the amount that she was overcharged.

Liability for Minors' Torts and Crimes

The law does not protect anyone, not even a minor, who has committed a tort or a crime. Minors are protected against their own inexperience, but not against their own wrongdoing. If a minor injures another person or another person's property, he or she is liable for damages and may be prosecuted by the state in a criminal action. A minor can be held liable for money damages in a tort action when he or she destroys property or appropriates it for himself or herself or for another, or causes another person to suffer a money loss through his or her negligence, or persuades another person to break a contract. A minor can also be held liable if he or she makes damaging statements in writing (tort of libel) or orally (tort of slander).

OBJECTIVE 3

Describe the operation of law as it relates to a minor's torts and crimes.

EXAMPLE 9.6

McDonnell, who was 17, looked much older because of his large size and full beard. When the merchant asked McDonnell's age, he claimed that he was 19 (legally an adult in this state). He bought a compact disc player for $240. After using the player for six months, McDonnell brought it back to the dealer and demanded the return of his money.

In most states, the dealer would have to return the money to McDonnell even though he did not know that he was dealing with a minor. The minor, despite the false representation of his age, may avoid the contract. The dealer, however, may sue him, charging the tort of fraud, and attempt to recover any damages that he suffered. In many states, when a minor disaffirms a contract and returns the goods, he or she can be held liable for damages to the goods.

Contracts of the Mentally Impaired

incompetent Being unable to make binding contracts due to having an unsound mind and being unable to safeguard one's own interests and affairs.

Persons of unsound mind are considered *incompetent* to make binding contracts because they are assumed to lack the mental capacity to safeguard their own affairs. Consequently, most of their contracts are considered voidable and cannot be enforced against them if they do not carry them out.

A mentally impaired person may sometimes have lucid periods during which he or she can exercise sound judgment. If the person entered into a contract during a lucid interval and the other party can prove it, he or she will be held to the contract. The cause of the impairment does not matter; it might be insanity, senility, brain injury, drugs, or alcohol.

A person with mental impairment is liable for the reasonable value of necessaries that person buys, unless he or she can return them. The person can recover his or her money or property on all other contracts, but the other party's consideration must be returned if at all possible.

A contract with a person who has been declared insane by the courts is void even if the sane person who contracted with the impaired individual did not know that he or she had been declared insane by the courts. When a court so classifies a person, it appoints a legal guardian to handle his or her affairs. Any contracts the impaired person makes thereafter are considered void, not simply voidable. Nevertheless, if a person who has been declared insane by the court purchases necessaries, most courts will hold the legal guardian liable for their reasonable value.

CONTRACTS OF PERSONS AFFECTED BY DRUGS OR ALCOHOL

OBJECTIVE 4

Assess the legal status of contracts made by intoxicated persons.

If a person makes a contract while so intoxicated or affected by drug use, that he or she is unable to understand the nature and effect of the contract, it is voidable at his or her option. The law considers the impaired person to have been mentally incompetent at the time the contract was made, hence, not bound by it. However, if the party, when no longer impaired, and within a reasonable time, chooses to carry out the contract, it has been ratified. If the contract is for necessaries, he or she must pay their reasonable value.

If a contract does not involve necessaries, the person who wishes to disaffirm it on the grounds that he or she was intoxicated or affected by drugs when the contract was made must either return the other party's consideration or prove that he or she lost possession of it while still impaired. Obviously, if the person disposed of the other party's consideration after returning to normal, the law would not permit disaffirmance of the contract because it had been ratified after regaining the power to contract.

CHAPTER SUMMARY

1. The age of majority is the age at which a person can make binding contracts. Until a person reaches the age of majority, he or she is not legally required to carry out most of his or her contracts because such contracts are voidable.

2. A minor can ratify a contract by an act that shows the minor intends to satisfy the terms of the contract. If a reasonable time passes after a minor reaches legal age and he or she has said nothing about disaffirming the contract, it is considered ratified and enforceable.

3. The law does not protect minors who have committed a tort or crime. A minor is held responsible for injury to other persons, damaged property, and damaging statements. In many states, even if a minor disaffirms a contract and returns the goods, he or she can be held liable for any damages to the goods.

4. If a person enters into a contract while so intoxicated that he or she is unable to understand the nature and effect of the contract, then the contract is voidable at his or her option.

Chapter 9 Assessment

MATCHING LEGAL TERMS

Match each of the following definitions with the correct term in the list below. Write the letter of your choice in the answer column.

- **a.** abandonment
- **b.** age of majority
- **c.** contractual capacity
- **d.** competent party
- **e.** disaffirmance
- **f.** emancipation
- **g.** incompetence
- **h.** minor
- **i.** necessaries
- **j.** ratification

1. Items considered essential for a person's well-being, such as food, shelter, clothing, medical care, and employment.   1. _____
2. Affirming, or agreeing to the terms of a contract entered into previously.   2. _____
3. A person who has not yet reached the age of majority.   3. _____
4. The state of a minor who has married or left home that renders the minor responsible for his or her contracts.   4. _____
5. The act of canceling a voidable contract.   5. _____
6. Legal incapacity to make a binding contract.   6. _____
7. Statutory legal age.   7. _____
8. A person of legal age and normal mentality who is capable of understanding the meaning of a contract.   8. _____
9. The ability of a party to make a contract.   9. _____
10. A minor's surrender of the special protection given to him or her by the law.   10. _____

TRUE/FALSE QUIZ

Indicate whether each of the following statements is true or false by writing *T* or *F* in the answer column.

11. A person's legal birthday is the same as the day on which his or her birthday is celebrated.   11. _____
12. A minor's contracts for necessaries are valid.   12. _____
13. A contract with a minor can be ratified by either party.   13. _____
14. Upon reaching legal age, a minor must ratify earlier completed contracts in writing.   14. _____
15. A minor is responsible for his or her torts and crimes.   15. _____
16. Contracts made while a person is intoxicated are voidable by either party.   16. _____
17. A person who is able to understand the meaning of a contract is considered a competent party.   17. _____
18. A contract made by a person while intoxicated must be ratified in writing within 30 days.   18. _____

Chapter 9 Assessment

19. A minor is considered emancipated, and hence responsible for his or her contracts, upon marriage.
19. _____

20. The responsibility of determining whether or not a person is competent rests with everyone who enters into a contract with the person.
20. _____

21. The law regards actions of minors that result in emancipation as abandonment.
21. _____

22. A minor's disaffirmance must be in writing to be effective.
22. _____

23. Ratification of minors' contracts must be in writing to be effective.
23. _____

24. In some states, a minor may avoid a contract, even if he or she falsely represented himself or herself.
24. _____

25. A contract ratification must ratify the entire contract.
25. _____

DISCUSSION QUESTIONS

Answer the following questions and discuss them in class.

26. Discuss what is meant by "age of majority" and how it affects the legal status of minors entering into contracts.

27. How is a contract with a minor affected by the minor's ratification of the contract?

28. A minor is held legally responsible if he or she injures another person or another person's property. Would it make a difference if the injury were accidental? Why or why not?

29. A minor purchased a desk, computer, and printer—all on sale. If he later attempted to purchase only the computer, the salesperson could legally refuse to limit the sale to one item on the grounds of the buyer's minority. In this case, what is the legal principle regarding partial ratification of the minor's contract?

Competent Parties   CHAPTER 9   139

Chapter 9 Assessment

30. A 17-year-old dancer signed a contract for a season with a ballet company. After rehearsals and two performances, the dancer received a better offer from another company. Can she terminate the current contract? Why or why not?

31. Contracts made by mentally incompetent persons are generally voidable. Are there any exceptions? If yes, explain.

THINKING CRITICALLY ABOUT THE LAW

Answer the following questions, which require you to think critically about the legal principles that you learned in this chapter.

32. Age of Majority The required age for obtaining a driver's license is usually lower than the age for drinking or voting. What is the rationale for this difference?

33. Minors' Contracts Is it fair that minors' contracts are voidable, whereas those of adults are legally binding? Why or why not?

34. Contracts of Emancipated Minors The contracts of emancipated minors are usually considered legally binding. Give an example to illustrate why this is necessary.

35. Contracts of Mentally Incompetent If a contract is made by a responsible adult who later becomes mentally incompetent, is the contract enforceable by either party? Explain your answer.

PART 2 Contracts

Chapter 9 Assessment

36. **A Question of Ethics** Is it fair and ethical for a minor to take advantage of the protection accorded by the law to breach a contract made with a person who believed the minor to have reached the age of majority? Explain your answer.

_____
_____
_____

CASE QUESTIONS

Study each case below and answer the questions that follow by writing *Yes* or *No* in the answer column.

37. **Minors' Contracts** Nguyen, 17 years old, purchased a used boat and over a six-month period made six of the payments. On the day before she celebrated her eighteenth birthday, she made the seventh payment. One month later, instead of making the regularly scheduled payment, she attempted to disaffirm the contract, claiming that she was a minor when she made the contract. (Nguyen lived in a state where the age of majority is 18.)

   a. Did Nguyen's first six payments indicate her ratification? a. _____
   b. Is this a contract for necessaries? b. _____
   c. Did the seventh payment serve to ratify the contract? c. _____
   d. Is it likely that Nguyen will be successful in her attempt to disaffirm the contract? d. _____

38. **Voidable Contract** Caroli, 17 years old, signed an agreement to buy a used computer from Egan for $450. While Caroli was on his way to pick up the equipment, Egan got an offer for $550 from someone else. When asked to complete the transaction, Egan told him he was unwilling to go through with the agreement because Caroli was a minor.

   a. Can Egan cancel the contract? a. _____
   b. Is this a voidable contract? b. _____
   c. Can Caroli cancel the contract? c. _____
   d. If Egan sells the computer to Caroli, can Caroli later return the computer? d. _____

39. **Contracts of the Mentally Incompetent** Jenna, who had been declared insane by the courts, purchased a high-powered sports car for $36,000. She made the purchase during a lucid interval, and her condition was not known to the seller. Jenna drove the car for several months, and then she returned it to the seller and claimed that her mental condition permitted her to avoid the contract.

   a. Was Jenna's contract valid at the time of purchase? a. _____
   b. Did Jenna's continued use of the car constitute ratification? b. _____
   c. Can the seller claim that the contract was valid because the car was a necessary? c. _____
   d. Will Jenna be successful in avoiding the contract? d. _____

Competent Parties   CHAPTER 9

Chapter 9 Assessment

CASE ANALYSIS

Study each of the following cases carefully and then briefly state the principle of law and your decision.

40. Contracts of the Mentally Incompetent Staples, following extensive injuries in an automobile accident, was declared mentally incompetent. He imagined himself to be in command of a large army engaged in protecting the country against an invasion. He ordered several large tents, sleeping bags, and other military supplies from a firm that specialized in selling such goods. When he failed to pay for the goods, the firm attempted to seize Staples' bank deposits and his disability pension. *Will the military supply firm be successful in its attempt to secure payment?*

Principle of law:

Decision:

41. Contracts of Emancipated Minors Doran, a young man of 17, married a 17-year-old woman. After the wedding they moved to another city, where they both found work and began to buy furniture and appliances. When they realized that they had been unwise in some of their purchases, they attempted to rescind the contracts, claiming they were minors. *Will the Dorans be successful in avoiding the contracts?*

Principle of law:

Decision:

42. Contracts of Intoxicated Persons Martinson borrowed money from Matz while Martinson was intoxicated. Later, when he was sober, Martinson was told that he had signed a note payable to Matz. Five years later, he indicated that he would not pay the note because of his intoxication. Two years after that, Matz sued to collect on the note. *Is it likely that Matz will collect on the note?* [*Matz v. Martinson,* 149 N.W. 370 (Minnesota).]

Principle of law:

Decision:

142   PART 2   Contracts

Chapter 9 Assessment

43. Contracts of the Mentally Incompetent Ortelere, a retired teacher, had built up a substantial amount in the retirement plan before she retired because of "involutional psychosis" (mental illness). She had previously specified that a lowered monthly retirement benefit would be paid to her so that her husband would get some benefit from the retirement plan if she died before he did. After her mental problems began, she changed her payout plan and borrowed from the pension fund. As a consequence of the changes she made, her husband lost his rights to benefits. Two months after she made the changes, she died. The husband sued to reverse the changes his wife had made, claiming that she was not of sound mind when she made them. *Will the changes in the plan be voided?* [*Ortelere v. Teachers' Retirement Board,* 250 N.E.2d 460 (Wisconsin).]

Principle of law:

Decision:

LEGAL RESEARCH

Complete the following activities. Then share your findings with the class.

44. Working in Teams In teams of three or four, interview several retailers of home appliances or furnishings to determine how they ascertain the age of customers who wish to enter into an installment contract for purchases.

45. Using Technology Using the Internet and search engines, compare the age of majority provisions in several states. Also, determine the differences in the legal ages required for various activities, such as marriage, driving, voting, and military service.

Competent Parties   CHAPTER 9   143

CHAPTER 10

LEGAL PURPOSE OF CONTRACTS

PERFORMANCE OBJECTIVES

After studying this chapter and completing the assessments, you will be able to:

1. Classify illegal agreements into three major categories.

2. Identify four kinds of agreements that are in violation of statutes.

3. Identify four kinds of agreements that are in violation of public policy.

4. Explain the provisions of two major laws governing business competition: the Sherman Antitrust Act and the Robinson-Patman Act.

5. Discuss government-granted franchises as a form of legally permissible restraints on trade and competition.

LEGAL TERMS

Sunday agreement
gambling agreement
interest
usury
unlicensed transaction
champerty
restraint of trade
monopoly power
government-granted franchise
franchisor
franchisee

LEGALITY AND THE PUBLIC INTEREST

As discussed in Chapter 6, legality of purpose is one of the essential elements of an enforceable contract. Although the parties to a contract are legally competent and have reached mutual agreement, the law still requires that the purpose of the agreement be legal and not contrary to the public interest.

CLASSIFICATIONS OF ILLEGAL AGREEMENTS

There are three broad classifications of illegal agreements: (1) agreements that are contrary to the common law, (2) agreements that have been declared illegal by statute, and (3) agreements that the courts have found to be against the security or welfare of the general public.

OBJECTIVE 1

Classify illegal agreements into three major categories.

EFFECT OF ILLEGALITY

An illegal agreement is usually considered void and unenforceable. However, if the contract is divisible—that is, if it has several unrelated parts—and if one or more parts have a legal purpose, then the legal components are usually enforceable. The part or parts that have an illegal purpose are not enforceable.

> **EXAMPLE 10.1**
> Revak contracted to make some major repairs and to add a room to one side of her house. After the contractor began the work, it was discovered that if the room were added, Revak would be in violation of local zoning ordinances. If the agreement had specified one price for all the work, the contract would be unenforceable. If the estimate and contract were sufficiently detailed, the part of the agreement that covered the remodeling would be enforceable and the part involving the added room would be unenforceable.

AGREEMENTS IN VIOLATION OF STATUTES

Agreements that violate government statutes are not enforceable by the courts. Examples of such agreements include (1) agreements made on Sundays or legal holidays, (2) gambling and wagering agreements, (3) usurious agreements, and (4) unlicensed transactions.

OBJECTIVE 2

Identify four kinds of agreements that are in violation of statutes.

Agreements Made on Sundays or Legal Holidays

Some state statutes and local ordinances regulate the creation and performance of contracts on Sundays and legal holidays. Many of these restrictions originate in religious customs and practices. In recent years, there has been a steady decline in the number of activities that are prohibited on Sundays and holidays.

In a small number of jurisdictions, a contract that is made on a Sunday but is to be carried on a weekday is invalid. In some states, a ***Sunday agreement*** must be ratified on a weekday. The contract is considered ratified if it is performed on a weekday or if the terms are restated on a weekday. Contracts made on a legal holiday can generally be performed on the next business day following the holiday. Examples of contracts that might be made on a Sunday or on a legal holiday and ratified on a weekday are contracts involving the payment of a note, the delivery of merchandise, and the repair of equipment.

Gambling and Wagering Agreements

All states have legislation that regulates gambling—that is, risking money or something of value on the uncertain outcome of a future event. A ***gambling agreement*** is one in which performance by one party depends on the occurrence of an uncertain event. Some states permit betting on certain kinds of horse or dog races; other states permit state-run lotteries. Where gambling agreements are permitted, the state closely regulates the nature of the betting and usually derives considerable revenue from it. Even in a state that permits betting on horse races, the bets must be placed with state-approved outlets, such as racetracks or off-track betting facilities operated or regulated by the state. Other bets in these states are illegal unless approved by state law and are, therefore, as unenforceable as they would be in a state that permits no gambling at all. In some states, gambling on Native American reservations is legal.

Usurious Agreements

Interest is the charge for using borrowed money, generally expressed as an annual percentage of the amount of the loan (principal). Nearly every state has laws that regulate interest charges. If a loan is made at an interest rate higher than that allowed by state law, the lender is guilty of ***usury,*** charging interest higher than the law permits. Such usurious agreements are illegal and void. In some states, usury laws do not apply to transactions between corporations. In many states, the usury statutes apply to retail installment credit sales and credit card transactions. Most states have varying usury rates, depending on the kind of loan.

Sunday agreement A contract made on a Sunday. In a small number of jurisdictions, such contracts are invalid unless they are ratified on a weekday.

gambling agreement An agreement in which performance by one party depends on the occurrence of an uncertain event.

interest The charge for using borrowed money, generally expressed as an annual percentage of the amount of the loan (principal).

usury Charging interest higher than the law permits.

EXAMPLE 10.2

> Nunez purchased a microwave oven from a local appliance dealer. Since he did not have a credit record, he agreed to pay the dealer $10 down and $10 per week for one year from the date of purchase. There were no other benefits to Nunez, such as delivery or an investigation of his credit. The price for a cash transaction was $200. When Nunez figured out how much it was costing him to finance the purchase through the dealer, he refused to make any more payments, claiming that the rate of interest was illegal. A court would likely rule that the interest charge was usurious.

Unlicensed Transactions

To protect the public, most states require persons engaged in certain businesses, professions, and occupations to be licensed. The requirements for a license usually include paying an annual fee and passing an examination—written, oral, or both—to ensure competency. Persons in licensed professions and occupations include doctors, dentists, lawyers, nurses, certified public accountants, pharmacists, plumbers, barbers, and teachers. An agreement with a person who does not have the required license is an *unlicensed transaction* and is generally illegal if the purpose of the statute is regulatory and enforcement of the licensing requirements is clearly in the public interest. If the purpose of the licensing requirement is solely to raise revenue for the jurisdiction, the absence of a license does not make the agreement void.

unlicensed transaction An agreement with a person who does not have a required license.

AGREEMENTS AGAINST PUBLIC POLICY

Some agreements are unenforceable because they are contrary to the interests of the public. Examples include agreements (1) that obstruct or pervert justice, (2) restrain marriage, (3) interfere with public service, and (4) defraud creditors and other persons.

OBJECTIVE 3

Identify four kinds of agreements that are in violation of public policy.

Agreements that Obstruct or Pervert Justice

Among the kinds of agreements that obstruct or pervert justice are the following: (1) an agreement to conceal a crime or not to prosecute a criminal—such as a thief if he or she returns the stolen property; (2) an agreement to encourage a lawsuit in which one or more of the parties has no legitimate interest, called *champerty;* (3) an agreement to give false testimony or to suppress evidence; (4) an agreement to bribe a juror or a court official; and (5) an agreement to refrain from testifying as a witness in a legal action.

champerty An agreement to encourage a lawsuit in which one or more of the parties has no legitimate interest.

> **EXAMPLE 10.3**
>
> Blasky, an investor and speculator, agreed to pay a percentage of his profits on stock trading to Gillian, who had access to confidential information. When the scheme was uncovered and Blasky was charged with violating federal securities regulations, he offered $10,000 to Gillian if Gillian would deny knowing about or being involved in Blasky's illegal activities. The contract was clearly unenforceable, because it was an agreement to give false testimony.

In the above case, even if the money was paid, neither side could sue the other. A court will not touch an illegal contract, even if one party is out of the money or service.

Agreements that Restrain Marriage

Agreements in restraint of marriage are void. For example, a promise to pay money to a child on the condition that he or she never marry would not be enforceable. If a child agreed to this arrangement and avoided marrying, he or she could not enforce the agreement.

Agreements that Interfere with Public Service

Agreements that attempt to bribe or interfere with public officials, obtain political preference in appointments to office, pay an officer for signing a pardon, require one of the parties to the agreement to break a law, or influence a law-making body for personal gain are examples of agreements that are illegal because they interfere with public service.

Although some clever schemes have been used to influence public officials, such as giving "no-show" jobs to relatives of political officials or making contributions to political campaigns, public officials and those who attempt to influence them are exposed and prosecuted every year. Often "vacations" are given as bribes. Not many of these activities involve specific contracts, but they are nevertheless illegal.

> **EXAMPLE 10.4**
>
> Furth, a government official, used his influence with the parking violations bureau to ensure that a particular firm received a contract for parking meters without competitive bidding. The manufacturer of the meters agreed to employ the official as a consultant when he left office. The agreement was clearly illegal and unenforceable.

Agreements to Defraud Creditors and Other Persons

Because agreements to defraud lack the element of legality of purpose, they are void and unenforceable. An example of an agreement to defraud another person might be an agreement to sell or give away property with the intention of defrauding creditors in anticipation of bankruptcy. Consider the case in Example 10.5.

> **EXAMPLE 10.5**
>
> Lachman, who had been operating a retail store at a loss for several years, agreed to give his brother-in-law substantial inventory with the understanding that after bankruptcy proceedings were concluded and his creditors were satisfied, the property would be returned to him. An agreement such as this is void and unenforceable.

Illegal Restraints of Trade

Competition in public sales and in bidding for contracts is essential in our market-oriented economy because the competition of a free market encourages lower prices, improved products, and better service. The law generally encourages competition, except in certain instances that will be discussed later in this chapter. Unless specifically permitted by law, agreements to suppress or eliminate competition are illegal and unenforceable. These kinds of agreements are said to be in *restraint of trade.*

Monopoly power is the term used to describe a situation in which one or more people or firms control the market in a particular area or for a certain product. A monopoly is generally illegal because it results in a restraint of trade.

Sherman Antitrust Act

In 1890, Congress passed the *Federal Antitrust Act,* also known as the *Sherman Antitrust Act.* This law and several amendments to it are still vigorously enforced against large and small businesses. It forbids certain agreements that tend to unreasonably lessen competition, fix prices, allocate territories, or limit production. Persons or businesses found guilty of such practices are liable to punishment by heavy fines and imprisonment, and the contracts will be judged to be void. While the act does not prohibit firms from growing large as a result of producing good products and utilizing effective management, if a firm's size allows it to dominate a market, the federal government can require it to be split into smaller businesses. Similar antitrust statues have been passed by most states to prohibit local anticompetitive practices.

> **EXAMPLE 10.6**
>
> The two drug stores in the village of Forque agreed between themselves that they would each service a particular section of the town and that each would charge customers the same low prices for certain

OBJECTIVE 4

Explain the provisions of two major laws governing business competition: the Sherman Antitrust Act and the Robinson-Patman Act.

restraint of trade A limitation on the full exercise of doing business with others.

monopoly power A situation in which one or more people or firms control the market in a particular area or for a particular product.

> prescription medicines. The purpose of the agreement was to create a monopoly and discourage competition from any new store that might wish to open in the town. This agreement would be found to be in restraint of trade and a violation of state law.

Robinson-Patman Act

The *Robinson-Patman Act* of 1936, which amended earlier antitrust legislation, makes it unlawful to discriminate, directly or indirectly, in matters involving product pricing, advertising, and promotion. It specifically prohibits sellers from discriminating among different purchasers of goods of like grade and quality under certain conditions. The purpose of the act is to ensure that no one customer has an advantage over others. A seller of goods can, however, legally charge a certain customer a lower price if the seller can prove that the lower price is a result of savings due to large-quantity sales to that customer. The act does not force the larger buyer to give up the advantages resulting from greater efficiency, but rather puts a limit on the use of the economic power that often results from large size.

> **EXAMPLE 10.7**
>
> Meadowbrook Fuel is a large national company that markets fuel oil in the city of Westerville. The company sells fuel oil in the area surrounding Westerville for a lower price than it does in the city, where it already controls a substantial share of the market and has little competition. The competition in the surrounding area is largely from small companies. Meadowbrook would be in violation of the Robinson-Patman Act for such discriminatory pricing practices.

LEGAL RESTRAINTS OF TRADE

OBJECTIVE 5

Discuss government-granted franchises as a form of legally permissible restraints on trade and competition.

government-granted franchise A legal monopoly in which a state or federal government grants a person or firm a license to conduct a specific business, usually an essential service.

Although federal and state legislation and many court decisions encourage competition, there are times when agreements in restraint of trade are in the public interest and are legally enforceable.

Government-Granted Monopolies

A *government-granted franchise* is another form of legal monopoly in which a state or the federal government grants a person or firm a license to conduct a specific—usually essential—business such as a bus line, railroad, electric power company, telephone company (including cellular service), TV cable service, and so on.

Such franchises are granted because it is in the public interest to limit the number of companies operating in an area if those companies provide a necessary service. These legal monopolies are subject to a greater degree of regulation than other businesses and are responsible to administrative agencies, boards, or public service commissions.

Private Franchises

A government-granted franchise should not be confused with a private franchise, which is a special kind of business organization involving a contractual relationship between a parent firm and an independent company. In the case of private franchises, the contractual relationship provides that the parent firm *(franchisor)* will supply certain services, such as management consulting, to the independent company *(franchisee)* and will allow the independent company to use the parent firm's name, join with others in national advertising, and secure various other benefits.

The private franchise is a form of business organization that is usually used in businesses such as fast-food chains, motels, automobile dealerships, and gasoline service stations.

franchisor The parent firm in a franchise agreement.

franchisee The independent company in a franchise agreement.

Zoning Regulations

A community may designate certain areas as zones for such uses as light industrial, industrial, commercial, and residential. While zoning regulations are intended to protect the citizens of a community, they may also act as legal restraints of trade because they restrict where and how businesses may operate.

Photo 10.1

The Franchise Relationship

A franchise relationship exists between a franchisor and a franchisee. *What are some of the benefits of owning and operating a franchise?*

Legal Purpose of Contracts CHAPTER 10 151

Environmental and Safety Regulations

Federal and state legislatures have enacted statutes to protect the health and welfare of the general population from the effects of pollution of the atmosphere and bodies of water. Safety regulations serve to protect the health and welfare of the general population of a community, customers, and employees. Like zoning regulations, discussed above, environmental and safety regulations also serve as legal restraints of trade because they place limits and restrictions on how a firm may operate.

CHAPTER SUMMARY

1 The three major categories of illegal agreements are **(a)** agreements that are contrary to the common law, **(b)** agreements that have been declared illegal by statute, and **(c)** agreements that have been found by the courts to be against the security or welfare of the general public.

2 Four kinds of agreements that violate statutes are **(a)** agreements made on Sundays or legal holidays, **(b)** gambling and wagering agreements, **(c)** usurious agreements, and **(d)** unlicensed transactions.

3 Four kinds of agreements that violate public policy are those that **(a)** obstruct or pervert justice, **(b)** restrain marriage, **(c)** interfere with public service, and **(d)** defraud creditors and other persons.

4 The Sherman Antitrust Act forbids agreements that tend to unreasonably lessen competition, fix prices, allocate territories, or limit production. The Robinson-Patman Act makes it unlawful to discriminate, directly or indirectly, in matters involving product pricing, advertising, and promotion.

5 A government-granted franchise is a form of legal monopoly in which a state or the federal government grants a person or firm a license to conduct a specific—usually essential—business. Such franchises are granted because it is in the public interest to limit the number of companies operating in the area. These monopolies are subject to extensive regulation.

Chapter 10 Assessment

MATCHING LEGAL TERMS

Match each of the following definitions with the correct term in the list below. Write the letter of your choice in the answer column.

- **a.** champerty
- **b.** franchisee
- **c.** franchisor
- **d.** gambling agreement
- **e.** government-granted franchise
- **f.** interest
- **g.** monopoly power
- **h.** restraint of trade
- **i.** unlicensed transaction
- **j.** usury

1. An agreement based on the uncertain outcome of some future event.   **1.** _____
2. The practice of charging a higher interest rate than that permitted by law.   **2.** _____
3. An agreement with a person who is required to have, but lacks, the approval of the state to practice his or her business, profession, or occupation.   **3.** _____
4. An agreement by a person to encourage or support a lawsuit in which he or she has no legitimate interest.   **4.** _____
5. The ability to control the market in a particular area or for a certain product.   **5.** _____
6. A legal monopoly granted to a firm or person to conduct a specific business such as a railroad or electric company.   **6.** _____
7. Actions or agreements intended to suppress or eliminate competition.   **7.** _____
8. The person or firm to whom a legal monopoly is granted.   **8.** _____
9. The charge for the use of borrowed money.   **9.** _____
10. A government or firm that grants a monopoly to another.   **10.** _____

TRUE/FALSE QUIZ

Indicate whether each of the following statements is true or false by writing *T* or *F* in the answer column.

11. A contract is always legal and enforceable if the parties are competent and if they have a mutual understanding.   **11.** _____
12. An agreement to perform an illegal act is void and unenforceable.   **12.** _____
13. All states prohibit all forms of gambling.   **13.** _____
14. Agreements that require the performance of acts against public policy are void.   **14.** _____
15. Agreements that restrain marriage are valid if both parties agree to all provisions.   **15.** _____
16. Agreements in restraint of trade can only be prosecuted under federal law.   **16.** _____

Chapter 10 Assessment

17. The government will always prosecute companies that wield monopoly power because competition is always deemed in the public's best interest. 17. _____

18. The Robinson-Patman Act prohibits price discrimination. 18. _____

19. The Sherman Antitrust Act prohibits agreements that tend to lessen competition. 19. _____

20. Zoning regulations may also act as legal restraints of trade because they restrict where and how businesses may operate. 20. _____

21. Environmental and safety regulations seldom act as legal restraints of trade even though they place limits and restrictions on how a firm may operate. 21. _____

DISCUSSION QUESTIONS

Answer the following questions and discuss them in class.

22. What are the three broad classifications of illegal agreements?

23. Provide an example of an agreement that has been made illegal by statute.

24. Is an illegal agreement enforceable? Why or why not?

25. Why are contracts made with individuals who are required to be licensed, but are not, usually unenforceable?

26. Legislation intended to protect the natural environment can have unexpected consequences and may serve as a disincentive to business. Explain your answer.

Chapter 10 Assessment

27. How does society benefit from the actions of governments granting monopolies for such services as telephone service, railroads, and so on?

THINKING CRITICALLY ABOUT THE LAW

Answer the following questions, which require you to think critically about the legal principles that you learned in this chapter.

28. Illegal Agreements Certain kinds of agreements, such gambling agreements, are illegal or highly regulated. What do you think is the primary motivation for such prohibitions?

29. Licensing Most states require people engaged in certain professions or businesses to be licensed. How do licensing requirements protect the public?

30. The Law and Minors Laws that protect minors were established during a very different time when minors seemed less mature and sophisticated than they are today. Evaluate whether the law as it applies to minors needs to be reexamined.

31. Environmental Protection Enforcement of laws that are intended to protect the environment sometimes has unforeseen economic effects, such as plant closings and unemployment. How should society attempt to balance between environmental and economic issues?

32. Competition Various federal and state laws are intended to encourage competition. Analyze and report on the benefits of competition to society.

Legal Purpose of Contracts   CHAPTER 10   155

Chapter 10 Assessment

33. **Restraint of Trade** Zoning regulations have the effect of restraining trade because they limit the activities of certain kinds of businesses. Explain how society benefits from such limitations.

34. **A Question of Ethics** The Robinson-Patman Act prohibits price discrimination. What were the ethical reasons that motivated the passage of this act?

CASE QUESTIONS

Study each case below and answer the questions that follow by writing *Yes* or *No* in the answer column.

35. **Gambling Agreements** Pickens was one of a group of four army veterans who met once a month to play poker. On one occasion, Pickens lost more than $1,000 and refused to pay, claiming that gambling debts are not collectible. The winner claimed that since the state had legalized off-track betting and had begun a lottery, gambling debts were now legal and collectible.

    a. Does the existence of state-approved gambling affect the legality of other forms of gambling? a. _____

    b. Can the winner of the gambling activity legally collect his winnings? b. _____

36. **Unlicensed Transactions** Rogan, who had worked for eight years as an electrician's helper, tried several times to pass the state-required electrician's test, but he failed each time. Still, he felt that he knew enough about his trade that he could perform the work of an electrician and accepted several jobs that required a fully licensed electrician. Duggan hired Rogin to install the wiring in a room addition. Just as Rogin was beginning work, Duggan learned that Rogin did not have a valid electrician's license and cancelled the contract. Rogin claimed that he should be paid anyway because he turned down other employment elsewhere to accept Duggan's work.

    a. Is the contract between Duggan and Rogin enforceable? a. _____

    b. Does it seem that Rogin should be paid for the work he and Duggan agreed he would do? b. _____

    c. Is Duggan partly to blame for the misunderstanding for having failed to ask to see Rogin's license? c. _____

Chapter 10 Assessment

CASE ANALYSIS

Study each of the following cases carefully and then briefly state the principle of law and your decision.

37. Usurious Agreements Alfino borrowed money from Yakutsk and agreed in writing to pay a rate of interest higher than that allowed by local law. Later, when Alfino was called upon to pay, he refused, claiming that the agreement was void because of the usurious rate. Yakutsk, the lender, sued to collect. Yakutsk agreed to accept the legal rate of interest and felt he was entitled to collect the debt. Alfino believed that the entire debt was void because of the illegality of the original agreement. *In view of Yakutsk's willingness to accept the legal rate of interest, can Alfino be compelled to pay?* [*Yakutsk v. Alfino,* 349 N.Y.S. 2d 718 (New York).]

Principle of law:

Decision:

38. Price Discrimination Morton Salt Company, a large producer of table salt, had an established price scale for its product based on the quantity of salt ordered in a 12-month period. Consequently, a firm that ordered a substantial quantity of salt paid less per package than a store that ordered a small quantity. Acting in response to complaints from small firms, the Federal Trade Commission investigated and determined that the lowest price offered by Morton Salt Company, although available to all customers, was practical only for five national customers who purchased in sufficiently large quantities to benefit from the lowest prices established. *Would the alleged price discrimination be covered under the Robinson-Patman Act?* [*FTC v. Morton Salt Co.,* 334 U.S. 37.]

Principle of law:

Decision:

39. Illegal Agreement Jason decided to declare bankruptcy because his financial situation was desperate and his only property was a nearly new car worth about $14,000. In an attempt to conceal the value of his property, he sold the car to his friend Dean for $2,000. He planned to buy the car back from Dean when the bankruptcy proceedings were concluded. *Is the sale of the car a valid contract?*

Principle of law:

Legal Purpose of Contracts   CHAPTER 10   157

Chapter 10 Assessment

Decision:
_____
_____

LEGAL RESEARCH

Complete the following activities. Then share your findings with the class.

40. Working in Teams In teams of three or four, interview several owners or managers of small businesses to learn about the experiences they have had attempting to operate the firm in an environment where there are various legal obstacles that must be overcome.

_____
_____
_____
_____
_____
_____
_____

41. Using Technology Use the Internet and search engines to investigate the Sherman Antitrust Act, the Robinson-Patman Act, and the various prosecutions under each.

_____
_____
_____
_____
_____
_____
_____
_____

CHAPTER 11

FORM OF CONTRACTS

PERFORMANCE OBJECTIVES

After studying this chapter and completing the assessments, you will be able to:

1. Provide examples of contracts that (a) should be in writing, (b) should not be in writing, and (c) must be in writing.

2. Describe how the parol evidence rule affects the addition of supplementary provisions to a written contract.

3. Identify the six types of contracts that the Statute of Frauds requires to be in writing.

4. Specify the five items of information that should be included in a written contract.

LEGAL TERMS

parol evidence rule
Statute of Frauds
executor
administrator
intestate
guaranty
antenuptial agreement
real property
auction sale
memorandum

THE REQUIREMENT OF PROPER FORM

The required elements of a valid contract were introduced in Chapter 6. These requirements are: (1) offer and acceptance, (2) mutual agreement, (3) consideration, (4) competent parties, (5) legality of purpose, and (6) proper form. Following the introduction of the essential elements, several chapters were devoted to the first five elements. In this chapter, the final element, proper form, is covered.

WHEN CONTRACTS SHOULD BE IN WRITING

Not all contracts should be in writing because many of them are so routine that putting them in writing would be a waste of time and effort. For example, a written contract is not needed when one is taking a bus ride, purchasing groceries, or ordering a meal in a restaurant. Some contracts *should* be in writing to protect against later disagreement, such as a contract for the sale of an automobile. Still others *must* be in writing because the law requires it for the contract to be enforceable.

OBJECTIVE 1(a-b)
Provide examples of contracts that (a) should be in writing, and (b) should not be in writing.

THE PAROL EVIDENCE RULE

The word *parol* as used in the **parol evidence rule** simply means "speech" or "words." Parol evidence refers to any supplementary evidence or conditions, written or oral, that a party wants to add to a written contract. The parol evidence rule states that any spoken or written words in conflict with what the written contract states cannot be introduced as evidence in a court of law.

parol evidence rule The rule that any spoken or written words in conflict with what the written contract states cannot be introduced as evidence in a court of law.

> **EXAMPLE 11.1**
> When Wlodyka signed a purchase agreement for a small garden tractor, the salesperson orally assured her that several attachments came with the purchase. However, when the tractor was delivered, the attachments were not included. The seller has no legal obligation to furnish the attachments if their inclusion was not specified in the original purchase agreement. If Wlodyka decides to sue the seller, the court will probably refuse to allow her to introduce testimony regarding the oral statements.

OBJECTIVE 2
Describe how the parol evidence rule affects the addition of supplementary provisions to a written contract.

Oral evidence introduced after a contract is signed is legally accepted if it clarifies some point in the written agreement. The

Uniform Commercial Code specifically states that the terms of a written contract may not be changed by evidence of any prior agreement, but the written terms may be explained or supplemented [UCC 2-202]. In a minority of states, however, even consistent oral statements may not be introduced into evidence if a contract is in writing.

The Statute of Frauds

Like the parol evidence rule, the **Statute of Frauds** is a confusing name for an important legal principle. The name is taken from the English law of 1677 called "An Act for Prevention of Frauds and Perjuries." The law specifies that certain kinds of agreements must be in writing to be enforceable. While there is some variation in its interpretation, most states agree on the main principle of the statute.

It is important to note that the Statute of Frauds does not prohibit a person from legally entering into oral contracts for certain kinds of agreements; it only specifies that certain contracts must be in writing to be enforceable. However, once a contract has been completed, it cannot be cancelled merely because it was not in writing—even if it should have been. The Statute of Frauds applies to executory contracts only, that is, to contracts that have yet to be performed.

Statute of Frauds A law requiring certain contracts to be in writing to be enforceable.

OBJECTIVE 1(c)

Provide examples of contracts that (c) must be in writing.

What Types of Contracts Must Be in Writing

The Statute of Frauds specifies six types of contracts that must be in writing to be legally enforceable. These contracts are agreements

- by an executor or administrator to pay the debts of a deceased person
- to answer for the debts of another
- that cannot be completed in less than one year
- made in contemplation of marriage
- to sell any interest in real property
- to sell personal property for $500 or more

Agreements by an Executor or Administrator to Pay Debts of a Deceased Person

The law recognizes that there are often many unsettled matters that need to be resolved when a person dies. An *executor* is a personal

OBJECTIVE 3

Identify the six types of contracts that the Statute of Frauds requires to be in writing.

executor A personal representative named in a will to handle matters involving the estate of a deceased person.

Form of Contracts CHAPTER 11

representative named in a will to handle matters involving the estate of the deceased person. An ***administrator*** is a personal representative named by the court to perform as the executor would in instances in which the deceased person has not left a will. (A person who dies without leaving a will is said to have died ***intestate.***) Either an executor or an administrator has legal authority to arrange for the distribution of the assets of a deceased person, and in such a position may be inclined to promise to pay debts of the deceased personally. The Statute of Frauds requires such a promise be in writing to be enforceable.

> **administrator** A personal representative named by the court to perform as the executor would in instances in which the deceased person has not left a will.
>
> **intestate** Having died without leaving a valid will.

EXAMPLE 11.2

Dellner was named executor in his father's will. After his father's death, Dellner was attempting to close the estate when a creditor demanded immediate payment of an old debt of $400. To avoid embarrassment for other members of his family, Dellner advised the creditor that he would pay the debt personally. Such a promise is not enforceable unless it is in writing.

Agreements to Answer for Debts of Another

A promise, or ***guaranty,*** to pay the debts or settle the wrongdoings of another if he or she does not make settlement personally is not enforceable unless it is written.

> **guaranty** A promise to pay the debts or settle the wrongdoings of another if he or she does not make settlement personally.

EXAMPLE 11.3

Mata, the president of Excel Products, Inc., orally promised to pay the corporation's debts from his own resources in an effort to calm several persistent creditors. Under the Statute of Frauds, such a promise must be in writing.

In some states, an oral promise to assume the debts of another, even if not a cosigner, is enforceable.

Agreements that Cannot Be Completed in Less than One Year

A contract that obviously cannot be completed within one year must be in writing. If the life of the contract is indefinite and there is a possibility of its being completed within a year, it need not be in writing.

EXAMPLE 11.4

Rizzi, a building contractor constructing a condominium, orally agreed with Pie-in-the-Sky, a food service company, to deliver coffee and lunch to the workers on the job until the construction was completed.

> Six months later, Rizzi cancelled the contract. When the food company complained, Rizzi said that the contract could not possibly have been completed within a year because the schedule called for completion in 18 months, and because it was impossible to complete the contract within a year, it should have been in writing to be enforceable.

If the building in the previous case had been scheduled for completion in nine months, but took 14 months because of delays, then the contract would not need to have been in writing to be enforceable.

Agreements Made in Contemplation of Marriage

A promise made by a person planning to marry, known as an *antenuptial agreement,* commonly known as a prenuptial agreement, is enforceable only if it is put in writing before the marriage takes place. This law applies to agreements by the parties to accept additional obligations not ordinarily included in the marriage contract, such as the rearing and custody of children.

antenuptial agreement A promise made by a person planning to marry that is enforceable only if it is put in writing before the marriage takes place.

Agreements to Sell Any Interest in Real Property

Real property, often called real estate, is land and items permanently attached to the land, such as buildings or trees. All contracts to sell real property or any interest in it must be in writing to be enforceable.

real property Land or items permanently attached to the land, such as buildings or trees.

EXAMPLE 11.5

> Abdula agreed to sell a portion of his property to his neighbor, Sasaki. Because they had known each other for many years, they agreed orally on the terms of the contract. When Abdula realized that the property had increased in value over the years, he changed his mind. Sasaki would have no legal recourse because a contract for the sale of any interest in real property must be in writing.

Agreements to Sell Personal Property for $500 or More

The English law of 1677 that served as the basis for the Statute of Frauds provided that a contract of sale for more than ten pounds sterling had to be in writing. This early law has found its way into today's UCC as a requirement that sales for $500 or more must be in writing [UCC 2-201]. The UCC also has other requirements for written contracts, which are discussed in later chapters.

EXAMPLE 11.6

> Suard, the owner of a clothing store, orally agreed to buy a made-to-order display case for $1,200 from Island Fixtures, a manufacturer of display and exhibit equipment. Because of a long-standing relationship

> between the parties to the contract, neither one demanded that the agreement be in writing. In most cases like this one, there would be no difficulty. Although Suard could back out of the deal, he values his reputation in the community and regards himself as a gentleman who keeps his word. Legally, however, the contract is unenforceable.

There are several exceptions to this requirement. Partial or full payment to the seller renders the contract enforceable because it shows the serious intent of the buyer, just as much as a written agreement does.

If, in the Example 11.6, Suard paid part of the sale price at the time of the agreement, he would be bound to it. Acceptance by the buyer or attempted delivery by the seller of the goods or part of them also indicates the serious intent of the parties and renders the oral contract enforceable.

In an *auction sale,* in which goods are sold to the highest bidder, the sale is completed at the fall of the hammer. The notation in the auctioneer's book, initialed by the buyer, is sufficient to meet the requirements for written contracts. In the case of auction bids made by telephone from another city, the bidder is required to sign an agreement in which he or she agrees to be bound by the telephone bids made.

auction sale A sale in which goods are sold to the highest bidder.

WHAT SHOULD BE INCLUDED IN A WRITTEN CONTRACT

OBJECTIVE 4
Specify the five items of information that should be included in a written contract.

Most important contracts are either printed or typewritten, and signed by hand by the parties to the agreement. (Electronically produced and signed contracts will be covered in Chapter 26.) A signature may include any symbol used by a contracting party intending to authenticate a written agreement. This can, for example, include a firm's logo or a purchase order. A valid agreement can be entirely handwritten as long as it is legible. It may even be a series of letters among several persons. It can be written on almost any surface with any material that makes a discernible mark, such as pen, pencil, or crayon.

A written contract or agreement, sometimes called a *memorandum,* should contain the following information:

memorandum A written contract or agreement.

1. names of the parties
2. purpose of the agreement
3. description of the consideration promised

PART 2   Contracts

Figure 11.1 Form of a Contract

A written contract, or agreement, contains five basic pieces of information. *Why does the law require that some contracts be in writing?*

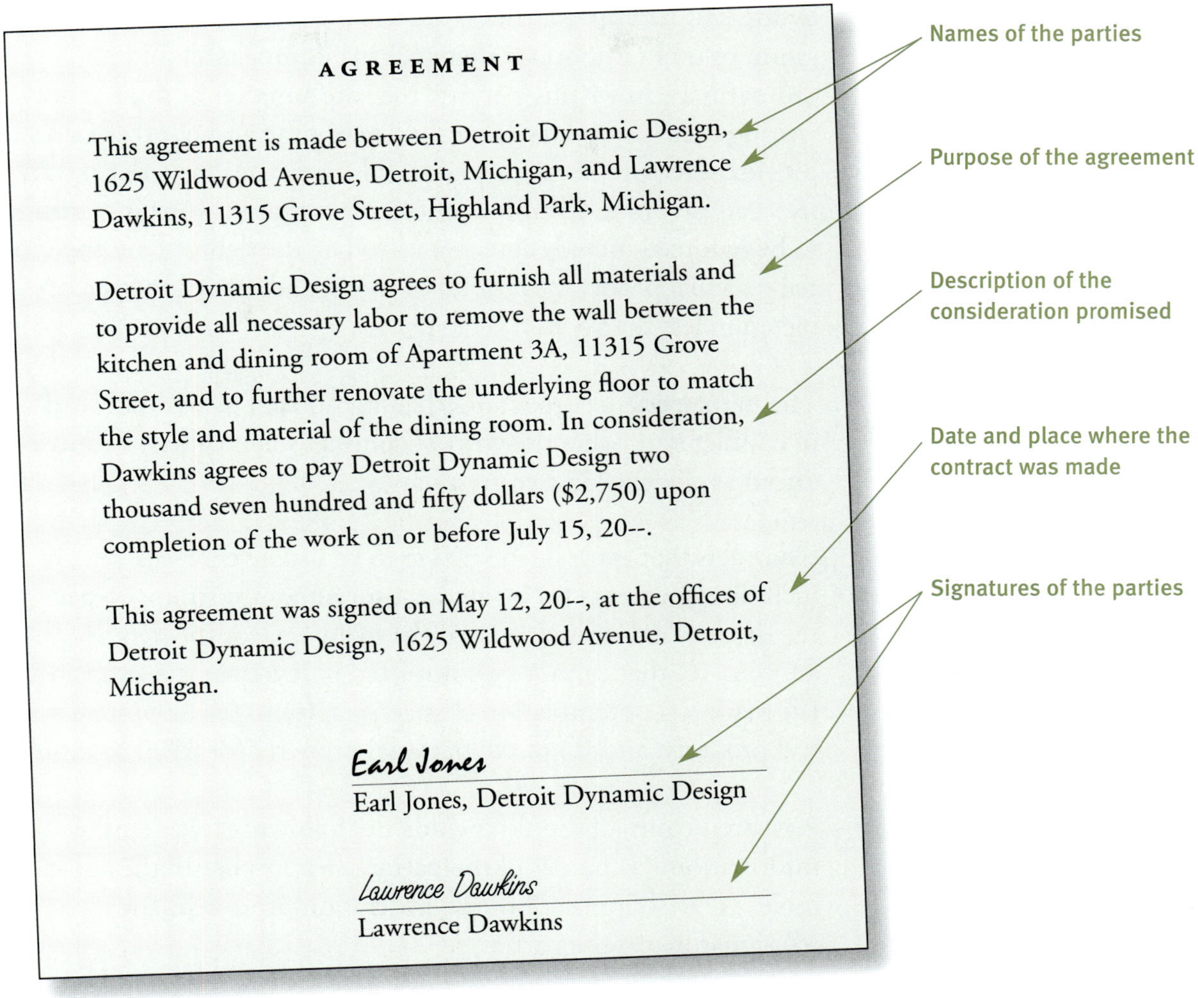

AGREEMENT

This agreement is made between Detroit Dynamic Design, 1625 Wildwood Avenue, Detroit, Michigan, and Lawrence Dawkins, 11315 Grove Street, Highland Park, Michigan.

Detroit Dynamic Design agrees to furnish all materials and to provide all necessary labor to remove the wall between the kitchen and dining room of Apartment 3A, 11315 Grove Street, and to further renovate the underlying floor to match the style and material of the dining room. In consideration, Dawkins agrees to pay Detroit Dynamic Design two thousand seven hundred and fifty dollars ($2,750) upon completion of the work on or before July 15, 20--.

This agreement was signed on May 12, 20--, at the offices of Detroit Dynamic Design, 1625 Wildwood Avenue, Detroit, Michigan.

Earl Jones
Earl Jones, Detroit Dynamic Design

Lawrence Dawkins
Lawrence Dawkins

- Names of the parties
- Purpose of the agreement
- Description of the consideration promised
- Date and place where the contract was made
- Signatures of the parties

4. date and place where the contract was made
5. signatures of the parties

In addition, a written contract may include a warranty, agreement to arbitrate, agreement to be bound by the laws of a specific state, acknowledgement that the buyer has inspected the goods, and the form of payment accepted.

CHAPTER SUMMARY

1 Some contracts should be in writing, although it is not required by the law. Examples include the sale of an automobile, heirloom, or other important items. Other contracts should not ordinarily be in writing because they are a matter of routine and writing them down would be a waste of time and effort. Examples include purchasing groceries, riding the bus, or ordering coffee at a restaurant. Examples of contracts that must be in writing to be enforced include agreements to pay the debts of another, to sell personal property for $500 or more, and that cannot be completed in less than a year.

2 The parol evidence rule states that any spoken or written words in conflict with what the written contract states cannot be introduced as evidence in a court of law.

3 Contracts that must be in writing to be legally enforceable include agreements **(a)** by an executor or administrator to pay the debts of a deceased person, **(b)** to answer for the debts of another, **(c)** that cannot be completed in less than a year, **(d)** made in contemplation of marriage, **(e)** to sell any interest in real property, and **(f)** to sell personal property for $500 or more.

4 A written contract should include the following five items of information: **(a)** names of the parties, **(b)** purpose of the agreement, **(c)** description of the consideration promised, and **(d)** signatures of the parties.

Chapter 11 Assessment

MATCHING LEGAL TERMS

Match each of the following definitions with the correct term in the list below. Write the letter of your choice in the answer column.

- **a.** administrator
- **b.** antenuptial agreement
- **c.** auctioneer
- **d.** executor
- **e.** guaranty
- **f.** intestate
- **g.** parol evidence rule
- **h.** personal property
- **i.** real property
- **j.** Statute of Frauds

1. The law that requires certain types of contracts to be in writing.   **1.** _____
2. Property, other than land and things permanently attached to it.   **2.** _____
3. The point of law that prevents oral changes to a written contract from being legally enforceable.   **3.** _____
4. The state of a person who dies without leaving a will.   **4.** _____
5. The personal representative appointed by a court to distribute the assets of the estate of the deceased.   **5.** _____
6. Land and things that are permanently attached to it.   **6.** _____
7. The personal representative named in a will to distribute the assets of the estate of the deceased.   **7.** _____
8. A promise to pay the debts or settle the wrongdoings of another.   **8.** _____
9. A person who conducts sales of articles in which individuals bid against one another.   **9.** _____
10. Promises made by persons planning to marry.   **10.** _____

TRUE/FALSE QUIZ

Indicate whether each of the following statements is true or false by writing *T* or *F* in the answer column.

11. Some types of contracts must be in writing to be enforceable.   **11.** _____
12. The parol evidence rule affects the enforceability of contracts that include oral or written changes in the terms of an existing contract.   **12.** _____
13. The Statute of Frauds specifies that certain kinds of contracts must be in writing.   **13.** _____
14. Oral or written evidence cannot legally be used to explain unclear portions of a contract.   **14.** _____
15. A valid contract can be entirely handwritten.   **15.** _____
16. Promises made in anticipation of marriage are enforceable.   **16.** _____

Chapter 11 Assessment

17. An agreement to guarantee debts of another must be in writing to be enforceable.   17. _____
18. The requirement of writing does not apply in auction sales.   18. _____
19. An agreement that cannot be completed within six months must be in writing.   19. _____
20. An agreement for the sale of personal property for over $500 must be in writing to be enforceable.   20. _____
21. An agreement for the sale of real estate must be in writing to be enforceable.   21. _____
22. An agreement by an administrator or executor to pay the debts of the deceased must be in writing to be enforceable.   22. _____
23. The Statute of Frauds applies only to contracts that have yet to be performed.   23. _____
24. The Uniform Commercial Code states that the terms of a written contract between merchants may be changed by evidence of a prior agreement.   24. _____
25. A valid contract must either by typed, printed, or written in pen.   25. _____

DISCUSSION QUESTIONS

Answer the following questions and discuss them in class.

26. What are the chief provisions of the Statute of Frauds? Can you suggest other agreements that should also be in writing?

27. What is the minimum dollar amount specified in the Uniform Commercial Code as a requirement for written contracts? Should this amount be greater? Explain your answer.

28. In auction sales, how is the legal requirement for a written contract satisfied? What problems might arise from this arrangement?

29. Why do you think a prenuptial agreement dealing with the custody of children would not be enforceable?

PART 2   Contracts

Chapter 11 Assessment

30. Why does the Statute of Frauds apply to executory contracts only, that is, contracts that have yet to be performed?

___

THINKING CRITICALLY ABOUT THE LAW

Answer the following questions, which require you to think critically about the legal principles that you learned in this chapter.

31. Parol Evidence Rule Even though the parol evidence rule prohibits any amendments to a contract, try to envision circumstances when this rule might be unreasonable.

___

32. Statute of Frauds Under the Statute of Frauds an oral promise to take on the debts of another is enforceable in some states. Can you think of any other activities that should be legally acceptable despite the fact that they are not in writing?

___

33. Personal Property A buyer makes a deposit on an item valued greater than $500, but is later forced to cancel the order. Arguing that there is no written contract, could the buyer expect a refund of the deposit?

___

34. Statute of Frauds Why must a contract that obviously cannot be completed within one year, be in writing?

___

35. A Question of Ethics A man dies intestate. The administrator of the estate refuses to pay the debts on the grounds that there is no written evidence of the obligation. Comment on the ethics of this situation.

___

Form of Contracts   CHAPTER 11   169

Chapter 11 Assessment

CASE QUESTIONS

Study each case below and answer the questions that follow by writing *Yes* or *No* in the answer column.

36. **Statute of Frauds** Coursey orally agreed to sell three acres of land to Oulette for $8,000. After Oulette had paid the $8,000 and the transfer had been officially recorded, Coursey received an offer of $9,000 for the land from another prospective buyer. Hoping to set aside the first transaction so that he could accept the second, higher, offer, Coursey attempted to cancel the sale to Oulette on the grounds that the Statute of Frauds required a written contract.

   a. Does the fact that there is evidence (the recording of the sale) indicate Coursey's agreement to the terms of the sale?   a. _____

   b. Will Coursey succeed in canceling the contract of sale?   b. _____

   c. Is the contract enforceable?   c. _____

37. **Statute of Frauds** Garcia, an independent computer consultant, was orally engaged by the Eastern Institute of Management, a publisher of management newsletters, to set up an office computer network that included needs assessment, employee training, and a desktop publishing system. The plan envisioned at least 18 months of work. Three months after he began work, Eastern paid Garcia for the work he had done and discharged him to hire another consultant, who appeared to have wider experience and greater expertise.

   a. Can Eastern Institute legally cancel this agreement?   a. _____

   b. If the work could have been done in six months, would the oral contract have been legally enforceable?   b. _____

38. **Parol Evidence Rule** Safran, the owner of an automobile repair shop, placed an order for an engine diagnostic machine from the Mountain Range Equipment Company. The salesperson, Rubinstein, orally assured Safran that a number of test programs for both gasoline and diesel engines would be included as part of the order. When the machine was delivered, the test programs were not included. When the buyer protested, Rubinstein claimed that Safran was mistaken and must have been thinking about another special offer the firm was running.

   a. Are the oral promises Rubinstein made that supplement the written contract of sale enforceable?   a. _____

   b. Is it likely that Safran will gain legal satisfaction?   b. _____

   c. Does the parol evidence rule allow introduction of oral revisions to a contract?   c. _____

CASE ANALYSIS

Study each of the following cases carefully and then briefly state the principle of law and your decision.

39. **Statute of Frauds** Anderson was seriously injured in a traffic accident. Anderson's daughter called a doctor, Lawrence, and told him to "give my father the best care you can give him, and I'll pay whatever you charge." The doctor provided the care, but the father died before the bill was paid. Lawrence attempted to collect for

170   PART 2   Contracts

Chapter 11 Assessment

his services from the father's estate. The executor of the estate refused to pay. Lawrence then attempted to collect from the daughter who had guaranteed payment. *Is the daughter legally responsible for the debts of her father if the agreement was not in writing?* [*Lawrence v. Anderson,* 184 A. 689 (Vermont).]

Principle of law:

Decision:

40. **Parol Evidence Rule** Dennison agreed to purchase land from Harden with the understanding that the land contained fruit trees. To prove that there were fruit trees on the property, Harden provided nursery reports stating that Pacific Gold peach trees were growing on the land. When Dennison discovered that the land contained valueless, shrubby trees and only a few of the fruit trees he had been expecting, he sued, charging breach of contract. At the trial, Dennison wanted to introduce the nursery reports as parol evidence to clarify the meaning of the "fruit trees" referred to in the contract. Harden resisted having the nursery report introduced to clarify the contract. *Was Dennison successful in his attempt to clarify the contract by adding the terms "fruit trees," or did Dennison get what he agreed to buy?* [*Dennison v. Harden,* 186 P.2d 908 (Washington).]

Principle of law:

Decision:

41. **Contract Essentials** Marti, the owner of an expensive sports car, agreed in writing to sell the car to Berini. Because both parties recognized that some necessary engine repairs were needed, their contract did not specify the sales price, intending to determine the cost of repairs first. The cost of repairs was later determined and the final price settled, but the price was never included in the contract. *Is this an enforceable contract?*

Principle of law:

Decision:

Form of Contracts   CHAPTER 11   171

Chapter 11 Assessment

42. Statute of Frauds Wang orally agreed to sell a thoroughbred horse to Presti for $60,000. When Presti sent a check in payment, Wang told him that he intended to hold the check for a month for tax purposes. Wang held the horse. While the check remained uncashed, a disagreement arose between Wang and Presti. Wang announced that he would not go through with the transaction and that, because the contract was oral, it was unenforceable. Presti claimed that his sending the check was payment and this action made the oral contract valid and enforceable. *Wang denied accepting payment. Is Presti's claim, that sending the check made the contract enforceable, valid?*

Principle of law:

Decision:

LEGAL RESEARCH

Complete the following activities. Then share your findings with the class.

43. Working in Teams There are numerous risks in the preparation of contracts. Some must be written as specified by the Statute of Frauds, while others need not be. In teams of three or four, interview owners or managers of several small businesses and ask about the procedures followed to minimize these risks.

44. Using Technology Using the Internet and search engines, investigate the parol evidence rule and the Statute of Frauds in two states. Contrast the differences.

172   PART 2   Contracts

CHAPTER 12

Operation of Contracts

PERFORMANCE OBJECTIVES

After studying this chapter and completing the assessments, you will be able to:

1. Distinguish between a third-party beneficiary and an incidental beneficiary, and outline the rights of each.

2. Interpret the legal concept of assignment of contracts and provide an example of a contract that is assignable.

3. Distinguish between the assignment of rights and the delegation of duties.

4. Identify three kinds of contracts that cannot be assigned.

5. Provide examples of contracts that may be assigned by a court.

6. Discuss novation and how it differs from assignment.

LEGAL TERMS

third-party beneficiary
incidental beneficiary
assignment
assignor
assignee
guarantor
personal-service contract
delegation
novation

Contracts Involving Third Parties

In the previous chapters on contracts, only contracts between two parties were discussed. The reason is that normally only the two parties to a contract have rights and duties under it. However, there are two important exceptions to this rule: (1) when the purpose of a contract is to benefit a third party, and (2) when rights that arise from a contract are legally transferred to a third party.

Rights of Third Parties

Third parties to a contract are those who are in some way affected by it but who are not among the parties to the contract. There are two ways in which third parties can be affected by a contract: if they are either (1) third-party beneficiaries, or (2) incidental beneficiaries.

Third-Party Beneficiaries

A **third-party beneficiary** to a contract has a legal right to the benefits resulting from the contract only if it is the intent of the contracting parties to benefit the third party. A life insurance policy is an example of a third-party contract.

> **EXAMPLE 12.1**
>
> Hamomoto contracted with an artist, Janet Frey, to create a painting of his family's farmhouse for $1,000. The painting was to be presented to his son as a birthday gift. Just before the painting was finished, Hamomoto died. The artist learned that she could sell the painting through an art gallery for several thousand dollars. She offered to return the portion of the fee already paid to Hamomoto's son (who is now the heir), but the son insisted that the artist fulfill the terms of the contract. The son, while not one of the contracting parties, is a third-party beneficiary and is entitled to receive the painting.

Incidental Beneficiaries

An **incidental beneficiary** is one who may benefit as an indirect consequence of a contract, although that was not the intent of the contracting parties. That is, the purpose of the contract is not to confer a benefit to a third party, but a third party does, in fact, benefit from it. Such parties have no rights in the contract, regardless of the size of their gain or benefit.

OBJECTIVE 1

Distinguish between a third-party beneficiary and an incidental beneficiary, and outline the rights of each.

third-party beneficiary
Someone who is not a party to a contract but is intended by the contracting parties to benefit as a consequence of a contract.

incidental beneficiary
Someone who will benefit as an indirect consequence of a contract, although that was not the intent of the contracting parties.

EXAMPLE 12.2

> Seaview Development Company planned to construct a marina and condominium on the shore of a lake. Philbus owned property adjacent to the planned development. Knowing that the value of his property was about to be greatly enhanced, Philbus began developing his own property and planned to open a number of stores and a restaurant to serve the people who would be attracted to the Seaview development. However, because of financial difficulties, Seaview cancelled their plans. Philbus suffered a loss as a consequence of Seaview's cancellation, but because he is an incidental beneficiary, he has no rights in the contract and no legal course of action.

Assignment of Rights/Delegation of Duties

In most states, the law permits a party to a contract to *assign* rights—that is, to transfer them to a third party and permit the third party to receive the benefits of the contract. This change of a contract is known as an **assignment**. The person who transfers his or her rights is known as the **assignor**; the third party to whom the rights are transferred is known as the **assignee**. A party to an existing contract may also appoint a third person to perform contractual duties; this appointment is referred to as a *delegation* (discussed later in this chapter).

A party may transfer his or her rights (assignment) and his or her duties (delegation), subject to several restraints (e.g., prohibition by law and personal service contracts). It is important to note that the term *duties* means tasks and performance, not responsibilities. A person who agrees to perform a particular task may generally delegate this task to someone else, but he or she is still responsible for getting it done. Consider Example 12.3, in which Higgins transfers his duty to Randall, but is still responsible for making sure that the duty is met.

EXAMPLE 12.3

> Higgins, a professor of finance, agreed to conduct a financial planning workshop for Randall, the president of a local club of retirees, for a fee of $1,200. Before conducting the workshop, Higgins assigned his right to the $1,200 to the Holiday Villa Motel, where he had held a number of workshops and to whom he owed $1,500. Holiday Villa was eager to agree to this arrangement because they were concerned about when Higgins would pay his bill. When the workshop was finished, Randall simply paid the $1,200 to Holiday Villa instead of to Higgins.

---

assignment The transfer of a contract right to a third party who can receive the benefits of the contract.

assignor The person who transfers his or her rights in an assignment.

assignee The third party to whom rights are transferred in an assignment.

OBJECTIVE 2

Interpret the legal concept of assignment of contracts and provide an example of a contract that is assignable.

OBJECTIVE 3

Distinguish between the assignment of rights and the delegation of duties.

Form of Assignment

An assignment may be either written or oral. If the original contract is required to be in writing under the Statute of Frauds, the assignment must also be in writing. Obviously, it makes good sense to put important assignments in writing, whether or not doing so is required by the Statute of Frauds.

Notice of Assignment

A party to a contract will not be obligated by an assignment made by the other party without his or her knowledge until notified. Using Example 12.3 to illustrate the process: It is the responsibility of Holiday Villa to notify Randall that Higgins made the assignment. In other words, the assignee (Holiday Villa) is responsible for notifying the other party to the contract (Randall) of the change that transferred Higgins' right to payment. After the assignee (Holiday Villa) has received a notice of assignment, he or she may demand a reasonable time to investigate its validity.

What Rights May Be Transferred

Most rights are assignable, except in cases in which the obligations of the parties would be significantly altered.

> **EXAMPLE 12.4**
>
> Suppose that, in the case of Professor Higgins' financial planning workshop, Randall contracted with Higgins, but then the retirees vetoed the idea of the workshop altogether because most of them had small incomes and little interest in financial planning. To salvage some value from the workshop to which he was already committed, Randall attempted to assign his right to have a workshop conducted to a different audience—a local group of bankers. Clearly, this assignment would not be acceptable to Higgins. Usually contracts for personal services are not assignable (delegable).

The Assignor's Guaranty

The assignor of a contract right, by assigning his or her right, becomes a *guarantor*—that is, one who guarantees the promises assigned. The Uniform Commercial Code states, "No delegation of performance relieves the party delegating of any duty to perform or any liability for breach" [UCC 2-210].

guarantor The party who guarantees the promises assigned.

Contracts that Cannot Be Assigned

Three types of contracts cannot be assigned: (1) contracts that include assignment restrictions, (2) assignments prohibited by law or public policy, and (3) contracts that require personal service.

Contracts that Include Assignment Restrictions
When parties to a contract include in the contract itself a specific provision forbidding assignment, both parties are prevented from assigning their rights or duties. A contract may prohibit only one party from assigning.

Assignments Prohibited by Law or Public Policy
Various state and federal statutes have been enacted to prohibit the assignment of certain contracts. For example, members of the armed services are prohibited from assigning their pay, and many state and local governments prohibit the assignment of salaries of public officials.

Contracts that Require Personal Service
If the services to be provided by a party to a contract are unique, they cannot be delegated. For example, artists, musicians, photographers, and athletes are hired because of their special personal skills, and consequently, their services under a contract cannot be assigned to anyone else. In most cases, an employment contract is considered a ***personal-service contract*** and may not be assigned. A personal-service contract is one in which a party hires a specific person to perform certain duties and who has a substantial interest in having only the hired person perform.

OBJECTIVE 4

Identify three kinds of contracts that cannot be assigned.

personal-service contract
A contract in which a party hires a specific person to perform certain duties and who has a substantial interest in having only the hired person perform.

Photo 12.1

Personal-Service Contracts

Most contracts for personal service involving the special or unique talents of one of the parties cannot be assigned. *What is the justification for this rule?*

Operation of Contracts   CHAPTER 12

delegation The appointment of a third party by a party to an existing contract to perform contractual duties that do not involve unique skills or abilities.

DELEGATION OF DUTIES

Just as a party's rights in a contract can be assigned to another party, a party's duties can be transferred to a third party if the duties do not involve unique skills or abilities. This transfer is known as a ***delegation*** of duties. If, however, there is no relationship of trust or confidence, or any other circumstance that would create a materially greater burden on the party whose services are being assigned, then even employment contracts may be assigned.

EXAMPLE 12.5

> Rensal Services had a three-year employment contract with Kopelek, an accountant. After working only one year, Rensal Services was sold to Pacific Accountants, Ltd., and Kopelek's contract was assigned to Pacific. Kopelek refused to work for Pacific, claiming that he had a special relationship with Rensal, and the working atmosphere was "almost family." The duties assigned to him by Pacific were substantially the same as before the sale of Rensal. Consequently, the assignment of Kopelek's contract would be legally enforceable.

ASSIGNMENT AND DELEGATION BY LAW

Rights or duties under a contract may be assigned by a court of law when a contracting party dies or becomes bankrupt.

OBJECTIVE 5

Provide examples of contracts that may be assigned by a court.

Death of a Contracting Party

When a party to a contract dies, all contractual rights are assigned to the administrator or executor of the estate. All rights to the collection of money, to demands for performance, and to the sale or purchase of real or personal property are assigned by law immediately upon the party's death. This assignment does not include personal-service contracts of the deceased, which are not delegable because of the unique nature of the services.

EXAMPLE 12.6

> Zarb, a composer, agreed in writing to sell an original musical score to Olney, a music promoter, for $65,000. One week before the completed score was to be delivered and payment made, Olney was killed in an accident. Meanwhile, Zarb got an offer of $75,000 for the score from a

> different promoter, and as a result stood to gain from not completing the transaction with Olney. The right to purchase the music, however, was assigned by law to Olney's executor, and Zarb must complete the transaction.

If, in Example 12.6, Zarb had agreed to teach a course in musical composition at a local college, neither the college nor the executor would have any rights under the contract, which was for personal services.

Bankruptcy of a Contracting Party

The laws dealing with bankruptcy provide that the assets and contracts of a bankrupt (legally recognized as unable to pay legitimate debts) person or business be assigned to the trustee in bankruptcy. The trustee is then empowered to sell the assets and exercise contract rights for the benefit of the creditors of the bankrupt person or firm.

NOVATION

When all parties to a contract agree to a significant change in the contract, the change is called a *novation.* Such a change actually creates a new contract that is simply based on the earlier one. A novation differs from an assignment in the following ways:

- A novation requires the mutual consent of all parties (the original parties to the agreement and/or any new third parties) just as a new contract does. However, an assignment can be made without the mutual consent of both contracting parties.
- A novation transfers all rights and obligations in a contract, but an assignment transfers only the rights of the assignor and still leaves the assignor with the duty of fulfilling his or her obligations under the contract.

As a result, a party to a contract who assigns his or her rights or delegates his or her duties to a third party is never free from the contract until it is completely executed. In contrast, if the third party enters the contract as a result of a novation, the party whose rights or duties are assumed is completely relieved of any obligations.

OBJECTIVE 6

Discuss novation and how it differs from assignment.

novation When all parties to a contract agree to a significant change to a contract.

CHAPTER SUMMARY

1 A third-party beneficiary to a contract has a legal right to the benefits resulting from the contract only if the contracting parties intend to benefit the third party. An incidental beneficiary is one who may benefit as an indirect consequence of a contract, although that was not the intent of the contracting parties. An incidental party has no rights in the contract.

2 An assignment occurs when a party to a contract transfers his or her rights under the contract to a third party and permits the third party to receive the benefits of the contract.

3 An assignment of rights entitles a party to receive the benefits of a contract. A delegation of duties obliges a third party to carry out the tasks and performance under the terms of the contract, provided they do not involve unique skills or abilities.

4 Three types of contracts that cannot be assigned include **(a)** contracts that include assignment restrictions, **(b)** assignments prohibited by law or public policy, and **(c)** contracts that require personal service.

5 A court can assign rights and duties under a contract when a contracting party dies or becomes bankrupt.

6 A novation occurs when parties to a contract agree to a significant change in the contract. A novation differs from an assignment because **(a)** unlike an assignment, it requires the mutual consent of all parties; and **(b)** a novation transfers all rights and obligations in a contract, but an assignment transfers only the rights of the assignor and still leaves the assignor with the duty of fulfilling his or her obligations under the contract.

Chapter 12 Assessment

MATCHING LEGAL TERMS

Match each of the following definitions with the correct term in the list below. Write the letter of your choice in the answer column.

- **a.** assignee
- **b.** assignment
- **c.** assignor
- **d.** bankrupt
- **e.** delegation
- **f.** guarantor
- **g.** incidental beneficiary
- **h.** novation
- **i.** personal service contract
- **j.** third-party beneficiary

1. A significant change in a contract that is made with the mutual consent of all parties. 1. _____
2. The transfer of duties to a third party by a party to a contract. 2. _____
3. A party who would benefit from the performance of a contract, but for whom the contract is not created. 3. _____
4. An outside party for whose benefit a contract is made by other parties. 4. _____
5. A party to a contract who transfers his or her rights to a third party. 5. _____
6. A contract in which the party who hired a specific person to perform certain duties has a substantial interest in having only the hired person perform. 6. _____
7. The state of a person or firm recognized to be unable to pay obligations. 7. _____
8. An outside party to whom contract rights are transferred. 8. _____
9. The transfer of contract rights by one of the parties. 9. _____
10. An assignor who guarantees or stands behind an assignment. 10. _____

TRUE/FALSE QUIZ

Indicate whether each of the following statements is true or false by writing *T* or *F* in the answer column.

11. A third-party beneficiary has a legal right to receive the benefits of a contract if it is the intent of the contract to benefit the third party. 11. _____
12. A third party who benefits incidentally from a contract has a right to the benefits if they exceed $500. 12. _____
13. The law in most states permits the assignment of most contract rights to a third party. 13. _____
14. The court may make assignments for bankrupt persons. 14. _____
15. An assignment must be in writing if the original contract was required by law to be in writing. 15. _____

Operation of Contracts CHAPTER 12

Chapter 12 Assessment

16. The assignment of certain contracts is forbidden by law. 16. _____

17. It is legally permissible to delegate contract obligations. 17. _____

18. Contracts that specifically prohibit assignment in their wording can still be assigned if the assignee is known to be a reputable person. 18. _____

19. Contracts for personal services may not be delegated unless there is agreement to the contrary. 19. _____

20. Contracts of employment are not assignable. 20. _____

21. A contracting party's duties as well as rights under a contract can be delegated. 21. _____

22. The assignment of contract rights or duties cannot be made by anyone other than one of the parties to a contract. 22. _____

23. Once a person delegates a contractual duty, he or she no longer has responsibility under the contract. 23. _____

24. A novation is a special kind of assignment where none of the parties to the contract is required to agree to its terms. 24. _____

25. The assignor of a contract right, by assigning his or her right, becomes a guarantor. 25. _____

DISCUSSION QUESTIONS

Answer the following questions and discuss them in class.

26. Distinguish between a third-party beneficiary and an incidental beneficiary.

27. Explain the legal concept of assignment of contracts and provide an example of a contract that is assignable.

28. Distinguish between the assignment of rights and delegation of duties.

Chapter 12 Assessment

29. Identify the three kinds of contracts that cannot be assigned.

30. Describe the circumstances in which a court might assign rights or duties under a contract.

31. Discuss novation and explain how it differs from assignment.

THINKING CRITICALLY ABOUT THE LAW

Answer the following questions, which require you to think critically about the legal principles that you learned in this chapter.

32. Third-Party Beneficiary Do you think a third-party beneficiary should be required to sign a contract as one of the parties involved? Why or why not?

33. Incidental Beneficiary Should an incidental beneficiary to a contract have any legal recourse if the contract is terminated? Explain your answer.

34. Personal-Service Contract Under what circumstances may the duties under a personal service contract be delegated?

Chapter 12 Assessment

35. Novation What are some advantages of using a novation over a contract assignment?

_____
_____
_____

36. A Question of Ethics Under the law, a bankrupt person is allowed to retain certain property—including his or her residence. Is it ethical for a bankrupt person to use the law to avoid payment on his or her legitimate debts, and still retain some, often valuable, property? Why or why not?

_____
_____
_____

CASE QUESTIONS

Study each case below and answer the questions that follow by writing *Yes* or *No* in the answer column.

37. Performance Liability Chang, a dealer in floral arrangements, contracted with Torres to provide delivery services in the local community. Torres discovered that his vehicles did not have the equipment to handle the work well, so he asked Chang if another delivery service, Rush Truk, would be acceptable to him. After some meetings with Torres and Rush Truk, Chang agreed to the change in delivery services.

   a. Is Torres responsible for the performance of Rush Truk?   a. _____

   b. Is this a valid assignment?   b. _____

   c. Is this an example of a novation?   c. _____

38. Beneficiary Benefits Franken, a college student, recognized that she was financially dependent upon her mother while she was in college. To protect against the risk of financial loss in the event of her mother's death, Franken persuaded her mother to take out an insurance policy naming her as the beneficiary.

   a. Is Franken an incidental beneficiary?   a. _____

   b. Is Franken a third-party beneficiary?   b. _____

   c. In the event of the mother's death, would Franken's college be judged to be a third-party beneficiary?   c. _____

39. Contractual Rights Westerfield contracted with Bradley Building Company for the construction of a ranch house as a wedding gift for his daughter. Before construction began, Westerfield died and Bradley announced that he would not build the house. The daughter brought suit in her own name to compel Bradley to build the house as it had contracted to do.

   a. Does the daughter have any rights in the contract between her father and Bradley Construction Company?   a. _____

   b. Can the daughter seek to have the court force Bradley Construction Company to construct the house or to pay damages to the daughter?   b. _____

184   PART 2   Contracts

Chapter 12 Assessment

40. Contract Assignment Rodrigos, the leader of a rock-and-roll group, agreed to provide music for the annual Park College Marketing Club dinner dance. On the night of the dinner dance, however, another, very amateurish group showed up and said that Rodrigos had assigned the contract to them and that they would play the engagement.

   a. Is a person who hires an outside entertainer required to accept the services of a substitute if it is impossible for the original party to perform? a. _____

   b. Are all contracts assignable? b. _____

   c. Can contracts for personal services be assigned? c. _____

CASE ANALYSIS

Study each of the following cases carefully and then briefly state the principle of law and your decision.

41. Assignable Contracts A restaurant, Pizza of Gaithersburg, Inc. (PG), agreed with Virginia Coffee Service (VCS) to have vending machines installed in PG's restaurants. The contract was to run for one year and was automatically renewable unless PG gave 30 days' notice. One year later, VCS was sold to Macke Company, including the contract with PG. PG cancelled the contract because of the change of ownership. Macke sued PG, claiming that VCS had delegated the duties to them and they were performing the duties previously done by VCS. PG claimed that the contract they had with VCS was a personal-services contract and was therefore not assignable. *Does Macke Company have a valid argument?* [*Macke Co. v. Pizza of Gaithersburg, Inc.*, 270 A.2d 645 (Maryland).]

Principle of law:

_____
_____
_____

Decision:

_____
_____

42. Third-Party Beneficiaries The employees of Powder Power Tools Corp. were represented by a labor union that had negotiated an agreement covering pay rates. A number of employees did not receive the higher rates of pay specified in the union contract. Springer, an employee, brought suit on behalf of those employees who did not receive the higher pay, claiming that they were third-party beneficiaries of the contract. The employer claimed that Springer could not sue because he was not a party to the contract. *Is it likely that Springer will be successful in his suit?* [*Springer v. Powder Power Tool Corp.*, 348 P.2d 1112 (Oregon).]

Principle of law:

_____
_____
_____

Chapter 12 Assessment

Decision:
_____
_____

43. Lost Benefits Birmingham Automotive Supply Company entered into a contract with the Excel Construction Company to build a chain-link fence around the property of the auto supply company. Included in the contract was a provision that the fence must be manufactured by Tornado Fence Company. Excel used another brand of fence, and Tornado sued Excel for the loss suffered, claiming that they were a third-party beneficiary to the contract. *Will Tornado be successful in their claim of loss suffered?*

Principle of law:
_____
_____
_____

Decision:
_____
_____

LEGAL RESEARCH

Complete the following activities. Then share your findings with the class.

44. Working in Teams Working in teams of three or four, interview the owners or managers of small businesses to determine whether they typically get involved in contract assignments.
_____
_____
_____
_____

45. Using Technology Using the Internet and search engines, investigate regulations or legislation that govern the assignment of certain contracts. What are some types of contracts typically controlled?
_____
_____
_____
_____

CHAPTER 13

DISCHARGE OF CONTRACTS

PERFORMANCE OBJECTIVES

After studying this chapter and completing the assessments, you will be able to:

1. Discuss termination of a contract by agreement.

2. Explain the three types of termination by performance.

3. Discuss the effect and validity of tender of performance.

4. Distinguish among termination by (a) impossibility of performance, (b) alteration, and (c) operation of law.

5. Provide examples of contracts terminated by breach.

6. Explain how contracts can be terminated to protect consumers.

7. Discuss the remedies of specific performance and injunction, and provide examples of situations that would be appropriate for each remedy.

LEGAL TERMS

substantial performance
tender of performance
tender of payment
impossibility of performance
material alteration
breach of contract
anticipatory breach
mitigate
promissory note
specific performance
restraining order
injunction

How Contracts Come to an End

Earlier chapters have described the formation and operation of contracts. This chapter is concerned with the termination, or end, of contracts.

Termination by Agreement

OBJECTIVE 1
Discuss termination of a contract by agreement.

A contract may provide for its termination after a certain period of time or upon the occurrence of a certain event.

> **EXAMPLE 13.1**
> Office Products agreed to act as a local distributor for Comet Typewriter Company for five years. The agreement required Office Products to sell typewriters, maintain an inventory of ribbons and other supplies, and provide repairs. In this case, the termination was provided for in the contract.

Suppose that after two years, Office Products found that the distributorship agreement was unprofitable and also that Comet was somewhat disappointed in Office Products' performance. If both firms agreed that canceling the contract was the best course of action, the contract could be terminated by mutual agreement even though the original contract did not provide for termination after two years. If only one party was dissatisfied with the contract, both parties would be bound by the terms of the agreement until the specified five years had passed.

Termination by Performance

OBJECTIVE 2
Explain the three types of termination by performance.

Complete and satisfactory performance of the terms of a contract will bring about its termination. When a contract is fulfilled, there is no need to provide for contract termination.

> **EXAMPLE 13.2**
> The Soft Sound Recording Studio agreed to record several radio commercials for Sachley Advertising Agency. When the work was completed on schedule and payment was made, the contract was considered terminated by performance.

Substantial Performance

If, in Example 13.2, the contract had been largely completed and only small details remained unfinished, then the contract would have been considered substantially performed. ***Substantial performance*** occurs when a party to a contract, in good faith, executes all of the promised terms and conditions of the contract with the exception of minor details that do not affect the real intent of their agreement. If an important part of a contract is not performed within the period of time specified in the contract, then the agreement may be cancelled, but the omission of a small detail entitles the injured party only to claim a proportionate reduction in the payment. Some states provide for a remedy only for a "material breach," and not for substantial performance.

Suppose that in Example 13.2, the commercials were completed, and the only unfinished work consisted of mailing the duplicated tapes to radio stations. Soft Sound would have substantially performed the contract and would be entitled to payment according to the terms of the contract, less the cost of the mailing. A court, applying the substantial performance standard, would probably award compensation to Soft Sound.

Performance by Payment of Money

Contracts that require the payment of money are not complete until the amount agreed upon has been paid. Even if the agreement provides that payment may be made by check, as most payments are, payment by check is considered conditional and subject to collection in cash. A party to a contract who pays by check is not relieved of the obligation for payment under the contract until the cash has been paid by the bank on which the check is drawn.

Tender of Performance

A ***tender of performance*** is an offer to perform and is considered evidence of a party's willingness to fulfill the terms of a contract. It applies equally to an offer to pay the required sum and to an offer to perform the required acts.

EXAMPLE 13.3

> Sunset Realty contracted with Clean Sweep to purchase janitorial services, including carpet cleaning, window washing, and general cleaning services. When personnel from Clean Sweep arrived for their evening's work, the manager of Sunset advised them that they would not be needed because a staff meeting was being held in the offices. Clean Sweep made a tender of performance, so although Sunset could not use the service, they were obligated to pay under the contract.

---

substantial performance When a party to a contract, in good faith, executes all of the promised terms and conditions of the contract with the exception of minor details that do not affect the real intent of their agreement.

OBJECTIVE 3

Discuss the effect and validity of tender of performance.

tender of performance An offer to perform that is considered evidence of a party's willingness to fulfill the terms of a contract.

tender of payment A money offer of payment of an obligation.

Effect of Tender When money is offered in payment of an obligation and is refused by the creditor, the debt is not cancelled, but penalties and interest cannot be charged beyond the date on which the offer of payment was made. Such an offer is known as *tender of payment.* If a tender of goods or the performance of an act is refused, the person making the offer is relieved of the obligation to perform and may sue the other party for breach of contract.

Valid Tender Certain requirements must be met for tender of money or performance to be valid.

First, tender must be made as specified in the contract. If the contract provides that payment or performance be made at a certain time or place, or to a particular person, these conditions must be met.

EXAMPLE 13.4

Phin ordered a truckload of Christmas trees from Spruce Tree Company to be delivered to his used-car lot on December 5. Because bad weather in Canada and Vermont affected the cutting schedule, the trees were not delivered until December 15. Phin refused delivery, claiming that he had already lost a considerable amount of business he had hoped to get, and he had dismissed the two college students he had hired to sell the trees. Phin had the right to refuse the tender because Spruce Tree failed to meet the conditions of the contract.

Second, when tender of payment is made, it must be for the exact amount. The mention of money in a contract implies payment in cash. Although checks are used in most business transactions, the seller has the right to refuse such a payment and to insist on cash.

Lastly, if the contract calls for the delivery of certain specific goods, only the tender of these particular goods will satisfy the contract.

OBJECTIVE 4

Distinguish among termination by (a) impossibility of performance, (b) alteration, and (c) operation of law.

impossibility of performance When unforeseen circumstances make it impossible to fulfill the terms of a contract. In these cases, the contract is considered void.

TERMINATION BY IMPOSSIBILITY OF PERFORMANCE

Unforeseen circumstances may make it impossible to fulfill the terms of a contract as originally agreed. In a case of *impossibility of performance,* the contract is considered void and the parties are discharged.

EXAMPLE 13.5

Solvey Brick Company, a manufacturer of standard building bricks used in construction, had a contract to supply several hundred thousand bricks to Ramon Construction. Ramon assumed that the bricks

> would be from Solvey's own production. The contract did not specify the source of the bricks. As Solvey was preparing to manufacture the bricks, the plant burned down. Solvey could buy the same type of bricks from another manufacturer and supply them to Ramon—probably at a loss. Most courts would rule that the subject matter was standard bricks, not specific bricks from Solvey's own production facilities, and would not excuse Solvey from its contractual obligations. There was no impossibility of performance.

In Example 13.5, Solvey would be required to perform, even at a loss. In fact, a business can protect against the risk of loss resulting from such an event by purchasing insurance.

The UCC makes a special provision for failure to perform when the goods under contract are destroyed. If the contract covers goods that have been identified (such as a particular article of merchandise) and if the goods are destroyed without fault of either party, the contract is cancelled. If the seller's source of supply or means of production creates only a partial inability to perform, the seller may tender only a portion of the goods under contract. Also, if the loss is only partial, the buyer may demand the right to inspect the damaged goods to decide whether to accept or reject them in their damaged state and claim an allowance for the damages [UCC 2-615].

Personal-Service Contracts

Death or disabling illness of a party to a contract terminates the obligation of the party to perform if it can be shown that the contract calls for a special skill or talent possessed by the deceased or ill person. Such contracts are known as personal-service contracts.

> **EXAMPLE 13.6**
>
> Iverson, a concert pianist, had a contract to perform at a summer music festival. Before the concert, she was stricken with a paralytic stroke and was unable to perform. Because her contract was for a personal service, she was excused from the contract.

TERMINATION BY ALTERATION

A deliberate change or alteration of an important element in a written contract that affects the rights or obligations of the parties is known as a ***material alteration*** and results in termination of the contract.

material alteration A deliberate change or alteration of an important element in a written contract that affects the rights or obligations of the parties.

EXAMPLE 13.7

Perry agreed to buy a vacant lot from Serio for $11,600. When the parties were about to close the transaction, it was discovered that the contract to purchase had been changed by Serio to $12,600. Her illegal act of changing the contract not only terminated the contract, but it also made Serio subject to criminal prosecution for the crime of forgery.

TERMINATION BY OPERATION OF LAW

If a law or regulation makes the performance of a contract illegal, the contract is void from the beginning. In fact, there is no contract. If, however, a law is passed *after* the parties enter into a contract that makes performance illegal, the contract is terminated by operation of law.

EXAMPLE 13.8

Burlington, a dealer in shrubbery and trees, agreed with DaVall, a grower in a foreign country, to import several hundred decorative shrubs. To prevent the spread of a plant disease, the U.S. Department of Agriculture enforced an embargo on this variety of shrub and refused to allow the shipment into the country. The parties are released from the agreement because of the impossibility of performance caused by the operation of law. Laws and regulations that increase the cost of performance, however, do not absolve the parties from their contractual obligations.

Suppose in Example 13.8 that a new regulation had been passed that required special packaging for imported plants, and that this packaging increased the total cost of the plants. In this case, the seller would not be relieved of her obligations, even if the added cost meant that she would lose money on the transaction.

OBJECTIVE 5

Provide examples of contracts terminated by breach.

breach of contract When a party to a contract refuses to perform as required by the contract or performs in an unsatisfactory manner.

TERMINATION BY BREACH OF CONTRACT

A *breach of contract* occurs when a party to a contract refuses to perform as required by the contract or performs in an unsatisfactory manner. There are three common ways in which contracts are breached:

- anticipatory breach, also known as anticipatory repudiation
- breach resulting from a deliberate or negligent act
- failure to perform an obligation

Anticipatory Breach

A party who announces an intention to break a contract is said to create an *anticipatory breach.* He or she has given notice of intention to break the contract even before being required to perform. Court decisions have allowed the injured party to bring suit for damages at the time of the announcement and have not required the party to wait until the time for performance has passed.

> **EXAMPLE 13.9**
>
> Zikmund, an actress, had agreed to appear in a supporting role in a play scheduled to open on February 1. However, on December 1, she announced that she would not be available because she had been given a starring role in a motion picture. The producer has a right to initiate a suit on December 1 for anticipatory breach, without waiting for the time the contract was to start.

anticipatory breach When a party to a contract announces his or her intention to break the contract in the future.

When a party has received notice from the other party of intent to breach, he or she cannot continue with the performance of the work or service covered by the contract; doing so would only increase the amount of damages. When a party breaches a contract, the injured party has the duty to *mitigate,* or lessen, the amount of damages.

> **EXAMPLE 13.10**
>
> Ebersol hired Weston Restorers to restore a 1936 Chevrolet to classic car condition. While Weston was still ordering and manufacturing needed parts, Ebersol announced that he had changed his mind and intended to break the contract. Weston cannot continue restoring the car and later sue for a greater amount than if he had stopped work when Ebersol breached. He can sue only for damages suffered up to the time he was notified of the anticipatory breach.

mitigate The obligation of the injured party to protect the other party from any unnecessary damages.

The law regarding anticipatory breach does not apply to promises to pay money at some future date. A person who renounces an obligation on a *promissory note* (a written promise to pay a specified sum of money) cannot be sued until after the due date of the first payment on the note, even if he announces his or her intention to breach before the first payment is due.

promissory note A written promise to pay a specified sum of money.

Breach Resulting from a Deliberate or Negligent Act

A contract is breached if one party deliberately or negligently stands in the way of performance. Consequently, if a party who has agreed to sell certain perishable foods negligently allows them to become damaged by freezing, he or she has committed a breach of contract.

EXAMPLE 13.11

Herrera hired Kotley to conduct marketing research at a shopping mall. They agreed that Kotley would interview shoppers selected at random and conduct a survey by using a questionnaire. Before the interviews began, Herrera changed his mind and destroyed the questionnaires. The contract was breached by Herrera's deliberate act. Herrera is subject to Kotley's suit for damages: the agreed fee to be paid to Kotley.

Failure to Perform an Obligation

A party who fails, after a reasonable time has passed, to perform contractual obligations has breached the contract. The breach occurs whether the party has completely or partially failed to perform. In the case of complete failure, the contract is terminated. Partial failure to perform may require the injured party to pay for the work that has already been done.

EXAMPLE 13.12

Suppose in Example 13.11 that Kotley did have access to the questionnaires, but conducted only half the number he had agreed to do. In this situation, it is doubtful that partial work would have much, if any, value to Herrera.

Photo 13.1

Breach of Contract

A lawyer has a professional obligation to act in the best interests of his or her client. *If an attorney fails to argue his or her client's case convincingly, should he or she be liable for a breach of contract?*

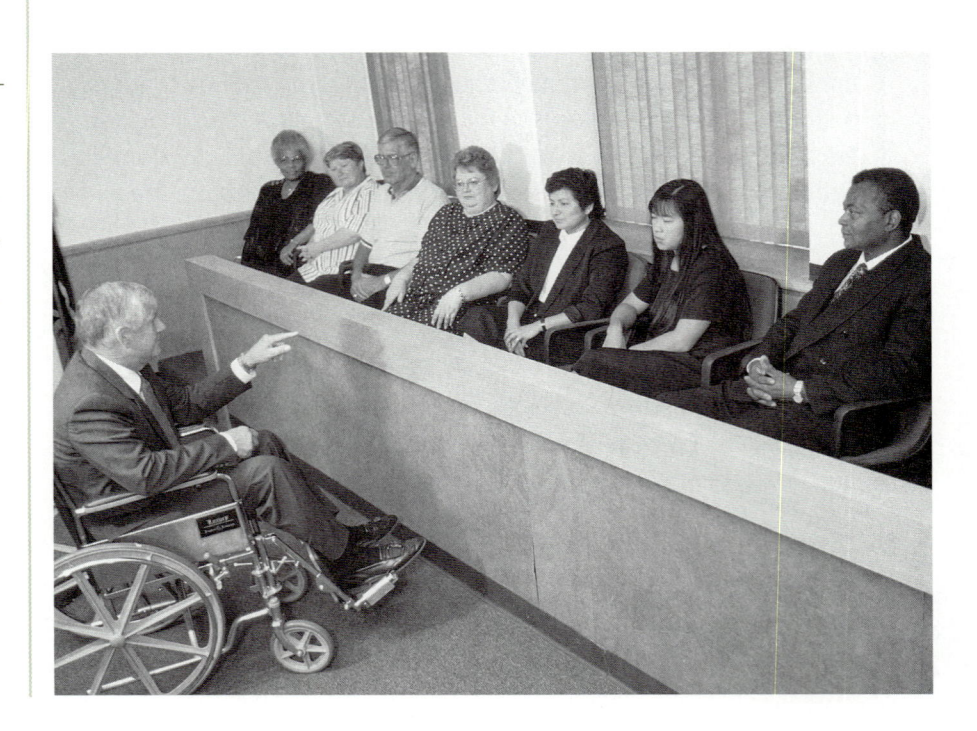

Breach Due to Frustration of Purpose

When unexpected circumstances develop that make a contract impossible to perform, the frustrated party can cancel the contract without paying damages.

> **EXAMPLE 13.13**
>
> Sigmund contracted to buy an historic house with hope of establishing a tourist lodge. While the sale was pending, the building was condemned as unsafe. Sigmund withdrew from the contract without penalty.

TERMINATION TO PROTECT A CONSUMER

To protect consumers against their own impulsiveness and various questionable sales techniques, a number of federal, state, and local laws and regulations allow consumers to terminate a contract under certain conditions. For example, the federal Consumer Credit Protection Act of 1968 gives a consumer the right to cancel a credit transaction within three days when the contract requires that the consumer pledge his or her home as a security deposit. A Federal Trade Commission regulation gives the consumer a "cooling-off" period of three days and the right to cancel contracts for either goods or services made in the consumer's home and to receive a full refund.

OBJECTIVE 6

Explain how contracts can be terminated to protect consumers.

REMEDIES FOR BREACH OF CONTRACT

Each party to a contract has the right to expect complete and satisfactory performance. When such performance is not made, the injured party may sue for a sum of money that will compensate for his or her loss. In all such claims for damages, the injured party must determine the damage in terms of money, and the court will determine if the claim is fair and adequate.

> **EXAMPLE 13.14**
>
> Nam Sang was to be married, and he and his fiancée planned a large reception. After inspecting several restaurants and catering halls, they reached an agreement with Westport Villa for the use of the facilities and for the food and beverage service. A week before the event, Westport cancelled the contract, claiming that they had overlooked an earlier commitment. Nam Sang found alternate facilities but for a fee $300 higher. After the event, Nam Sang sued for damages of $300—the difference between the contract price and the higher fee he had to pay as a result of Westport's breach. A court would likely rule in Nam Sang's favor.

Discharge of Contracts CHAPTER 13 195

OBJECTIVE 7

Discuss the remedies of specific performance and injunction, and provide examples of situations that would be appropriate for each remedy.

specific performance A court order directing a person to perform—or not perform—as he or she agreed to do in a contract.

restraining order A court order prohibiting the performance of a certain act. In some states, a restraining order is temporary.

injunction A restraining order that in some states is permanent.

Specific Performance

Sometimes a judgment of money damages will not really repay an injured party for a breach of contract. In some cases, the injured party may sue for *specific performance,* that is, a court order directing a person to perform—or not to perform—as he or she agreed to do. To obtain an order of specific performance, the injured party asks the court to order the other party to do what he or she promised to do. For example, if a contract is made for the sale of some unique item, such as an antique or real estate, the buyer can bring an action for specific performance if the seller attempts to breach the contract. A court order for specific performance serves as a remedy in cases in which an award of money damages for a breach of contract cannot adequately compensate the injured party.

Courts almost never order specific performance of a contract for personal services, partly because it is difficult to ensure the performance of someone who is being forced to work after a dispute, in that any loyalty or normal relationship is nearly impossible to achieve. Also, courts do not wish to impose what might be viewed as involuntary servitude.

An order for specific performance may be obtained not only in cases of breach of contract for the sale of unique goods or real estate, but also in cases in which the purchaser is not able to obtain elsewhere the goods called for by the contract.

> **EXAMPLE 13.15**
>
> Resol bought and remodeled a restaurant and named it the Packard Roadster. He contracted with Timmons, a collector of classic cars, to purchase a 1932 Packard for $9,600, which he planned to display in the front window of the restaurant. He also registered the name, had signs made, and ran advertising announcing the grand opening. Sensing an opportunity to sell the vehicle to another buyer for a higher price, Timmons attempted to cancel the contract. There was no point in suing for damages, Resol thought—how would he place a dollar value on the hardship the cancelled sale would cause? Instead, Resol sought an action of specific performance that required Timmons to sell the car as he had agreed to do. Because the product is unique, the court would likely grant a decree of specific performance.

Restraining Order or Injunction

Whereas a decree of specific performance is a court order requiring the performance of a certain act, a *restraining order,* or *injunction,* is a court order prohibiting the performance of a certain act. In some states, a restraining order is temporary and an injunction is permanent.

EXAMPLE 13.16

> Segal sold a heavily wooded parcel of land to Hargett, who claimed that he wanted to use it as a hunting preserve. Hargett agreed to refrain from cutting down the trees for a period of 15 years. One year after the sale, Hargett decided to build a shopping mall on the property, which would require cutting down the trees. Segal began legal action, but was concerned that the trees would be destroyed by the time the case was heard. She therefore sought a temporary restraining order to stop all work at the site.

If, as a result of the legal action taken by Segal, it was found that Hargett had indeed violated the contract, the court could make the temporary restraining order a permanent or mandatory restraining order or injunction. That would bar Hargett from cutting down the trees for the period specified by the contract. If Hargett failed to obey either the temporary or mandatory injunction, his actions would put him in contempt of court. He could then be fined or even jailed.

CHAPTER SUMMARY

1 A contract can be terminated by agreement if both parties agree that it should end.

2 The three types of termination by performance are **(a)** substantial performance, in which the contract has been largely completed and only small details remain, **(b)** performance by payment of money, in which the agreed upon payment has been paid, and **(c)** tender of performance, in which is the offer to pay the required sum or to perform the required acts.

3 If tender of goods or performance is refused, the person making the offer is relieved of the obligation to perform and may sue the other party for breach of contract. To be valid, tender must **(a)** be made as specified in the contract; **(b)** when made, it must be for the exact amount; and **(c)** if the contract calls for the delivery of specific goods, only tender of these goods will satisfy the contract.

4 Contracts can be terminated by impossibility of performance when unforeseen circumstances make it impossible to fulfill the terms of a contract as originally agreed. Termination by alteration occurs when an important element in a written contract that affects the rights or obligations of the parties is changed. A contract can also be terminated by operation of law if a law passed after the parties had entered into a contract makes performance illegal.

5 Contracts terminated by breach occur when a party to a contract refuses to perform as required by the contract or performs in an unsatisfactory manner. Three common ways in which contracts are breached are by **(a)** anticipatory breach, **(b)** a deliberate or negligent act, and **(c)** failure to perform an obligation.

6 Some contracts can be terminated to protect consumers because the law hopes to protect them against their own impulsiveness, questionable sales techniques, and similar problems. For example, the Consumer Credit Protection Act of 1968 gives consumers the right to cancel a credit transaction within three days when the contract requires that the consumer pledge his or her home as a security deposit. An FTC regulation also gives consumers a "cooling-off" period of three days and the right to cancel contracts made in the consumer's home and to receive a full refund.

7 The remedy of specific performance is a court order that a person perform (or not perform) as he or she agreed to do. The remedy of injunction is a court order that prohibits performance of a certain act.

Chapter 13 Assessment

MATCHING LEGAL TERMS

Match each of the following definitions with the correct term in the list below. Write the letter of your choice in the answer column.

- **a.** anticipatory breach
- **b.** impossibility of performance
- **c.** material alteration
- **d.** mitigation
- **e.** promissory note
- **f.** specific performance
- **g.** restraining order or injunction
- **h.** substantial performance
- **i.** tender of payment
- **j.** tender of performance

1. A written promise to pay a specified sum of money. 1. _____
2. The completion of a contract except for some small details. 2. _____
3. A change of an important term in a contract that affects the rights or obligations of the parties. 3. _____
4. An offer to perform acts required by a contract. 4. _____
5. An offer of payment made to fulfill the terms of a contract. 5. _____
6. Inability to fulfill the terms of a contract due to extreme forces. 6. _____
7. Cancellation of a contract due to an announcement of intention to breach before the time for performance. 7. _____
8. A court decree that prohibits the performance of a certain act. 8. _____
9. A court order that directs the performance of a certain act. 9. _____
10. The duty of an injured party to lessen the amount of damages. 10. _____

TRUE/FALSE QUIZ

Indicate whether each of the following statements is true or false by writing *T* or *F* in the answer column.

11. A contract can be terminated in accordance with provisions in the contract itself. 11. _____
12. A consumer can terminate a contract made in the home with a door-to-door salesperson within three days. 12. _____
13. Complete and satisfactory performance of a contract will bring about its termination. 13. _____
14. A contract must be completely performed in all its details in order to be considered terminated. 14. _____
15. A tender of performance may not relieve a contracting party of his or her obligation to perform. 15. _____

Discharge of Contracts CHAPTER 13 199

Chapter 13 Assessment

16. A consumer has three days to cancel a contract in which his or her home has been pledged as security.

16. _____

17. Death or disabling illness of a party to a contract terminates the contract if such requires the particular skill or talent of the contracting party.

17. _____

18. A deliberate material alteration of a contract that affects the rights or obligations of the parties is cause for termination of the contract.

18. _____

19. If a law or regulation makes the performance of a contract illegal, the parties are released from their obligations.

19. _____

20. A party to a contract is released from his or her obligations if a law is passed that increases the cost of performing the contract.

20. _____

21. Except for promissory notes, the injured party in a contract may bring suit whenever he or she receives notice that the other party intends to breach the contract.

21. _____

22. A contract is breached if one party deliberately or negligently stands in the way of satisfactory performance.

22. _____

23. When one party to a contract receives notice of the other party's intent to breach, he or she may continue with the performance of work or service covered by the contract. Later he or she may sue for damages resulting from the completed contract's having been breached.

23. _____

24. An action for specific performance is a request that the court direct a party to perform a particular act agreed upon in a contract.

24. _____

25. A court order directing a person to refrain from performing a particular act is an injunction.

25. _____

DISCUSSION QUESTIONS

Answer the following questions and discuss them in class.

26. Discuss termination of a contract by agreement.

27. Explain how a contract is terminated by performance.

Chapter 13 Assessment

28. Provide examples of contracts terminated by impossibility of performance.

29. Explain how a contract might be terminated by breach.

30. Explain how a contract might be terminated to protect a consumer.

31. Compare and contrast the remedies of specific performance and injunction.

THINKING CRITICALLY ABOUT THE LAW

Answer the following questions, which require you to think critically about the legal principles that you learned in this chapter.

32. Contract Termination by Performance Contract termination by performance seems so final. Do you think that the parties to a contract should be given an opportunity to change their minds if circumstances change after the required performance?

33. Contract Termination by Impossibility of Performance It's possible for one of the parties to a contract terminated by impossibility of performance to suffer some injury or loss as a result. Should the law recognize this possibility and provide some form of redress?

Chapter 13 Assessment

34. Contract Termination by Breach The law provides a remedy for a party injured by the breach of a contract, but the usual remedy, a lawsuit that awards money damages, does not always give the injured party the level of redress appropriate to the situation. What other remedies are available and how effective are they?

_____
_____
_____

35. Personal Service Contracts Death or disabling illness of a party to a personal service contract requiring a special skill or talent, terminates the contract. How would a concert promoter, who had sold tickets and rented a hall, protect against a loss that would likely result from the termination of a contract with a renowned pianist?

_____
_____
_____

36. A Question of Ethics To protect consumers against their own impulsiveness and various questionable sales techniques, a number of federal, state, and local laws and regulations allow consumers to terminate a contract under certain conditions. Is it ethical for a consumer to take advantage of this protection, when his or her own good judgment should have suggested avoidance of the contract?

_____
_____
_____

CASE QUESTIONS

Study each case below and answer the questions that follow by writing *Yes* or *No* in the answer column.

37. Substantial Performance Central City Garage Builders contracted with Morgan for the construction of a two-car garage and an attached greenhouse of similar size. The garage was built on schedule, but because of a shortage of special materials, it appeared that the construction of the greenhouse would be delayed for several months. Central City requested payment for the entire contract.

   a. Does Central City have a legitimate claim that it had performed substantially?   **a.** _____

   b. Can Central City claim that it was prevented from completing the project because of impossibility of performance?   **b.** _____

   c. Would Central City have a right to request payment for the portion of the contract that was completed?   **c.** _____

38. Revoked Contract Scher, a homeowner, purchased a vacuum cleaner from a door-to-door salesperson. When the salesperson demonstrated the machine in her home, it seemed to work very well. After signing the contract, she checked several consumer magazines at the public library and learned that the company was

Chapter 13 Assessment

noted for its deceptive practices and that the demonstration machine was specially constructed and not the same type the consumer gets.

   a. Does Scher have the opportunity to terminate the contract?   a. _____

   b. Was the contract Scher signed a valid one?   b. _____

   c. Is the contract voidable?   c. _____

39. Breach of Contract Chiu agreed to sell his custom-built sailboat to Graham for $60,000. Before delivery, Chiu received another offer for $68,000 and wrote to Graham that he had decided not to sell his boat after all.

   a. Can Graham seek a decree of specific performance?   a. _____

   b. Would a suit for money damages completely satisfy Graham?   b. _____

   c. Can Chiu avoid Graham's suit by claiming that he was merely selling to the highest bidder?   c. _____

CASE ANALYSIS

Study each of the following cases carefully and then briefly state the principle of law and your decision.

40. Impossibility of Performance Bunge, a grain dealer, contracted with Recker, a farmer, to purchase 10,000 bushels of soybeans at $3.35 per bushel. The contract did not specify where the beans were to have been grown, except that they were to be grown in the United States. As a result of crop failure, Recker was unable to deliver the beans, even with several extensions of the deadline. Finally, Recker admitted that he could not deliver, claiming impossibility of performance. In the meantime, the market price had increased from the $3.35, the agreed price, to $5.50 at the time agreed for delivery. Bunge sued for the difference between $3.35 and the market price at the time agreed for delivery. *Will Recker be excused from his contractual obligations, or should he be held responsible for delivering as agreed?* [*Bunge Corp. v. Recker,* 519 F.2d 449 (8th Cir.).]

Principle of law:

_____

_____

Decision:

_____

_____

41. Option to Settle Laclede Gas Company purchased propane gas from Amoco Oil Company and sold it to various residential subdivisions. After the contract had been in operation for some time, Amoco refused to supply any more gas. Laclede was unable to find another supplier willing to enter into a long-term contract such as Laclede had with Amoco. Management of Laclede felt that money damages would not provide a reasonable settlement. *What would be a reasonable resolution of Laclede's problem?* [*Laclede Gas Co. v. Amoco Oil Co.,* 522 F.2d 33 (8th Circ.).]

Chapter 13 Assessment

Principle of law:
_____
_____

Decision:
_____
_____

42. **Breach of Sale** Dahl, the owner of a machine shop, agreed to manufacture 22 valves for $460 each for Capobianco. When six valves were finished and shipped, Capobianco advised Dahl of his intention to cancel the contract. Dahl went on to build the remaining valves according to the contract. *Will Dahl be successful in his suit for the entire amount?*

Principle of law:
_____
_____

Decision:
_____
_____

LEGAL RESEARCH

Complete the following activities. Then share your findings with the class.

43. **Working in Teams** In teams of three or four, interview owners or managers of small businesses to learn some typical contracts in which the firms have been involved and how they were terminated.
_____
_____
_____
_____
_____

44. **Using Technology** Using the Internet and search engines, investigate "contract termination" and other terms used in the chapter.
_____
_____
_____
_____
_____

PART 2 Contracts

PART III
SALES, AGENCY, AND CONSUMER PROTECTION

CHAPTER 14	Transfer of Title
CHAPTER 15	Sales
CHAPTER 16	Agency and Employment
CHAPTER 17	Warranties and Product Liability
CHAPTER 18	Professional Responsibility

CHAPTER 14

TRANSFER OF TITLE

PERFORMANCE OBJECTIVES

After studying this chapter and completing the assessments, you will be able to:

1. Explain how title relates to the concept of ownership.

2. Distinguish between real and personal property, and indicate which is subject to the law of sales.

3. Describe how title passes, and discuss how bills of sale, bills of lading, and warehouse receipts are involved in the passing of title.

4. Explain the law governing title to lost or stolen goods, and sales by persons having wrongful possession of goods.

5. Define the principle of estoppel, and provide examples of how this principle is applied in various situations.

6. Describe the passage of title to fungible goods.

LEGAL TERMS

title
real property
personal property
bill of sale
bill of lading
straight bill of lading
order bill of lading
warehouse receipt
conditional sale
conditions precedent
conditions subsequent
estoppel
remote party
wrongful possession
fungible goods

Title

Many business transactions that involve disputes are like a game of musical chairs. The person left standing when the music stops is the one who loses. Similarly, legal disputes often involve the determination of who is holding title when a loss occurs.

Prior to the Uniform Commercial Code, the concept of title was crucial in making determinations of the rights and responsibilities of the parties to a contract, and perhaps even more important, who bore the risk of loss. The UCC has reduced the significance of title, but it remains important in many instances.

The Right of Ownership

The concept of private property is one of the foundations of our economic and social system. The laws of our country recognize the right of individuals to own property.

Title, as it relates to property, is intangible—you cannot see it or feel it. Title is ownership and the right to possess something, unless you have given up the right to possess the property by renting it to someone else. As a result, if you own something—a house, car, or suit—you have title to it. When you sell something, you sell not only the property, but also the intangible right of ownership called title. The automobile *certificate of title,* used in many states, is not title but rather proof of title. Sometimes an exchange of letters or a department store bill of sale can be used as proof of ownership, or title.

Kinds of Property

The two main classifications of property, introduced in Chapter 11, are real property and personal property.

Real Property

Real property, sometimes called *real estate,* is land and all articles permanently attached to it, such as buildings and trees.

Personal Property

Personal property is all kinds of property other than real property, such as an automobile, clothing, a computer, and so on. Personal property can be tangible, that is, it can be seen and touched like the examples just cited. Personal property can also be intangible, such as a patent, a copyright, or ownership in a corporation—things that

---

OBJECTIVE 1

Explain how title relates to the concept of ownership.

title Ownership and the right to possess something, unless the right to possess property has been given up by renting it to someone else.

OBJECTIVE 2

Distinguish between real and personal property, and indicate which is subject to the law of sales.

real property The land and all articles permanently attached to it, such as buildings and trees.

personal property All kinds of property other than real property, such as an automobile, clothing, a computer, and so on. It can be tangible or intangible.

cannot be seen or touched. Only personal property—tangible or intangible—is affected by the law of sales and the Uniform Commercial Code. Real property is governed by a separate branch of law, known as the *law of real property*, which is covered in Chapter 21. The sales of services are not considered property at all, and contracts for services are considered ordinary contracts.

How Title Passes

There are a variety of ways in which title can pass. Involved in the passage of title are the legal concepts of a bill of sale, a bill of lading, and a warehouse receipt.

Bill of Sale

A **bill of sale** is simply a written statement that the seller is passing ownership to the buyer. The bill of sale need not be an elaborate legal document—a handwritten note is as effective as a lengthy legal document. The important thing to remember is that the description of the goods should be as complete as possible. For example, if you bought a computer from a neighbor, a simple note describing the goods involved in the transaction as "a computer" would probably be adequate. However, if the note included a more complete description, such as "one Apple iBook® G3-600, Serial No. 175274," you would be further protected from a claim of ownership by another person.

Bill of Lading

A **bill of lading** is a document prepared by the carrier or the shipper for goods to be shipped by land or water. In the case of goods shipped by air, an *air bill* is prepared. One copy of the document is signed by the carrier—such as a trucking firm, a railroad, or an airfreight company—when the carrier accepts the goods for shipment. The bill of lading or air bill is both a receipt for the goods and a contract with the carrier.

There are two kinds of bills of lading. The most common is a **straight bill of lading,** which is simply a receipt for the goods to be shipped and an acknowledgment that the goods have been received and will be transported to the destination indicated. A bill of lading is not negotiable.

An **order bill of lading,** in addition to being a receipt as just described, is negotiable; that is, the bill of lading is proof of title and can be used to transfer title from one person to another. A negotiable order bill of lading can be used to ensure that the carrier will not

---

OBJECTIVE 3

Describe how title passes, and discuss how bills of sale, bills of lading, and warehouse receipts are involved in the passing of title.

bill of sale A written statement that the seller is passing ownership to the buyer.

bill of lading A document prepared by the carrier or the shipper for goods to be shipped by land or water; if shipped by air, an air bill is prepared.

straight bill of lading A receipt for the goods to be shipped and an acknowledgement that the goods have been received and will be transported to the destination indicated.

order bill of lading A receipt similar to a straight bill of lading, only negotiable and proof of title that can be used to transfer title from one person to another.

deliver the goods until the receiver surrenders the original copy of the bill of lading to the carrier. Because it would be nearly impossible for anyone to possess the original order bill of lading without the shipper agreeing to it, such a document is proof of ownership. Bills of lading are covered by Article 7 of the Uniform Commercial Code.

> **EXAMPLE 14.1**
>
> Eastern Jewelry Manufacturers in New York agreed through an exchange of letters to sell 50 expensive bracelets to a jeweler in Peoria, Illinois. Eastern Jewelry completed an order bill of lading, turned the shipment over to a trucking line, and notified the Peoria jeweler that the merchandise was being shipped. The shipper gave the original bill of lading to his bank, which in turn sent it to a cooperating bank in Peoria. The Peoria jeweler was instructed by mail to pay the agreed-upon sales price of the merchandise to the Peoria bank to obtain the original copy of the order bill of lading. When the Peoria jeweler paid the money to the bank, he was given the original bill of lading, which he then surrendered to the trucking firm on or before delivery was made.

Warehouse Receipt

A *warehouse receipt* is much like a bill of lading except that the goods involved are not being transported but merely stored. There are two kinds of warehouse receipts. A *nonnegotiable warehouse receipt* is like a straight bill of lading—it is simply a receipt for the goods to be stored. A *negotiable warehouse receipt,* like the negotiable order bill of lading, requires that the original copy be presented to the warehouser before the goods will be surrendered to someone claiming them. Also, like an order bill of lading, a negotiable warehouse receipt is proof of ownership.

warehouse receipt Much like a bill of lading except that the goods are not being shipped but merely stored.

> **EXAMPLE 14.2**
>
> Suppose that, in the preceding case, the purchaser of the jewelry was located in the same community as the manufacturer. The transaction would be similar to the one in the preceding case. The warehouser would play the same role as the truck line, but a cooperating bank would probably not be involved in the transaction.

When Title Passes

Title to goods pass when the parties intend and at the moment when they unconditionally agree to sell specific goods that are in a deliverable state.

Intent

In the eyes of the law, title passes when the parties intend it to pass. How does one prove what one intended? Suppose that a person bought a boat and arranged to pick it up the following day. Before the buyer had a chance to pick it up, the boat was destroyed by fire. Quite likely, the seller would claim that he intended title to pass at the time of the transaction, making the buyer bear the loss. The buyer, on the other hand, would probably say that he intended title to pass when he picked up the boat, making the seller bear the loss. To minimize such disagreements, rules for determining the intent of the parties have been established.

> **EXAMPLE 14.3**
>
> Castelli agreed in writing to purchase Piak's car for $8,000. They both agreed that Castelli would return the following day with license plates and take the car away. In the eyes of the law, title passed at the time of agreement, even though the parties may have taken a few minutes to complete the necessary documents, such as a bill of sale and the check for payment of the car.

Specific Time

Although it may take some time to complete the documents that signify the passing of title, title itself passes in a single instant. The law provides guides to determine the exact time at which title passes. Ordinarily, title passes when the parties have agreed unconditionally to sell specific goods that are in a deliverable state.

CONDITIONAL PROMISES

conditional sale A sale with contract provisions that specify conditions that must be met by one of the parties.

A *conditional sale* is a sale with contract provisions that specify conditions that must be met by one of the parties. Title does not generally pass until these conditions are met. The two types of conditions generally found in contracts for conditional sales are conditions precedent and conditions subsequent.

Conditions Precedent

conditions precedent Conditions in a sales contract that must be met before title passes.

When a sales contract provides that specific conditions must be met before title passes, the agreement contains *conditions precedent.*

> **EXAMPLE 14.4**
>
> Suppose that, in Example 14.3, Castelli agreed to purchase Piak's car if Piak had new tires installed. Title would pass when the tires were

installed. If anything had happened to the car before the tires were installed, Piak would have to bear the loss.

Conditions Subsequent

When a sales contract provides that specific conditions must be met after title has passed, it is said to contain **conditions subsequent.** A right-of-return provision in a sales contract is an example of a condition subsequent that gives the buyer the right to *revest,* or transfer back, title to the seller if the buyer is not satisfied after making the purchase.

conditions subsequent
Conditions in a sales contract that must be met after title has passed.

EXAMPLE 14.5

Returning to Examples 14.3 and 14.4, suppose that the parties agreed that Castelli would purchase the car, but would have the right to return it to Piak if it did not have enough power to pull a travel trailer that Castelli had ordered. Whether the car would be adequate for this purpose would not be known until the trailer was delivered. If the sales contract included this condition and upon delivery of the trailer it was discovered that the trailer did not have enough power, Piak would be obliged to take the car back, and title would be revested in her.

LOST AND STOLEN GOODS

When someone possesses something, ownership is presumed, but it is possible to have possession of goods without having title, just as it is possible to have title without having possession. A thief has no title to goods he or she has stolen, and therefore cannot pass title to anyone else. The real owner of stolen goods has not passed title to anyone, and even an innocent purchaser who bought the goods in good faith would have to return them to the original owner.

A person who finds an article has a good title against anyone except the true owner. Anyone who buys an article from someone who has found it must be prepared to surrender the article to the true owner. However, it is often difficult to prove ownership of a lost article. Local police departments and insurance agents' associations have mounted campaigns to help people identify their property by using a tool that engraves identifying information on property.

OBJECTIVE 4
Explain the law governing title to lost or stolen goods and sales by persons having wrongful possession of goods.

EXAMPLE 14.6

Fortuna, a businesswoman, left a laptop computer in an airline waiting room, where it was found by Moreno. Because the computer had a serial number that matched the one on her bill of sale, Fortuna was able to prove ownership and recover her property.

Photo 14.1

Lost and Found

If someone finds an item, the finder has good title to it against anyone except the true owner. *What are some of the safeguards you can take so you can establish true ownership if something you have lost is found?*

OBJECTIVE 5

Define the principle of estoppel, and provide examples of how this principle is applied in various situations.

estoppel A bar to using contradictory words or acts in asserting a claim against another.

TRANSFER OF TITLE BY ESTOPPEL

Under certain circumstances, it is possible for title to goods to be passed by a nonowner who does not have title. In these cases, title is said to pass by estoppel. *Estoppel* is a bar to using contradictory words or acts in asserting a claim against another. As the concept of estoppel is used in discussions of title, the title holder is estopped—legally prevented—from claiming ownership of the property as a result of certain actions taken by the title holder. The Uniform Commercial Code, in UCC 2-202 and UCC 2-403, deals with the rights of persons who acquire questionable title:

For title to pass by estoppel, the purchaser must be able to prove the following:

1. The purchase was made in good faith. That is, the buyer believed the seller to be the owner or one appointed to act for the real owner.

2. The purchase was made from one in rightful possession.
3. Value was given by the buyer for that which he or she now claims ownership under the principle of estoppel.

Examples of Estoppel

The following examples illustrate how the principle of estoppel is applied.

Transfer of Money or Commercial Paper Made Out to Bearer

When the owner of cash or commercial paper (such as a check) makes it payable to bearer, who then gives it to a third person, the original owner cannot demand the return of the money from a third party to whom it was given in exchange for something of value.

> **EXAMPLE 14.7**
>
> Schultz gave his brother-in-law, Robb, $250 cash and asked him to buy a CD player because Robb could use his employee discount. Instead, Robb bought himself a suit. Schultz cannot demand the return of the cash from the person who sold the suit.

Transfer of Property to a Seller Dealing in the Same Type of Goods

When the owner of goods entrusts property to a person who sells the same type of goods and that person sells the property to an innocent third party, the owner is estopped from recovering the goods from the third party.

> **EXAMPLE 14.8**
>
> Unger left a power lawnmower at a garden shop for repair and service, and the owner of the shop sold the mower to another customer. Unger would be estopped from recovering the mower from the innocent third-party purchaser. Unger can, however, sue the owner of the garden shop for the value of the mower.

Transfer of Property to a Seller Permitted to Appear as the Real Owner

If the owner of property gives possession of it to a second party and allows that person to act as the real owner, the rightful owner cannot recover the property if the second party sells the property to an innocent third party.

> **EXAMPLE 14.9**
>
> Suppose that Unger, in Example 14.8, borrowed a lawnmower from his neighbor to use while his own was being repaired. Unger then sold the borrowed mower to a gardener who was working on his lawn. The

neighbor would be estopped from recovering the lawnmower from the gardener. However, the neighbor could bring legal action against Unger.

Transfer of Proof of Ownership to an Unauthorized Seller If the owner of goods entrusts proof of ownership to someone in possession of the goods, the goods cannot be recovered by the true owner from an innocent purchaser.

EXAMPLE 14.10

Returning again to Example 14.8, suppose that the neighbor who loaned the mower to Unger also gave him the bill of sale (proof of ownership). If Unger then sold the mower to another neighbor, the rightful owner would be estopped from recovering the mower from the innocent purchaser because Unger, the unauthorized seller, had proof of ownership.

SALES BY PERSONS HAVING RIGHTFUL POSSESSION

A salesperson in a store, service station, restaurant, and so on, is known as a *remote party*. Such individuals have the right to make legitimate sales as representatives of the owner of the goods, although they themselves are not titleholders. A salesperson has the express or implied permission of the titleholder of the merchandise to sell it. Similarly, agents acting on behalf of principals can pass title without holding title themselves.

remote party Someone with the right to make legitimate sales as a representative of the owner of the goods, although they themselves are not titleholders.

SALES BY PERSONS HAVING WRONGFUL POSSESSION

Unlike the situations described previously, in which possession of goods was transferred with the permission of the owner, situations of *wrongful possession* occur when property, such as stolen goods, is transferred without permission of the owner. The titleholder, or rightful owner, of stolen goods is never estopped. That is, he or she is never prevented from exercising a claim to the goods, even if the person in possession of them is an innocent purchaser of the property.

wrongful possession When property, such as stolen goods, is transferred without permission of the owner.

EXAMPLE 14.11

Brilley, a shipping clerk employed by Action Auto Parts, stole an automobile engine and sold it to a friend, Petras. After Action Auto

> discharged Brilley, the owners suspected that Petras had possession of the stolen engine, which they could prove was their property by its serial number. With the aid of the police, they recovered the stolen engine. Even if Petras had sold the engine to Jones, who sold it to Smith, Action Auto could recover the property at any point when it could be found because Action Auto never lost title to it.

Transfer of Title to Fungible Goods

Fungible goods are goods that are generally sold by weight or measure. Examples are wheat, sugar, flour, gasoline, oil, and so on. A unit of such goods is like any other unit. Consequently, 1,000 gallons of No. 2 fuel oil in a storage tank that holds many thousands of gallons is like all the other 1,000 gallons of No. 2 oil in the tank. Nevertheless, it is important to determine when title to such fungible goods passes. Generally, the following rules apply.

- If goods are ordered and the building, tank, storage yard, or grain elevator from which they are to come is not specified, this general rule of title passing applies: Title passes when the goods become ascertained, that is, when they become clearly identifiable. As a result, when a person simply orders 1,000 gallons of No. 2 fuel oil, title passes when the 1,000 gallons are delivered or at least separated from the larger mass.
- If a buyer orders a specific quantity of fungible goods from a specific mass—for example, if the preceding order for fuel oil specified that it be from "Hunterspoint Storage Yard"—then title passes at once, even before the portion ordered is separated from the rest. In the eyes of the law, the buyer acquires immediate title to an undivided share of the specific mass because the units of oil are all the same and no selection is necessary to identify the particular units that the buyer is purchasing.

fungible goods Goods that are generally sold by weight or measure.

OBJECTIVE 6

Describe the passage of title to fungible goods.

EXAMPLE 14.12

> Rural Cannery received an order from Fisk Supermarkets for 1,000 cases of canned peas bearing the Fisk label. The cannery normally packaged such goods for many supermarkets and had an abundant supply of canned peas. After they received this order, the cannery began placing Fisk labels on cans of peas. Title to the canned peas passed to Fisk when the labels were affixed to the cans.

CHAPTER SUMMARY

1. Title, as it relates to property, is intangible. It represents ownership and the right to possess something, unless that right has been given up.

2. Real property is land and all articles permanently attached to it, such as buildings and trees. Personal property is all kinds of property other than real property. Only personal property is governed by the law of sales.

3. There are a variety of ways in which title can pass. A bill of sale is a written statement that the seller is passing ownership to the buyer. A bill of lading is a document prepared by the carrier or shipper for goods to be shipped by land or water. A warehouse receipt is like a bill of lading except that the goods involved are not being transported but merely stored. Title passes when the parties intend and at the moment when they unconditionally agree to sell specific goods that are in a deliverable state.

4. A thief has no title to goods that he or she has stolen, and consequently cannot pass title, even to innocent purchasers. Someone who finds lost goods has title to them against anyone but the true owner. A person without good title to goods cannot transfer title, except in cases of transfer of title by estoppel.

5. Estoppel is a bar to using contradictory words or acts in asserting a claim against another. Examples of estoppel include transfer of money or commercial paper made out to the bearer, transfer of property to a seller dealing in the same type of goods, transfer of property to a seller permitted to appear as the real owner, and transfer of proof of ownership to an unauthorized seller.

6. Title to fungible goods passes when the goods become clearly identifiable. In cases in which a specific quantity is ordered from a specific mass, title passes at once, even before the portion ordered is separated.

Chapter 14 Assessment

MATCHING LEGAL TERMS

Match each of the following definitions with the correct term in the list below. Write the letter of your choice in the answer column.

- **a.** bill of sale
- **b.** certificate of title
- **c.** condition subsequent
- **d.** condition precedent
- **e.** estoppel
- **f.** fungible goods
- **g.** order bill of lading
- **h.** personal property
- **i.** real property
- **j.** remote party
- **k.** straight bill of lading
- **l.** warehouse receipt

1. A carrier's receipt for goods accepted for shipment. 1. _____
2. A written statement that the seller is passing, or transferring, ownership to a buyer. 2. _____
3. A carrier's receipt for goods accepted for shipment that ensures that the goods will not be delivered unless the original bill of lading is surrendered. 3. _____
4. A provision in a contract that requires the performance of a specific act before title passes. 4. _____
5. A salesperson authorized to sell merchandise for a merchant. 5. _____
6. Land and articles permanently attached to it. 6. _____
7. A provision in a contract that requires the performance of a specific act after title passes. 7. _____
8. A bar that prevents a person from denying the truth of a fact that has become settled by actions of a party. 8. _____
9. Goods generally sold by weight or measure, such as grain or gasoline, in which each unit is like all others. 9. _____
10. A document that is proof of ownership. 10. _____
11. Possessions other than real property, such as jewelry. 11. _____
12. Evidence of ownership provided by a storage facility. 12. _____

TRUE/FALSE QUIZ

Indicate whether each of the following statements is true or false by writing *T* or *F* in the answer column.

13. A bill of sale must be prepared on a specific legal form. 13. _____
14. Title is proof of ownership as shown by a bill of sale. 14. _____
15. Personal property is land and anything attached to it. 15. _____
16. A straight bill of lading is an instrument used to collect money owed. 16. _____

Transfer of Title   **CHAPTER 14**   217

Chapter 14 Assessment

17. The general rule of law regarding the passing of title is that title passes when the parties intend it to pass.
17. _____

18. A handwritten bill of sale may be an effective legal document.
18. _____

19. Estoppel is a legal principle that can prevent an owner from recovering his or her own property under certain circumstances.
19. _____

20. An air bill is similar to a bill of lading except that it covers a shipment made by air.
20. _____

21. Conditions precedents are required acts that must be performed before title passes.
21. _____

22. A person who finds an article has good title against anyone else except the true owner.
22. _____

23. The owner of cash who entrusts it to another cannot demand the return of the money from a third party to whom the money was given in exchange for something of value.
23. _____

24. Title to goods can never pass to another without the consent of the owner.
24. _____

25. Conditions subsequent are required acts that must be performed after a contract is signed.
25. _____

26. Title to fungible goods passes when they are delivered.
26. _____

27. The owner of personal property cannot recover it from an innocent third party who purchased it from a seller in possession of the property and who was entrusted with proof of ownership by the real owner.
27. _____

DISCUSSION QUESTIONS

Answer the following questions and discuss them in class.

28. Distinguish between real and personal property and indicate which is subject to the law of sales.

29. Explain how title and certificate of title relate to ownership.

30. Explain how title passes and discuss how bills of sale, bills of lading, and warehouse receipts are involved in the passing of title.

Chapter 14 Assessment

31. Explain the law governing title to lost or stolen goods and sales by persons having wrongful possession of goods.

32. Discuss the principle of estoppel and provide examples of how this principle is applied in various situations.

33. Explain the passage of title to fungible goods.

THINKING CRITICALLY ABOUT THE LAW

Answer the following questions, which require you to think critically about the legal principles that you learned in this chapter.

34. Title An important application of the concept of title relates to who is holding title when a loss occurs. Are there other ways of determining who should bear a loss in a business transaction? Explain your answer.

35. Conditions Precedent A contract stipulates that certain conditions must be met before title can pass. A seller might wish to hasten the passage of title to minimize the risk of loss and the cost of insurance to indemnify such losses. Consider a typical sales transaction and suggest steps a seller might take to accelerate title transfer.

36. Estoppel It seems that passage of title by estoppel might deny the rights of an innocent, though inattentive, property owner. Should a legitimate title holder lose title because of inattention? Why or why not?

Transfer of Title **CHAPTER 14**

Chapter 14 Assessment

37. Remote Parties How can a buyer in a store know whether he or she is dealing with a titleholder or a remote party? Does it make a difference? Who does a buyer hold responsible for problems?

_____
_____
_____

38. A Question of Ethics Is it ethical for a person who is not a title holder to act as one who has title to goods, thereby misleading a prospective buyer? Explain your answer.

_____
_____
_____

CASE QUESTIONS

Study each case below and answer the questions that follow by writing *Yes* or *No* in the answer column.

39. Passage of Title Crowley, a building contractor, ordered 500 bags of cement from Litvak Building Supply. It was agreed that Litvak would deliver to a building site and title would pass when delivery was made. Before the bags of cement could be loaded on a delivery truck, a railroad derailment destroyed much of the supply company's inventory.

   a. Must Crowley bear the loss and recover damages from the railroad?   **a.** _____

   b. Is the requirement of delivery to a building site a condition precedent?   **b.** _____

   c. Did title to the bags of cement pass at the time the order was placed?   **c.** _____

40. Estoppel Hollander purchased a computer from a pawnshop for use in his real estate office. Several weeks later, Diem, one of Hollander's customers, mentioned that the computer looked familiar and asked if he could examine it. After checking the underside of the machine, he pointed to his Social Security number, which had been engraved on the metal frame by his insurance agent. Diem demanded the return of the computer, claiming that it had been stolen from him and that he could produce the original sales slip.

   a. Can Diem legally recover the computer?   **a.** _____

   b. Can a rightful owner be estopped from recovering his or her property from an innocent purchaser?   **b.** _____

   c. Could the pawnshop have given good title to Hollander?   **c.** _____

41. Condition Precedent Fallon agreed in writing to purchase a used truck from Sunset Motors with the understanding that a snowplow attachment be added. When Fallon attempted to take delivery of the truck, he found that the plow attachment had not been added. He refused to accept delivery. Sunset protested that the plow attachment was being shipped from Minnesota and that it would be installed when it arrived. Sunset demanded that Fallon accept the truck.

   a. Can Fallon legally refuse to accept the truck?   **a.** _____

b. Is this an example of a condition precedent? b. _____

c. Is the contract enforceable? c. _____

42. Certificate of Title Forell, a resident of Des Moines, purchased for the unusually low price of $4,000, a nearly new Buick automobile from a visitor from Cleveland, who explained that he was in town to take delivery of another automobile that he had just inherited from his late father. The seller produced a certificate of title. After Forell had possession of the Buick automobile for several months, he sold it to Bates for $3,800. Bates had had the car for two months, when he was pulled over by the police for a minor traffic violation. The police checked the car's Vehicle Identification Number in their computer, which showed that the car had been stolen from Santiago in Cleveland and that the certificate of title was forged. When Santiago learned that his car had been located, he claimed ownership.

a. Will Santiago be able to recover his automobile? a. _____

b. Will the certificate of title Forell obtained from the out-of-town seller entitle him to ownership? b. _____

c. Was Forell a good-faith purchaser? c. _____

CASE ANALYSIS

Study each of the following cases carefully and then briefly state the principle of law and your decision.

43. Title to Stolen Goods Patterson was on a group vacation tour when he discovered that his camcorder video camera was not where he had left it on the tour bus. Later on the tour, Patterson noticed another vacationer, Carlsen, with a similar camcorder. When Carlsen was confronted, he claimed that he had found the camera at one of the tour bus stops. When Patterson produced a bill of sale with a serial number that matched the one on the disputed camera, Carlsen refused to surrender it, claiming that since he had found it, it was his. *Will Patterson be able to retain possession of his lost camcorder?*

Principle of law:

_____

_____

Decision:

_____

_____

44. Remote Party Kiang, a sales representative working for Prat's Appliances, sold a refrigerator to Pogany. After several weeks, Pogany changed her mind and wanted to repudiate the sales contract. Her argument was that a valid contract did not exist because Kiang did not possess title to the refrigerator and therefore could not convey title to her. *Will Pogany be allowed to repudiate the sales contract?*

Principle of law:

_____

_____

Chapter 14 Assessment

Decision:
_____
_____

45. Passage of Title Hughes purchased a new Lincoln Continental automobile from Al Greene, Inc., an authorized new car dealership. On the day of the sale, Hughes made a cash down payment and signed a purchase contract and an application for title certificate. The understanding was that Hughes would take immediate possession of the car and return in a few days for new-car preparation and the installation of a CB radio. On the way home from the dealer, Hughes wrecked the car. The certificate of title had not yet been issued by the state. The buyer, Hughes, claimed that title had not yet passed, since the title certificate had not yet been issued. *Who must bear the loss?* [*Hughes v. Al Greene, Inc.,* 418 N.E.2d 1355 (Ohio).]

Principle of law:
_____
_____

Decision:
_____
_____

LEGAL RESEARCH

Complete the following activities. Then share your findings with the class.

46. Working in Teams In teams of three or four, interview several real estate agencies and discuss title and title insurance.
_____
_____
_____
_____
_____

47. Using Technology Using the Internet and search engines, investigate the expression "transfer of title," used in this chapter.
_____
_____
_____
_____
_____
_____

CHAPTER 15

SALES

PERFORMANCE OBJECTIVES

After studying this chapter and completing the assessments, you will be able to:

1. Discuss the concept of title as it concerns sales contracts.

2. Distinguish between a contract for sale and a contract to sell, and provide examples of each.

3. Discuss the difference between entire and divisible contracts.

4. Describe the special requirements of contracts for labor and materials.

5. Provide examples of two kinds of sales with the right of return.

6. Discuss auction sales and conditional sales.

7. Discuss shipments made f.o.b. destination and f.o.b. shipping point.

8. Explain both sellers' and buyers' remedies for breach of sales contracts.

LEGAL TERMS

contract for sale
existing goods
future goods
contract to sell
contract for labor and materials
contract for sale with the right of return
sale on approval
sale or return
auction sale
conditional sales contract
f.o.b. shipping point
f.o.b. destination
stoppage in transit
replevin
cover

OBJECTIVE 1

Discuss the concept of title as it concerns sales contracts.

THE LAW OF SALES

Because the law of sales affects so many individuals and businesses, Article 2 of the Uniform Commercial Code is quite comprehensive. It does not, however, include investment securities (covered by Article 8 of the UCC), real estate, or services. Contracts for services are considered ordinary contracts and are not covered by the UCC.

In the case of transactions involving both goods and services, courts look to the predominant portion of the contract to determine whether it is a sales contract for goods or a services contract for repairs, which incidentally includes the parts necessary to make the repairs.

The term *title,* introduced in Chapter 14, as used in contracts for sale, refers to ownership. Consequently, having title to something usually means having the right to possess it. However, there are important exceptions. For example, if *A* leases *B* a car, then *B* has the right to possess, while *A* retains ownership. The concept of title is important in the law of sales. Equally important are the remedies for *breach of contract,* that is, breaking a contract.

OBJECTIVE 2

Distinguish between a contract for a sale and a contract to sell, and provide examples of each.

contract for sale A legally enforceable agreement that has as its purpose the immediate transfer of title to personal property in return for consideration.

CONTRACT FOR SALE

A **contract for sale** is a legally enforceable agreement that has as its purpose the immediate transfer of title to personal property in return for consideration. The contract may be for a present sale of goods or for a sale of future goods, that is, goods that are not yet in existence or manufactured. A sale, according to the Uniform Commercial Code, is the passing of title from the seller to the buyer for a price [UCC 2-106]. Payment for goods can be in the form of money, goods, or the performance of services [UCC 2-304].

> **EXAMPLE 15.1**
>
> Jesup agreed to sell an amateur radio transmitter to Moncada for $750. Moncada paid the agreed price and Jesup gave him the equipment.

This agreement is an executed contract for sale, and title (ownership) to the transmitter passed when the money was paid to Jessup. If Moncada, after purchasing the transmitter, left it with Jesup for a day while he arranged delivery and it was damaged, destroyed, or stolen during that time, the loss would be Moncada's.

224   PART 3   Sales, Agency, and Consumer Protection

> **EXAMPLE 15.2**
>
> Suppose that, in Example 15.1, the parties had agreed that the sale of the radio equipment would be completed when Moncada had passed his FCC amateur's examination. The transaction would be viewed as an agreement in which both parties intended title to pass when Moncada passed the examination. If anything happened to the equipment in the meantime, Jesup would suffer the loss.

Contract to Sell

Goods that physically exist and are owned by the seller at the time of sale are considered *existing goods.* Goods that do not exist at the time of the sales transaction, but are expected to come into the possession of the seller, are considered *future goods.* Examples of such future goods include growing crops and timber, unborn livestock, goods not yet manufactured, and so on. An agreement to sell future goods is considered a *contract to sell,* in contrast to a contract for sale. The distinction between existing and future goods is important because a person cannot sell goods to which he or she does not hold title, and no one can hold title to goods that do not yet exist.

existing goods Goods that physically exist and are owned by the seller at the time of sale.

future goods Goods that do not exist at the time of the sales transaction, but are expected to come into the possession of the seller.

contract to sell An agreement to sell future goods.

> **EXAMPLE 15.3**
>
> Kierman paid a $500 deposit to Mondrus, a breeder of pedigreed dogs, who agreed to sell Kierman a male puppy from the next litter of his prized terrier for $1,200. Before the terrier gave birth to the expected litter, it was killed in a fire that destroyed the kennel. Kierman demanded the return of his deposit, claiming that title to the puppy did not pass until delivery was made. Mondrus demanded the balance of the agreed price of $1,200, claiming that the unborn puppy belonged to Kierman from the time of their agreement.

The courts have heard many such cases, and in almost every one they have held that title to such future goods remains with the seller. In Example 15.3, Kierman would get back his deposit and Mondrus would bear the loss.

Oral, Written, and Implied Contracts

Sales contracts may be oral, written, or implied. As pointed out in Chapter 11, contracts for $500 or more must be in writing to be enforceable [UCC 2-201]. The complete agreement need not be in writing, but there must be some evidence of the intention of the parties. The contract must also be signed by the affected parties.

ENTIRE AND DIVISIBLE SALES CONTRACTS

Entire and divisible contracts were introduced in Chapter 6, and examples were provided to show the difference between them. The significance of the distinction between entire and divisible sales contracts can be seen in numerous business transactions.

OBJECTIVE 3

Discuss the difference between entire and divisible contracts.

> **EXAMPLE 15.4**
>
> Management Mode, a publisher of newsletters, decided to switch from using an outside typesetter to internal desktop publishing to save the cost of typesetting and to speed up their operation. The firm ordered personal computers from Compu-Writ for each of their editors and writers, appropriate word-processing software, desktop publishing software, in-house training, and laser printers. Delivery of the equipment and software was scheduled to be made within 30 days of placing the order. Delivery of the laser printers was delayed for two months.

Because all of the components were included in the same order—an entire contract—payment for the contract would not be required until the whole order was filled. Payment for the portion of the order delivered—the computers—would not be due when they were delivered. On the other hand, if the computers and printers were in separate orders—a divisible contract—payment for the computers would be due when delivery was made, even though they were useless without the printers. Paying for the computers before they could be used would be an unwise use of the firm's financial resources because the money that would be tied up in the computers could be earning interest instead.

CONTRACTS FOR LABOR AND MATERIALS

OBJECTIVE 4

Describe the special requirements of contracts for labor and materials.

contract for labor and materials A sales contract for goods of special design, construction, or manufacture.

A sales contract for goods of special design, construction, or manufacture is neither a contract for sale nor a contract to sell. Such a contract is considered a *contract for labor and materials.* A contract for labor and materials, even though it involves $500 or more, need not always be in writing to be enforceable. This rule is an exception to the Uniform Commercial Code requirement that contracts of $500 or more be in writing. The UCC provides that "if the goods are to be specially manufactured for the buyer and are not suitable for sale to others," the requirement of a written contract does not necessarily apply [UCC 2-201(3)]. The contract will not be binding if the buyer repudiates (cancels) the contract and the seller receives the notice before he or she has made either a substantial beginning in manufacturing the goods or before he or she has made commitments for their procurement. If, however, the seller has begun manufacture or commitment, the cancelation is not effective [UCC 2-201(3)].

> **EXAMPLE 15.5**
>
> Manhattan Bakery orally contracted with Foremost Conveyor Company for the design and construction of a special conveyor system to be installed in the shipping room of the bakery. After the conveyor was designed, built, and ready to be installed, Manhattan Bakery had a change of manager. The new manager canceled the order, claiming that it was invalid because it was not in writing. Foremost Conveyor can recover damages from the bakery for breach of contract because the cancelation was not received before work on the conveyor system had begun.

SALES WITH RIGHT OF RETURN

Certain kinds of goods are frequently sold on a trial basis. Because a sales brochure and a demonstration, for example, will typically not persuade a business person that a certain office machine will be an asset to the business, a short trial period during which the buyer can use the machine is often arranged. As a result, a ***contract for sale with the right of return*** gives the buyer both title to the goods and the opportunity to return them to the seller at a later time.

A merchant might prefer to sell for cash with no return privilege. But if the seller's competitors are willing to allow prospective customers a trial period, other sellers must also do so to remain competitive. In this kind of selling arrangement, it is important to determine who owns the merchandise while it is in the prospective buyer's possession, in the event of loss or damage.

Sale on Approval

When a contract provides for the sale of goods subject to the buyer's approval, the transaction is a ***sale on approval***. The goods remain the property of the seller until the buyer has expressed approval of the goods. Title and risk of loss remain with the seller. The buyer may indicate approval orally or in writing, or by retaining the goods for more than a reasonable time [UCC 2-326].

OBJECTIVE 5

Provide examples of two kinds of sales with the right of return.

contract for sale with the right or return A contract for the sale of goods that gives the buyer both title to the goods and the opportunity to return them to the seller at a later time.

sale on approval A contract for the sale of goods subject to the buyer's approval.

EXAMPLE 15.6

The sales representative of Scrub 'n' Clean Equipment was trying to persuade the manager of Riverdale Car Wash to install a new type of car wash brush. The cost of the brushes and uncertainty about their effectiveness made the car wash manager hesitant to make a commitment to buy until he had the opportunity to try the equipment. The sales representative agreed to let the car wash use four brushes for two months on approval.

Both parties in this case agreed to a sale on approval. After using the brushes for a month or two, the car wash manager could agree to purchase them, and at such time title would pass to the car wash. It is not wise for a potential buyer to let the trial period slip by on the assumption that the seller does not mind or that he or she is getting something for nothing. The buyer must notify the seller of his or her decision to return the goods, if that is the intention, within the time agreed upon for trial of the goods, or within a reasonable time if no time has been agreed upon. If notification is not given during that period, the user's continued, prolonged use of the goods on approval could be interpreted as implied consent to buy, and the user could be held responsible for the goods and obligated to pay for them.

Sale or Return

Most goods sold by reputable merchants can be returned for a variety of reasons unless the sale is clearly identified as final or the circumstances of the return are unreasonable. Often a merchant will agree to a *sale or return,* that is, an agreement whereby the seller will accept the return of goods at the request of the buyer to maintain goodwill, rather than because the seller is legally obliged to accept the returned goods. The sale of goods can be made with the understanding that the purchaser takes title to the goods but has the right to return them within a specified or reasonable time. In such cases, the purchaser must assume all the obligations of ownership while the goods are in his or her possession.

sale or return An agreement whereby the seller will accept the return of goods at the request of the buyer to maintain goodwill, rather than because the seller is legally obliged to accept the returned goods.

EXAMPLE 15.7

Suppose that, in Example 15.6, the manager of Riverdale Car Wash was sure that the new brushes were what he wanted and needed. Suppose also that the funds were available for the planned purchase of the brushes and that a purchase order for the brushes was issued. If the brushes did not prove satisfactory, the manager could probably still return them. The major distinction between this example and the

> previous one is that, in this instance, title to the brushes is in the hands of the purchaser, who would be held responsible for loss or damage of the equipment. Not only would the parties to the agreement have an interest in who held title, but the insurance carriers for the car wash and the supplier, Scrub 'n' Clean, would also have an interest in who held title.

OTHER KINDS OF SALES

Two additional kinds of sales are auction sales and conditional sales.

Auction Sales

Auction sales were introduced in Chapter 11. At an **auction sale,** the buyer is the party making the offer, or bid. The seller is the owner of the goods, who has engaged an auctioneer to gather bids from interested parties with the hope of selling to the highest bidder. The bidder's offer is accepted when the auctioneer says, "One, two, three—sold!" and at the same time lets the hammer fall. A bidder may retract a bid at any time before the hammer falls, and such retraction does not revive any previous bid. If a bid is made while the hammer is falling, the auctioneer may use his or her discretion to reopen the bidding or declare the goods sold under the bid made as the hammer was falling [UCC 2-328(2)].

You may have heard stories about expensive pieces of property being sold at auction for a pittance simply because no one offered a higher bid. This possibility occurs only at an *auction without reserve*—one at which the goods must be sold to the highest bidder and may not be withdrawn after bidding has begun [UCC 2-328(3)]. An *auction with reserve* gives the auctioneer the right to withdraw the goods at any time before announcing completion of the sale if reasonable bids are not made. If a *reserve amount* has been established, it will be announced by the auctioneer before bidding begins, or it will be disclosed in posters or catalogs listing the goods to be auctioned.

The legal requirement that sales of property for $500 or more be in writing is satisfied by the notations made in the auctioneer's sales book. In the case of telephone bids made from distant branches of the auction house, the bidder must sign an agreement that sets out the conditions under which he or she agrees to pay any accepted bid.

Online auctions are available on the Internet, and unlike actual auctions during which a buyer can inspect goods to be auctioned, the online auction relies on the reputation of the seller, photographs to display goods, and e-mail for bidding. Items offered for sale can be

OBJECTIVE 6

Discuss auction sales and conditional sales.

auction sale A sale in which the buyer is the party making the offer, or bid.

offered with a reserve so that the sale price must be equal to or greater than the reserve.

Conditional Sales

Some sales contracts include conditions that must be met either before or after the sale is completed. In most instances, the conditions deal with arrangements for payment. A ***conditional sales contract*** is one way of selling merchandise with the condition that title will remain with the seller until the purchase price has been paid. The buyer cannot legally resell goods purchased in this manner because title has not passed; a person cannot sell goods to which he or she has no title. The seller can *repossess* the goods (take back property through judicial action) if the buyer does not pay in the time agreed.

conditional sales contract A sales contract that includes conditions that must be met either before or after the sale is completed.

DELIVERY

Many transactions require shipment of the goods purchased. The manner in which the goods are shipped affects the passing of title. Title to goods that are shipped by private carrier or delivered by the seller passes at the time of delivery to the buyer. If the buyer arranges for delivery, title passes when the buyer, or his or her agent, picks up the goods. However, in the case of goods that are shipped by *common carrier*—someone who is in the business of transporting goods or persons, whether by rail, truck, plane, or any other mode of transportation—title passes to the purchaser according to the conditions covered in the following discussion.

OBJECTIVE 7

Discuss shipments made f.o.b. destination and f.o.b. shipping point.

Sales f.o.b. Shipping Point

The abbreviation *f.o.b.* means "free on board." When goods are sold ***f.o.b. shipping point,*** title to the goods passes from the seller to the buyer when the carrier receives the shipment, and it is understood that the buyer will pay the transportation charges. From that point, the goods belong to the buyer, and in the event of loss or damage, the buyer must attempt to recover any loss from the carrier. Further, the buyer is responsible for paying the seller for the merchandise even if he or she never receives it [UCC 2-239].

f.o.b. shipping point Title to goods passes from the seller to the buyer when the carrier receives the shipment and it is understood that the buyer will pay the transportation charges.

f.o.b. destination Title passes from the seller to the buyer when the goods are delivered to the buyer.

Sales f.o.b. Destination

Title to goods shipped ***f.o.b. destination*** passes when the goods are delivered to the buyer. In the event of their loss or damage en route, the seller must attempt to recover any loss from the carrier. In such a case, the cost of transporting the goods is paid to the carrier by the seller, but is usually included in the buyer's invoice or is billed to the buyer separately.

This method of shipment offers the buyer somewhat more advantage. For example, in case of a lost or damaged shipment, the buyer can quickly call the seller and arrange for a duplicate shipment. The buyer's money is not tied up in goods not received, and the buyer is spared the inconvenience of filing a claim with the carrier.

REMEDIES FOR BREACH OF SALES CONTRACTS

The law provides a number of remedies to protect the buyer and the seller in disputes involving sales contracts. It is important to note that remedies are available for only a limited time. The Uniform Commercial Code provides a *statute of limitations,* that is, a time limit after which the usual legal remedies are no longer available. The UCC provides that, in the absence of negligence or fraud (for which there are different statutes of limitations), legal action to remedy a breach of sales contract must be started within four years [UCC 2-275].

Sellers' Remedies

A seller has a number of remedies at law depending on the circumstances of the case. The most common circumstances are covered in the following discussion.

When the Buyer Refuses to Accept Delivery of the Goods

When the buyer refuses to accept delivery of the goods, the seller may do one of the following:

1. Store the goods for the buyer and sue to recover the sales price if the goods are not readily resalable to another customer [UCC 2-704].
2. Resell the goods immediately if they are perishable or if their market value might depreciate rapidly. Also, the seller can sue the buyer for the difference between the price the goods brought in the resale and the price the buyer had agreed to pay for them plus incidental damages [UCC 2-706].
3. Retain the goods and sue the buyer for the difference between the contract price and the market price at the time the buyer refused to honor the contract [UCC 2-706].

EXAMPLE 15.8

Georgio placed an order with Med-Lab Manufacturing Company for medical laboratory testing equipment of special design. When the

> **OBJECTIVE 8**
>
> Explain both sellers' and buyers' remedies for breach of sales contracts.

> equipment was ready for shipment, Georgio notified Med-Lab of her intention to cancel the order. Med-Lab has the right to hold the equipment for Georgio and sue for the agreed purchase price.

If the equipment was not of special design and could be sold to others, Med-Lab could return the equipment to stock for sale to others and sue Georgio for damages resulting from Georgio's breach. In this case, the damages would be limited to the profit Med-Lab would have made on the sale if there had been no breach.

When the Buyer Refuses to Pay the Purchase Price
When the buyer refuses to pay the purchase price, the seller may do one of the following:

1. If the seller still has possession of the goods, he or she can resell them after a reasonable period of time and sue for any damages incurred.
2. If the merchandise has already been delivered to the buyer, he or she can sue for the purchase price.

> **EXAMPLE 15.9**
> Molstad bought a laser printer from Computer Universe Company, agreeing to pay cash for it. Computer Universe insisted on retaining possession of the printer until the invoice amount was paid in full. When Molstad failed to pay within the agreed time, Computer Universe sold the printer to Fishman at a lower price because of a general lowering of prices that took place between the time Molstad agreed to buy and the time it was sold to Fishman. Computer Universe sued Molstad for the difference between the price Molstad had agreed to pay and the price paid by Fishman. If the printer had been sold on credit and the credit period had expired, Computer Universe could have sued for the contract price.

When the Buyer is Insolvent
Sometimes, after goods have been shipped to the buyer but before actual delivery has been made by the carrier, the seller learns that the buyer is *insolvent*—that is, has ceased to pay his or her debts.

When the buyer is insolvent, the Uniform Commercial Code provides the seller with the right of **stoppage in transit.** Stoppage in transit is the right of an unpaid seller to stop goods in transit and order the carrier to hold them for the seller. This right to interrupt the shipment of goods to the buyer exists for both f.o.b. shipping point sales and f.o.b. destination sales [UCC 2-705].

stoppage in transit When the buyer is insolvent, the right of an unpaid seller to stop goods in transit and order the carrier to hold them for the seller.

To exercise this right of stoppage in transit, the seller must satisfy the common carrier that the buyer is insolvent. If the seller's information proves unfounded, both the seller and the carrier are subject to suit for damages. For this reason, the carrier should require the seller by contract to accept full responsibility for any loss that it may suffer as a result of a suit by the purchaser.

> **EXAMPLE 15.10**
>
> An order of books was en route to Readers' Haven bookstore, timed to arrive in time for a well-promoted author's autographing party. The seller, Words in Print, notified the carrier not to deliver the books, claiming that it had received information from a reliable source that the buyer, Readers' Haven, was insolvent. Later it was revealed that the information was in error. Both the publisher and the carrier are subject to Readers' Haven's suit for damages.

Buyers' Remedies

The Uniform Commercial Code provides a buyer with certain remedies depending on the specific circumstances [UCC 2-711].

When the Wrong Quantity is Delivered The buyer may reject delivery of a smaller quantity of merchandise than was ordered and sue for damages, or may accept the quantity delivered and sue for damages, which would be the lost profits that would have resulted from the sale of the undelivered portion. If a larger quantity of goods is delivered than was ordered, the buyer may reject the entire shipment, accept only what was ordered and reject the rest, or accept the entire shipment and pay for it at the contract price.

> **EXAMPLE 15.11**
>
> Woodbury Way, an appliance store, ordered 100 microwave ovens from an importer. By mistake, the importer shipped 200. Woodbury Way was delighted to learn that he had an unexpected bargain because the wholesaler's price was going to be increased as a result of changes in the foreign exchange rate. The buyer has the right to keep the entire shipment and pay for it at the contract price.

When the Goods are not as Ordered The buyer may revoke the contract and return the goods that are substantially not as ordered. If the goods have already been paid for, the buyer may demand a refund of the purchase price, and in most states, sue for damages for breach of warranty (a legally binding guarantee). Alternatively, the buyer may keep the goods and sue for damages for any loss resulting from the seller's breach of contract. If the goods are of a higher quality than what was ordered, the buyer could reject the order or keep the order and pay the contract price.

> **EXAMPLE 15.12**
>
> Susuki purchased and paid for a standby electric generator for emergency use at his factory. The seller assured Susuki that the generator would produce enough power to keep his essential operations running during a power failure. When the generator was tested, however, it failed to produce sufficient power. Susuki could demand a refund. In this instance, Susuki could probably not show that he had suffered injury, so a suit for damages would be unlikely.

When the Seller Fails to Deliver the Goods When title has passed to the buyer for goods that the seller has failed to deliver, the buyer has the following remedies:

1. The buyer can sue for damages by bringing a tort action charging conversion. As explained in Chapter 4, conversion is a tort that results when a person has unlawfully assumed ownership of property that belongs to another. The amount of damages sought would be the value of the goods at the time of the seller's failure to deliver.
2. If the goods are unique, such as a one-of-a-kind work of art, and the buyer wants the particular goods that are specified in the contract, the buyer can seek a court order of *specific performance*. Such an order requires the seller to deliver the goods specified in the contract or face being held in contempt of court [UCC 2-716].
3. Another remedy available to a buyer who wishes to obtain goods that are rightfully his or hers, rather than money damages, is to sue to obtain them by bringing an action of **replevin**, that is, an action to recover possession of specific goods wrongfully taken or detained by another [UCC 2-716]. In such an action, the court will order the sheriff to seize the goods and deliver them to the buyer.
4. The Uniform Commercial Code also permits a buyer to ***cover***, that is, to buy similar goods elsewhere to substitute for those not delivered by the seller. If the buyer chooses to cover, he or she may demand from the seller, as damages, the difference between the cost of cover (what he or she paid for the replacement goods) and

replevin An action to recover possession of specific goods wrongfully taken or detained by another.

cover When the seller fails to deliver the goods, the right of a buyer to buy similar goods elsewhere to substitute for those not delivered by the seller.

PART 3 Sales, Agency, and Consumer Protection

the contract price, plus any incidental expenses, less expenses saved as a result of the seller's breach [UCC 2-712].

EXAMPLE 15.13

> Andrews, a retail electronics dealer, purchased and paid for 60 compact disc players of an advanced design from a wholesaler. The CD players were in stock and delivery was promised. Clearly, title had passed. Because of a sharp increase in the manufacturer's prices, the wholesaler refused to deliver the players as agreed in the contract. Andrews can sue the distributor for the difference between the contract price and the higher market price at the time of the wholesaler's refusal to deliver. If she is seeking money damages, her suit will be an action for conversion. Alternatively, if the sets are in short supply and she is more interested in getting the CD players than in a money settlement, she can seek an order of specific performance. Or she can institute an action of replevin for delivery of the CD players. If the CD players are available elsewhere at a higher price, she could "cover" by buying at the higher price and sue the wholesaler for the difference between the contract price and the price of the "cover." The suit could also seek repayment of expenses such as the additional cost of transportation from a distant seller.

If title has not yet passed to the buyer, his or her remedy when the seller refuses to deliver at the time and place stated in the contract is a suit for breach of contract. The amount of damages would be the difference between the contract price and the market price at the time delivery was refused. The Uniform Commercial Code also permits payment of other damages that the buyer can prove, less any expenses saved as a result of the seller's breach [UCC 2-713].

EXAMPLE 15.14

> Duft, the owner of a business school, ordered 30 computers from Latimer, a supplier of office equipment, at a price of $875 each. A week before the time agreed for delivery, Latimer got an order for 30 of the same kind of computers from an insurance company that had relocated to the city. The second buyer agreed to pay a price of $1,150 each. Sensing an opportunity to increase his profit, Latimer refused to fill Duft's order. While it would be difficult to determine the amount of damages, Duft could sue for damages that would include the loss resulting from the loss of tuition that would have been paid by students who would have enrolled in the school if the computers had been delivered as promised.

CHAPTER SUMMARY

1 The term *title*, as it is used in contracts for sale, refers to ownership. Having title to something usually means having the right to possess it.

2 A contract for sale is a legally enforceable agreement that has as its purpose the immediate transfer of title to personal property in return for consideration. A contract to sell is an agreement to sell future goods.

3 An entire contract is one in which all of the components of the agreement are included in the same order; a divisible contract is one in which components of an agreement are in separate orders.

4 A contract for labor and materials is a sales contract for goods of special design, construction, or manufacture. These contracts need not always be in writing, and they can be canceled before a substantial beginning or commitment to procurement has been made.

5 A contract for sale with the right of return is an agreement that gives the buyer both title to the goods and the opportunity to return them to the seller at a later time.

6 An auction sale is one in which the buyer is the party making the offer, or bid. A conditional sale is one in which certain conditions must be met before or after the sale is completed.

7 In sales f.o.b. shipping point, title to the goods passes from the seller to the buyer when the carrier receives shipment and it is understood that the buyer will pay the transportation charges. In sales f.o.b. destination, title to goods passes when the goods are delivered to the buyer.

8 Seller's remedies and buyer's remedies for breach of a sales contract depend on the circumstances. The UCC provides a statute of limitations in which legal action for breach of contract must be started.

Chapter 15 Assessment

MATCHING LEGAL TERMS

Match each of the following definitions with the correct term in the list below. Write the letter of your choice in the answer column.

- **a.** conditional sales contract
- **b.** contract for labor and materials
- **c.** contract to sell
- **d.** insolvency
- **e.** reserve amount
- **f.** sale on approval
- **g.** sale or return
- **h.** title
- **i.** statute of limitations
- **j.** stoppage in transit

1. Ownership of goods and the right to possess them. 1. _____
2. A contract for the sale of goods of special design, construction, or manufacture. 2. _____
3. A contract for sale that gives the buyer the title to goods and the opportunity of returning them to the seller at a later time. 3. _____
4. A sales agreement whereby the seller retains title and the buyer can return the goods. 4. _____
5. An agreement for the sale of future goods. 5. _____
6. An amount used at auction sales that specifies the lowest acceptable bid. 6. _____
7. A sales agreement whereby the seller retains title until the buyer pays for the goods. 7. _____
8. A time limit after which legal remedies are no longer possible. 8. _____
9. A state in which a person is unable to pay his or her debts. 9. _____
10. The right of an unpaid seller to stop goods in transit and order the carrier to hold them for the seller. 10. _____

TRUE/FALSE QUIZ

Indicate whether each of the following statements is true or false by writing *T* or *F* in the answer column.

11. Contracts for sale can be oral or written, express or implied. 11. _____
12. A contract for sale differs from a contract to sell primarily in the point at which title passes. 12. _____
13. In most cases of the sale of future goods, title remains with the seller until the goods are in a deliverable state. 13. _____
14. Goods that physically exist and are owned by the seller at the time of sale are considered existing goods. 14. _____
15. A contract for the sale of various unrelated articles is considered a divisible contract. 15. _____
16. A contract for labor and materials must always be in writing, regardless of the amount of money involved. 16. _____

Chapter 15 Assessment

17. When goods are sold on approval, the buyer has title during the trial period.   17. _____

18. The buyer of goods sold on approval can indicate his or her consent to keep the goods by retaining them for longer than the agreed time or a reasonable time.   18. _____

19. A buyer whose goods are not delivered within a reasonable time has the right to "cover," that is, to purchase substitute goods from another seller.   19. _____

20. The title to goods sold on approval passes to the buyer at the time of sale.   20. _____

21. A contract for special manufacture, construction, or design of goods is considered a contract for labor and materials.   21. _____

22. The notations in an auctioneer's book of sales of more than $500 satisfies the requirements of the Uniform Commercial Code that such contracts be in writing to be enforceable.   22. _____

23. A common carrier is a firm in the business of transporting goods or persons by rail, truck, plane, or any other mode of transportation.   23. _____

24. Title to goods shipped f.o.b. shipping point remains with the seller until delivery is made to the buyer.   24. _____

25. The buyer of goods that have been shipped f.o.b. destination must bear the loss if the goods are lost or damaged in transit.   25. _____

DISCUSSION QUESTIONS

Answer the following questions and discuss them in class.

26. How can a contract for future goods provide price flexibility for the seller? How can it provide predictability to the buyer?

27. Why is it important to determine when title passes?

28. A contract for sale with the right of return gives the buyer both title to the goods and the opportunity to return them to the seller at a later time. What are the benefits to the seller of this type of sales transaction?

Chapter 15 Assessment

29. When a contract provides for the sale of goods subject to the buyer's approval, the transaction is a sale on approval. What are the benefits to the seller of this type of sales transaction?

30. Discuss advantages and disadvantages to both sellers and buyers of shipping f.o.b. destination and f.o.b. shipping point.

31. Explain both sellers' and buyers' remedies for breach of contract.

THINKING CRITICALLY ABOUT THE LAW

32. Contract for Labor and Materials A contract for labor and materials need not be in writing, even if it is over $500. Does the buyer of repair services enjoy the same level of legal protection as if it were in writing? Why or why not?

33. Internet Auction Compare and contrast online auctions with actual live auctions.

34. Sellers' Remedies How might a seller avoid pitfalls in selling to unknown buyers?

35. Buyers' Remedies How might a buyer avoid pitfalls in buying from unknown sellers?

Chapter 15 Assessment

36. A Question of Ethics Is it fair for a buyer to ask a seller to hold merchandise while the buyer shops for a better price? Why or why not?

_____

_____

_____

CASE QUESTIONS

Study each case below and answer the questions that follow by writing *Yes* or *No* in the answer column.

37. Contract for Labor and Materials Rios furnished Stern, a carpenter, with a set of sketches for a cabinet she wanted built. They orally agreed on a price of $1,000, the type of wood to be used, and the delivery date. Before Stern had begun work or obtained the necessary materials, Rios cancelled the agreement, saying that she planned to move to another apartment and would not need the cabinet.

    a. Was this a contract for sale?   **a.** _____

    b. Was this a contract for labor and materials?   **b.** _____

    c. Is this a contract to sell?   **c.** _____

    d. Will Stern be successful in a suit for damages?   **d.** _____

38. Divisible or Entire Contracts Miro, the owner of a supermarket, contracted with Market Supply Company for one complete checkout counter, including a cash register. After the counter was installed, but before the cash register was delivered, Market Supply Company demanded payment for the checkout counter. Miro refused to pay, claiming that he had contracted for a complete checkout counter, including the cash register, and he would pay when the cash register was installed.

    a. Was this a sales contract?   **a.** _____

    b. Was this a divisible contract?   **b.** _____

    c. Was this an entire contract?   **c.** _____

    d. Does Market Supply have grounds for suit to collect for the portion of the order that was delivered?   **d.** _____

39. Sales Contracts Eamons offered to sell his sailboat, complete with boat trailer, to Fitzgerald for $3,000. Fitzgerald agreed to the offer, gave Eamons a deposit of $100, and said that he would pay the balance when he came back with his car to pick up the boat and trailer. While Fitzgerald was away, the boat caught fire and was destroyed.

    a. Was this a contract for sale?   **a.** _____

    b. Did the parties intend title to pass when Fitzgerald picked up the boat?   **b.** _____

    c. Must Eamons bear the loss?   **c.** _____

    d. Was this a contract to sell?   **d.** _____

Chapter 15 Assessment

CASE ANALYSIS

Study each of the following cases carefully and then briefly state the principle of law and your decision.

40. Substitute Goods Gagne made a good living selling snacks, hamburgers, and refreshments at athletic events. He placed a written order with Pacific Container Company for 4,000 Styrofoam containers to be used to package hamburgers. Gagne requested delivery for three days before the last big football game of the season, and Pacific promised to meet the date. Two days before the game, the order still had not been delivered. In desperation, Gagne ordered 4,000 similar containers from another firm. When his order from Pacific finally arrived, he refused to accept delivery or to pay for it. Pacific Container sued to collect the purchase price. *Is Pacific likely to collect?*

Principle of law:

_____

_____

Decision:

_____

_____

41. Auction Sales Bundeson, a farmer, attended an auction of used farm equipment and successfully bid $1,600 for a tractor. When he returned home, he learned that a real estate developer was eager to buy his farm and build a shopping center on the property. Bundeson agreed to sell his farm, but then realized that he would not need the tractor he had just purchased and that it would be to his advantage to avoid the sale. He notified the auctioneer that he would not go through with the sale because the Uniform Commercial Code required a written contract for personal property sales of $500 or more. *Will Bundeson succeed in avoiding the contract?*

Principle of law:

_____

_____

Decision:

_____

_____

42. Contract for Services Gates contracted with Mennonite Deaconess Home & Hospital for the installation of a new, "one-ply roofing system." The work was to be done by an installer chosen by Mennonite but approved by Gates. When the work was nearly complete, but before Gates had approved the work, the hospital paid the installer 90 percent of the balance due. After inspection, Gates did not approve, and in addition, the roof leaked and had to be replaced at the hospital's expense. The hospital claimed that Gates was responsible for the quality of the work. Gates claimed that he could not be held accountable because the Uniform Commercial Code does not cover service contracts. *Did the contract involve goods or services, and will Gates be held responsible?* [*Mennonite Deaconess Home & Hospital Inc. v. Gates Engineering Co.,* 363 N.W.2d 155 (Nebraska).]

Chapter 15 Assessment

Principle of law:
_____
_____

Decision:
_____
_____

LEGAL RESEARCH

Complete the following activities. Then share your findings with the class.

43. Working in Teams In teams of three or four, interview owners or managers of small businesses to determine what problems they face in their roles as buyers or sellers.
_____
_____
_____
_____
_____

44. Using Technology Using the Internet and search engines, investigate online auctions to determine the operating rules of the various sites. Select one site and briefly summarize the rules.
_____
_____
_____
_____
_____

CHAPTER 16

Agency and Employment

PERFORMANCE OBJECTIVES

After studying this chapter and completing the assessments, you will be able to:

1. Identify the parties to an agency agreement, and describe the relationship of the parties.
2. Classify the major kinds of agents, and discuss the four ways in which an agency may be created.
3. Describe the duties of (a) an agent to a principal, (b) a principal to an agent, (c) a principal to third parties, and (d) an agent to third parties.
4. Differentiate between disclosed principal, partially disclosed principal, and undisclosed principal.
5. Explain how an agency may be terminated.
6. (a) Differentiate between the principal-agent and employer-employee relationship, and (b) describe the duties of an employer and employee to each other.
7. Distinguish independent contractors from agents.

LEGAL TERMS

agent
principal
contract of agency
power of attorney
attorney in fact
express authority
implied authority
apparent authority
irrevocable agency
workers' compensation
independent contractor

OBJECTIVE 1

Identify the parties to an agency agreement, and describe the relationship of the parties.

agent A person authorized to act on behalf of another and subject to the other's control in dealing with third parties.

principal A person who authorizes an agent to act on her or his behalf and subject to her or his control.

contract of agency An agreement between a principal and an agent by which the agent is vested with authority to represent the principal.

PRINCIPAL-AGENT RELATIONSHIPS

It is often necessary or desirable for a person or firm to be represented by another in business or personal dealings with third parties. This relationship is called a principal-agency relationship. The person who represents another is known as the *agent.* The person the agent represents or for whom he or she performs duties is called the *principal.* An agreement between a principal and an agent by which the agent is vested with authority to represent the principal is known as a *contract of agency.* Many, but not all, employees act as agents of their employers. Often an agent is not specifically referred to as an agent, and similarly, some people or firms referred to as agents or as an agency are not really agents at all. For example, an automobile dealership may be referred to as an agency when the dealer may, in fact, be only a seller of the manufacturer's product. As a result, it is important to distinguish between an agency relationship and other forms of relationships.

WHO MAY APPOINT AN AGENT

Any person or corporation that has the legal right to perform an act may delegate its performance to another. Certain acts of a personal character, however, such as voting, serving on juries, rendering professional services, and holding public office, may not be delegated to others.

Any person who is competent to contract may appoint an agent to make contracts for him or her. A minor who has appointed an agent may avoid the contract of agency in some states, just as he or she may avoid other kinds of contracts as discussed in Chapter 9. In some instances, courts have held that minors who operate businesses are bound by the contracts they make. So, too, is a minor who operates a business and whose agent enters into contracts with third parties. In other cases, contracts made with third parties by a minor's agent are voidable at the option of the minor-principal.

EXAMPLE 16.1

Diego, a minor who owned an auto repair shop, employed Fogel, an adult, as head mechanic. Fogel contracted with Mid-City Auto Supply for the purchase of needed supplies and equipment. When the order was delivered, Diego refused to accept it. In some states, Diego has a right to avoid the contract, just as if he had entered into the contract himself.

Who May Be Appointed as an Agent

Anyone who is legally competent to act for himself or herself may also serve as an agent for another. Minors and others who lack the capacity to contract on their own (discussed in Chapter 8) may still be considered competent to represent other persons as agent's if they are capable of properly carrying out an agent's duties.

> **EXAMPLE 16.2**
>
> Jutson, a minor, was employed by Quong as a buyer in the young men's department of a retail clothing store. Jutson's duties included making contracts with third parties in the name of his employer. Jutson's contracts are binding on Quong because of the legal relationship of principal and agent that exists between them. Jutson is expected to exercise good judgment and discretion in making contracts for his employer, just as any other agent would be.

Classes of Agents

Agents are usually classified according to the nature of their relationship with their principals.

General Agent

A *general agent* is a person authorized to assume complete charge of his or her principal's business or who is entrusted with general authority to act for the principal in all business-related matters.

Special Agent

A *special agent* is a person delegated to act only in a particular transaction, under definite instructions, and with specific limits on the scope of his or her authority. Examples of special agents are real estate firms that have been given authority to manage property of an owner, lawyers who have been given authority to manage the financial affairs of a client, and auctioneers who have been designated to represent a seller. Typically, the average real estate broker is not an agent if his or her responsibility is limited to locating a buyer or seller of real property.

Creation of Agency

An agency may be created by agreement, ratification, necessity, or by operation of law.

OBJECTIVE 2

Classify the major kinds of agents and discuss the four ways in which an agency may be created.

Agency by Agreement

The most common method of creating an agency is by contract, or agreement. A contract of agency usually states the rights and duties of the principal and the agent, the duration of the agency, and any other agreements made between the parties. Generally, an agency contract may be oral or written, express or implied. The requirements of the Statute of Frauds, discussed in Chapter 10, concerning the kinds of contracts that must be in writing, also apply to contracts of agency. A contract appointing an agent must be in writing, for example, if the appointment is to extend beyond a year.

The legal document that formally creates an agency is called a *power of attorney.* The precise legal term for the person appointed as agent is *attorney in fact.* When an agent, say Nancy Williams, signs documents on behalf of her principal, say Susan McGowan, the signature is: "Susan McGowan, by Nancy Williams, her attorney in fact."

power of attorney An instrument in writing by which one person, as principal, appoints another person as agent and confers the authority to perform certain specified acts on behalf of the principal.

attorney in fact The person appointed as agent when the power of attorney is exercised.

Agency by Ratification

An *agency by ratification* results when a principal approves an unauthorized act performed by an agent or an act done in the principal's name by an unauthorized person. The ratification must apply to the entire act. A principal cannot accept the benefits of such a transaction and refuse to accept the obligations that are a part of it. A ratification occurs after the fact, while authorization occurs before the fact.

Agency by Necessity

An *agency by necessity* is created when circumstances make such an agency necessary. Although a family relationship does not normally give members of a family the right to act as agents for one another, the law in some states recognizes an agency by necessity when one spouse fails to support the other spouse or any minor children. In these states the spouse, acting as agent for the other spouse, may purchase necessities for himself or herself and the children, even against the will of the nonsupporting spouse, and thereby make the other spouse responsible for payment. Similarly, a minor may purchase necessities if a parent fails to provide them. In other states, current legislation specifies that both the husband and wife are responsible for the support of their minor children.

Agency by Operation of Law

An *agency by operation of law* is created when a court finds the need for an agency to achieve a desired social policy. For example, a child's parent may not be providing the child with certain necessities of life. In this case, a court may appoint an agent, like a guardian, with the authority to purchase whatever necessities the parent has failed to provide. Under such a court-directed agency, the parent would be bound by reasonable contracts made by the agent.

Authority of an Agent

An agent may perform only those acts that have been authorized by the principal or court. If an agent exceeds the authority, he or she can become personally liable unless the unauthorized act was reasonably assumed by a third party to be within the powers delegated to the agent. Just as third parties can be justified in assuming that an agent has certain authority, so, too, an agent can be justified in assuming that he or she has certain authority not specifically stated in the contract of agency. While the courts have an interest in protecting the property and the interests of the principal, they also have an interest in protecting the property and interests of third parties who may have had good reason to rely on the apparent authority of the agent. The authority of an agent can be express, implied, or apparent.

Express or Implied Authority

The authority of an agent to perform the duties that are specifically stated in the contract of agency is known as *express authority,* that is, the authority that has been given by the principal, either orally or in writing. Authority can also be implied by the agency relationship. *Implied authority* is the authority an agent reasonably assumes he or she has that relates to the express authority granted by the principal. If, for example, the agency agreement gives the agent the express authority to purchase goods for the principal, it is implied that the agent can purchase the goods by using the principal's credit. It is easy to confuse implied authority with apparent authority, discussed below. Remember that *implied authority* is the relationship between principal and agent in which the principal implies the authority. This authority is sometimes called "incidental authority." For example, if *A* appoints *B* as an agent and asks *B* to purchase a car for him, *B* has the implied authority to fill the tank with gasoline.

Apparent Authority

The authority that a third party may reasonably assume an agent possesses is known as *apparent authority.* It would be reasonable, for

express authority An agent's authority that the principal voluntarily and specifically sets forth as oral or written instructions in an agency agreement.

implied authority The authority of an agent to perform acts that are necessary or customary to carry out expressly authorized duties.

apparent authority An accountability doctrine whereby a principal, by virtue of words or actions, leads a third party to believe that an agent has authority but no such authority was intended.

example, for a third party to assume that a retail store manager has the authority to set prices, hire salespeople, and purchase merchandise, because the customs of the business usually give store managers this kind of authority. On the other hand, it would be unreasonable for the owner of a multistory building to assume that a store manager had the authority to sign a 20-year lease.

EXAMPLE 16.3

Kertz, the manager of the dress department of a large store, offered a 25 percent reduction on the prices of all merchandise in her department during an end-of-season sale. Although her contract did not specifically give her the authority to reduce prices, such authority is apparent from her duties and responsibilities and from the custom of the business.

Agent's Torts and Crimes

A principal is liable for the torts and crimes of the agent if they are committed at the direction of the principal or while the agent is performing authorized duties during the ordinary course of the business. Thus, if an agent makes a fraudulent statement in a contract within the scope of his or her authority, the principal is responsible. Whether an agent commits a tort or crime willfully, recklessly, or negligently, the fact of the principal's liability is the same. A principal is not released from liability or penalty, for example, if the agent is negligent in the performance of duties and causes injury to another. Although the principal may be liable for an agent's torts or crimes committed while acting within the scope of his or her authority, the agent is not relieved of liability.

EXAMPLE 16.4

Suppose that, in Example 16.3, Kertz purchased, and intended to resell, stolen merchandise. The owner was fully aware of the nature of the merchandise, so both the agent and the principal were subject to criminal prosecution. On the other hand, if only Kertz knew that the merchandise was stolen, the principal would not be subject to prosecution since this was not within the scope of Kertz's authority.

OBJECTIVE 3(a)

Describe the duties of an agent to a principal.

DUTIES OF AN AGENT TO PRINCIPAL

An agent must obey all the principal's reasonable and lawful orders and instructions within the scope of the agency contract. He or she may not perform any act that would betray the principal's trust. The agent may not act for both parties to a contract without consent. The agent may not buy his or her own property for the principal, sell the principal's property to himself or herself, or compete with the principal without the principal's knowledge and consent.

An agent is presumed to possess the qualifications needed to carry out the work of the agency as agreed. The agent is liable for losses to the principal resulting from the agent's incompetence. An agent must keep accurate accounts of his or her transactions conducted as part of the agency agreement. All profits from contracts made by the agent belong to the principal unless other provisions are made in the agency agreement.

EXAMPLE 16.5

Nagy, a sales representative employed by Gilman Products, was authorized to enter into contracts for the installation of burglar alarms. His responsibilities included negotiating prices for the complete installation and arranging for local workers to install the alarms. General guidelines were established for the usual prices of the equipment sold and the fees to be paid for the installation. On the sale of a system to Ballwin, Nagy correctly gauged Ballwin's urgent need for the alarm and his high income. The price quoted was considerably higher than usual for an installation of this kind. Nagy was also fortunate in locating a handyman who was willing to do the work for much less than the usual rate. While there was a very substantial profit because of the higher sales price and the lower installation cost, the higher profits all belong to Gillman (the principal).

DUTIES OF A PRINCIPAL TO AGENT

The principal must pay the agent the compensation agreed in the contract. If a person acts as agent for more than one party with their knowledge, the agent is entitled to receive compensation from each.

A principal must reimburse the agent for any money advanced by the agent in carrying out the principal's instructions and for debts legally paid to third parties on behalf of the principal.

If an agent is in possession of the principal's property or goods, the agent may enforce a right to compensation by placing a lien and refusing to surrender the goods to the principal until payment has been made.

The principal must reimburse the agent for any loss or damage suffered by the agent in the legitimate performance of duties.

OBJECTIVE 3(b)

Describe the duties of a principal to an agent.

EXAMPLE 16.6

> Hillman was employed as a sales representative by the General Merchandise Company. As part of his agreement with the company, he received salary, commission, and traveling expenses. The car that Hillman used was supplied by the company. While on a business trip, Hillman finished his work early and took a side trip to visit friends 75 miles off his normal route. A hit-and-run driver damaged the car through no fault of Hillman. It cost $500 to have it repaired. The company need not reimburse Hillman for the expenditure because the expenditure was an expense unrelated to the discharge of his duties.

DUTIES OF A PRINCIPAL TO THIRD PARTIES

OBJECTIVE 3(c)
Describe the duties of a principal to third parties.

A principal is responsible to third parties for all agreements made by the agent on behalf of the principal if the agent acted within the scope of his or her authority, either express or implied. If, however, the agreement was not authorized by the principal, and if it was obviously or apparently outside the scope of the agent's employment, the principal is not liable. Third parties are liable to the principal on all lawful contracts made with him or her by the agent.

DUTIES OF AN AGENT TO THIRD PARTIES

OBJECTIVE 3(d)
Describe the duties of an agent to third parties.

The relationship between agents and third parties, and whether an agent can be held personally responsible, is influenced by a number of factors, including the degree to which a principal is disclosed.

Disclosed Principal

OBJECTIVE 4
Differentiate between disclosed principal, partially disclosed principal, and undisclosed principal.

If an agent represents a *disclosed principal,* that is, a principal whose identity is known to the third party, the agent can be held personally responsible if the agent exceeds his or her authority.

If an agent exceeds his or her authority, either actual or apparent, in making contracts for the principal, the agent becomes personally liable for damages to any third party who suffers injury. The agent has warranted (guaranteed) his or her authority, and by exceeding it, cannot bind the principal.

Agents are also liable when they make contracts in their own names. To escape personal liability, an agent must disclose to third parties that he or she is merely an agent. This fact can be revealed by signing a contract, "Louise Smith, by Susan Jacobs, Agent" or by merely signing the principal's name.

Partially Disclosed Principal

It is not sufficient for the agent to sign his or her own name and the title, "Agent." If the agent does so, he or she will have to assume responsibility. If an agent exceeds his or her authority, the principal must disclaim responsibility before the agent can be held responsible.

When the agent acts on behalf of an unknown principal and informs the third party that he or she is acting on behalf of another, the principal is known as a *partially disclosed principal.* Because the third party does not know the identity of the principal, the contract is with the agent and the agent is a party to the contract.

Undisclosed Principal

When a third party is not informed and is unaware that the agent is acting as agent for someone else, the unidentified or unknown principal is known as an *undisclosed principal.* In the event of a dispute, a third party can hold the agent responsible. If a contract concerns the sale of goods, for example, the agent is, in fact, the seller. If the third party learns the identity of the principal after entering into the contract with the agent, the third party can hold either the principal or the agent, or both responsible.

> **EXAMPLE 16.7**
>
> Watanabe, as agent for Allegheny Supply, purchased 500 bags of Portland cement from Northwest Cement without disclosing his agent status. After shipment, Watanabe attempted to cancel the order. Northwest Cement can sue Watanabe because he became a party to the contract when he neglected to disclose his principal during his dealings with Northwest. If Northwest Cement learned that Watanabe was an agent for Allegheny, Northwest might choose to sue Allegheny instead, or it could sue both Allegheny and Watanabe.

TERMINATION OF AGENCY

Agency is a type of contract, and like other contracts, may be terminated by agreement, by performance, or by operation of law.

When an agency contract is terminated by an act of the parties, either the principal and the agent have mutually agreed on termination, the principal has dismissed the agent, or the agent has given up the position.

If an agency exists "at will," the principal has the right to revoke the agency agreement and discharge the agent for incompetence, disloyalty, or similar shortcomings, or for no reason at all.

OBJECTIVE 5

Explain how an agency may be terminated.

A principal who dismisses an agent must give notice of the termination of the agency to all third parties who are accustomed to doing business with the agent or who have knowledge of the appointment. Failure to do so will render the principal liable on any further contracts made by the agent in the principal's name because the agent would still have apparent authority in the eyes of third parties until they have been notified.

A principal may not revoke an agency contract if the agent has an interest in the subject matter of the agency in addition to the remuneration (e.g., salary, commissions) that he or she receives for services. Such a contract is an ***irrevocable agency,*** or an agency coupled with an interest. An agency agreement that authorizes an agent to sell specific property, deduct commissions, and apply the proceeds to the credit of a debt that the principal owes the agent is an example of an irrevocable agency. Partners are agents for each other and cannot dismiss each other.

irrevocable agency An agency contract that cannot be terminated by a principal in which the agent has an interest in the subject matter of the agency in addition to the remuneration that he or she receives for services.

EXAMPLE 16.8

A manufacturer of office machines offered Irving, for $25,000, a three-year exclusive agency to sell a new model of fax machine. Irving accepted the offer and paid the money. The manufacturer-principal cannot revoke the agreement until the end of the three-year period. This contract is an agency coupled with an interest.

The agency relationship may be terminated by death, insanity, illness, impossibility of performance, or bankruptcy. With the exception of an agency coupled with an interest, the death of either party terminates the agency contract immediately.

DIFFERENCES BETWEEN PRINCIPAL-AGENT AND EMPLOYER-EMPLOYEE RELATIONSHIPS

The legal principles governing the relationship of principal and agent and of employer and employee are, in many respects, the same. The main difference between principal-agent and employer-employee relationships is the employer's power to control the activities of the employee. Whereas an agency agreement brings about a relationship between a principal and a third party that results in a contract, an employee has no such rights or powers. An employee acts under the employer's direction and subject to the employer's control.

The employer controls not only what shall be done by the employee but also how it shall be done. If, however, an employee is required

OBJECTIVE 6(a)

Differentiate between the principal-agent and employer-employee relationship.

to perform duties for the employer that necessitate the exercise of judgment and discretion and that result in a contractual relationship between the employer and a third party, then the employee has the status of an agent even without a formal contract of agency.

> **EXAMPLE 16.9**
>
> Stein operated an automobile repair shop and frequently sent a beginning mechanic, Lopez, to the local auto parts distributor to pick up parts needed for repairs. The cost of the parts was charged to Stein's account, which he paid periodically.

Clearly, Lopez is an employee, not an agent. If Lopez bought parts for his own use, the parts distributor could still collect from Stein because an employer is responsible for the acts of employees performed within the scope of the employee's duties. If Stein had directed Lopez to negotiate an agreement for a quantity discount on parts with the supplier for future purchases, Lopez would have become an agent.

Some employees are agents, while others are not. Some agents are also employees, and some are not. The two relationships are judged independently.

DUTIES OF EMPLOYER AND EMPLOYEE TO EACH OTHER

An employer must pay an employee the amount agreed on, subject to company policy, union contracts, and government mandates, for his or her services. The employer must protect the employee by providing a safe and sanitary place to work, proper tools and machinery for the job to be performed, careful and competent employees with whom to work, and an environment free of harassment. The employer must warn the employee of any danger that exists in connection with the work. Under ***workers' compensation,*** any employee who is injured in the course of employment is permitted to recover for injury regardless of its cause unless the injury was due to the injured person's gross negligence or intentional act. An employee must obey his or her employer's lawful orders concerning the employment, exercise good faith toward the employer, and do his or her work carefully and conscientiously.

The acts of an employee committed while performing duties are considered the acts of the employer. The employer is liable, therefore, to third parties for injuries caused by an employee, whether the acts are willful or negligent, provided that they were committed by the employee within the ordinary course of employment.

OBJECTIVE 6(b)

Describe the duties of an employer and an employee to each other.

workers' compensation
Worker protection provided for by state statutes that compensates covered workers or their dependents for injury, disease, or death that occurs on the job or as a result of it.

An employee is liable personally for wrongful acts that result in injuries to a third party, whether they are intentional or the result of negligence.

> **EXAMPLE 16.10**
>
> Marek was employed in the shipping department of Margo Stores, Inc. Normally, customers did not come into the shipping department. However, one day Otler came to the department to pick up a shipment, and Marek carelessly ran into him with a hand truck and injured Otler's leg. Both Margo Stores and Marek are liable to Otler for the injury. As a practical matter, an injured third party who is interested in receiving a financial settlement will usually sue the employer, since the employer generally has more financial resources as well as insurance.

Independent Contractors

An *independent contractor* is a person or firm that performs services for another. Examples of independent contractors are freelance writers and photographers, private-duty nurses, painters, and plumbers. Independent contractors are not under the direct control of the person

---

independent contractor One who contracts to do a job and who retains complete control over the methods employed to obtain completion.

Photo 16.1

Independent Contractors

Individuals and companies often prefer to hire independent contractors instead of full-time employees. *What are some of the reasons for this preference?*

PART 3   Sales, Agency, and Consumer Protection

who engages them. It is important to distinguish between employees and independent contractors because employees usually cannot sue their employers for on-the-job injuries (workers' compensation laws generally prohibit such actions), whereas independent contractors can sue in such cases. An employer is responsible for an employee's torts committed within the scope of employment. The person who engages an independent contractor, on the other hand, is not responsible for the contractor's torts.

OBJECTIVE 7
Distinguish independent contractors from agents.

EXAMPLE 16.11
> Chu, a retired magazine editor, was engaged by Fifth National Bank to write and edit a monthly employee newspaper. She often spent time in the offices of the bank interviewing various staff members, but was paid a flat fee for each issue of the newspaper. Chu would not be considered a member of the bank's staff and did not have the legal status of an employee.

If Chu were to libel someone in her writing, the bank would not be responsible for the tort (although the bank would probably be named as a co-defendant in a suit). Also, if Chu were injured while in the offices of the bank, she would not be prevented, as an employee would be, from suing the bank for its negligence.

CHAPTER SUMMARY

1 The person who represents another is known as the agent. The person the agent represents or for whom he or she works is called the principal. An agreement between a principal and an agent by which the agent is vested with authority to represent the principal is known as a contract of agency.

2 The major kinds of agents are general agents, special agents, and independent contractors. An agency can be created by agreement, ratification, necessity, or operation of law.

3 **(a)** An agent has a duty to obey all of the principal's reasonable and lawful orders and instructions within the scope of the agency contract. **(b)** The principal must pay the agent the compensation agreed upon in the contract. He or she must also reimburse the agent for any money advanced by the agent in carrying out the principal's instructions and for debts legally paid to third parties.

The principal must also reimburse the agent for any loss or damage suffered by the agent in the legitimate performance of duties. **(c)** A principal is responsible to third parties for all agreements made by the agent on behalf of the principal if the agent acted within the scope of his or her authority, either express or implied. **(d)** The duties of a principal toward third parties depend on whether the principal is disclosed, partially disclosed, or undisclosed.

4 A disclosed principal is one whose identity is known to the third party. When the agent acts on behalf of an unknown principal and informs the third party that he or she is acting on behalf of another, the principal is known as a partially disclosed principal. When a third party is not informed and is unaware that the agent is acting as an agent for someone else, the unidentified or unknown principal is known as an undisclosed principal.

5 Agency can be terminated by agreement, performance, or operation of law. Specific reasons may include death, insanity, illness, impossibility of performance, or bankruptcy.

6 **(a)** The main difference between principal-agent and employer-employee relationships is the employer's power to control the activities of the employee. **(b)** An employer must pay an employee the amount agreed on for his or her services, and provide the employee with a safe and sanitary workplace, proper tools for the job to be performed, and careful and competent employees with whom to work. The employer must also warn an employee of any danger that exists in connection with the work. The employee must obey his or her employer's lawful orders concerning employment, exercise good faith toward the employer, and do his or her work carefully and conscientiously.

7 Unlike employees, independent contractors can sue their employer for on-the-job injuries. An employer is also liable for an employee's torts, but not those of an independent contractor, that are committed within the scope of employment.

Chapter 16 Assessment

MATCHING LEGAL TERMS

Match each of the following definitions with the correct term in the list below. Write the letter of your choice in the answer column.

- **a.** agent
- **b.** agency by necessity
- **c.** agency by ratification
- **d.** apparent authority
- **e.** attorney in fact
- **f.** express authority
- **g.** contract of agency
- **h.** disclosed principal
- **i.** implied authority
- **j.** irrevocable agency
- **k.** partially disclosed principal
- **l.** power of attorney
- **m.** principal
- **n.** undisclosed principal
- **o.** workers' compensation laws

1. The party in an agency contract who represents another.   1.____
2. A principal whose existence and identity is not known to third parties.   2.____
3. The legal document that formally creates an agency.   3.____
4. The party in an agency contract who delegates power to another.   4.____
5. An agreement between a principal and an agent in which the agent is vested with authority to represent the principal.   5.____
6. An agency coupled with an interest in the subject matter of the contract services.   6.____
7. The authority possessed by an agent that may be reasonably assumed by a third party.   7.____
8. The authority possessed by an agent that is specifically stated in the agency contract.   8.____
9. A principal who is known to third parties.   9.____
10. The precise legal term for an agent.   10.____
11. The agency that results when a person approves an unauthorized act done in the principal's name by a person who has no authority to act as agent.   11.____
12. The agency that results when a person fails to support his or her spouse or minor children.   12.____
13. The authority an agent reasonably assumes he or she has that relates to the express authority granted by the principal.   13.____
14. A principal whose identity is not known to a third party who knows he or she is dealing with an agent.   14.____
15. Legislation that requires employers to pay for the care and treatment of workers who are injured or become ill in the course of employment.   15.____

Agency and Employment   CHAPTER 16

Chapter 16 Assessment

TRUE/FALSE QUIZ

Indicate whether each of the following statements is true or false by writing *T* or *F* in the answer column.

16. A general agent is a person authorized to assume complete charge of his or her principal's business.

    16. _____

17. Workers' compensation laws are designed to ensure that all employees are paid fairly.

    17. _____

18. An agent is reasonable in assuming that he or she has the authority that is related to the responsibilities covered in the contract of agency.

    18. _____

19. An agent is liable to the principal for any losses that result from the agent's neglect or incompetence.

    19. _____

20. A principal is liable for an agent's torts and crimes if they were committed in the ordinary course of the agent's performance of authorized duties.

    20. _____

21. An agent representing a partially disclosed principal becomes a party to the contract.

    21. _____

22. In a contract between an agent and a third party, the agent can be held responsible to the third party if the identity of the principal is not disclosed.

    22. _____

23. An employee who performs only mechanical acts under the employer's direction and is subject to the employer's control is still legally an agent.

    23. _____

24. Acts of an employee while performing duties of employment are considered the acts of the employer.

    24. _____

25. An independent contractor is not covered by workers' compensation laws that normally cover employees.

    25. _____

DISCUSSION QUESTIONS

Answer the following questions and discuss them in class.

26. Identify the parties to an agency agreement and describe the relationship of the parties.

    _____

    _____

27. Classify the major kinds of agents and discuss the three ways in which an agency may be created.

    _____

    _____

    _____

Chapter 16 Assessment

28. Differentiate between disclosed principal, partially disclosed principal, and undisclosed principal.

29. Explain how an agency may be terminated.

30. Differentiate between the principal-agent and employer-employee relationships, and describe the duties of an employer and employee to each other.

31. Distinguish independent contractors from agents.

THINKING CRITICALLY ABOUT THE LAW

Answer the following questions, which require you to think critically about the legal principles that you learned about in this chapter.

32. Agency It is often difficult for a third party to distinguish between an agent and an employee. Are there times when it is important to distinguish between the two? Should there be a clear identification system established? Explain your answer.

33. Agent's Liability A principal is liable for the torts and crimes committed by an agent if he or she is performing authorized duties. To what extent should the agent also be liable?

Agency and Employment   CHAPTER 16

Chapter 16 Assessment

34. **Undisclosed Principal** Does it seem likely that a third party would be suspicious if an agent disclosed the existence but not the identity of his or her principal? Explain your answer.

   _____
   _____
   _____

35. **Employees as Agents** Does it place an unnecessary burden on third parties to determine whether he or she is dealing with an agent or an employee? Why or why not?

   _____
   _____
   _____

36. **A Question of Ethics** In some states, an agent's contracts may be voided if he or she is acting for a principal who is a minor. Is this fair to a third party with whom the contract is signed? Explain your answer.

   _____
   _____
   _____

CASE QUESTIONS

Study each case below and answer the questions that follow by writing *Yes* or *No* in the answer column.

37. **Agent or Employee** Apex Truck Company had an established rule that its truck drivers were not allowed to carry passengers in the trucks. Further, this rule was included in the contract between the union and the company. Peterman, a driver for Apex, enjoyed the company of a friend and invited him to ride in his truck on a day's delivery trip. As a result of Peterman's carelessness during the trip, the truck was involved in a collision, and his friend was seriously injured.

   a. Is the employer responsible to third parties for injuries caused by an employee in the normal performance of employment? a. _____

   b. Would Peterman be held responsible for the injuries? b. _____

   c. Is an employer liable to third parties for all actions of an employee? c. _____

38. **Apparent Authority** A shipper asked a truck driver to deliver a shipment of chemicals and to protect them from freezing while in route. The driver assured the shipper that the chemicals would be carried in heated trucks. When the shipper learned that the shipment had been damaged in transit by freezing, she demanded payment from the trucking company.

   a. Did the truck driver have the authority to assure the shipper that the chemicals would be protected from freezing? a. _____

   b. Would the trucking company be responsible for the damaged chemicals? b. _____

   c. Did the truck driver have apparent authority? c. _____

   d. Was the truck driver acting as an agent? d. _____

Chapter 16 Assessment

39. **Agency by Necessity** The Chalmers family lived in poverty. In spite of their destitute condition, Chalmers' wife bought several articles of jewelry for herself and an expensive painting for their home. When the retailer attempted to collect payment, Chalmers refused to pay. The merchant claimed that Mrs. Chalmers was acting as an agent for Mr. Chalmers.

   a. Is this an example of agency by necessity?

   b. Is this an example of agency by ratification?

   c. Will the retailer succeed in collecting from Mr. Chalmers?

   d. Does the law recognize agency by necessity when a spouse makes essential purchases?

   a. _____
   b. _____
   c. _____
   d. _____

CASE ANALYSIS

Study each of the following cases carefully and then briefly state the principle of law and your decision.

40. **Responsibility of Employer** Franklyn, a clerical employee of Woodbury Manufacturing Company, told Buron that he was an agent of the company and made a contract on behalf of Woodbury. Later Woodbury repudiated the contract and claimed that Franklyn had no authority to enter into a contract. Buron sued Franklyn, who claimed that he really thought he had the authority. Franklyn pointed out that at no time did he tell Buron he had the authority that Buron thought he did. *Will Buron succeed in her suit?*

   Principle of law:

   _____
   _____

   Decision:

   _____
   _____
   _____

41. **Undisclosed Principal** Ferrara made a contract with Perret without informing her that he was acting on behalf of National Steel Wire Company. Ferrara had the authority, as provided in his contract of agency with National. The contract was breached, and Perret sued National. National claimed that Perret cannot sue because her contract was with Ferrara, not with National. *Will Perret be successful in her suit of National?*

   Principle of law:

   _____
   _____

   Decision:

   _____
   _____
   _____

Chapter 16 Assessment

42. **Agency** Blodgett, while walking on a public sidewalk, was injured when a large piece of wood fell from a construction job at the offices of Olympic Savings and Loan Association. Drury Construction Company was doing the work. Blodgett sued both Olympic and Drury, claiming that Drury was an agent for Olympic. Olympic denied both responsibility for the injury and the existence of an agency relationship with Drury. *Will Blodgett succeed in her suit against Olympic?* [*Blodgett v. Olympic Savings and Loan Association,* 646 P.2d 139 (Washington).]

Principle of law:

Decision:

LEGAL RESEARCH

Complete the following activities. Then share your findings with the class.

43. **Working in Teams** In teams of three or four, interview managers of small businesses to determine whether the firm is a sole proprietorship, partnership, corporation, franchisee, or agency. In the case of an agency, discuss the nature of the agent's relationship with the principal including agent's authority and other matters.

44. **Using Technology** Using the Internet and search engines, investigate "contract of agency" and identify key terms in such a contract. List these terms and briefly explain why they are important.

PART 3 Sales, Agency, and Consumer Protection

CHAPTER 17

WARRANTIES AND PRODUCT LIABILITY

PERFORMANCE OBJECTIVES

After studying this chapter and completing the assessments, you will be able to:

1. Explain the term *warranty*, and distinguish between express and implied warranties.
2. Provide examples of two kinds of express warranties and three kinds of implied warranties.
3. Explain the effect of warranties offered after a transaction has been completed.
4. Explain disclaimers and the requirements for them to be legally valid.
5. Explain the provisions of the Magnuson-Moss Warranty Act.
6. Describe product liability and the tort on which it is based.
7. Identify the kinds of businesses that can be charged with product liability.
8. Explain the legal reasoning behind the concept of strict liability and weigh its consequences for businesspeople and consumers.

LEGAL TERMS

warranty
express warranty
implied warranty
custom of the marketplace
puffing
disclaimer
implied warranty of merchantability
implied warranty of fitness of purpose
full warranty
limited warranty
product liability
strict liability

OBJECTIVE 1

Explain the term *warranty,* and distinguish between express and implied warranties.

warranty A guarantee or promise made by the manufacturer or seller that the goods or services offered really are what they are claimed to be, or that goods or services are what a reasonable person has a right to expect.

express warranty An explicit, specifically stated promise.

implied warranty A guarantee suggested or inferred from known facts and circumstances.

OBJECTIVE 2

Provide examples of two kinds of express warranties and three kinds of implied warranties.

PROTECTING CONSUMERS AND THIRD PARTIES

A seller or manufacturer has a significant legal responsibility to buyers and users of goods and services, as well as to third parties. These obligations are covered by the law of sales, contract law, the Uniform Commercial Code, and tort law. Together, these various applications of the law provide remedies to buyers and users of goods and services, and to third parties who suffer financial or physical injury. Two important aspects of the law concern warranties and product liability. These topics will be covered in this chapter.

A *warranty,* as the term is used in the UCC, is a guarantee or promise made by the manufacturer or seller that the goods and services offered really are what they are claimed to be, or that the goods or services are what a reasonable person has a right to expect. As discussed in greater detail in this chapter, one warranty that is recognized by the UCC is an *express warranty,* that is, an explicit, specifically stated promise [UCC 2-313]. Another recognized warranty is an *implied warranty,* which is a guarantee suggested or inferred from known facts and circumstances [UCC 2-312 to 2-315]. A seller of goods makes an implied warranty that he or she actually holds title, that is, owns the goods.

Like many other areas of the law, rights and obligations are all subject to the courts' applications of the law. In addition, the law is always changing as new legislation is passed and as the courts make decisions that break new ground, sometimes overruling decisions made in earlier, similar cases.

While the law dealing with warranties is intended to protect the general public, it often has the effect of limiting the seller's obligations and responsibilities. For example, a warranty for an appliance might state that the manufacturer will replace it if it fails during the first 90 days. While this promise may be a benefit to the buyer, it also relieves the manufacturer of any obligation if the appliance fails after 90 days. However, if a manufacturer or seller issues statements limiting a warranty to provide less protection than the law requires, such statements may discourage a buyer from legal action, but they do not have the force of law and the manufacturer or seller is still responsible for breaches of warranty.

EXPRESS WARRANTIES

Express warranties can be made in many ways, including by promise, description, sample, or model. They can also be made before or after a sale. However, not everything that a salesperson communicates can be construed as a warranty, and sometimes salespeople can disclaim express warranties.

Express Warranty by Promise

An *express warranty* is an explicit, definite promise by the seller that the goods will have certain characteristics. An express warranty that is made by the seller to the buyer and becomes part of the basis of the agreement creates an explicit warranty that the goods will be as promised. If a written warranty is vague and indefinite, the court may apply the **custom of the marketplace,** or what such a warranty usually means in similar transactions [UCC 2-313(1)(a)].

Interpretations of the UCC requirement that the warranty be part of the basis of the agreement mean that the buyer must have relied on the promise and did not dismiss it as merely sales talk.

It is not required that a seller make a specific written or oral statement of warranty for an express warranty to exist. Actions of the seller may also be considered express warranties.

custom of the marketplace
What a warranty usually means in similar transactions.

> **EXAMPLE 17.1**
>
> Wiggins, a homeowner, asked Grosso Lumber for a quantity of outdoor plywood. The seller delivered 10 sheets of plywood, and in so doing the seller warranted that the plywood was suitable for outdoor use.

Express Warranty by Description, Sample, or Model

The Uniform Commercial Code [UCC 2-313(1)(b)] states that any description of goods that is made part of the basis of the agreement creates an express warranty that the goods will conform to the description. A manufacturer of electric wire, for example, that accepts orders for No. 8 electric wire would be held to have warranted that the wire shipped will in fact be No. 8.

The UCC also states that any sample or model that is made part of the basis of the agreement creates an express warranty that the whole of the goods will conform to the sample or model [UCC 2-313(1)(c)]. A buyer may refuse delivered goods if the goods are not the same as described by the seller or do not conform to the sample or model used by the seller to effect the sale.

> **EXAMPLE 17.2**
>
> Clawson Appliance had on display a General Electric microwave oven Model JE 48. Prospective buyers were encouraged to examine the appliance, take measurements, and make note of technical specifications.

> By using this model as a basis for the sale, Clawson warranted that any oven it sold would be substantially the same as the model.

The Timing of the Express Warranty

While most express warranties are made before or during a sales transaction, written or oral statements issued by the seller after the transaction has been completed can also be interpreted as express warranties. Marketers recognize the uneasiness that many buyers experience after having made a buying decision. "Did I make the right decision?" "Should I have purchased the Ford instead of the Buick?" In an effort to reduce this uneasiness, sellers often send mailings to assure buyers that they did indeed make a wise purchase. These statements can also be regarded as express warranties.

The Effect of Sellers' "Puffing"

The UCC states that "it is not necessary to the creation of an express warranty that the seller use formal words such as 'warrant' or 'guarantee' or have a specific intention to make a warranty, but an affirmation merely of the value of the goods or a statement purporting to be merely the seller's opinion or commendation of the goods does not create a warranty" [UCC 2-313(2)]. Consequently, sales talk, or "*puffing*," however sincere and persuasive, is not a warranty. This is true even if the buyer relies on such statements.

EXAMPLE 17.3
A salesperson in an appliance store told a customer that the washing machine she was considering "is the best in the world and will be trouble-free for many years to come." Such a statement is considered a mere expression of opinion—puffing, not a warranty—and would be unenforceable.

Only when statements of fact about quality of merchandise, construction, price, durability, performance, effectiveness, and safety are made part of the contract and later prove false may the buyer bring action against the seller.

Disclaimers of Express Warranties

Toward limiting the effect of express warranties, some sellers put specific limitations in the warranty. Such a denial or repudiation in an express warranty is known as a *disclaimer* and serves to limit the effectiveness of a warranty. Suppose, for example, that a manufacturer claims a pump will deliver a certain number of gallons of water per

---

OBJECTIVE 3
Explain the effect of warranties offered after a transaction has been completed.

puffing Sales talk that merely expresses a seller's opinion or commendation of the goods, and does not constitute a warranty.

OBJECTIVE 4
Explain disclaimers and the requirements for them to be legally valid.

disclaimer A denial or repudiation in an express warranty that places specific limitations in the warranty.

minute. A disclaimer may say, "Warranty does not cover applications where water must be pumped into storage tanks." The UCC provides that modifications of warranties that limit their effect are unenforceable (UCC 2-316).

Another example of a disclaimer is when oral warranties are given and then followed by a written document containing a disclaimer. This might happen when a salesperson is attempting to be persuasive and promises more orally than the firm is willing to promise in writing.

IMPLIED WARRANTIES

In addition to the provisions dealing with express warranties, the Uniform Commercial Code also makes specific references to *implied warranties,* which are those warranties not made explicitly, but that a buyer might reasonably expect a seller to honor. Implied warranties relate to the title and quality of goods.

Title

The UCC provides that "the title conveyed shall be good, and its transfer rightful: and the goods shall be delivered free from any security interest or other lien or encumbrance of which the buyer has no knowledge" [UCC 2-312(1)(a, b)]. This passage simply means the seller promises that (1) he or she is the real owner of the goods offered for sale, (2) the seller has the right to sell the goods, and (3) there are no claims or liens of any kind against the goods that might later cause the seller to lose title to someone else who might claim ownership or an interest in the goods.

EXAMPLE 17.4

Futaba bought a used car from Jalik, a college friend, for $4,800. A short time later, a local bank notified Futaba that Jalik owed $700 to the bank, had used the car as security for the loan, and the indebtedness was recorded at the appropriate county office. As a result, the bank had an interest in the car. Futaba may sue his former friend for his loss on the grounds that the implied warranty of title had been breached.

Quality

The law recognizes two types of warranties of quality: (1) warranties of merchantability, which are given solely by merchants; and

(2) warranties of fitness for a particular purpose, which apply more generally, to merchants as well as to others.

Implied Warranty of Merchantability

The law assumes that the goods sold by a merchant-seller are fit to be sold or resold, and therefore carry an *implied warranty of merchantability.* A "merchant" is anyone who deals in goods of the kind being sold in the ordinary course of business or who presents himself or herself as having the skills or knowledge relating to the goods [UCC 2-104(1)]. The UCC provides that when a merchant sells goods, he or she warrants that the goods will:

- pass without objection in the trade under the contract description
- be fit for the ordinary purposes for which such goods are sold
- be adequately contained, packaged, and labeled as the agreement may require
- conform to the promises or statements of fact made on the container or label [UCC 2-314(2)]

This implied warranty is probably the most important warranty from the viewpoint of the buyer. It imposes a general duty upon the merchant-seller to furnish goods that are at least of minimum acceptable quality.

Implied Warranty of Fitness for Particular Purpose

If a seller, at the time of making a contract, knows or has reason to know any particular purpose for which the goods are required and that the buyer is relying on the seller's skill or judgment in selecting or furnishing suitable goods, there is an *implied warranty of fitness of purpose.* That is, the goods must be fit for their intended use [UCC 2-315].

> **EXAMPLE 17.5**
>
> Business Printers, Inc., was seeking a new high-speed press that would be suitable for printing high-quality, four-color brochures. Bonhomme, the manufacturer's representative, thinking more of his commission than the needs of his customer, recommended a particular press. When the press was delivered and installed, Business Printers discovered that it printed only black. Clearly, Bonhomme violated the manufacturer's implied warranty of fitness of purpose.

It must be noted, however, that an implied warranty of fitness exists even if the buyer does not make his or her intended use of the merchandise known to the seller. To recover for breach of the implied warranty of fitness of purpose, a buyer must prove that (1) the seller knew

implied warranty of merchantability The law's assumption that goods sold by a merchant-seller are fit to be sold and are adequate for the ordinary purposes for which such goods are sold.

implied warranty of fitness of purpose The law's assumption that goods are fit for their intended use.

or had reason to know the buyer's purpose, (2) the seller knew or had reason to know that the buyer was relying on the seller's skill or judgment, and (3) that the buyer did rely on the seller's skill or judgment.

Disclaimers of Implied Warranties

The two important implied warranties of merchantability and of fitness for a particular purpose may be disclaimed in several ways. The UCC provides specific rules that must be followed by a seller who wants to avoid the responsibility of the implied warranties. A disclaimer of the warranty of merchantability must mention the word *merchantability*. If the disclaimer is in writing, it must be conspicuous; that is, it cannot be buried in the fine print of the contract [UCC 2-316]. In fact, most states require a specific type size.

Disclaimers of the warranty of fitness for a particular purpose must be in writing and must be conspicuous. Such warranties are excluded by the use of expressions such as "as is" or "with all faults," or other language that would call the buyer's attention to the exclusion of warranty [UCC 2-316].

MAGNUSON-MOSS WARRANTY LEGISLATION

Even with the protection provided by the Uniform Commercial Code, consumers were not always protected adequately. In 1975, Congress passed the Magnuson-Moss Warranty Act to reduce or eliminate many different kinds of consumer abuses relating to warranties.

Provisions of Magnuson-Moss

The Magnuson-Moss Warranty Act applies only when written warranties are made voluntarily on consumer products that cost more than $10. The act requires that such warranties must be labeled as either "full" or "limited." The act applies only to purchases by consumers of tangible personal property normally used for personal, family, or household purposes, and not to commercial or industrial transactions. Because the act is a federal law, it affects only warranties on products that are sold in interstate commerce.

The type of warranty to which the act applies is much more narrowly defined than is an express warranty under the UCC. Specifically, warranties covered by the act are (1) any written statement of fact made by a seller to a purchaser relating to the quality or performance of a product and stating that the product is free of defects or that it will meet a specified level of performance over a period of time; or (2) a written promise to "refund, repair, replace, or take other action"

OBJECTIVE 5

Explain the provisions of the Magnuson-Moss Warranty Act.

if a product fails to meet written specifications. Obviously, express warranties that are not in writing, such as those created by verbal description or by sample, continue to be governed solely by the UCC, even though a consumer transaction is involved.

Distinction Between Full and Limited Warranty

The Magnuson-Moss Act makes a distinction between a *full warranty* and a *limited warranty.*

Full Warranty A *full warranty* promises that a defective product will be repaired without charge and within a reasonable time after a complaint has been made. If the product cannot be repaired within a reasonable time, the consumer may have either a replacement product or a refund of the purchase price. The consumer is not required to do anything unreasonable, such as ship a heavy product back to the factory, to obtain warranty service. In addition, a full warranty applies to anyone who owns the product during the warranty period, not just the original buyer. No time limitation can be placed on a full warranty.

Limited Warranty A written warranty that does not meet the minimum requirements of a full warranty must be designated as a ***limited warranty.*** If only a time limitation distinguishes a limited warranty from a full warranty, then the act permits the seller to indicate this fact by such language as "full 12-month warranty."

PRODUCT LIABILITY

The two main avenues of redress for injured parties are breach of warranty and liability for the tort of negligence. The various warranties described previously provide that certain remedies, available to a buyer of goods, can be shown to be warranted in one way or another as part of a contract. The law also provides other remedies in cases in which a person has been injured by a defective product. The liability of a manufacturer or seller for injury to users and third parties is known as *product liability.*

Tort Law

The tort of negligence was introduced in Chapter 4. If the buyer, user, or a third party can prove that he or she suffered injury as a result of the negligent design or manufacture of a product, a court will often award damages under tort law.

---

full warranty The promise that a defective product will be repaired without charge and within a reasonable time after a complaint has been made.

limited warranty A written warranty that does not meet the minimum requirements of a fully warranty.

OBJECTIVE 6

Describe product liability and the tort on which it is based.

product liability The liability of a manufacturer or seller for injury to users and third parties.

EXAMPLE 17.6

> Grimshaw, a 13-year-old girl, was a passenger in a Ford Pinto driven by a neighbor. The Pinto stalled, and while motionless, was hit from behind by another car. Moments later, the Pinto's fuel tank exploded, with the result that the driver was killed and Grimshaw was burned over 90 percent of her body. Grimshaw's family sued Ford Motor Company, claiming that Ford was negligent in designing the Pinto so that the fuel tank was in a dangerous position, with "conscious disregard of public safety." The jury awarded the family of the driver $666,000 and Grimshaw $2,841,000 as compensation for her injuries. In addition, the jury awarded Grimshaw another $125,000,000 as punitive damages (that is, to punish Ford). The judge, feeling that the punitive award was excessive, lowered it to $3,500,000.

While not every negligence suit results in such high awards, there are many cases in which the injured party has been awarded more than a million dollars.

Reasons for Product Liability Injury Claims

Certain product characteristics often become the basis of claims against manufacturers and sellers.

Product Flaw A product flaw has been defined as an abnormality or a condition that was not intended, and that makes the product more dangerous than it would have been had it been produced as intended.

Failure to Warn It is believed that a product can cause injury as a result of manufacturers' or sellers' failure to warn users of dangers inherent in the product.

Design Defect It has been claimed that a product that caused injury was essentially hazardous if it was more dangerous than a buyer with ordinary knowledge would know. As a result, a hazard that is not obvious to an ordinary person would be considered a design defect even if the hazard were obvious to a trained technician or engineer.

Who Can Be Held Liable for Product-Related Injuries?

The most obvious target of an injured party is the manufacturer of the defective product. However, others in the channel of distribution have also been found liable. Retailers are particularly vulnerable when the manufacturer is insolvent or is a corporation that has been dissolved, or is unreachable—such as a manufacturer in a foreign country.

OBJECTIVE 7

Identify the kinds of businesses that can be charged with product liability.

Consequently, retailers need to be particularly careful to choose manufacturers that act responsibly and are also financially secure.

In addition to the risks faced by retailers, others involved in the distribution of products found to be defective also face risks of being held liable. This group includes manufacturers of component parts, assemblers of products, endorsers of products, licensors of trademarks, and licensors of patents.

Strict Liability

Strict liability (sometimes called *absolute liability*) is liability without the necessity of proving fault. Under traditional tort law, the injured party had to prove that the manufacturer was negligent in producing a product. It was often difficult for injured parties to prove negligence for several reasons, and the defenses of manufacturers were often effective. The financial burden to society and the hardships suffered by injured parties that resulted were of grave concern to many legal scholars and jurists. In 1944, California Supreme Court Judge Trayner, and in 1969 California Justice Peters, suggested that it should not be necessary for an injured person to prove negligence. They believed that the manufacturer is in a better position than the user of a product to prevent injuries because the manufacturer has the opportunity to design safe products. Also, they felt that the manufacturer is in a position to pay for the damages suffered by a user of a product, regardless of whether the manufacturer was in fact negligent, because the manufacturer can buy insurance that pays the injured party. The manufacturer can then pass on the cost of insurance to all users of the product.

Today, the concept of strict liability is generally accepted. Still, there is considerable activity in various state legislatures with a view toward "tort reform" and other efforts to curb abuses of the system. One consequence of strict liability is that companies are sometimes hesitant to introduce new or innovative products because of the fear of strict liability lawsuits.

OBJECTIVE 8

Explain the legal reasoning behind the concept of strict liability and weigh its consequences for businesspeople and consumers.

strict liability Liability without the necessity of proving fault.

CHAPTER SUMMARY

1. A warranty is a guarantee or promise made by the manufacturer or seller that goods or services offered are what they are claimed to be or what a reasonable person has a right to expect. An express warranty is explicitly stated, whereas an implied warranty is suggested or inferred from known facts or circumstances.

2 Express warranties can be made by promise, description, sample, or model. Implied warranties include that of ownership when title is passed, and of merchantabilty and fitness for a particular purpose in contracts for the sale of goods.

3 Warranties can be disclaimed in several ways. To be disclaimed, the implied warranty of merchantability must be in writing, conspicuous, and in most states, in font of a certain size. Warranties of fitness for a particular purpose must be in writing, conspicuous, and use language such as "as is" or "with all faults."

4 The Magnuson-Moss Warranty Act is aimed to reduce or eliminate different kinds of consumer abuses relating to warranties.

5 Oral or written assurances offered after a transaction has been completed can be interpreted as an express warranty.

6 Product liability is the liability of a manufacturer or seller for injury to users and third parties. These claims are based on the tort of negligence and may pertain to a product flaw, failure to warn, or design defect.

7 Parties that can be held liable for product-related injuries include manufacturers, retailers, and others involved in the distribution chain such as component manufacturers, assemblers, endorsers, and licensors of trademarks or patents.

8 Strict liability for defective products is based on the idea that manufacturers are best positioned to prevent injuries because they have the opportunity to design safe products, can most easily pay for injuries resulting from their products, and can purchase insurance that pays injured parties. However, the consequences are that costs are passed along to consumers in the form of higher prices, and businesses are often hesitant to introduce new and innovative products for fear of strict liability suits.

Chapter 17 Assessment

MATCHING LEGAL TERMS

Match each of the following definitions with the correct term in the list below. Write the letter of your choice in the answer column.

- **a.** disclaimer
- **b.** express warranty
- **c.** full warranty
- **d.** implied warranty
- **e.** limited warranty
- **f.** product liability
- **g.** strict liability
- **h.** warranty of fitness for particular purpose
- **i.** warrant of merchantability
- **j.** warranty of title

1. A warranty provided by law for the protection of the buyer and not specifically included in the agreement.

2. An implied warranty that goods are suitable for the specific purpose for which they are sold.

3. An application of tort law in which a manufacturer can be held liable for injuries regardless of whether fault can be proven.

4. A denial or repudiation of an express warranty made at the time of sale.

5. An implied warranty that the seller actually owns the goods sold.

6. The liability of a manufacturer for injury to users and third parties.

7. An implied warranty that goods sold are fit for the ordinary purpose for which they are intended.

8. A written or oral promise or statement regarding goods sold.

9. Under the Magnuson-Moss Act, a warranty that requires a seller to repair or replace a defective product without charge within a reasonable time.

10. Under the Magnuson-Moss Act, the designation that must be used if a warranty does not meet the minimum requirements.

TRUE/FALSE QUIZ

Indicate whether each of the following statements is true or false by writing *T* or *F* in the answer column.

11. Warranties are promises or statements made by manufacturers or sellers.

12. The concept of product liability concerns the liability of manufacturers or sellers for injury caused by their products.

13. Any warranty can be cancelled if the seller claims that it is causing him or her to lose money.

14. A specific oral promise made by a seller is an implied warranty.

Chapter 17 Assessment

15. The Uniform Commercial Code clearly specifies requirements that manufacturers or sellers must follow in making disclaimers.   15. _____
16. Sales talk, or puffing, is considered a warranty.   16. _____
17. The implied warranty of merchantability means that all merchants warrant their goods to be of the highest quality.   17. _____
18. There is an implied warranty of title with the sale of merchandise that means the seller actually owns the goods.   18. _____
19. The court can apply the custom of the marketplace when a warranty is vague and indefinite.   19. _____
20. The sale of food involves the implied warranty of merchantability.   20. _____
21. Promises and statements issued after the sale have no effect on the warranty of a product.   21. _____
22. A disclaimer of a warranty of fitness for a particular purpose is effective if it includes such expression as "as is" or "with all faults."   22. _____
23. An alteration that a buyer might make in a product is known as a product flaw.   23. _____
24. Courts have held that manufacturers and sellers have a duty to warn users of dangerous or hazardous characteristics of a product.   24. _____
25. Only manufacturers can be held liable in product liability lawsuits.   25. _____

DISCUSSION QUESTIONS

Answer the following questions and discuss them in class.

26. Explain the term *warranty* and distinguish between express and implied warranties.

_____
_____
_____

27. Provide examples of two kinds of express warranties and three kinds of implied warranties.

_____
_____
_____

28. Explain disclaimers and the requirements for them to be legally valid.

_____
_____
_____

Chapter 17 Assessment

29. Explain the provisions of the Magnuson-Moss Warranty Act.

30. Describe product liability and the tort on which it is based.

31. Identify the kinds of business that can be charged with product liability.

32. Explain the legal reasoning behind the concept of strict liability, and weigh its consequences for business people and consumers.

33. Explain the effect of warranties offered after a transaction has been completed.

THINKING CRITICALLY ABOUT THE LAW

Answer the following questions, which require you to think critically about the legal principles that you learned in this chapter.

34. Product Liability Where should the responsibility lie for product safety—manufacturers, retailers, users, or government regulators? Explain your answer.

35. Disclaimers What is the primary objective of warranty disclaimers? Explain your answer.

PART 3   Sales, Agency, and Consumer Protection

Chapter 17 Assessment

36. Disclaimers Should the law distinguish between a reasonable basis for a warranty disclaimer and one that attempts to substantially negate the warranty? Why or why not?

37. Oral Warranties How would the law distinguish between oral statements of warranty and "puffing?"

38. A Question of Ethics Is it ethical to promote as a selling point, the seemingly generous provisions of a warranty, when it merely restates what the law requires? Explain your answer.

CASE QUESTIONS

Study each case below and answer the questions that follow by writing *Yes* or *No* in the answer column.

39. Warranty Buynoski, the operator of a restaurant, served a dinner to Costas. Costas had nearly finished her soup when she found several metal chips in the bottom of her bowl. When Costas showed the chips to Buynoski, the restaurant owner was very apologetic and offered not to charge for the meal. Costas, still angry at the risk to which she had been exposed, said, "I'll see you in court!"

    a. Does Costas have a case involving a warranty?   a. _____

    b. Had Buynoski offered an express warranty?   b. _____

    c. Could Costas claim an implied warranty of fitness of purpose?   c. _____

40. Disclaimer Liang was about to purchase an air-conditioner for her apartment at a close-out sale at Irving Appliance. The salesperson assured her that the unit was large enough to cool the apartment she described. The price was right, but she was nervous when the salesperson said, "Remember that you're taking this unit 'as is'." When she found that the unit would not cool the apartment, she returned to the store, where she claimed that the unit had been sold with an implied warranty of fitness for a particular purpose. The salesperson reminded her that he had said, "as is."

    a. Can the oral disclaimer void the implied warranty of fitness for a particular purpose?   a. _____

    b. Is there an implied warranty still in effect?   b. _____

    c. Is Liang reasonable in her demand?   c. _____

Chapter 17 Assessment

41. **Product Liability** Eddington operated a toy store and carried merchandise from both domestic as well as foreign manufacturers. As the holiday season approached, he found that he could reduce his costs by importing a stuffed toy from a developing country. One of the toys was responsible for an injury to a child, and the parents brought a product liability suit, charging Eddington. He claimed that he was unaware of the defects of the toy, since he did not manufacture it, but only sold it.

   a. Were the parents of the injured child right to bring suit against Eddington instead of the manufacturer? a. _____

   b. Can a seller be held liable for defective products? b. _____

   c. Is there anyone else who could be named in the suit? c. _____

42. **Warranty** Pathek sold a pair of skis to Whelan, making no specific warranties or promises of any kind other than letting Whelan examine and try them. In fact, Pathek did not own the skis; he had only rented them. When the true owner claimed them, Whelan demanded his money back. Pathek defended his actions by stating that he had made no warranty of any kind.

   a. Did Pathek give an implied warranty of title? a. _____

   b. Will Whelan be able to recover his money? b. _____

   c. Did Pathek give an express warranty of any kind? c. _____

CASE ANALYSIS

Study each of the following cases carefully and then briefly state the principle of law and your decision.

43. **Warranty** Walters bought a power lawnmower. Attached to the engine was a tag that read in part, "For 90 days from purchase date Power Engine Company will replace for the original purchaser, free of charge, any part or parts found, upon examination at any Factory Authorized Dealer, to be defective under normal use and service." Two weeks after purchase the starter mechanism broke, and Walters returned her machine to the Factory Authorized Dealer. *Can the dealer be compelled to repair the mower?*

   Principle of law:
   _____
   _____

   Decision:
   _____
   _____

44. **Warranty** Adano Restaurant Supply, which sells only to commercial customers, sold 200 plastic dishes to Airport Diner. When the owner of the diner attempted to wash the dishes in the dishwasher, they were distorted by the heat. Airport Diner claimed that there was an implied warranty of fitness for a particular purpose, since most restaurants used the same type of dishwasher it did. When the owner bought the dishes from Adano, he assumed that they could be washed with the equipment in his restaurant. *Does Airport Diner have a legal remedy?*

Chapter 17 Assessment

Principle of law:

Decision:

45. Disclaimer Ferguson contracted to buy a quantity of knitting yarn. After receipt, he cut it and knitted it into sweaters. At this point, he discovered color variations from one piece to another. Ferguson refused to pay the agreed price, claiming that the yarn had been sold with a warranty of merchantability. The seller, Wilson Trading Corporation, sued to collect the contract price and pointed out that the sales contract provided, "no claims . . . shall be allowed if made after weaving, knitting, or processing, or more than 10 days after receipt of shipment. . . ." Ferguson viewed the time-limit clause as modifying the warranty of merchantability, which was stated explicitly elsewhere in the contract, and that the disclaimer was in conflict with the warranty. *Will the disclaimer be viewed as negating the warranty?* [*Wilson Trading Corp. v. David Ferguson, Ltd.,* 244 N.E.2d 685 (New York).]

Principle of law:

Decision:

LEGAL RESEARCH

Complete the following activities. Then share your findings with the class.

46. Working in Teams In teams of three or four visit an appliance retailer. Check the warranties on various products to find out their duration, disclaimers, and any other related information. What safety information is included?

47. Using Technology Using the Internet and search engines, find additional information about the Magnuson-Moss Warranty Act.

Warranties and Product Liability CHAPTER 17 279

CHAPTER 18

Professional Responsibility

PERFORMANCE OBJECTIVES

After studying this chapter and completing the assessments, you will be able to:

1. Discuss why the malpractice of professionals is considered more serious than the negligence by nonprofessionals.

2. Discuss the four elements of negligence.

3. Provide examples of professional malpractice that might be caused by accountants, architects, attorneys, engineers, financial planners, insurance agents and brokers, nurses, physicians, and psychiatrists.

4. Explain how the malpractice or negligence of a professional might cause injury to third parties.

5. Distinguish between insurance agents and insurance brokers.

6. Explain how professionals protect themselves against the losses that might result from being found liable for malpractice or negligence.

LEGAL TERMS

professional
malpractice
consortium
churning
whole life insurance
term insurance

Professional's Liability

All competent parties are liable for their negligence or their failure to meet their contractual obligations. This chapter is devoted to the liability of a special category of persons—professionals—because their work poses great risk of injury and the need for redress (remedy).

A *professional* is a person who does highly specialized work that depends on special abilities, education, experience, and knowledge. Professionals generally are members of state and national professional societies, such as bar associations or medical societies, that establish entry requirements, set standards for performance, and discipline members. Many professionals must pass a state-administered examination and gain accreditation, certification, or a license before they are permitted to work in their field.

While nearly everyone is subject to a lawsuit for negligence, suits by injured parties charging malpractice or negligence can involve professionals, such as doctors, dentists, accountants, attorneys, and others. In some cases, third parties can also sue if they are able to show, among other things, that they suffered injury as a result of a professional's malpractice.

OBJECTIVE 1

Discuss why the malpractice of professionals is considered more serious than the negligence of nonprofessionals.

professional A person who does highly specialized work that depends on special abilities, education, experience, and knowledge.

Liability for Malpractice and Negligence

Malpractice is a subdivision of negligence that refers to a professional's improper or immoral conduct in the performance of his or her duties through carelessness or ignorance. The term is usually applied to physicians, dentists, lawyers, or accountants. One could think of malpractice as a special kind of negligence of which certain professionals are accused. Perhaps this distinction between malpractice and other kinds of negligence stems from the fact that the performance of certain professionals is known as a practice and the people served are called patients or clients rather than customers. For the purpose of this discussion, however, there is little difference between malpractice and negligence, which was first introduced in Chapter 4.

malpractice A subdivision of negligence that refers to a professional's improper or immoral conduct in the performance of his or her duties through carelessness or ignorance.

Who Can Be Charged With Negligence

Almost anyone can be charged with, and found liable for, negligence that causes injury to others. Perhaps the most widely discussed legal actions for negligence involve healthcare providers—physicians, surgeons, psychiatrists, dentists, and nurses. The list of professionals, however, includes many others, such as attorneys, architects, accountants, clergy, financial planners, engineers, insurance agents, and almost anyone who, in the performance of his or her professional duties, may cause injury to others.

ESSENTIALS OF NEGLIGENCE

A claim of negligence must prove that four elements existed; if even one of these is not present, an action for negligence will be dismissed. The required elements are as follows:

1. A relationship existed in which the actor (the person performing the service) had a duty to another party, and if the actor neglected to perform the duty, the other party would be harmed or would not receive the benefit that might be expected.
2. The actor breached the standard of care or performance.
3. The failure of the actor to perform according to the standard was the direct or proximate cause of the injury.
4. The injured party suffered a loss from the failure of the actor to perform his or her duty.

PROFESSIONAL MALPRACTICE LIABILITY

The following discussion explains how specific professionals can commit malpractice or engage in behavior that might result in charges of negligence.

Liability of Healthcare Providers

The malpractice of medical professionals occurs when their actions demonstrate that they have failed to observe accepted standards of performance, and as a result, the patient suffers injury or death. Negligent performance might involve a physician's incorrect diagnosis of a patient's condition, failure to order appropriate tests, failure to prescribe appropriate medications, or an incorrect prognosis. Medications prescribed must be appropriate in terms of treatment and with due concern for possible side effects. A physician can also be liable for failing to inform a patient of the risks involved in a particular treatment or operation, or of other alternatives available.

Normally the negligence of a physician does not cause injury to third parties, except in cases in which his or her negligence results in the patient's death or permanent disability. In such cases, the physician

---

OBJECTIVE 2

Discuss the four elements of negligence.

OBJECTIVE 3

Provide examples of professional malpractice that might be caused by accountants, architects, attorneys, engineers, financial planners, insurance agents and brokers, nurses, physicians, and psychiatrists.

can be held liable to a surviving spouse, children, or parents for wrongful death. If the physician's negligence results only in the patient's disability, a spouse can claim the loss of companionship, or **consortium.**

A psychiatrist who learns from a patient that he or she intends to do harm to another has the legal responsibility to inform the possible victim and the police. Failure to do so would be considered negligence.

Although nurses customarily work under the supervision of physicians, a nurse can be found negligent, for example, for incorrectly administering prescribed medications or failing to properly monitor a patient's condition.

EXAMPLE 18.1

> Simmons, a nurse-anesthetist, was charged with negligence in administering a spinal anesthetic that resulted in a patient's paralysis. Expert testimony introduced at the trial showed that it was standard practice to place a pillow under the patient's head when giving a spinal anesthetic to prevent the rise of the anesthetic in the spinal canal. Simmons failed to use the pillow. She was held to have been negligent.

Pharmacists who dispense drugs other than those specifically prescribed by qualified professionals can also be charged with negligence if the incorrectly dispensed drugs cause injury to the legal user. Pharmacists are also liable if they dispense multiple medications that, when taken together, cause injury.

Liability of Accountants and Financial Planners

Accounting professionals are liable to their clients and to third parties when they fail to observe established standards for their profession, and if such failure has caused clients or third parties to suffer a loss.

An accountant is liable to a client when, as a result of his or her negligence, for example, he or she fails to discover or conceals evidence that a client's employee has been embezzling funds, or if the accountant fails to file appropriate and timely tax returns with the result that penalties are assessed against the client.

Previously, it was generally held that an accountant had a responsibility only to his or her client. In recent years, however, accountants' liability has grown to the extent that they have been found liable to third parties who have relied on the accountant's work, such as creditors or investors.

OBJECTIVE 4

Explain how the malpractice or negligence of a professional might cause injury to third parties.

consortium Companionship, usually of a spouse.

> **EXAMPLE 18.2**
>
> The accounting firm of Casey and Ming prepared an analysis and audit of the Reference Publishing Company that was used in securing a loan from First National Bank. The report showed that Reference was a solvent firm in good financial condition, although it actually was not. First National relied on the report in making the requested loan. In spite of the loan, Reference Publishing failed and the loan could not be repaid. First National sued Casey and Ming charging negligence. Casey and Ming claimed that the bank had no course of action against it because Reference Publishing had retained their firm and their only duty of care was to their client. It was held that because the use of the audit in securing a loan from a bank was a reasonably foreseeable event, First National did, indeed, have a cause of action against Casey and Ming.

In Example 18.2, if Casey and Ming's inaccurate audit resulted from deliberate actions, and with full knowledge of the inaccuracies, it would not have been the tort of negligence, but rather the tort of fraud, and may have subjected the firm to criminal prosecution as well.

Financial planning is a relatively new profession in which practitioners attempt to advise their clients, who are usually individuals rather than businesses, on the best ways to manage their financial affairs. The work of financial planners involves an initial analysis of the client's personal situation, including age, income, dependents, current assets, and obligations. The analysis leads to recommendations that typically involve insurance, investments, and pensions. When the client relies on the financial planner's recommendations and suffers a loss, the financial planner can be sued for negligence. Most lawsuits against financial planners so far have involved accusations of negligence in recommending various forms of investments and insurance. Some financial planners are licensed to buy and sell securities. The practitioner can be sued if he or she engages in ***churning,*** that is, unreasonable buying or selling of securities to generate commissions.

churning The unreasonable buying or selling of securities to generate commissions.

Liability of Architects and Engineers

Architects design and supervise the construction of buildings and other structures. The engineering profession includes many specialties, including mechanical, electrical, and civil engineering. Each specialty involves work that, if done negligently, could result in injury. Engineers usually design complicated devices or installations, such as bridges and power-generating stations. Both architects and engineers are subject to lawsuits for negligence if their work results in injury to parties with whom they have contracted or to third parties.

Typically, architects and engineers are licensed by the states and must demonstrate their competence by passing various examinations and providing evidence of a certain level of education. These professionals do not actually build structures but design them and often supervise the construction. If an architect, for example, negligently designs a building and supervises its construction, and during or after construction it turns out that some of the windows fall out on windy days, the architect is liable to both the firm that hired the architect and to any innocent passerby who may have been killed or injured by the falling windows, or to the spouse or children of the innocent victim.

Liability of Attorneys

An attorney is liable to a client if he or she fails to exercise due care in handling a client's affairs. If the attorney is in general practice, the standard of performance is that of other attorneys engaged in similar practices in the area. If the attorney is in a specialized practice such as real estate or immigration law, it is the performance of other attorneys engaged in similar practice by which he or she will be judged.

An attorney can be negligent if he or she fails to act in a timely fashion in filing claims or bringing suit before the statute of limitations (a legal time limit) prevents such suit. Negligence can also be established if an attorney fails to properly investigate matters related to a client's case, such as seeking clear title to property in real estate matters.

Photo 18.1

Liability of Attorneys

An attorney is liable to his or her client if he or she fails to act with due care in managing a client's affairs. *What are some ways in which a lawyer can fail to exercise a sufficient degree of professional responsibility?*

Most instances of attorney malpractice involve only the attorney and his or her client. In recent years, however, in some states third parties have successfully sued attorneys who have negligently drawn wills with the result that a third party failed to inherit property as intended. In other cases, attorneys have been held liable to third parties when an attorney planned an estate in such a way that higher taxes were required as a result of the attorney's negligence.

Liability of Insurance Agents and Brokers

Insurance agents (representatives of companies) and insurance brokers (representatives of insurance buyers) are deemed to possess superior knowledge of insurance and to have the ability to use their expertise to protect buyers against various kinds of losses. As a result, buyers of insurance look to agents and brokers to recommend appropriate coverage. When an agent or broker fails to recommend appropriate insurance and the buyer suffers a loss that could have been prevented or lessened, the agent or broker can be charged with negligence.

Negligence on the part of insurance agents and brokers generally relates to their alleged failure to recommend the purchase of either the right kind of insurance to protect against a specific type of loss, or failure to recommend appropriate amounts of insurance. Negligence of agents and brokers can occur in the fields of both life insurance as well as property/casualty insurance.

OBJECTIVE 5

Distinguish between insurance agents and insurance brokers.

EXAMPLE 18.3

Ted Gurchi was concerned about the welfare of his wife and two children and what would happen to them in the event of his untimely death. He discussed his concerns with a life insurance agent, who recommended a whole life policy with a face value of $100,000. For the same cost, Gurchi could have purchased $700,000 of term insurance. Within a year Gurchi was killed in an automobile accident. The proceeds of the policy, $100,000, barely replaced Gurchi's earnings for two years. When the widow realized how little benefit she received as compared to the benefits she would have received had her late husband purchased term insurance, she sued the agent and the insurance company for whom the agent worked, charging that the agent had sold her husband an inappropriate form of insurance. Both the agent and the company were found liable for negligence.

The preceding case rested on the agent's recommendation of a ***whole life insurance*** policy with a face value of $100,000. (A whole life policy is a relatively costly form of insurance protection, but it

whole life insurance
A relatively costly form of insurance protection that includes a savings feature.

includes a savings feature.) For the same premium, Gurchi could have purchased $700,000 of **term insurance** (pure insurance with no savings feature). Also, the agent probably received a higher commission for selling the whole life policy.

term insurance A form of pure life insurance that does not include a savings feature.

> **EXAMPLE 18.4**
>
> Petras was involved in an accident with an uninsured driver. He then learned that his insurance policy had only minimum coverage and was inadequate to cover his loss. He also learned that for an additional $5 per year, he could have had more coverage that would have covered the complete loss. Petras sued the agent for negligence in failing to inform him about other insurance options available.

Other Professionals' Liability

Most other types of professionals are subject to suit for negligence when they fail to perform according to the standards expected of them. Educators and schools have been sued for failure to educate students to an expected level.

Directors and officers of corporations have been successfully sued for breach of their duty resulting from negligence, error, or omission. Stockholders may sue officers and directors, demanding reimbursement from the firm for damages resulting from an action or inaction by an officer or director. Third parties such as creditors, competitors, and the government may also bring suits.

REDUCING PROFESSIONALS' RISK OF LIABILITY

Nearly all professionals carry some form of liability insurance to protect against the possibility of being adjudged negligent. But more than insurance should be considered. Many professional groups conduct workshops and training sessions to help members of the profession reduce the risks that lead to negligent actions and the lawsuits that frequently result. Associations of insurance agents, for example, instruct their members on how best to conduct themselves in dealing with clients to minimize the risk of negligence.

OBJECTIVE 6

Explain how professionals protect themselves against the losses that might result from being found liable for malpractice or negligence.

CHAPTER SUMMARY

1. Professional malpractice is considered more serious than the negligence of nonprofessionals because of the special and serious nature of their work poses a greater risk of injury to the public.

Professionals typically require special abilities, education, experience, and knowledge, making it especially important that they exercise these qualities in a responsible manner.

2 The four elements of negligence are **(a)** a relationship existed in which the actor had a duty to another party, and if the actor neglected to perform the duty, the other party would be harmed or would not receive the benefit that might be expected; **(b)** the actor breached the standard of care or performance; **(c)** the failure of the actor to perform according to the standard was the direct or proximate cause of the injury; and **(d)** the injured party suffered a loss from the failure of the actor to perform his or her duty.

3 Examples of professional malpractice include an architect who fails to design a structure with proper materials; an attorney who fails to inform a client of his or her legal options; a financial planner who fails to explain investment risks; an insurance agent who fails to recommend the right kind of insurance; a physician who fails to prescribe the proper treatment; and a psychiatrist who fails to alert the police and intended victim of a client's plan to cause harm.

4 Malpractice can cause injury to third parties in a variety of ways. Examples include: **(a)** in healthcare, when malpractice causes the death to a parent or spouse; **(b)** in insurance, when malpractice causes hardship on surviving family members; **(c)** in accounting, when malpractice harms creditors or investors who relied upon an accountant's assessment of a company's books; and **(d)** in architecture, when malpractice causes a third party to be injured on premises designed by an architect.

5 Insurance agents represent companies; insurance brokers represent insurance buyers.

6 Professionals can protect themselves against losses resulting from being found liable for malpractice or negligence by buying liability insurance. Many professional groups conduct workshops and training sessions to help professionals reduce the risks that lead to negligent conduct and the lawsuits that often result.

Chapter 18 Assessment

MATCHING LEGAL TERMS

Match each of the following definitions with the correct term in the list below. Write the letter of your choice in the answer column.

- **a.** malpractice
- **b.** professional
- **c.** term insurance
- **d.** whole life insurance

1. A form of life insurance that is pure insurance, with no savings feature.   1. _____
2. A professional's improper or immoral conduct in the performance of his or her duties, whether through intent, carelessness, or ignorance.   2. _____
3. A person who performs highly specialized work requiring special abilities, education, experience, and knowledge.   3. _____
4. A form of life insurance that includes a savings feature.   4. _____

TRUE/FALSE QUIZ

Indicate whether each of the following statements is true or false by writing *T* or *F* in the answer column.

5. Malpractice refers to the negligence of physicians, architects, attorneys, accountants, and other professionals.   5. _____
6. Only professionals such as doctors and lawyers can be charged with negligence.   6. _____
7. For a charge of negligence to be successful, it must be proved that a relationship existed in which the provider of services had a duty to another, that the provider neglected to perform the duty, and that the other party was harmed or did not receive the benefit that was expected.   7. _____
8. For a charge of negligence to be successful, it must be proved that a standard of care or performance has been established.   8. _____
9. A psychiatrist who learns from a patient that the patient intends to do harm to another has the legal duty to inform the intended victim or the police.   9. _____
10. For a charge of negligence to be successful, it must be proved that the failure of the provider to perform according to the established standard was the direct cause of injury.   10. _____
11. Nurses cannot be found to be negligent because they work under the direct supervision of a doctor.   11. _____
12. For a charge of negligence to be successful, it must be proved that the injured party suffered damages as a result of the failure of the provider to perform his or her duty according to the established standard.   12. _____

Professional Responsibility   CHAPTER 18   289

Chapter 18 Assessment

13. Accounting professionals have a duty only to their client.

13. ____

14. An accountant who deliberately falsifies financial data can be charged only with negligence.

14. ____

15. An insurance agent or broker can be charged with negligence only if he or she cancels a policy.

15. ____

16. An insurance agent or broker can be charged with negligence for failing to recommend appropriate amounts of insurance coverage.

16. ____

17. An architect who designed a building that is later destroyed in a windstorm cannot be charged with negligence because architects have no control over the weather.

17. ____

18. Clergy cannot be charged with negligence because they have a calling.

18. ____

19. Directors and officers of corporations can be charged with breach of their duty resulting from action or inaction.

19. ____

DISCUSSION QUESTIONS

Answer the following questions and discuss them in class.

20. Discuss why the malpractice of professionals is considered more serious by society than negligence by nonprofessionals.

21. Of the four elements of negligence discussed in the text, is one of them more critical than the others? Why?

22. Explain how the malpractice or negligence of a professional might cause injury to third parties.

23. What are some injuries suffered by third parties for which accountants can be found liable?

Chapter 18 Assessment

24. Distinguish between insurance agents and brokers. Do you think that one should bear greater responsibility than the other for advising buyers about their insurance needs? Explain your answer.

25. What are some ways that professionals can reduce their risk of negligence lawsuits?

THINKING CRITICALLY ABOUT THE LAW

Answer the following questions, which require you to think critically about the legal principles that you learned in this chapter.

26. Professional Negligence Does the licensing of professionals guard against negligence? Give the pros and cons.

27. Malpractice Insurance Does having malpractice insurance lessen the care taken by professionals? Explain.

28. Liability Insurance Because most professionals carry liability insurance, what is the role of the insurance industry in ensuring the competency of professionals?

29. Conduct of Financial Advisors Where should the line be drawn between a reasonable number of securities transactions and churning? Explain your answer.

Professional Responsibility   CHAPTER 18   291

Chapter 18 Assessment

CASE QUESTIONS

Study each case below and answer the questions that follow by writing *Yes* or *No* in the answer column.

30. Accountants Liability Franklin Weiss, an accountant, prepared the usual accounting records for Malucic, the operator of a clothing store. Malucic, using the records prepared by Weiss, entered into negotiations with Walling for the sale of the business. After the transaction was complete, Walling discovered that the business potential had been greatly exaggerated and there was little chance the clothing store would ever reach the potential suggested by the records. Walling felt that he had been deceived by the accountant's financial reports.

   a. Does Walling have a course of action against Malucic? a. _____

   b. Does Walling have a course of action against Weiss? b. _____

   c. Do accountants have a responsibility to persons other than their clients? c. _____

31. Malpractice Philasen underwent a minor operation for the removal of his tonsils. Serious complications developed when he was administered penicillin, to which he was allergic. The doctor denied responsibility because he did not know about the allergy.

   a. Does it seem that Philasen has a cause of action against the doctor? a. _____

   b. Does it seem that Philasen has a cause of action against the hospital? b. _____

   c. Was Philasen partly responsible for failing to voluntarily tell the doctor of his allergy? c. _____

32. Negligence Cho, an architect, designed a large ranch house for Spadacini. Within two years after construction, the house began to tilt to one side. When questioned, Cho said that it was not his fault because it was designed properly and the problems must be the fault of the contractor. Spadacini produced the original contract, which called for Cho to supervise the work of the contractor.

   a. Can the architect be held responsible for the substandard work of the contractor? a. _____

   b. Does the architect have a course of action against the contractor? b. _____

   c. Can Spadacini share some of the blame for not supervising the work as well? c. _____

CASE ANALYSIS

Study each of the following cases carefully and then briefly state the principle of law and your decision.

33. Malpractice Rosemary Smith was represented by Jerome Lewis, an attorney, in a divorce action against General Clarance Smith. General Smith was employed by the California National Guard and, as a state employee, belonged to the State Employees' Retirement System. Lewis advised Mrs. Smith that her husband's retirement benefits were not community property and thus would not be considered in the litigation or distributed by the trial court. Six months after the divorce was final, Lewis petitioned the court to amend the

Chapter 18 Assessment

decree because of his mistake in not including the retirement benefits as community property in the divorce action. It was pointed out that major authoritative reference works, which attorneys routinely consult for a brief and reliable discussion of the law, provided that vested retirement benefits were generally subject to community-property treatment. The court refused Lewis, and Rosemary Smith brought suit against Lewis for malpractice. *Will Lewis be found to be guilty of malpractice?* [*Smith v. Lewis,* 530 P.2d 589 (California).]

Principle of law:

_____

_____

Decision:

_____

_____

34. Negligence During construction at Alma College, an inadequately reinforced wall of an excavation caved in and killed Clark, a worker employed by the general contractor, Beard. The contract between the architect, Sarvis, and Beard provided that Sarvis had supervisory authority over the construction and thus had the responsibility for the safety of all workers at the site. The administrator of Clark's estate brought suit against Sarvis, charging negligence. *Will a suit against the architect succeed?* [*Swarthout v. Beard,* 190 N.W.2d 373 (Michigan).]

Principle of law:

_____

_____

Decision:

_____

_____

35. Negligence Mansfield contacted his insurance agent to obtain an automobile insurance liability policy to be effective as of February 10. On February 14, Mansfield was involved in an accident while operating his car. The agent provided a policy with an effective date of February 24, which did not cover the loss resulting from the accident. Mansfield charged the agent with a breach of the contract to procure insurance as well as negligence in the performance of his responsibilities. *Will Mansfield succeed in his suit?* [*Mansfield v. Federal Services Finance Corp.,* 111 A.2d 322 (New Hampshire).]

Principle of law:

_____

_____

Decision:

_____

_____

Chapter 18 Assessment

36. **Negligence** Chard completed an educational program in financial planning and was awarded the certification offered by a national association of financial planners. He set up a business to offer his financial planning services to the general public. One of his first clients, Roblee, sought Chard's advice on investments and insurance. Chard prepared a written report that included a recommendation to purchase shares in a real estate venture. Because Chard neglected to verify the financial status of the real estate venture, Roblee lost a significant amount of the money he had invested in the venture. With almost no prospect of ever recovering the investment, he sued Chard, charging negligence. *Is Roblee likely to succeed in the suit?*

Principle of law:

Decision:

LEGAL RESEARCH

Complete the following activities. Then share your findings with the class.

37. **Working in Teams** Working in teams of three or four, interview the risk manager of a medium-sized business to learn how insurance is used as a part of an overall risk management strategy. The discussion should include various forms of insurance, such as life insurance including key person, property-casualty including professional liability, and so on.

38. **Using Technology** Using the Internet and search engines, investigate a case of professional liability and the basis on which it was decided. Also, research selected terms from the text, particularly the related expression *wrongful death*.

294 PART 3 Sales, Agency, and Consumer Protection

PART IV

PROPERTY

CHAPTER 19	Real and Personal Property
CHAPTER 20	Bailments
CHAPTER 21	Landlord-Tenant Relations
CHAPTER 22	Wills, Intestacy, and Trusts

CHAPTER 19

Real and Personal Property

PERFORMANCE OBJECTIVES

After studying this chapter and completing the assessments, you will be able to:

1. Distinguish between real and personal property.
2. Describe the responsibilities of a finder of lost or abandoned property.
3. Distinguish between lost and mislaid personal property.
4. Discuss both gifts *inter vivos* and *in causa mortis*.
5. Explain how someone can acquire property by accession.
6. Discuss severalty ownership, tenancy in common, joint tenancy, tenancy by the entirety, and community property.
7. Distinguish between freehold and leasehold estates.
8. Describe the characteristics of the several types of freehold estates as they relate to ownership interest.
9. Explain the characteristics of various kinds of deeds, and transfers of real property through eminent domain and adverse possession.

LEGAL TERMS

real property
personal property
gift
accession
joint tenancy
tenancy by the entirety
tenancy in common
community property
easement
freehold estate
leasehold estate
fee simple
life estate
leasehold estate
deed
eminent domain
adverse possession

What is Property?

To many people, the term *property* suggests land. Actually, property should be viewed more broadly because it also includes tangible goods such as cars, furniture, and clothing. And there are also other, intangible possessions, such as a patent, the right to drill for oil on someone else's land, and a copyright of a creative work such as a book. These intangibles are also property. Consequently, the broad term *property* includes both tangible and intangible personal property.

Distinguishing Between Real and Personal Property

The law distinguishes between real and personal property and governs each in different ways.

Real Property

Under common law, ownership of real property extended from the center of the earth to the highest point in the sky. A person owned not only a portion of the earth's crust but also the ground under it and the airspace above it. As a result, **real property** comprises not only land, but also includes minerals such oil, iron ore, and other rights. In addition, real property includes any permanent additions to the land, such as houses, buildings, and trees.

Personal Property

Personal property describes property, other than land, both tangible and intangible. Tangible property includes such items as furniture, clothing, books, and so on. Intangible personal property includes such things as patents, copyrights, goodwill, trademarks, and service marks.

When Does Real Property Become Personal Property?

Because real property consists of land and things permanently attached to it, it follows that when things are removed from real property, they become personal property. When a tree is cut down, for example, it becomes personal property. So, too, grain growing in a field becomes personal property when it is harvested.

When Does Personal Property Become Real Property?

Personal property such as trees or shrubbery purchased at a nursery become real property when they are planted. Similarly, personal

OBJECTIVE 1

Distinguish between real and personal property.

real property The ground and everything permanently attached to it, including land, buildings, trees and shrubs; the air space above the land, and ground below are also included.

personal property Tangible and intangible property that is not real property.

property such as lumber and bricks become real property when they are used in a building erected on real property.

> **EXAMPLE 19.1**
>
> Blanchard owned one-half acre of vacant property. He hired a contractor to build a house on the property and to plant various trees and shrubs. A year later, Blanchard became dissatisfied with the planting, uprooted the trees and shrubs, and sold them to a neighbor. In this case, the building materials and trees were personal property that became real property. When the trees and shrubs were uprooted, they became personal property again.

ACQUIRING TITLE TO PERSONAL PROPERTY

Title to personal property is the actual ownership of property, not just the evidence of ownership, such as a certificate of title. Title (ownership) can be transferred from one person to another in a number of ways, including sale, gift, inheritance, finding lost property, and other ways that will be discussed later in this chapter.

Finding Lost Personal Property

The saying, "Finders keepers, losers weepers," has no basis in law. The finder of lost property holds it in trust, that is, in safekeeping, at least for a time, for the real owner. As a result, the finder is a custodian acting for the true owner. The finder of lost property has ownership rights superior to everyone except the true owner.

Responsibility of the Finder Someone who finds property has a legal responsibility to try to make reasonable efforts to return the property to its rightful owner. Statutes in many states provide that if the finder of lost property has made a reasonable effort to locate the owner without success within a period specified by statute, then the property belongs to the finder.

Distinction Between Lost and Mislaid Property Courts have frequently made a distinction between lost and mislaid property. An object has been "mislaid," rather than lost, when it was intentionally left in a certain place and then forgotten by the owner. Objects forgotten in this way are considered to have been transferred willingly and placed in the custody of the person with whom the object was left; as a result, they are not lost at all. On the other hand, an object that has

OBJECTIVE 2

Describe the responsibilities of a finder of lost or abandoned property.

OBJECTIVE 3

Distinguish between lost and mislaid personal property.

not been intentionally left in the custody of someone else, and then forgotten, is considered lost, not mislaid.

> **EXAMPLE 19.2**
>
> McAvoy, a customer in Medina's barbershop, found a briefcase containing certain valuables that had been left there by another customer. A dispute arose as to who should get the briefcase and its contents. The court awarded possession to Medina, stressing that the owner had intentionally left the briefcase and then forgotten it, and for that reason had entrusted it to Medina's care.

Property Found in Public versus Private Places Courts have also made a distinction between objects found in a private portion of a person's property and objects found in areas open to the public. An owner of property that is not open to the public is presumed to want both possession of the place itself and whatever it contains. In an area that is open to the public, however, the finder is more likely to gain ownership of a found object than is the owner of the land.

> **EXAMPLE 19.3**
>
> Patillo, a worker for a swimming pool maintenance company, was cleaning the pool at the Red River Motel when he found a valuable diamond ring. Both Patillo and the owner of the motel, Calkins, claimed ownership. The court decided that because Calkins had the right to say that the pool should be cleaned in any way he thought fit, and to direct what should be done with anything found in the pool, Calkins should be presumed to have an intent to exercise control over any object found in or on it. The finder, Patillo, would probably have been granted possession if the ring had been found in the parking lot or on the floor in the motel lobby.

Statutory Remedies Many states have enacted statutes that govern who owns lost and mislaid property. Typically, these statutes require the finder of lost or mislaid property to notify a specific government official who maintains records of the property found. If by the end of a period of time set by statute the true owner does not claim the property, title is given to the finder. If the true owner does not come forward and the finder does not claim ownership, the property becomes the property of the state after a period of time specified in the statute.

Abandoned Property

Personal property is considered abandoned when the owner disposes of it with the apparent intention of disclaiming ownership.

Title to such property is assumed by the first person who takes control over it.

Gifts

A ***gift*** is the voluntary transfer of property by one person to another without consideration or payment of any kind.

Inter Vivos **Gifts** While giving gifts is a common act, it takes on added dimensions when viewed from a legal standpoint. There are three requirements for property to be transferred as a gift:

- The person giving the gift (the donor) must intend to make a gift.
- The gift, or a written statement of the donor's intention, must actually be delivered to the person who is to receive the gift (the donee).
- The donee must accept the gift.

The donor cannot cancel the gift if these requirements are met. A gift that meets these requirements is known as an *inter vivos* gift (between the living).

Gifts *In Causa Mortis* A gift given by a living person, who expects to die from a known cause, is known as a gift *in causa mortis* (in contemplation of death). If the donor does not die from the expected cause or dies as a result of some other cause, the gift can be reclaimed.

OBJECTIVE 4

Discuss both gifts *inter vivos* and *in causa mortis*.

gift The voluntary transfer of property by one party to another without consideration or payment of any kind.

Photo 19.1

***Inter Vivos* Gifts**

An *inter vivos* gift cannot be canceled by the donor if certain requirements are met. *What are the three requirements?*

PART 4 Property

EXAMPLE 19.4

> Eisermann suffered from terminal cancer. Recognizing the seriousness of his condition, he signed over several valuable stock certificates to his son, despite the objections of his wife and other children. On the way home from the hospital, he was killed in an automobile accident. The executor of his estate could justifiably claim that the gift *in causa mortis* to the son should be revoked and that the stock certificates should be included in the estate.

Accession

Accession is the right of an owner of property, such as plants or animals, to any increase in the property. The owner of a cow, for example, owns the calves born to the cow.

accession The right of an owner of property to any increase in the property.

OWNERSHIP OF PROPERTY

The concept of title was discussed in Chapter 14, where it was explained that title is actual ownership, not just evidence of ownership, such as a certificate of title. At this point, different forms of ownership will be introduced. Many of the following descriptions of single and multiple ownership apply to both personal and real property.

OBJECTIVE 5

Explain how someone can acquire property by accession.

INDIVIDUAL AND MULTIPLE OWNERSHIP OF PERSONAL PROPERTY

Personal property can be owned individually or by multiple owners. Different laws apply in each case.

Severalty Ownership

When all the rights of ownership in a particular piece of property are held by one person, the ownership is held in *severalty*. (Contrary to what the word *severalty* suggests, *several* in this context means separate).

OBJECTIVE 6

Discuss severalty ownership, tenancy in common, joint tenancy, tenancy by the entirety, and community property.

Multiple Ownership

For various reasons, it is sometimes desirable for several people to own personal property jointly. However, certain types of property, such as businesses, boats, cars, and planes, cannot be divided among the owners. Obviously, one of the co-owners of an airplane could not very well

Real and Personal Property CHAPTER 19 301

claim the wings of the plane and indicate that the engine belonged to the other owner.

Joint Tenancy A *joint tenancy* exists when two or more persons own equal shares of personal property. The death of one person transfers his or her interest to the surviving joint tenants.

In cases of joint tenancy, owners have an *undivided interest;* that is, each owner can claim ownership of the entire estate, subject to the equal rights of the other joint tenants. Generally, a person's part interest in property may be sold just as a severalty interest may be sold, unless specifically prohibited. To underscore the intention of the parties, agreements generally include the phrase, "with right of survivorship." In this sense, *survivorship* means that in the case of one owner's death, ownership of the portion owned by the deceased passes to the survivors.

> **EXAMPLE 19.5**
>
> McGrath and Connell were partners who owned a retail business and the real property on which the store was built as joint tenants. Each owner had a wife and children. McGrath died and Connell assumed McGrath's ownership of the business and the property. McGrath's wife and children inherited nothing.

Tenancy by the Entirety A *tenancy by the entirety* is a form of joint ownership of property by husband and wife in which both have the right to the entire property, and upon the death of one, the other has title (the right of survivorship).

Tenancy in Common A *tenancy in common* is a form of joint ownership of property by two or more persons. The ownership interest of any one of the owners can be sold, transferred, or inherited just as in the case of joint tenancy. The distinction of tenancy in common is that an owner's interest does *not* pass to the persons who share ownership at the time of his or her death. Rather, the interest of a tenant in common passes to that person's heirs.

Community Property Some states have enacted statutes that provide that property acquired during a marriage is the **community property** of both husband and wife; that is, the property acquired belongs to both parties. Statues vary in the determination of what happens to property at the time of death or divorce. Generally, it is provided that property owned by either party before the marriage or property

joint tenancy When two or more persons own equal shares of personal property.

tenancy by the entirety A form of joint ownership of property by husband and wife in which both have the right to the entire property, and upon the death of one, the other has title.

tenancy in common A form of joint ownership of property by two or more persons in which any owner's interest can be sold, transferred, or inherited.

community property Property that is acquired during a marriage.

received as gifts or inheritances by either party remains the property of the individual and does not become community property.

Real Property

Real property is distinguished from personal property in a number of ways. Unlike most forms of personal property, the supply of land is limited. Moreover, land is unique, and one piece of land is not the same as any other. One piece, for example, may contain valuable minerals and another might have little value.

Land

As stated previously, the law relating to real property treats land as extending down to the center of the earth, and also includes things that are permanently attached to it, such as houses, buildings, and trees. Moreover, rights to land include the airspace above the land to an indefinite height, subject to the rights of aircraft in flight that do not pose a hazard to persons or property on the land. Land also includes rights to minerals such as oil, coal, or iron ore, except in states where the state retains an interest in certain minerals.

Buildings and Fixtures

A *building* is a structure built on land. Such a structure can be almost any building permanently placed on or beneath the surface of the land. When items of personal property are added to land, or to buildings in such a way that they become a part of the building, they are known as *fixtures*. Shrubbery, trees, and satellite antennae are examples of fixtures.

Rights in Land Other Than Ownership

Rights in land can be separated from the land itself, except in the case of easements. Consider the following examples.

Subterranean Rights The right to extract minerals, such as oil or coal, is known as *subterranean rights*. The right to extract minerals can be sold without altering the ownership of the land itself.

Air Rights The right to build on or over the land is known as *air rights*. Air rights are of particular significance in crowded urban areas where the right to erect a building over some other use of the land might be sold. An example of such use would be the sale of the right to erect an apartment building over railroad tracks or a highway.

easement A right or interest in land granted to a party to make beneficial use of the land owned by another.

Easements

An *easement* is a right or interest in land granted to a party to make beneficial use of the land owned by another. The distinction between easements and other rights is that easements "run with the land." That is, they cannot be sold or transferred once they are recorded. An example of an easement is the right granted to a public utility company to enter the land of another to maintain telephone or electrical equipment or lines.

Licenses

The owner of land may grant a party the right to enter the land for a specific purpose. For example, a landowner may grant someone the right to build a temporary stand to sell fruit and vegetables or souvenirs to passing motorists, or the owner of a service station may license someone to sell Christmas trees on a portion of the property. Generally, the landowner receives payment or a share of profits in exchange for the license. Licensing agreements may be written or oral. The temporary interest created in the land does not run with the land.

> **EXAMPLE 19.6**
> The Downtowner Motel allowed Rubin to use a small area of the lobby to display and sell his sculptures. The arrangement required Rubin to pay the motel owner a small commission on the sculptures sold. After several years, the motel manager informed Rubin that the arrangement was over. Rubin disagreed, claiming that the arrangement was a lease. In this instance, the arrangement was clearly a license, not a lease.

OWNERSHIP INTERESTS IN REAL PROPERTY

Interests in real property can represent either ownership or possession. The term *estate* is used to identify the interest or the right a person has in real property. An estate can be either a ***freehold estate***, by which a person owns the land for life or forever; or a ***leasehold estate***, by which a person has an interest in real property that comes from a lease. A leasehold estate is not ownership, but only the right to possess real property subject to the provisions of a lease.

OBJECTIVE 7

Distinguish between freehold and leasehold estates.

freehold estate An estate in which a person owns the land for life and forever.

leasehold estate An estate in which a person has an interest in real property that comes from a lease.

Freehold Estates

There are a number of ways in which freehold estates can be held that provide absolute ownership lasting for either the lifetime of the holder or forever. Consequently, a holder of a freehold estate in land can transfer the estate (ownership) by sale, by gift, or by leaving it to his or her heirs. A holder of a freehold estate can also create and transfer an interest in the estate that lasts for only a lifetime. Such an estate, called a life estate, will be discussed later in the chapter.

Estate in Fee Simple The owner of a freehold estate who holds it absolutely is said to hold it in *fee simple.* The owner of a freehold estate who holds real property in fee simple can sell it, give it away, or leave it to his or her heirs. The person to whom it is transferred then owns it in fee simple. The holder of a freehold estate in fee simple is not, however, allowed to use the property in any way that violates local zoning rules, or the rights of others, or restrictive covenants in the deed. For example, a restrictive covenant in a deed may prohibit the alteration, destruction, or removal of a historic structure. Any restrictive covenant must be for a lawful purpose. A restrictive covenant prohibiting a sale because of the race of the prospective buyer, for example, would not be lawful.

Life Estates A person who holds a freehold estate (ownership interest) owns the property only for his or her lifetime and holds a *life estate* in the property. A life estate is usually created by deed (the document used to transfer ownership in real property) or by inheritance.

If real property is transferred from *A* to *B* for *B*'s lifetime, what happens when *B* dies? The property is then returned to *A,* if he or she is still alive, or to *A*'s heirs. The interest that *A* holds while *B* is still alive is known as a *reversion estate* because the property reverts to *A* upon *B*'s death. But suppose that *A* decides that upon *B*'s death, the property should belong to *C*. Then *C* has a *remainder estate*.

Leasehold Estates

An estate that does not involve an ownership interest in real property is known as a *leasehold estate.* A leasehold estate provides the holder with certain rights during the period covered by the lease. Leaseholds are discussed further in Chapter 21, "Landlord-Tenant Relations."

TRANSFER OF REAL PROPERTY

The transfer of real property is, in many ways, more complex than the transfer of personal property. Consequently, a number of specialized terms are used. A *deed* is the instrument, or document, that conveys an interest in real property between parties. The parties are: the *grantor,* the party who conveys real property; and the *grantee,* the party to whom the property is conveyed. Unlike a contract, no consideration is required to effect a transfer of real property. Real property, like personal property, can be sold or given as a gift. A deed, however, is needed in any kind of transfer of ownership.

OBJECTIVE 8

Describe the characteristics of the several types of freehold estates as they relate to ownership interest.

fee simple When an owner of a freehold estate holds it absolutely, meaning he or she can sell it, give it way, or leave it to his or her heirs.

life estate A freehold estate in which a person has an ownership interest only for his or her lifetime.

leasehold estate An estate that does not involve an ownership interest in real property.

deed The instrument, or document, that conveys an interest in real property between parties.

OBJECTIVE 9

Explain the characteristics of various kinds of deeds, and transfers of real property through eminent domain and adverse possession.

Types of Deeds

Deeds can be classified by the kind of ownership interest being transferred. A *quitclaim* deed transfers whatever interest a grantor has in real property, if any. It states that the grantor claims no interest in the property for which the deed is given.

Quitclaim deeds are often used when transferring property to family members, divorcing spouses, or in other transactions between people well known to each other. Quitclaim deeds are also used to clarify questions of full title when a person has a possible but unknown interest in the property. Quitclaim deeds do not warrant good title.

A *warranty deed* is one in which the grantor claims that he or she has title, and that the property is free of the claims of others. There are two kinds of warranty deeds. One is broad and makes a number of assurances; the other limits the assurances to specific matters.

A *bargain and sale deed* simply says, "I grant the property to you." No particular warranties are given, but state statutes assume that certain implied warranties are present.

Delivery and Recording of Deeds

When a deed has been completed and signed by the grantor, it must be delivered to the grantee to bring about a legally enforceable transfer of ownership. Most such deliveries are made in person in a real estate broker's or lawyer's office, but no particular form of delivery is required. The deed can be handed to the grantee (buyer), mailed to him or her, or given to another person with instructions for delivery.

Recording a deed with the appropriate public official, such as a county recorder of deeds, is not legally required, but it is an important step that notifies everyone of its existence and minimizes the possibility of another person's claim to the property surfacing at a later date.

Other Transfers of Real Property

Property can also be transferred from one party to another by eminent domain or by adverse possession.

Eminent Domain Real property can be taken from an owner by action of government or other public authority for the benefit of the public. Such actions are taken when a governmental body wishes to build a highway or school, for example, and the needed property is privately held. When private property is taken by **eminent domain,** compensation is made at the fair market value of the property. In the event of a dispute, the owner can pursue remedies available through state and federal courts.

eminent domain When ownership of real property is taken by the government and the previous owner is compensated at the fair market value of the property.

Adverse Possession Title to land can be acquired as a result of a person's use of land over a period of time. For title to pass through ***adverse possession,*** it must be proved that there was actual and exclusive continuous possession or use, the possession must have been for a period of years specified by state statute (typically 10 years), possession must have been open and known to the owner, and with hostility and adversely (that is, without the owner's permission).

adverse possession When title to land is acquired by a person's exclusive, continuous, open, known, and hostile use of the property over a period of time.

> **EXAMPLE 19.7**
> An alley owned by a retail store was commonly used to park cars with full consent of the owner. A driver was surprised one day to find that she was blocked from her favorite parking place by a chain. Upon inquiry, the store owner explained that to retain full ownership of the alley, he as required to briefly demonstrate his ownership. However, the driver would be welcome to park there the following day.

CHAPTER SUMMARY

1. Real property is the ground and everything permanently attached to it, including land, buildings, trees and shrubs; the air space above the land, and ground below are also included. Personal property is everything, tangible and intangible, that is not real property.

2. A finder of lost property has a responsibility to make a reasonable effort to find the true owner. However, property that is abandoned with the apparent intention of disclaiming it belongs to the first person who takes control of it.

3. An object is considered mislaid, rather than lost, when it has been intentionally left in a certain place and then forgotten by the owner. If an object has not been intentionally left in the custody of someone else, it is considered lost.

4. A gift *inter vivos* is one between the living; a gift *in causa mortis* is given by a living person who expects to die from a known cause.

5. Accession is the right of a property owner to any increase in the property. For example, if a pregnant animal gives birth to a calf, the owner of the mother owns both animals.

6 Severalty ownership exists when all the rights of ownership in property are held by one person. Joint tenancy occurs when two or more people own equal shares in property. Tenancy in common is a form of ownership by two or more people in which the ownership interest of any one party can be sold, transferred, or inherited. Tenancy by the entirety is a form of joint ownership by husband and wife in which both have a right to the entire property and each has the right of survivorship. Community property is property acquired during marriage and that belongs to both husband and wife.

7 A freehold estate is one in which a person owns the land for life or forever. A leasehold estate is one in which a person has an interest in real property that comes from a lease.

8 One type of freehold estate is an estate in fee simple, in which the owner of a freehold estate holds it absolutely. A second type of freehold estate is a life estate, in which the owner owns the estate only for his or her lifetime.

9 A deed is an instrument that conveys an interest in real property between parties. Types of deeds include a quitclaim deed, warranty deed, and bargain and sale deed. Real property can also be transferred by eminent domain (when it is taken by the government and the owner is compensated) or adverse possession (when land is acquired as a result of a person's actual, continuous, open, known, and hostile use of land for a certain period of time).

Chapter 19 Assessment

MATCHING LEGAL TERMS

Match each of the following definitions with the correct term in the list below. Write the letter of your choice in the answer column.

- **a.** accession
- **b.** adverse possession
- **c.** gift *in causa mortis*
- **d.** eminent domain
- **e.** fee simple
- **f.** freehold estate
- **g.** grantee
- **h.** *inter vivos* gift
- **i.** joint tenancy
- **j.** leasehold estate
- **k.** life estate
- **l.** quitclaim deed
- **m.** severalty
- **n.** subterranean rights
- **o.** tenancy in common

1. A gift between the living.
2. The right of an owner of property to the production of the property—a calf born to a cow, for example.
3. Ownership of property held by one person.
4. A gift given in anticipation of death.
5. A document of transfer of real property.
6. Absolute ownership of real property.
7. The right of a governmental or public body to acquire privately held real property needed for a public purpose.
8. An interest in real property that concerns ownership.
9. The person to whom real property is conveyed.
10. The interest a person has in real property that lasts a lifetime.
11. An interest in real property that concerns possession.
12. A form of co-ownership of property in which one owner's share of the property passes to the other owners upon his or her death.
13. The passing of title to land that can result from a non-owner's use of the land.
14. The right to extract minerals from land.
15. A form of joint ownership of property in which one owner's share of the property can be sold, transferred, or passed to heirs.

TRUE/FALSE QUIZ

Indicate whether each of the following statements is true or false by writing *T* or *F* in the answer column.

16. *Property* refers to both personal and real property.
17. Fixtures are additions to personal property.

Real and Personal Property CHAPTER 19

Chapter 19 Assessment

18. Personal property can be either tangible or intangible. 18. _____

19. There is no distinction between lost and mislaid personal property. 19. _____

20. A finder of personal property has a responsibility to try to return the property to the rightful owner. 20. _____

21. Title to abandoned property resides with the state. 21. _____

22. Some state statutes provide that property acquired before a marriage is the community property of both husband and wife. 22. _____

23. An easement is the right or interest in land granted for the benefit of one party to make beneficial use of the land of another, such as the right of a utility company to enter land to erect power lines. 23. _____

24. The person who holds a life estate in real property can sell absolute ownership or pass it on to his or her heirs. 24. _____

25. A grantor of a life estate in real property maintains a reversion estate. 25. _____

DISCUSSION QUESTIONS

Answer the following questions and discuss them in class.

26. Distinguish between real and personal property.

27. Discuss both *inter vivos* and *in causa mortis* gifts.

28. Discuss severalty ownership, tenancy in common, joint tenancy, and community property.

29. Discuss real property including land, buildings, and fixtures.

Chapter 19 Assessment

30. Identify and provide examples of rights in real property.

31. Explain the characteristics of various kinds of deeds, and transfers of real property through eminent domain and adverse possession.

THINKING CRITICALLY ABOUT THE LAW

Answer the following questions, which require you to think critically about the legal principles that you learned in this chapter.

32. Real and Personal Property Why do you think it is necessary to distinguish between real and personal property?

33. Sale of Property The transfer of real property is much more complex than the transfer of personal property. What could be done to simplify real property transactions?

34. Gifts Can a gift given *in causa mortis* be assumed to be as freely given as a gift given *inter vivos*? Why or why not?

35. Multiple Ownership of Real Property Various forms of multiple ownership of real property, i.e., *joint tenancy, tenancy by the entirety, tenancy in common,* have evolved from our English legal roots. Are these designations relevant today? Explain your answer.

Chapter 19 Assessment

36. **A Question of Ethics** An ocean front community wanted to limit the use of its beach to residents only. A group contested this exclusion, claiming the ocean was public property. Is it fair for residents to exclude nonresidents from access to the beach? Why or why not?

_____
_____
_____
_____

CASE QUESTIONS

Study each case below and answer the questions that follow by writing *Yes* or *No* in the answer column.

37. **Property Ownership** Roche and Hecht owned a boat, which they used for weekend fishing trips. Since both were married and had children, they set up their agreement to own the boat in such a way that if either one died, from any cause, the heirs of the deceased party would inherit his interest.

   a. Is this an example of joint tenancy?   a. _____

   b. Is this an example of tenancy in common?   b. _____

   c. Does Hecht's interest in the boat indicate a severalty interest?   c. _____

38. **Found Property** Weber, a customer at a restaurant owned by Hegler, found a wallet on the floor under the table. It contained money but no identification. In an attempt to return it to its rightful owner, Weber gave it to Hegler with the understanding that if the owner did not return, or could not be located, she would claim it. Weber returned to claim the wallet a month later, but Hegler refused to give it to her claiming it as his own.

   a. Does Weber have a lawful claim to the wallet?   a. _____

   b. Does Hegler have a lawful claim to the wallet?   b. _____

   c. Would a court regard the wallet as misplaced?   c. _____

39. **Community Property** LeRoi and her husband, Pillsbury, each had substantial assets before they were married. In addition, they jointly purchased a home with the income they earned during their four-year marriage, and during their marriage LeRoi inherited a small fortune. After four years, they agreed to divorce. The marriage ceremony and divorce action were both in a state with community property laws.

   a. Is the property owned by both husband and wife before marriage considered community property?   a. _____

   b. Is LeRoi's inheritance considered community property?   b. _____

   c. Is the home considered community property?   c. _____

Chapter 19 Assessment

40. **Real and Personal Property** Noguchi and his wife purchased a newly built development house that had no lawn or any other landscaping. Over several years, they spent many weekends landscaping with expensive and exotic shrubbery and trees. Because of a transfer to another city, the Noguchis were forced to sell their house. At the time of the sale they had a large camping tent in the yard, which they used to store lawn furniture. After the sale but before moving away, the Noguchis uprooted several shrubs to take with them. The buyer objected to the removal, claiming that the shrubbery and the tent were real property and were included in the sale of the house. Noguchi claimed that the shrubbery and tent were all personal property.

   a. Is the shrubbery real property? a. _____

   b. Is the house real property? b. _____

   c. Is the tent real property? c. _____

CASE ANALYSIS

Study each of the following cases carefully and then briefly state the principle of law and your decision.

41. **Adverse Possession** When Bryer bought a suburban house, the real estate salesperson pointed to a decorative stone fence as the boundary of the property. Because Bryer had several dogs he wanted to keep on his property, he erected a chain-link fence on what he believed to be the property line. His neighbor watched the work being done and even helped with the construction. Twenty years later, as a result of a new survey by the town, it was discovered that the fence was 18 inches inside the neighbor's property. *Can Bryer claim ownership of all the property on his side of the fence?*

   Principle of law:

   _____
   _____

   Decision:

   _____
   _____

42. **Easement** Rae owned a farm and each summer allowed a neighbor, Fuller, to set up a stand on his property to sell worms to people who drove by on their way to fish in the nearby lake. After 10 years of regularly using the small piece of property, Rae and Fuller had a dispute and Rae forbade Fuller from using his land again. Fuller claimed that he now had the right to continue using the small piece of property as he had in the past, insisting that an easement had been created. *Did Fuller's continued use of the property create an easement?*

   Principle of law:

   _____
   _____

   Decision:

   _____
   _____

Chapter 19 Assessment

43. **Gifts** Harry and Marilyn Owen were divorced after a short marriage, and an agreement to divide assets was made by the parties. In addition to the division of personal property as agreed to and as recorded by the court, Marilyn claimed ownership of a Chevrolet automobile and one-half of a $24,000 certificate of deposit, insisting that they were both gifts from her former husband, Harry. Harry purchased both the car, registered in his name, and the certificate before the marriage. He denied having given the car and a one-half interest in the certificate of deposit. *Does it appear that the requirements of an inter vivos gift have been met, and will Marilyn be awarded the disputed property?* [Owen v. Owen, 351 N.W.2d 139 (South Dakota).]

Principle of law:

Decision:

LEGAL RESEARCH

Complete the following activities. Then share your findings with the class.

44. **Working in Teams** Working in teams of three or four, interview personnel at the nearest governmental authority (federal, state, or local) that handles cases of eminent domain, or the taking of private property for public use. Structure the interview so that condemnation procedures are discussed plus some recent cases.

45. **Using Technology** Using the Internet and search engines, research a recent case involving a dispute over real or personal property. Write a one- or two-page paper summarizing the nature of the dispute, the basic facts involved in the case, and the reasons for the court's decision.

PART 4   Property

CHAPTER 20

BAILMENTS

PERFORMANCE OBJECTIVES

After studying this chapter and completing the assessments, you will be able to:

1. List the six typical reasons for transferring goods and creating a bailment.
2. Discuss the importance of acceptance, possession, and return of goods as they apply to bailments.
3. Distinguish among and provide examples of (a) bailment for the sole benefit of the bailee, (b) bailment for the sole benefit of the bailor, (c) mutual-benefit bailment, and (d) constructive bailment.
4. Discuss the level of care a bailee is required to give for each of several kinds of bailments.
5. Discuss the special requirements of mutual-benefit bailments concerned with (a) storage, (b) parking lots, (c) work and services, (d) hotels, and (e) common carriers.

LEGAL TERMS

bailment
bailor
bailee
bailment for the sole benefit of the bailee
bailment for the sole benefit of the bailor
mutual-benefit bailment
warehouser
bailee's lien
hotelkeeper
transient
common carrier
consignor
consignee
carrier's lien
constructive bailment

What Is a Bailment?

Earlier chapters have examined numerous kinds of agreements and contracts for many different purposes. A bailment is a special kind of contract that is widely used in business and in personal affairs. Specifically, a **bailment** is a transaction in which the owner of tangible personal property transfers it (not as a gift) to another party while still retaining ownership. For example, taking clothes to a dry cleaner transfers the goods but not ownership (or title) to them.

Characteristics of Bailments

A bailment allows the owner of personal property to transfer possession of it to another individual for any of the following purposes:

1. *Sale.* A manufacturer ships goods on consignment to sell or return. (A *consignment* is temporary custody of property given by an owner to a seller with the expectation that the seller will sell the goods.)
2. *Transportation.* A shipment by a transporter of goods, for example, a truck line.
3. *Repair or service.* A car left at a service station.
4. *Rental.* A rented car or rented skis.
5. *Storage.* Goods placed in a warehouse or checkroom, or a car left in a parking lot.
6. *Security for a loan.* Valuable goods left with a lender as security for a loan.

In these cases, the person who retains ownership and transfers possession is the **bailor;** the person who receives the goods is the **bailee.** The agreement reached between these parties is a bailment.

Bailment Created by Possession of Goods

Actual ownership of goods is not necessary to create a bailment. Anyone in possession of goods can create the bailment relationship and become a bailor—a borrower, a finder, or even a thief.

EXAMPLE 20.1

Castro rented a car to use during a business trip. While making a sales call at a downtown firm, Castro parked the car in a parking garage. The parking attendant surrendered the car to someone else by mistake. The parking garage was still responsible for the car and its contents, even though Castro was not the owner.

---

bailment A transaction in which the owner of tangible personal property transfers it (not as a gift) to another party while still retaining ownership.

OBJECTIVE 1

List the six typical reasons for transferring goods and creating a bailment.

bailor The party in a bailment who retains ownership and transfers possession of the goods.

bailee The party in a bailment who receives the goods.

OBJECTIVE 2

Discuss the importance of acceptance, possession, and return of goods as they apply to bailments.

Bailee Must Intend to Possess Goods

The transfer of goods from bailor to bailee must actually take place. Unless there is some other understanding, the bailee must actually accept the goods.

> **EXAMPLE 20.2**
>
> Goldstein had her car serviced regularly at Centre Service Station and knew the owner well. One evening, after the station had closed and all the employees had gone home, Goldstein parked on the station property while she attended a social function. When she returned, the car was gone. The owner of Centre Service denied responsibility because no bailment existed. The service station owner is correct because the station did not accept the car.

Bailee Must Return Identical Goods

Except for a bailment that requires alteration, such as a suit left for cleaning and alterations, or when fungible goods, such as grain or fuel oil, are stored, the identical goods must be returned.

> **EXAMPLE 20.3**
>
> Roth left her stereo receiver with Radio Masters for repair. As a result of an error, her receiver was repaired and given to another customer, who left town and could not be located. The owner of the repair shop offered Roth another, higher-quality receiver instead. Roth refused, claiming that the replacement would not fit in the space available in her shelving unit. Radio Masters must replace the exact item left for repair or pay damages.

KINDS OF BAILMENTS AND CARE DURING CUSTODY

The law concerning bailments provides for certain rights and duties of both bailor and bailee, depending on the kind of bailment. Bailments are often classified into four categories:

- *Bailments for the sole benefit of the bailee.* An example of this kind of bailment is when you borrow an article, such as a calculator, from a friend.
- *Bailments for the sole benefit of the bailor.* An example of this type of bailment is when you agree to store a friend's car in your garage while he or she is on vacation.
- *Bailments for the benefit of both the bailee and the bailor.* An example of this sort of bailment, also called a mutual-benefit bailment, is when you leave your car in a parking garage.

OBJECTIVE 3

Distinguish among and provide examples of (a) bailment for the sole benefit of the bailee, (b) bailment for the sole benefit of the bailor, (c) mutual-benefit bailment, and (d) constructive bailment.

OBJECTIVE 4

Discuss the level of care a bailee is required to give for each of several kinds of bailments.

bailment for the sole benefit of the bailee A bailment relationship in which only the bailee receives any benefit from the relationship.

bailment for the sole benefit of the bailor A bailment that exists when the bailor entrusts an article to the bailee for storage or safekeeping without charge, as a favor.

OBJECTIVE 5

Discuss the special requirements of mutual-benefit bailments concerned with (a) storage, (b) parking lots, (c) work and services, (d) hotels, and (e) common carriers.

- *Constructive bailments.* An example of this kind of bailment is when goods, such as an umbrella, are thrust upon you by a person who unintentionally leaves property behind in your home.

Bailments for the Sole Benefit of the Bailee

A ***bailment for the sole benefit of the bailee*** usually results in a borrowing or lending transaction. The person who borrows an article (the bailee) gets the only benefit. However, the owner (the bailor) must warn the bailee of any defects or hazards that might exist. Because the bailee is getting something for nothing, the law generally expects the bailee to exercise *great or extraordinary care* in using the article.

EXAMPLE 20.4

Fordyce loaned his car to a friend, Dyani, to use while taking a short trip. Fordyce knew but failed to mention that the brakes were worn and needed repair. Dyani was injured when the brakes failed and the car crashed into a tree. Fordyce would be held liable for failure to warn Dyani of the unsafe brakes.

However, if in Example 20.4, Dyani had been drinking alcohol and was at fault for the accident, he could be held liable for failing to use the necessary degree of care.

Bailments for the Sole Benefit of the Bailor

A ***bailment for the sole benefit of the bailor*** exists when the owner (the bailor) entrusts an article to another person (the bailee) for storage or safekeeping without charge, as a favor. Because the bailee is doing a favor for the bailor, the law requires that he or she exercise only *slight care* in taking care of the article.

EXAMPLE 20.5

Berens was going away for several months and asked a friend, Moreno, to care for a valuable painting. Moreno left the painting leaning against the wall in a spare room. While he was out for an evening, it the painting was stolen. Moreno would not be liable because he was required to provide only slight care. If Moreno had hung the painting in his living room, thereby gaining some benefit, he would have been required to use ordinary care because it would have been a mutual-benefit bailment, discussed next.

Mutual-Benefit Bailments

By far the most common bailment is the kind in which consideration is present. Recall from Chapter 8 that consideration is the exchange of promises by the parties to an agreement to give up something of value that they have a right to keep, or to do something they are not otherwise required to do.

A *mutual-benefit bailment* is one in which both the bailee and bailor derive some benefit, and as a result, each has rights and duties. The bailor has the duty to warn the bailee of any defects in the property that could cause harm. The bailee has the duty to exercise *reasonable or ordinary care* in using the property. Each party has the right to expect the other party to fulfill the duty imposed on him or her.

mutual-benefit bailment A bailment in which both the bailee and the bailor derive some benefit, and as a result, each has rights and duties.

> ### EXAMPLE 20.6
> Zubin rented a truck to use in moving his household furniture. The truck rental firm failed to inform Zubin that the hydraulic lift was not working properly, with the result that a container of dishes fell from the lift and broke. Zubin, however, failed to perform his duty of care because he allowed the engine to overheat and thereby become damaged. Each party had duties and rights that were not fulfilled.

Bailment for Storage Both individuals and businesses sometimes need to put certain articles in storage. The person or firm that provides storage facilities is known as a **warehouser.** The Uniform Commercial Code provides that when goods are turned over to a warehouse for storage, the warehouser will provide a receipt for the goods and will accept the responsibility for loss of, or damage to, the goods caused by a lack of care that a reasonable person would exercise under similar circumstances [UCC 7-204].

warehouser A person or firm that provides storage facilities.

Parking-Lot Bailment Parking a car in a parking lot or parking garage is a common transaction. It is important to remember, however, that a bailment is created only if the parking-lot attendant actually has control of the car. If a customer parks his or her own car, locks it, and retains the key, a bailment does not exist—only a rental of space. In most cases, the parking lot has no responsibility for the car. However, even when the customer locks his or her own car and retains the key, if the parking lot provides a substantial number of attendants and makes express or implied assurances that security will be provided, the court may interpret the facts of the case as suggesting that the parking lot had, in fact, gained control of the car and that a bailment existed.

> ### EXAMPLE 20.7
> Mandel was often disturbed when he would witness parking-lot attendants recklessly driving cars with much squealing of tires and racing of engines. For this reason, he preferred to patronize "park-and-lock"

> garages. On one occasion, he left his car in such a lot, and when he returned, he found that the car had been broken into and the radio and cellular telephone had been stolen. The court would find in this case there was not a bailment because the attendant had no control over the car and the transaction was merely a rental of space.

If, in Example 20.7, the parking lot had several attendants who were parking and moving cars of customers who had left their keys, the attendants admitted that there had been break-ins, and if the attendants assured Mandel that "we'll keep an eye on your car," then it is likely that a court would find that a bailment did exist.

Bailment for Work and Services When one person turns over property to another with the understanding that certain work is to be performed on the property, a bailment for work and services is created. For example, when the owner of a car (bailor) leaves it at a garage (bailee) to have repairs made, or the owner of some fabric turns it over to a tailor to have a garment made, a bailment for work and services is created.

In transactions of this kind, there are actually two legal relationships. The bailor-bailee relationship is concerned with the care of the property. The contractual relationship is concerned with the kind and quality of work done and the payment for services performed. The bailee in a bailment for work and services is entitled to hold, and if necessary, to sell the property if the bailor does not pay for the services or work done. This provision of the law is known as a *bailee's lien.* (A *lien* is a claim against the property of another as security for a debt.)

bailee's lien The right of the bailee in a bailment for work and services to hold, and if necessary, to sell the property if the bailor does not pay for the services or work done.

> **EXAMPLE 20.8**
>
> Surry instructed the service manager of an automobile service station to perform a tune-up and "check it over carefully and get it ready for the winter." When Surry picked up the car, he was given a bill for $385, which included numerous repairs and parts. He refused to pay and the service station refused to release the car, claiming a bailee's lien. The service station has the right to hold the bailor's property until Surry pays for the services done. Ultimately, a court would have to decide what was reasonable to get the car ready for winter.

Hotel Bailments A bailment relationship exists between a guest (as bailor) and a hotelkeeper (as bailee) with regard to the guest's property that is specifically placed in the care of the hotelkeeper. A *hotelkeeper,* sometimes called an *innkeeper,* is in the business of offering lodgings or temporary shelter to guests and transients. The shelter may be in a

hotelkeeper A person or firm in the business of offering lodgings or temporary shelter to guests and transients.

hotel, motel, or tourist home. A ***transient*** is a guest whose stay is relatively uncertain—a day, a week, a month, or more. Under common law, the hotelkeeper's liability for the property of guests was near absolute, but state statutes today limit a hotel's liability to that of an ordinary bailee or limit liability to the amount listed in a posted notice in the room. Typically, a hotel will have a sign on the room door stating that the hotel's liability extends only to property deposited in the hotel safe. Such statutes also allow the hotel to place a dollar limit on the hotel's liability.

Common-Carrier Bailments A ***common carrier*** is an individual or firm in the business of transporting goods between certain points as allowed by the various state commissions that regulate the carriers. The common carrier must accept all shipments that it is authorized to handle. When a shipper, also known as a ***consignor,*** turns goods over to a common carrier, a mutual-benefit bailment is created that is terminated only when the carrier delivers the goods to the party designated by the shipper. The party receiving the goods is known as the ***consignee.*** The mutual-benefit bailment gives the carrier (the bailee) certain rights and duties:

1. The right to determine and enforce reasonable rules and requirements concerning the operation of its services. For example, a carrier may refuse to accept improperly packed goods, or during certain times of the year, it may refuse to accept goods that could be damaged by freezing temperatures.
2. The right to payment for services provided. The carrier has a legal right to hold a shipment until payment is made. Withholding payment for transportation charges enables the carrier to hold goods on the basis of a ***carrier's lien.***
3. The right to payment from either the consignor or consignee when the carrier's equipment is rendered unavailable while it is being loaded or unloaded.

Constructive Bailments

There are instances in which goods are thrust upon a bailee who does not have any choice about whether he or she wishes to serve as bailee. An example would be a guest in your home who accidentally leaves his or her property behind, or a package addressed to your neighbor that is accidentally delivered to you. Many people would argue that such instances are not bailments at all. Still, the courts have been unwilling to dismiss the idea of a bailment altogether. As a result, the idea of an involuntary, or ***constructive bailment,*** has evolved.

---

transient A guest whose stay is relatively uncertain.

common carrier An individual or firm in the business of transporting goods between certain points as allowed by the various state commissions that regulate carriers.

consignor The person or party shipping goods in a bailment relationship.

consignee The person or party receiving goods in a bailment relationship.

carrier's lien A carrier's legal right to hold a shipment until payment is made.

constructive bailment A bailment in which goods are thrust upon a bailee who does not have any choice about whether he or she wishes to serve as bailee.

CHAPTER SUMMARY

1 The six typical reasons for creating a bailment are sale, transportation, repair or service, rental, storage, and security for a loan.

2 The transfer of goods from bailor to bailee must actually take place, and absent an understanding otherwise, the bailee must actually accept the goods for a bailment to exist. Except for a bailment that requires alteration, a bailee must return identical goods to the bailor.

3 **(a)** A bailment for the sole benefit of the bailee occurs when only the bailee benefits from the agreement. **(b)** A bailment for the sole benefit of the bailor occurs when only the bailor benefits from the agreement. **(c)** A mutual-benefit bailment is one in which both the bailee and bailor benefit. **(d)** A constructive bailment occurs when goods are thrust upon a bailee who does not have a choice about whether he or she wishes to serve as bailee.

4 The degree of care due in a bailment depends on the type of bailment involved and the consideration involved. In a bailment for the sole benefit of the bailee, the bailee is getting something for nothing and is expected to exercise great or extraordinary care in using the property. In a bailment for the sole benefit of the bailor, the bailee receives no benefit and must exercise only slight care. In a mutual-benefit bailment, the bailor is required to exercise reasonable and ordinary care. In constructive bailments, the bailee is usually expected to exercise reasonable care.

5 **(a)** Mutual-benefit bailments concerning storage involve leaving goods in the care of a warehouser. **(b)** Such bailments for parking lots usually involve parking a car in a parking lot of in a garage, and in the care of a parking-lot attendant. **(c)** Mutual-benefit bailments for work and services occur when one person turns over property to another for certain work to be performed on the property. **(d)** In the context of hotel bailments, a mutual-benefit bailment is created when a guest leaves property in the care of a hotelkeeper. **(e)** A mutual-benefit bailment with common carriers occurs when an individual or firm gives a common carrier property to be transported between certain locations.

Chapter 20 Assessment

MATCHING LEGAL TERMS

Match each of the following definitions with the correct term in the list below. Write the letter of your choice in the answer column.

- **a.** bailee
- **b.** bailment
- **c.** bailor
- **d.** carrier's lien
- **e.** common carrier
- **f.** consignee
- **g.** consignor
- **h.** constructive bailment
- **i.** lien
- **j.** transient

1. A relationship concerned with the transfer of possession of personal property without the passage of title. 1. _____
2. A relationship in which the bailee comes into possession by having goods thrust upon him or her. 2. _____
3. An individual or firm in the business of transporting goods between certain points for anyone. 3. _____
4. A person or firm who ships goods. 4. _____
5. A claim against the property of another as security for a debt. 5. _____
6. A person to whom goods are shipped. 6. _____
7. The person in a bailment relationship who transfers possession of goods to another. 7. _____
8. The person whose stay in a place of lodging is indefinite. 8. _____
9. The claim of a carrier against the owner of property for unpaid transportation charges. 9. _____
10. The person who receives goods as part of a bailment relationship. 10. _____

TRUE/FALSE QUIZ

Indicate whether each of the following statements is true or false by writing *T* or *F* in the answer column.

11. A bailment requires that title pass at the time the bailment is created. 11. _____
12. Bailments can be express or implied. 12. _____
13. Anyone in possession of goods can create a bailment relationship. 13. _____
14. A bailment for the sole benefit of the bailee usually exists in agreements for the rental of equipment. 14. _____
15. In a bailment for the sole benefit of the bailee, the bailee is required to extend only slight care. 15. _____

Bailments   CHAPTER 20   323

Chapter 20 Assessment

16. The lack of consideration invalidates a mutual-benefit bailment. **16.** _____

17. Except for storage transactions, the Uniform Commercial Code does not cover bailments. **17.** _____

18. The bailee in a bailment for work and services is entitled to hold and sell the property if the bailor does not pay for work or services done. **18.** _____

19. The relationship between a consignor and a carrier is a bailment for the sole benefit of the bailor. **19.** _____

20. A hotelkeeper has almost total liability for the property of guests. **20.** _____

21. A bailment relationship exists if a parking-lot operator allows a motorist to lock a car and retain the key. **21.** _____

22. When goods are stored in a warehouse, the warehouser becomes the bailor. **22.** _____

23. In a mutual-benefit bailment the bailee is required to extend extraordinary care. **23.** _____

24. When fungible goods are stored, the identical goods must be returned. **24.** _____

25. A bailment cannot be created without the agreement of both bailor and bailee. **25.** _____

DISCUSSION QUESTIONS

Answer the following questions and discuss them in class.

26. Discuss the six typical reasons for transferring goods and creating a bailment.

27. Discuss the importance of acceptance, possession, and return of goods as they apply to bailments.

28. Distinguish between (a) bailment for the sole benefit of the bailee, (b) bailment for the sole benefit of the bailor, (c) mutual-benefit bailment, and (d) constructive bailment. Provide examples of each.

Chapter 20 Assessment

29. Discuss the special requirements of mutual-benefit bailments concerned with (a) storage, (b) parking lots, (c) work and services, (d) hotels, and (e) common carriers.
_____
_____
_____

30. Discuss the level of care a bailee is required to give for each of several kinds of bailments.
_____
_____
_____

31. Discuss constructive bailments and explain how they differ from other kinds of bailments.
_____
_____
_____

THINKING CRITICALLY ABOUT THE LAW

Answer the following questions, which require you to think critically about the legal principles that you learned in this chapter.

32. Mutual Benefit Bailment A car in a parking garage is damaged and the attendant disclaims responsibility. In theory the owner of the car (bailor), would seem to have the law on his or her side, but can he or she prove his or her claim? What redress does the law provide?
_____
_____
_____

33. Care of Bailments The law of bailments requires that the bailee extend either slight care, reasonable care, or extraordinary care—depending on the circumstances. Why does the law allow such variations?
_____
_____
_____

34. Hotel Bailments A guest's laptop computer is stolen from her hotel room. Should the hotel bear some responsibility for the loss? Explain your answer.
_____
_____
_____

Chapter 20 Assessment

35. Common Carrier Bailments Should a common carrier be required to accept *all* goods for shipment that it is authorized to transport? Can there be grounds for refusing some shipments? Why or why not?

36. A Question of Ethics A man injured himself while using a rented power tool. The renter had ignored safety warnings, but refused to admit it. The owner denied that he knew of the defects in the power tool despite being aware of them. Is one party behaving more unethically than the other? Explain your answer.

CASE QUESTIONS

Study each case below and answer the questions that follow by writing *Yes* or *No* in the answer column.

37. Bailment Ky operated a service station on a road near the Canadian border. As a favor to customers, he frequently stored, without charge, certain items that travelers preferred not to take into Canada. Rowan had planned to cross the border for a day's visit but did not wish to take with her a bolt of fabric she had in her car. She left the fabric with Ky, saying that she would pick it up later in the day.

  a. Is the service Ky offers a bailment for the sole benefit of the bailee?   a. _____

  b. Is Ky the bailor?   b. _____

  c. Is Ky required to extend slight care?   c. _____

  d. Is Rowan the bailee?   d. _____

38. Bailment Ziess, a college student, owned some furniture, a portable TV, and a small refrigerator. At the end of the spring semester, she arranged to store her property in a storage room in her dorm building without charge by the college. The college made it clear that all storage was at students' risk.

  a. Is this storage arrangement a bailment for the sole benefit of the bailee?   a. _____

  b. Is this arrangement a mutual-benefit bailment?   b. _____

  c. Can Ziess take any action against the college in the event of loss of her property?   c. _____

39. Bailment Kenworth took his expensive watch to Gervey Jewelry for repairs and cleaning. During the week in which the watch remained with the jeweler, it was placed in the store's vault each night. One night, burglars were able to bypass the burglar alarm, break into the store, and use explosives to open the vault. Kenworth's watch was among the goods stolen. Kenworth brought suit, charging that Gervey should have provided greater care in this bailment. Specifically, he charged that Gervey should have had a 24-hour security guard.

Chapter 20 Assessment

   a. Is this an example of a mutual benefit bailment? a. _____
   b. Did Gervey provide ordinary care of the bailed property? b. _____
   c. Is it likely that a court would rule in favor of Kenworth? c. _____

CASE ANALYSIS

Study each of the following cases carefully and then briefly state the principle of law and your decision.

40. Parking Lot Bailment Wall parked his car in the parking lot at O'Hare Airport in Chicago. After he received a parking ticket from a ticketing dispensing machine, an automatic gate was raised and he entered the lot and parked his car in a space of his choosing. On the reverse side of the parking ticket was printed: "This is a lease of parking space only and not a bailment." When he returned the next day, he discovered that his car was missing and was presumed stolen. The car was later found, but had been extensively damaged by the thieves. Wall brought suit for $1,846, claiming that a bailment existed and that the parking-lot operator was responsible. *Did a bailment exist and is the parking-lot operator responsible for Wall's loss?* [*Clifford L. Wall et al., v. Airport Parking Company of Chicago,* 244 N.E.2d 190 (Illinois).]

Principle of law:

_____

_____

Decision:

_____

_____

41. Bailment Noble, a resident of Washington, D.C., ordered a stereo tuner from a store in Maine. The unit was shipped and was received by McLean, the receptionist/switchboard operator in Noble's apartment building. She placed the tuner in a small room where packages for tenants were kept. When Mrs. McLean went off duty at 4 P.M., the package was still in the room. By the next day it was gone; only the empty box in which the unit had been shipped was found outside the building. Noble brought suit, claiming that a bailment existed. The landlord, Bernstein, denied responsibility and pointed out a provision in the lease that the landlord is not responsible for the property of tenants and that, even if an employee of the landlord does store, move, or handle tenant's property, he or she does so as the tenant's agent. *Did a bailment exist, and is Bernstein responsible for the loss?* [*Howard Bernstein, et al. v. Richard Noble,* 487 A.2d 231 (District of Columbia).]

Principle of law:

_____

_____

Decision:

_____

_____

Chapter 20 Assessment

42. **Bailment** Gilder entered a parking garage enclosed within the Washington Hilton Hotel, where he was directed to a space by an attendant. Some of the spaces were designated for park-and-lock, and others were not. He locked the car and kept the keys. When Gilder entered the garage, he saw a number of employees—a manager, a cashier, and three attendants. After Gilder parked his car, he opened the trunk in plain view of a group of employees, placed his lady friend's cosmetic bag in it, and locked the trunk. Upon his return, he found the trunk lid damaged from being pried open. Gilder brought suit, charging the garage with failure to provide adequate care. On appeal, the garage denied responsibility, claiming that there was no bailment. *Did a bailment exist, and is the garage responsible?* [*Parking Management, Inc. v. Mark Gilder,* 343 A.2d 51 (District of Columbia).]

Principle of law:

Decision:

LEGAL RESEARCH

Complete the following activities. Then share your findings with the class.

43. **Working in Teams** In teams of three or four, visit a range of hotels and motels to determine their policies regarding stolen or missing property. Ask particularly about experiences with guests' complaints.

44. **Using Technology** Using the Internet and search engines, look for legal cases involving bailments or sample bailment contracts. Briefly record your findings.

CHAPTER 21

LANDLORD-TENANT RELATIONS

PERFORMANCE OBJECTIVES

After studying this chapter and completing the assessments, you will be able to:

1. Distinguish between a lease and a license.

2. Explain the purposes and effects of covenants and conditions in a lease.

3. Describe the four types of tenant interests in real property.

4. Discuss the rights and duties of landlords and tenants.

5. Explain several reasons for the termination of leases.

6. Explain how liability is determined and whether the landlord or tenant is likely to be found liable.

LEGAL TERMS

landlord
tenant
lease
lessor
lessee
covenants
conditions
periodic tenancy
tenancy for years
tenancy at will
tenancy at sufferance
warranty of habitability
quiet enjoyment
eviction
assignment
sublease

Renting a Residence

Part of the American dream is a "home of your own." For many people, however, home ownership is either an unattainable dream or an unattractive choice. Renting a house or an apartment, therefore, is often the best available option.

In Chapter 19, leasehold estates were introduced as possession interests in real property and distinguished from ownership interests-freehold estates. This chapter examines landlord-tenant relations and the major points of law that concern this relationship.

The Landlord-Tenant Relationship

The relationship between **landlord** (the owner of real property who gives up his or her right of possession) and **tenant** (the person who agrees to pay for the use of real property) involves a tenant's possession, use, and control of real property in exchange for payment—that is, rent. The document in which the terms of the agreement are spelled out is the **lease.** The property owner is the landlord, or **lessor,** and the party who contracts to lease the property is the tenant, or **lessee.**

landlord The owner of real property who gives up his or her right of possession.

tenant The person who agrees to pay for the use of real property.

lease The document in which the terms of a rental agreement are written.

lessor The property owner.

lessee The party who contracts to lease the property.

The Difference Between a Lease and a License

Both leases and licenses give nonowners certain rights in real property. A lease transfers to a lessee the right of possession; a license does not. A license merely gives a person (the licensee) the right to use real property and can be cancelled at the will of the landowner. As a result, a lease creates an estate (interest) in real property; a license merely gives permission to use it.

OBJECTIVE 1

Distinguish between a lease and a license.

Essential Elements of the Landlord-Tenant Relationship

The essentials of the landlord-tenant relationship are:

- The tenant can occupy a landlord's property only with the consent of the landlord.
- The tenant's rights in the property are inferior to those of the landlord.
- The property must revert (be returned) to the landlord at the termination of the lease.
- The parties must agree that the tenant has a right of immediate possession.

The Lease is the Basis of the Relationship

The landlord-tenant relationship can be created by an express or implied contract. While oral contracts of lease are valid under common law, most state statutes and the Statute of Frauds require written leases in instances in which the term of the lease is greater than one to three years.

Covenants The lease often includes *covenants,* which are agreements or promises made by either the landlord or tenant to do certain things, such as when a tenant promises to use the property for certain purposes or a landlord promises to make certain repairs and to assure the tenant's quiet enjoyment.

Conditions A lease may also contain *conditions,* or restrictions, that limit the use of the property. If the lease stipulates that the premises will be used as a retail bookstore, for example, a nightclub would not be permissible. The landlord may cancel the lease if a tenant fails to respect the conditions specified.

The Law Relating to Leases Under common law, the parties to a lease were relatively free to include whatever terms were agreed to by the parties. Increasingly, however, leases are subject to legal restrictions. Also, because leases are now viewed more often as contracts, commercial leases are subject to certain provisions of the Uniform Commercial Code regarding unconscionability [UCC 2-302].

TYPES OF TENANT INTERESTS IN REAL PROPERTY

The type of possession interest a tenant has in real property can vary considerably depending on the agreements between the parties and the provisions of the lease. The following types of possession interests are most common.

Periodic Tenancy

A *periodic tenancy* is a possession interest in which the lease continues for successive periods for the same length of time—weekly, monthly, or annually. A periodic tenancy is somewhat open-ended because it is automatically renewed at the end of the period unless the landlord or tenant gives notice of his or her intent to not renew the lease.

OBJECTIVE 2

Explain the purposes and effects of covenants and conditions in a lease.

covenants Agreements made by either a landlord of a tenant to do certain things.

conditions Restrictions that limit the use of the property.

OBJECTIVE 3

Describe the four types of tenant interests in real property.

periodic tenancy A possession interest in which the lease continues for successive periods for the same length of time.

Tenancy for Years

The most common type of possession interest is a ***tenancy for years.*** This type of lease is for a specific period of time—weeks, months, or years. A tenancy of this type automatically terminates on the stated expiration date.

Tenancy at Will

A ***tenancy at will*** is a possession interest in which no specific time of lease is agreed upon. The lease continues indefinitely until one of the parties notifies the other of a desire to terminate. Modern statutes provide that the landlord must give the tenant notice of his or her intent to terminate the lease. Sometimes such notice must be in writing.

Tenancy at Sufferance

A ***tenancy at sufferance*** exists only in one limited situation: when a tenant wrongfully extends his or her tenancy beyond the term agreed upon. Tenancy at sufferance is really not a true tenancy at all because the status of the tenant in this situation is rather uncertain. The landlord can either choose to evict the tenant and treat him or her as a trespasser, or hold the tenant to another term of the lease.

EXAMPLE 21.1
> Segura rented a house from Daly for two years. At the end of the lease, Segura was in no hurry to vacate the premises. The two parties discussed staying on, but nothing was agreed upon and no additional rent was paid. Segura's status was a tenancy at sufferance. Daly could evict Segura, or hold him to another term of the lease, even though Segura had not indicated any wish to stay.

RIGHTS AND DUTIES OF THE PARTIES

The rights and duties of the parties are spelled out in the lease and are expanded upon by relevant law and regulations.

Landlord's Warranty of Habitability

A warranty, as related to the sale of goods discussed in Chapter 16, is a promise or guarantee made by the seller that the goods or services offered are what he or she claims they are—or what a reasonable person has a right to expect. In the case of the landlord-tenant relationship, the law assumes another kind of promise—an implied ***warranty of habitability.*** This warranty means that the landlord

---

tenancy for years The most common type of possession interest in which the lease is for a specific period of time.

tenancy at will A possession interest in which no specific time of lease is agreed upon.

tenancy at sufferance A tenancy that exists only when a tenant wrongfully extends his or her tenancy beyond the term agreed upon.

OBJECTIVE 4
Discuss the rights and duties of landlords and tenants.

warranty of habitability An implied warranty in which the landlord guarantees that the premises are reasonably fit for occupancy and that there are no defects that would impair the health, safety, or well being of the occupants.

guarantees that the premises are reasonably fit for occupancy and that there are no defects that would impair the health, safety, or well being of the occupants of the premises.

EXAMPLE 21.2

Katya had been living in a college dormitory for three years and decided to rent an off-campus apartment for her senior year. Somewhat naïve and eager to be independent, she hurriedly signed a one-year lease and moved in soon afterward. It was not long before she had cause to regret her decision. She discovered that she had the unwelcome company of mice. There was no hot water and no heat in the winter. The door lock was defective and the windows could not be locked, with the result that an intruder stole her computer. When she moved out after one month, the landlord sued, claiming that she had violated the terms of the one-year lease. Katya claimed, and the court agreed, that the landlord had breached his warranty of habitability.

Landlord's Right to Rent, Possession, and to Evict

The landlord (lessor) has the right to collect the agreed-upon rent as provided in the lease. Also, the landlord has the right to regain possession of the property, in good condition, at the end of the lease. In addition, the landlord has the right, subject to limitations by local and

Photo 21.1

Warranty of Habitability

The law provides tenants with an implied warranty of habitability. *What does this warranty guarantee?*

Landlord-Tenant Relations CHAPTER 21 333

state statutes, to evict a tenant for nonpayment of rent, illegal use of the premises, or other material violations of the terms of the lease.

> **EXAMPLE 21.3**
> Itoh leased an apartment from Fodor, with the expressed intention of living there himself. Within three months, he began to use the apartment as a gathering place for drug users and prostitutes. Other tenants complained to Fodor, who shortly thereafter began an eviction action. Fodor would be successful in evicting Itoh.

Landlord's Right to Keep Fixtures and Permanent Improvements

A tenant may wish to make improvements by attaching fixtures to the land or to the premises. Two issues are raised by such actions:

- Does the tenant have the right to make attachments?
- Does the tenant have the right to remove the fixtures he or she attached at the end of the lease?

Generally, the tenant has the right to make reasonable changes in the leased property to make it suitable for use under the circumstances. Whether the tenant has the right to remove fixtures at the end of the lease depends largely on whether removing them would damage the landlord's interest. For example, it might not be reasonable for a tenant to add new wiring if the lease is for one year. However, it might be reasonable for a tenant with a long-term lease to add a patio.

Landlord's Duty to Mitigate Damages

In most states, a landlord has a duty to make reasonable efforts to reduce his or her losses resulting from a tenant's *abandonment* (the voluntary surrender of possession of leased premises). A landlord must make a reasonable effort, for example, to find a new tenant to occupy the abandoned premises. If the landlord fails to do so, the tenant might be relieved of his or her obligation under the lease to pay the rent for the remaining time of the lease.

> **EXAMPLE 21.4**
> Polin rented an apartment for one year for $800 per month. After occupying the apartment for two months, she was transferred to another city and abandoned her rented apartment. The landlord made no attempt to rent the vacated apartment, instead using the time to make repairs and paint it. After nearly a year had passed, the landlord

> brought suit to collect the rent that would have been paid by Polin had she not abandoned the premises. It is unlikely that a court would award the full amount of lost rent because the landlord had an obligation to mitigate damages and to rent the apartment. Of course, the landlord could sue for the difference between the lower rent and the rent specified in Polin's lease, plus any foreseeable reasonable expenses associated with finding a new tenant.

Tenant's Right of Quiet Enjoyment

Most written leases include covenants, expressly or implied, of *quiet enjoyment* of the premises. This right includes the use of the leased premises without unreasonable interference from the landlord or third parties. While the landlord is not usually responsible for the actions of third parties over which he or she has no control, some courts have held that the landlord was responsible for the actions of a tenant who denied another tenant his or her right to quiet enjoyment.

quiet enjoyment The right to use the leased premises without unreasonable interferences from the landlord or third parties.

Tenant's Right to Acquire and Retain Possession

When agreeing to lease property, the lessor (landlord) promises that the lessee (tenant) will have possession of the premises on the agreed date. If the premises are occupied or under construction, the landlord must take reasonable steps to ensure that the premises are available when they are supposed to be.

The tenant has the right to possess the leased premises for the duration of the lease. If the landlord interferes with the tenant's right of possession by evicting him or her without a court order of eviction, the tenant has the right to terminate the lease. An *eviction* is an action that denies the tenant the use of the premises. An *actual eviction* occurs when the tenant is denied the physical use of the premises.

eviction An action that denies the tenant the use of the premises.

A *constructive eviction* results when the tenant's use or enjoyment of the property has been substantially lessened as a result of certain actions, conditions, or behavior on the part of the landlord or other tenants. A tenant's use or enjoyment would be substantially lessened, for example, by excessive noise, foul odors, or the use of nearby premises for illegal purposes. When the tenant claims constructive, rather than actual eviction, he or she cannot terminate the lease or stop paying rent unless he or she abandons the premises.

Tenant's Right to Assign or Sublease

The act of a tenant who transfers his or her interest in the property is commonly referred to as a sublease. Actually, however, when a tenant transfers his or her *entire* interest in the *entire* premises for the

assignment When a tenant transfers his or her entire interest in the entire premises for the remaining length of the term of the lease.

sublease A transfer of the tenant's interest for part of the term of the lease and/or part of the premises.

OBJECTIVE 5

Explain several reasons for the termination of leases.

OBJECTIVE 6

Explain how liability is determined and whether the landlord or tenant is likely to be found liable.

remaining length of the term of the lease, it is an *assignment.* On the other hand, a *sublease* is a transfer of the tenant's interest for *part* of the term of the lease and/or *part* of the premises. Most leases provide that a tenant may not assign or sublease without the landlord's consent. Also, a provision may be added stating that a landlord may not unreasonably refuse consent for an assignment or sublease.

Termination of Leases

A lease may be terminated for several reasons beyond the most common one—the expiration of the lease. Abandonment and breaching the terms of the lease are two other valid reasons.

Tenant's Abandonment

If the tenant has abandoned the premises, he or she is not relieved of the obligation to pay the agreed rent. If, however, the landlord has violated his or her duty to provide the tenant with quiet enjoyment, the tenant may abandon the premises under the doctrine of constructive eviction, and this action will terminate the lease.

Termination by Breach

Most leases contain a provision that gives the landlord the right to terminate the lease if the tenant fails to pay rent or violates any other material lease provision—for example, making excessive noise, disturbing other tenants, or using residential premises for business purposes. However, the tenant's breach must be *material,* that is, involve an important matter. It is unlikely that a court would allow a termination if the tenant is only a few days late with a rent payment.

Tort Liability

When a person is injured on leased premises, the question of liability arises. Generally, the person in control of the area in which the injury took place is held to be responsible. The landlord remains in control of common areas, such as hallways, stairways, and laundry rooms.

EXAMPLE 21.5

Bonder, a new tenant in an apartment building owned by Mei, suffered serious injuries when he fell on a broken step while descending a stairway in his apartment building. The landlord was held liable for Bonder's injuries because he was negligent in failing to keep the stairway in good condition.

The tenant is responsible for injuries occurring in his or her own leased premises. Apartment dwellers' insurance policies protect the tenant policyholder against liability losses resulting from injuries that occur in the tenant's premises, but not losses that result from injuries that occur in common areas or in the physical structure itself.

CHAPTER SUMMARY

1. A lease transfers to a lessee the right of possession; a license does not. A license only gives the licensee the right to use real property and can be cancelled at will by the landowner.

2. Covenants are promises by either the landlord or the tenant to do certain things. Conditions are restrictions on the use of the property.

3. The four kinds of tenant interests in real property are the following: **(a)** periodic tenancy (a possession interest in which the lease continues for the same length of time), **(b)** tenancy for years (a lease for a specific period of time), **(c)** tenancy at will (a possession interest in which no specific time of the lease is agreed upon, and **(d)** tenancy at sufferance (when a tenant wrongfully extends his or her tenancy beyond the term agreed upon.

4. The law imposes on the landlord the warranty of habitability and the duty to mitigate damages if a lease is breached. In return, the landlord has the right to rent, possession, evict, and keep fixtures and permanent improvements to the property. Tenants have the right to property that is reasonably fit and safe for occupancy, to the quiet enjoyment of the premises, and to acquire, possess, lease, or assign the premises subject to the terms of the lease.

5. The most common reason that a lease is terminated is by expiration. Leases can also be terminated by abandonment or by breach of the terms of the lease.

6. Liability is generally determined by who has control of the premises at the time and place of injury. The tenant is responsible for injuries occurring in his or her own leased premises. The landlord is responsible for injuries that occur in common areas.

Chapter 21 Assessment

MATCHING LEGAL TERMS

Match each of the following definitions with the correct term in the list below. Write the letter of your choice in the answer column.

- **a.** abandonment
- **b.** assignment
- **c.** condition
- **d.** covenant
- **e.** eviction
- **f.** lease
- **g.** lessee
- **h.** lessor
- **i.** periodic tenancy
- **j.** quiet enjoyment
- **k.** sublease
- **l.** tenancy at will
- **m.** tenancy at sufferance
- **n.** tenancy for years
- **o.** warranty of habitability

1. The legal term in a landlord-tenant relationship that refers to the landlord. 1. _____
2. The agreement between landlord and tenant. 2. _____
3. The legal term in a landlord-tenant relationship that refers to the tenant. 3. _____
4. A promise made by a landlord or a tenant in a lease. 4. _____
5. A restriction in a lease that allows cancellation if a tenant fails to honor the limitation. 5. _____
6. A lease in which the lease period continues for successive periods for the same length of time. 6. _____
7. A lease for a specific period of time—weeks, months, or years. 7. _____
8. A lease in which no specific time has been agreed. 8. _____
9. The status of a tenant who extends tenancy beyond the term of the original lease. 9. _____
10. A landlord's promise that the premises are reasonably fit for occupation and that there are no defects that would impair the health, safety, or well-being of the occupants. 10. _____
11. A tenant's voluntary surrender of leased premises. 11. _____
12. The right of a tenant to use the premises without unreasonable interference from the landlord or third parties. 12. _____
13. An action of the landlord that denies the tenant the use of the premises. 13. _____
14. An act of a tenant that transfers his or her entire interest in premises for the entire term of the lease. 14. _____
15. An act of a tenant that transfers his or interest in premises for part of the term of the lease. 15. _____

TRUE/FALSE QUIZ

Indicate whether each of the following statements is true or false by writing *T* or *F* in the answer column.

16. A tenant can legally occupy a landlord's property only with the consent of the landlord. 16. _____

PART 4   Property

Chapter 21 Assessment

17. The tenant's rights in rented property are superior to those of the landlord.

17. _____

18. The landlord-tenant relationship can be created by express or implied contract.

18. _____

19. The unconscionability clause of the Uniform Commercial Code can be applied to the landlord-tenant relationship.

19. _____

20. A tenancy at sufferance describes the relationship that exists when a tenant extends his or her stay beyond the terms of the lease.

20. _____

21. A warranty of habitability is the tenant's promise that he or she will inhabit the property according to the terms of the lease.

21. _____

22. If a tenant abandons the premises, the landlord is permitted to continue charging rent without taking any other action.

22. _____

23. The covenant of quiet enjoyment refers to a tenant's promise to remain quiet after 10 P.M.

23. _____

24. A tenant usually has the right to assign or sublease the leased property with the landlord's consent.

24. _____

25. A landlord is liable for all injuries that occur on the leased premises.

25. _____

DISCUSSION QUESTIONS

Answer the following questions and discuss them in class.

26. Discuss the difference between a lease and a license, and state the advantages and disadvantages of each.

27. If a tenant chooses to use leased premises for purposes other than the ones stipulated in the lease, why would a new agreement be required?

28. If a landlord should fail to make the repairs promised in the lease, what recourse does the tenant have?

Landlord-Tenant Relations CHAPTER 21

Chapter 21 Assessment

29. Should a tenant have the right to remove fixtures he or she has added to the premises? Why or why not?

30. Explain several reasons for termination of leases.

31. Explain how liability for injuries suffered by a tenant's guests in common areas is determined and whether the landlord or tenant is likely to be found liable.

THINKING CRITICALLY ABOUT THE LAW

Answer the following questions, which require you to think critically about the legal principles that you learned in this chapter.

32. Landlord's Rights Under what circumstances should a landlord have the right to withhold his or her permission to assign or sublet premises?

33. Tenant's Rights Most residential leases prohibit the premises being used for business purposes. Would activities such as writing, dressmaking, or accounting be sufficient reason for eviction?

34. Warranty of Habitability What recourse does a tenant have when the landlord fails to provide reasonable habitability?

PART 4   Property

Chapter 21 Assessment

35. Liability of Landlord Under what circumstances is the landlord liable for injuries suffered by a tenant as a victim of a crime in his or her premises?

36. A Question of Ethics Are tenants justified in withholding rent on the grounds that another tenant's behavior has interfered with their right to quiet enjoyment?

CASE QUESTIONS

Study each case below and answer the questions that follow by writing *Yes* or *No* in the answer column.

37. Tenancy Maldanado rented office space in a commercial building for a period of one year and agreed to pay the rent monthly. At the end of the year, neither Maldanado nor the landlord gave the other notice of intention not to renew the lease, but instead engaged in negotiations for several months concerning the terms of a new lease. During the period of negotiations, Maldanado paid the same rent that he had during the lease, and the landlord accepted the payments.

    a. Was a tenancy at sufferance created?   a. _____

    b. Was the first year of the lease a periodic tenancy?   b. _____

    c. Was a new periodic tenancy created automatically?   c. _____

38. Landlord Rights Patsos rented a vacant warehouse for five years with the stated purpose of opening a wholesale meat-distribution business. It was necessary to install a number of large refrigerators and other kinds of equipment to process and store meat. At the end of the five years, Patsos decided to build his own warehouse and did not renew the lease. The day he began to remove his equipment, the landlord appeared and stopped the activity, claiming that the equipment was permanently installed and thus were fixtures—and that they therefore belonged to the landlord.

    a. Is it likely that a court would consider the refrigerators and other equipment to be fixtures and therefore the property of the landlord?   a. _____

    b. Is the determination of whether the landlord's property will suffer damage an issue in this case?   b. _____

    c. Is there any way that Patsos could have conducted his business without installing the equipment?   c. _____

Landlord-Tenant Relations   **CHAPTER 21**

Chapter 21 Assessment

39. Conditions of Lease Perez rented a vacant building to operate a movie theater that specialized in art and classic films. After several months, it was apparent that the business was doomed to failure, and in an attempt to salvage his business, Perez changed his policy and began showing pornographic films. The change helped the business but attracted a different clientele. The landlord began an eviction action, claiming that Perez had violated terms of his lease.

a. Is it likely that the landlord will be successful in evicting Perez?

b. Would the landlord have difficulty in proving his claim?

c. Could the disagreement have been prevented by more specific terms in the lease agreement?

a. _____

b. _____

c. _____

CASE ANALYSIS

Study each of the following cases carefully and then briefly state the principle of law and your decision.

40. Covenants Knight purchased an apartment building that was occupied by tenants Hallsthammer, Decaprio, and Breit. The day after acquiring the building, Knight informed the tenants that their rent was being increased. A week later, Breit, on behalf of himself and other tenants, informed Knight that the tenants intended to withhold their rent because of the state of disrepair of the building. In their complaint, the tenants cited wall cracks, peeling paint, water leaks, heating and electrical fixture problems, broken or inoperable windows, rodents and cockroaches, and lack of sufficient heat. The tenants accused Knight of a breach of his warranty of habitability, and for this reason they withheld rent payments. Knight defended his actions, stating that the tenants had not given him time to remedy the problems. *Does it seem likely that the court would support the actions of the tenants?* [*Knight v. Hallsthammer,* 623 P.2d 268 (California).]

Principle of law:

_____

_____

Decision:

_____

_____

41. Liability An intruder entered through a window and attacked McCutchen in her apartment. McCutchen sued the landlord, Ten Associates, for failure to provide adequate security and failure to warn her of the risk of intrusion through a window. Ten Associates claimed that they had no way of anticipating an intruder. Evidence was introduced that revealed the landlord knew or should have known of a prior attack and numerous intrusions through apartment windows. *Does it appear that Ten Associates was negligent in providing for the security of tenants?* [*Ten Associates v. McCutchen,* 398 So.2d 860 (Florida).]

Principle of law:

_____

_____

Chapter 21 Assessment

Decision:
_____
_____

42. Landlord Responsibility Harmon, the owner of a suburban house, rented it for one year to Wagner and his wife, who had just moved into the city from another state. Within two months of moving into the house, the Wagners divorced and both husband and wife moved to smaller residences. The house remained vacant for nine months. At the end of one year, Harmon brought suit to collect the rent for ten months. Wagner protested, claiming that the landlord should have tried to rent to someone else. The landlord said that it was Harmon's responsibility to sublease the house. *Is it likely that Harmon would be successful in his suit?*

Principle of law:
_____
_____

Decision:
_____
_____

LEGAL RESEARCH

Complete the following activities. Then share your findings with the class.

43. Working in Teams In teams of three or four, investigate whether your local community has a housing court. What are some of the landlord-tenant disputes decided by this court?
_____
_____
_____

44. Using Technology Using the Internet and search engines, investigate sample leases. What are some of the covenants and conditions contained in these leases?
_____
_____
_____

CHAPTER 22

Wills, Intestacy, and Trusts

PERFORMANCE OBJECTIVES

After studying this chapter and completing the assessments, you will be able to:

1. Identify the purpose of a will.
2. Use the correct language when discussing a will.
3. Discuss the types of gifts covered by a will.
4. Identify the requirements for a valid will.
5. Discuss the primary requirements for testamentary capacity.
6. Discuss and provide examples of undue influence.
7. Explain the way a court distributes the estate of someone who dies intestate.
8. Discuss the purposes of trusts and identify the major types.
9. Explain the role and responsibilities of a trustee.

LEGAL TERMS

decedent
will
testator
personal representative
intestate
beneficiary
legacy
bequest
testamentary capacity
undue influence
living will
codicil
trust
trustee

THE PURPOSE OF A WILL

The law in the United States with regard to wills, estates, and trusts has been developed to achieve certain objectives that are quite unlike those of the common law that existed in England prior to the early twentieth century. Much of early English law and tradition concerning wills and estates was intended to maintain a feudal system in which all land belonged to the king.

In this country, the law recognizes the concept of private property and the right of an individual to dispose of property as he or she wishes. Moreover, it reflects an attempt by the state to protect the family of the deceased person, who is known as the **decedent,** by providing for the needs of a surviving spouse and children, even if the decedent failed to do so.

A **will** is a person's declaration of how he or she wishes property to be distributed upon his or her death. The primary purpose of a will is to allow an individual to designate what will happen to his or her property after death. This intention of the decedent is known as *testamentary intent.*

The law, reflecting both recent tradition and current public policy, states that when a person dies, arrangements will be made to pay his or her final expenses, such as the cost of an appropriate burial, medical expenses, taxes, and legitimate debts. Also, the person's property will be disposed of and applied to payment of these expenses, with the remainder to be distributed as the deceased wished or as the law provides.

THE LANGUAGE OF WILLS

The person who makes the will is known as the **testator.** The court is responsible for accepting a will that meets all statutory requirements and for supervising the operation of a will is the *probate court.* The person responsible for settling the affairs of the decedent is known as the ***personal representative.***

If the personal representative has been named in the will of the deceased, he or she is known as the *executor.* If the executor is deceased, or if the decedent died without making a will, or the executor named in the will is lacking in capacity, the court will appoint a personal representative who is known as the *administrator.* The personal representative is responsible for managing the affairs of the estate with prudence. He or she may be held liable for any loss suffered by the estate as a result of misconduct or lack of judgment.

OBJECTIVE 1
Identify the purpose of a will.

decedent A deceased person.

will A person's declaration of how he or she wishes property to be distributed upon his or her death.

OBJECTIVE 2
Use the correct language when discussing a will.

testator The person who makes a will.

personal representative The person responsible for settling the affairs of the decedent.

intestate The state in which a person dies without a will.

beneficiary An individual who receives gifts of personal or real property by will.

OBJECTIVE 3
Discuss the types of gifts covered by a will.

legacy A gift of money by will.

bequest A gift of personal property by will.

OBJECTIVE 4
Identify the requirements for a valid will.

For various reasons, some people do not execute a will. When a person dies without a will, he or she is said to have died *intestate* (without a will).

The term *heir* is broad and refers to a person who inherits property either under a will or from someone who dies intestate. Currently, there is seldom a distinction between individuals who receive gifts of personal or real property by will. Each person is known as a **beneficiary**.

TYPES OF GIFTS

A gift of money is known as a **legacy;** a gift of personal property is known as a **bequest**—but the two terms are often used synonymously. Currently, the term *bequest* includes all types of gifts. It can be *specific,* such as "I give my gardener, John Brown, all the hand and power tools in my garage and workshop." A bequest that does not identify a specific item of property can be *general,* such as "I give my son, Kevin, $10,000." A gift can even be *residuary,* such as "The balance of my estate I leave to my brother, Joseph."

REQUIREMENTS OF A VALID WILL

A will must comply with legal requirements intended to ensure that the wishes of the testator (previously females were known as "testatrix") are met and that there are no obstacles to the transfer of the property as the decedent intended. The law governing wills varies by state, but most states specify certain requirements.

Requirements of Writing

In most cases, a will must be in writing, dated, and signed to be effective. The writing need not be formal, provided it meets certain requirements. A *holographic will,* for example, is one that is completely handwritten. Holographic wills have been challenged because they included some words that were not handwritten, such as the printing on stationery, or words or names that were printed rather than written. In some states, even a will without witnesses would be accepted as valid. However, a holographic will must be signed and dated.

A *nuncupative will,* that is, an oral will, might be valid in only the most rare of circumstances. A transcript of a tape recording of a decedent's voice, offered as a holographic will, was held to be invalid.

PART 4   Property

A formal, typewritten, or printed will must be signed by the testator and witnessed. In most states, there are no age requirements for witnesses, but they must be legally competent. That is, minors may witness a will if they have an adequate understanding and could testify regarding the facts related to the execution of the will if necessary. The number of witnesses required varies, depending on local statutes. It is necessary, however, that the witnesses see the testator sign the document because they may be called upon later to attest that they actually saw the testator sign. For this reason, it is generally advisable to have witnesses who are younger than the testator and who live nearby (not that all younger persons will outlive the testator, but it more likely that they will). It is expected that witnesses will be satisfied that the testator is of sound mind at the time of signing. Frequently, testators videotape themselves and their witnesses during the signing of the will to demonstrate competence and the presence of witnesses. However, videotaped wills in themselves are not valid.

In some states, witnesses cannot be beneficiaries. Most states require the testator to inform the beneficiaries that he or she is signing a will.

Testamentary Capacity

Just as contracts require competent parties, the law relating to wills requires ***testamentary capacity;*** that is, a testator must be of sound mind and legal age. There is some variation among the states as to the minimum age. In most states, the age of majority is 18. While the testator's age is something that can be determined easily, a person's mental capacity is not so readily provable. It is essential that the testator be of sound mind when the will is made, although, as often happens, mental capacity may deteriorate with the passing years. Also, the testator may lack the mental capacity to, say, operate a business, but he or she may have sufficient capacity to determine the distribution of his or her estate. If it can be established that the testator lacked testamentary capacity, the will is void.

Undue Influence

The expression ***undue influence*** describes the unfair and improper pressure that might be applied to a testator to change his or her true wishes for the disposition of property. Undue influence can take many forms, from threats of harm to more subtle suggestions. It is often difficult for a court to decide whether the attention given to an elderly parent, for example, is undue influence on the part of a relative or is simply loving concern shown by one of the parties named in the will.

OBJECTIVE 5

Discuss the primary requirements for testamentary capacity.

testamentary capacity The requirement that a testator be of sound mind and legal age.

OBJECTIVE 6

Discuss and provide examples of undue influence.

undue influence The unfair and improper pressure that might be applied to a testator to change his or her true wishes for the disposition of property.

Living Wills

Advancing medical technology can prolong life even when there is no chance of recovery. Many are opposed to their lives being prolonged by artificial life support. In response to these concerns, a number of states have enacted legislation allowing individuals to execute a ***living will***. A living will is a document in which a person directs his or her physician and/or health proxy to forgo certain extraordinary (heroic) medical procedures if, for example, the person is dying or permanently unconscious. The effect of a valid living will is to permit a terminally ill patient to die with dignity and to protect the physician or hospital from liability for withdrawing or limiting life support.

living will A document in which a person directs his or her physician and/or health proxy to forgo certain extraordinary medical procedures in especially dire circumstances.

REVOKING AND REVISING WILLS

During the lifetime of the testator, there is often a need to revoke or revise a will.

Revisions

Any alterations to a will, such as erasures, words crossed out, or handwritten insertions, usually invalidate the document. To make legal changes in a will, a separate document, called a ***codicil***, is prepared to revoke, alter, or revise the will. The execution of a codicil is very much like writing a new will. It must be witnessed and dated. There is no limit on the number of codicils that can be made. In the case of a relatively simple, straightforward will, it is often just as easy to execute an entirely new will. Also, with the use of word processing, it is easy to recall the existing will and make whatever changes are desired. On the other hand, a lengthy, complex will may be revised by writing a codicil.

codicil A document, separate from the will, in which a person can make legal changes to his or her will.

> **EXAMPLE 22.1**
>
> Kassim, a widower, executed a will in which he left his entire estate to his two children, Robert and Susan, equally. As the years passed, Robert struggled to make ends meet. Susan, on the other hand, enjoyed financial success. Kassim felt that Robert needed money more than Susan. To change the distribution of his estate so that a greater portion went to Robert, Kassim executed a new will.

Revocations

Many wills include a statement that the testator is revoking all previous wills. Even without such a statement, the most recent will, if valid, automatically revokes all prior wills made by the testator.

Revocations by operation of law can include those that result from marriage or remarriage of the testator, divorce or annulment of a marriage, and the birth or adoption of children after the will was made, all of which can change the disposition of gifts.

INTESTACY

When a person dies without a will, or had a will that fails to dispose of property properly, he or she is said to have died intestate. What happens, then, to personal and real property that belonged to the deceased? The law of the state in which the deceased person domiciled (lived) governs the disposition of his or her property, even if the death may have occurred elsewhere. These laws vary by state. Generally, a surviving spouse and children receive the entire estate. But even this seemingly fair division can create problems, as shown in Example 22.2.

OBJECTIVE 7

Explain the way a court distributes the estate of someone who dies intestate.

EXAMPLE 22.2

> Kaslick, a man of modest means, died intestate, leaving his wife, who had no marketable skills, and two young children. Under state law, Kaslick's estate was divided in half between the wife and the two children. Because of their ages, the children's share was held in trust until they reached the age of majority. As a result, the wife not only had to support herself but also the children with her one-half of the estate because the children's half was not available to her. If Kaslick had prepared a will, he might have left the entire estate, or at least most of it, to the wife, with perhaps a smaller amount to the children.

If a person dies intestate leaving a spouse but no children, the surviving spouse receives the entire estate. If there are children but no surviving spouse, the children receive the estate. State laws on intestacy cover other situations, such as when a person dies without either spouse or children. In these cases, other relatives, including parents, grandchildren, brothers, and sisters, are included in the distribution.

EXAMPLE 22.3

> Aiken, a young student without assets who believed he did not need a will, was killed in an airplane crash. Most likely, he would not have wanted to have the millions of dollars paid as a settlement to his estate given to a father who abandoned him as an infant.

If no surviving heirs or ancestors of the deceased can be found, the decedent's property passes to the state.

OBJECTIVE 8

Discuss the purpose of trusts and identify the major types.

trust A device or mechanism that permits personal or real property to be held by one party, the trustee, for the benefit of another, the beneficiary.

trustee A person who is entrusted with the management and control of another's property or the rights associated with that property.

TRUSTS

In some ways, a trust has some of the characteristics of a will: it allows a person to control the disposition of his or her property after death. A ***trust*** is a device or mechanism that permits personal or real property to be held by one party, the ***trustee***, for the benefit of another, the *beneficiary*. One of the benefits of a trust is that it allows the legal title of property to be separated from the benefits of ownership. A trust allows parents, for example, to transfer benefits, such as income derived from property, to children and still withhold actual ownership until the children are older (and presumably wiser).

Another use for a trust would be if, for example, A put property in trust for B's lifetime so that she could benefit from the income the property might produce, and at B's death, the property would then pass on to C.

Types of Trusts

Generally, there are two main types of trusts. A *testamentary trust* is created by a will. It only becomes effective upon the death of the testator. The names of the parties—beneficiaries and trustee—are specified in the will.

EXAMPLE 22.4

> Neurman, a wealthy merchant, was concerned that if he died, his three grown—but irresponsible—children would quickly squander their inheritances. To avoid the problems he foresaw, he set up a testamentary trust in his will that provided that his entire estate, after paying final expenses, would be placed in trust and that the trustee would pay each of his children a yearly allowance.

Note that, in Example 22.4, the final disposition of the property is still undetermined. What happens to the property held in trust when the last of the children dies? To avoid such difficulties, a trust must provide for final distribution of the property after the objective of the trust has been met.

A *living trust,* (also known as an *inter vivos* trust) is established while the person who wishes to set up the trust, known as the *settlor,* is still alive. The settlor transfers the legal title to the property to a trust to be held for the benefit of either a beneficiary or the settlor himself or herself.

PART 4   Property

The Role of the Trustee

The responsibility of the trustee is that of a fiduciary, and as suggested by the name, one of great trust. He or she must manage the property according to the wishes of the settlor, who may be deceased. Appointment as a trustee should not be accepted unless one has the temperament, knowledge, and skills necessary to minimize the risks inherent in the position. Typically, banks, trust companies, attorneys, and other fiduciary organizations offer professional skills in the administration of trusts.

OBJECTIVE 9

Explain the role and responsibilities of a trustee.

Trustee's Powers The trustee has certain powers granted by law or by the trust instrument itself. Powers usually granted by law include the authority and responsibility to invest trust property; to sell, exchange, or rent property; to contract with others in matters relating to the trust; to borrow funds by using trust property as security; and to distribute income to beneficiaries.

Trustee's Duties The trustee has the duty to maintain appropriate records and to provide a full accounting of the trust property; to pay taxes; and to use good judgment in managing the property, including making good investment decisions. The trustee may purchase securities that are of very low risk and that appear on a document referred to as a *legal list*.

Trustee's Accountability A trustee whose performance of duty in managing the trust property is called into question can be held liable unless a court rules that the trustee used good judgment.

CHAPTER SUMMARY

1. The purpose of a will is to recognize the concept of private property and give a person the right to dispose of his or her property as he or she wishes. A will is also important toward protecting the family of a deceased person.

2. You should be familiar with the meaning of terms used in discussing wills, including *testator, personal representative, executor, administrator, intestate,* and *beneficiary.*

3 A gift of money is called a legacy and a gift of personal property is known as a bequest, although both terms are often used synonymously. A bequest can be specific, general, or residuary.

4 The requirements for a valid will vary by state, but often include that the will be written, dated, signed, and witnessed. The testator must also have testamentary capacity and be free from undue influence.

5 The primary requirements of testamentary capacity are that the testator be of legal age and of sound mind when the will is created.

6 Undue influence is the unfair and improper pressure that might be applied to a testator to change his or her true wishes for the disposition of property.

7 When a person dies intestate, the law of the state in which the deceased was domiciled govern the disposition of his or her property. Usually, a surviving spouse and children receive the entire estate. When there are neither, relatives, including parents, grandchildren, brothers, and sisters, are then included in the distribution.

8 The purpose of a trust is to allow a person to control the disposition of his or her property after death by having it held by one party, the trustee, for the benefit of another, the beneficiary. Two kinds of trusts are a testamentary trust, which is created by a will, and a living trust, which is established while the settlor is still alive.

9 A trustee has a fiduciary duty to manage property according to the wishes of the settlor. Powers usually include the ability to sell, exchange, or rent property, borrow funds, contract with others in matters pertaining to the trust, and to distribute income to beneficiaries. Duties include maintaining records of the property, providing a full accounting of trust property, and using good judgment.

Chapter 22 Assessment

MATCHING LEGAL TERMS

Match each of the following definitions with the correct term in the list below. Write the letter of your choice in the answer column.

- **a.** beneficiary
- **b.** bequest
- **c.** codicil capacity
- **d.** decedent
- **e.** devise
- **f.** executor
- **g.** holographic will
- **h.** *inter vivos* trust
- **i.** intestate
- **j.** personal intent
- **k.** residuary settlor
- **l.** testamentary capacity
- **m.** testamentary intent
- **n.** testator
- **o.** representative

1. The legal term for a deceased person. 1. _____
2. The individual who is named either in a will or appointed by a court to administer an estate. 2. _____
3. A gift of real property left in a will. 3. _____
4. A gift of personal property left in a will. 4. _____
5. The wishes of a person for the distribution of his or her property as expressed in a will. 5. _____
6. The person named in a will to administer the estate. 6. _____
7. A person who makes a will. 7. _____
8. A person who receives gifts of personal property in a will. 8. _____
9. The balance of an estate remaining after specific distributions have been made. 9. _____
10. A completely handwritten will. 10. _____
11. The requirement that a person be of legal age and sound mind to prepare a will. 11. _____
12. A document that revokes, changes, or revises a will. 12. _____
13. The state of a person who dies without a will. 13. _____
14. A trust set up while a person is still living. 14. _____
15. A person who sets up a trust. 15. _____

TRUE/FALSE QUIZ

Indicate whether each of the following statements is true or false by writing *T* or *F* in the answer column.

16. The probate court is responsible for supervising the operation of a will and the settling of an estate. 16. _____
17. When a person dies intestate, the court appoints an executor to settle the estate. 17. _____

Wills, Intestacy, and Trusts **CHAPTER 22** 353

Chapter 22 Assessment

18. A tape recording is an acceptable form of a will. 18. _____

19. Generally, it is good practice to have witnesses to a will who are younger than the person making the will. 19. _____

20. A person of any age can make a will. 20. _____

21. Making a codicil has similar requirements to making a new will. 21. _____

22. The primary purpose of setting up a trust is to avoid paying taxes. 22. _____

23. An *inter vivos* trust is created by a will. 23. _____

24. A trustee who fails to use prudent judgment in managing a trust can be held liable. 24. _____

25. A trustee does not have authority to make investments. 25. _____

DISCUSSION QUESTIONS

Answer the following questions and discuss them in class.

26. Discuss the reasons a person prepares a will.

27. Discuss types of gifts and devises covered by a will.

28. Explain each of the requirements of a valid will.

29. Explain why the law requires the testator to have testamentary capacity.

30. Charges of undue influence are frequently made by those who are denied benefits in a will. What steps might a testator take, while still alive, to reduce the likelihood of these charges being made?

354   PART 4   Property

Chapter 22 Assessment

31. Explain the way the court distributes the estate of someone who dies intestate.

THINKING CRITICALLY ABOUT THE LAW

Answer the following questions, which require you to think critically about the legal principles that you learned in this chapter.

32. Wills and the Law Should the law dictate that a person must provide for a spouse and children either by a will or by state law of intestate succession? Why or why not?

33. Testamentary Intent If a person dies intestate, is there any way their heirs could prove his or her testamentary intent? Explain your answer.

34. Holographic Will Why should a holographic will be legally valid, while a transcript of a voice- or video-recorded will is invalid?

35. Trusts What are the alternatives available to a testator considering the establishment of a testamentary trust?

36. A Question of Ethics What is the fairest way to distribute the children's portion of an estate: to bequeath equal shares to each child, or to make the distribution reflect each individual child's needs?

Wills, Intestacy, and Trusts CHAPTER 22

Chapter 22 Assessment

CASE QUESTIONS

Study each case below and answer the questions that follow by writing *Yes* or *No* in the answer column.

37. Testamentary Capacity Gruen suffered from Alzheimer's disease (a form of mental illness that occurs as a result of old age and is progressive) and lived in a nursing home. His sister, whom he had not seen since they were teenagers, instituted proceedings to have him declared mentally incompetent. A physician testified that Gruen was permanently mentally disabled and that the condition would get progressively worse. Gruen's sister was appointed his guardian. Six months later, Gruen executed his last will, leaving his entire estate to his sister. When he died, Gruen's other relatives challenged the will, claiming that Gruen had lacked testamentary capacity.

    a. Does it appear that Gruen had testamentary capacity?   a. _____

    b. Does it appear that the will embodied testamentary intent?   b. _____

    c. Does it appear that the sister exerted undue influence?   c. _____

38. Requirements of a Valid Will Popov despised lawyers and refused to have one prepare a will. Instead, he went online, got information on estate planning, and wrote a will in his own handwriting in which he left his entire estate to his brother and one dollar to each of his three children. The will was not witnessed by anyone. After his death, his children challenged its legality and validity.

    a. Are witnesses necessary for a handwritten will to be valid?   a. _____

    b. Is this an example of a holographic will?   b. _____

    c. Will the validity of the will be accepted by the court?   c. _____

39. Trusts Harley set up a trust, naming himself as trustee, and transferred his entire estate to the trust. The trust was intended to provide him with a lifetime income. After his death, the income from the trust would be paid to his wife. After her death, the income from the trust would go to three of their four children, after which the trust would be terminated. The trust specifically stated that one child, Nancy, was not named in the trust because other arrangements had been made for her. When the trust began paying to the three children, but not Nancy, she challenged the validity of the trust, claiming that the trust was a testamentary trust and did not comply with the state statute on wills.

    a. Was this a testamentary trust?   a. _____

    b. Was this an *inter vivos* trust?   b. _____

    c. Will Nancy succeed in overturning the trust?   c. _____

Chapter 22 Assessment

CASE ANALYSIS

Study each of the following cases carefully and then briefly state the principle of law and your decision.

40. Executor Misconduct Corbin was named as executor in his father's will. While going through his late father's papers, he discovered a promissory note made by Fulsom in the amount of $10,000 that reflected a personal loan the decedent had made before he died. Rather than include the note in the estate's assets, Corbin approached Fulsom and indicated that he would accept $5,000 cash in exchange for the note. Obviously, Folsom's payment would not be included in the assets of the estate. One of the heirs discovered the cash payment and brought suit, charging misconduct. *Will Corbin be required to cover the loss suffered by the estate?*

Principle of law:

_____

_____

Decision:

_____

_____

41. Responsibilities of Personal Representatives Aversa, personal representative of her late father's estate, was presented with evidence that there was still $12,000 owing on his automobile. Rather than have the car taken, she borrowed $6,000 and refinanced the balance. Objection was made on the grounds that she had exceeded her authority. *Is it likely that the court will approve her actions?*

Principle of law:

_____

_____

Decision:

_____

_____

42. Trustee Responsibilities The trustees of a labor union pension fund delivered various stocks and bonds to a bank under an agreement that provided the bank would act as the trustees' agent in investing the fund's assets. The agreement also provided that the bank was "authorized to invest any assets . . . of the investment fund or to dispose of any such asset or property and invest the proceeds of such disposition, as in its absolute and uncontrolled discretion it deems suitable." The results of the bank's investments were disappointing. The trustees claimed that because trustees may not delegate their power, the bank breached its contract of agency by making unauthorized investment decisions that decreased the value of the fund. *Does it appear that the trustees delegated power to the bank to make the investments?* [*Local Union 422, U. A. of Joliet v. The First National Bank of Joliet,* 417 N.E.2d 1077 (Illinois).]

Chapter 22 Assessment

Principle of law:
_____
_____

Decision:
_____
_____

43. Testamentary Intent Before Dora Diggs, a widow, died, she left a handwritten document that said, "I want Tom R. Preston and Mattie Price to be the administrators (executors) to settle my estate." Following this passage, she listed various assets. A dispute arose about whether the decedent, Diggs, intended to give Preston and Price general power to dispose of her property. If this were the interpretation, Preston and Price would be the beneficiaries. Other relatives claimed: (1) the document was not really a will at all, (2) Diggs merely wanted to name executors, (3) the document lacked testamentary intent, and (4) Diggs died intestate. If this were the case, state law would determine the distribution of property. The other relatives would benefit if this position were the decision of the court. *Did the disputed document fail to qualify as a will because of the lack of testamentary intent?* [*Preston v. Preston,* 617 S.W.2d 841 (Texas).]

Principle of law:
_____
_____

Decision:
_____
_____

LEGAL RESEARCH

Complete the following activities. Then share your findings with the class.

44. Working in Teams In teams of three or four, interview the trust department of local banks to learn how they handle trusts and perform as executors of estates.
_____
_____
_____

45. Using Technology Using the Internet and search engines, investigate cases include issues of testamentary intent, testamentary capacity, holographic wills, and intestacy. Briefly record your findings.
_____
_____
_____
_____

PART 4   Property

PART V

COMMERCIAL PAPER

CHAPTER 23 Introduction to Commercial Paper

CHAPTER 24 Transfer and Discharge of Commercial Paper

CHAPTER 23

INTRODUCTION TO COMMERCIAL PAPER

PERFORMANCE OBJECTIVES

After studying this chapter and completing the assessments, you will be able to:

1. Explain the two ways in which commercial paper differs from ordinary contracts.
2. Distinguish between the two basic kinds of commercial paper: orders to pay (checks and drafts) and promises to pay (notes).
3. List and explain the essentials and nonessentials of commercial paper.
4. Describe cashier's checks and traveler's checks.
5. Discuss the law and liability as applied to bad checks and to forged, raised, or altered checks.
6. Explain the rules and procedures for stopping payment on a check.
7. Discuss electronic funds transfers, automatic teller machines, and point-of-sale systems.

LEGAL TERMS

commercial paper
promissory note
check
draft
negotiability
order instrument
certified check
cashier's check
traveler's check
bad check
forged check
raised check
postdated check
electronic funds transfer (EFT)

Characteristics of Commercial Paper

Commercial paper is a term widely used in law to describe a number of legally binding and commercially acceptable documents, such as checks and notes, that are used to transfer money from one person to another. These documents are negotiable—that is, they are freely transferable—and they circulate throughout our commercial system almost as readily as cash. Commercial paper is also sometimes referred to as *negotiable instruments.* A negotiable instrument is an unconditional written promise to pay, or pay to the order of another party, a certain sum of money on demand or at a definite time. Negotiable instruments are highly trusted and play an important role in everyday individual and business transactions.

Commercial paper (negotiable instruments) consists of contracts, but they differ from ordinary contracts in two important ways: the presumption of consideration and assignability.

Presumption of Consideration

The law presumes that commercial paper is issued for value, that is, for consideration. A party to a simple contract who is seeking to enforce the promise contained in the agreement must prove that he or she gave consideration; however, a party to commercial paper who is trying to collect payment does not. Instead, the person trying to avoid payment must prove that he or she received no consideration.

Negotiability versus Assignability

As described in Chapter 12, ordinary contracts may usually be assigned, but the assignee, or person to whom rights are transferred, may receive only those rights held by the person making the assignment (the assignor) at the time of the transfer. In addition, the person who has acquired assigned rights to a contract must notify the other party to the contract of the assignment. These conditions do not apply to transferred (negotiated) commercial paper. The person to whom commercial paper is transferred may acquire a better right to it than the person who made the transfer. For example, if commercial paper that has been found or stolen is sold (transferred) to an innocent person for value, that person becomes the legal owner with title enforceable even against the rightful owner—unlike the innocent receiver of found or stolen jewelry who cannot acquire title. In addition, in some cases the person receiving the instrument can receive money on the instrument when the transferring person could not.

commercial paper A number of legally binding and commercially acceptable documents that are used to transfer money from one person to another.

OBJECTIVE 1

Explain the two ways in which commercial paper differs from ordinary contracts.

KINDS OF COMMERCIAL PAPER

There are many different kinds of commercial paper. The two basic types of commercial paper are orders to pay (checks and drafts) and promises to pay (notes).

Promises to Pay

A ***promissory note*** is, as the name suggests, a written note or letter in which one person promises to pay a certain amount of money to another at a definite time. A simple promissory note would be one saying, "I, John Jones, promise to pay to the order of Frieda Smith $100 in 60 days." If Frieda Smith should need the $100 before the 60 days have passed, she could take this written promise to a bank or to another person, and if the bank or other person felt that John Jones would keep his promise, Smith could then transfer, or negotiate, her interest in the promise to the bank, or to the other person, in exchange for $100. Smith would then have the money she needed without having to wait for it, and the bank or the other person would be entitled to receive Jones's $100 at the time promised.

Checks A ***check*** is a written order drawn on a bank by a depositor that requests the bank to pay, on demand and unconditionally, a definite sum of money to the bearer of the check or to the order of a specified person. Try to think of a check for $50 from Frieda Smith to John Jones simply as a letter from Smith to her bank saying something like this: "Look, Mr. Banker, you're holding some of my money and I want you to pay $50 of it to John Jones." The banker would first ask Jones to sign his name on the back of the check—that is, to endorse it—to indicate that he had received the $50, and then he would pay Jones the $50, as directed by Smith. Additional discussion of indorsements is presented in Chapter 24.

Drafts, or Bills of Exchange Whereas a check is a letter to a bank instructing it to pay money to a certain person, a ***draft***, or *bill of exchange*, is an unconditional written order to a person or bank instructing him or her to pay money to another, third person. Drafts are often used in certain kinds of businesses.

EXAMPLE 23.1

Frey traveled for extended periods, and not wanting to delay payments to utility companies during his absences, authorized his bank to make periodic payments of specified amounts.

OBJECTIVE 2

Distinguish between the two basic kinds of commercial paper: orders to pay (checks and drafts) and promises to pay (notes).

promissory note A written note or letter in which one person promises to pay a certain amount of money to another at a definite time.

check A written order drawn on a bank by a depositor that requests the bank to pay, on demand and unconditionally, a definite sum of money to the bearer of the check or to the order of a specified person.

draft An unconditional written order to a person or bank instructing him or her to pay money to another, third person.

The Meaning of "Pay to the Order of"

If the check from Frieda Smith to John Jones was worded, "Pay to John Jones," the banker could not do otherwise; but if the check said, "Pay to the order of John Jones," it would mean, "Pay this money to John Jones or do whatever else he wants you to do with it." These few key words, *Pay to the order of,* give commercial paper **negotiability,** that is, the ability to be transferred freely from one person to another and be accepted as readily as cash. As a result, Jones can tell the banker, "I don't really want the money Smith is telling you to give me. I want you to pay it to Brown instead."

An item of commercial paper containing the key words of negotiability, *pay to the order of,* or their equivalent, is an **order instrument.** Checks, drafts, and notes are some examples of order instruments.

negotiability The ability to be transferred freely from one person to another and be accepted as readily as cash.

order instrument An item of commercial paper that contains the key words of negotiability, *pay to the order of,* or their equivalent.

Parties to Commercial Paper

The parties involved in a promissory note have particular names. The person who makes the promise is called the *maker.* If the maker has someone else add his or her name to the promise, to strengthen it, the other person is known as the *comaker.* The person to whom the promise is made is the *payee.*

The person who draws or creates a draft or bill of exchange is the *drawer* and corresponds to the maker of a note. The drawer actually draws or attempts to draw money from a second person. The person who receives the order to draw or to pay is the *drawee.* As a result, a bank is the drawee of all checks drawn on accounts held by it. The payee of a draft or bill of exchange is the same person as the payee of a note—the party who receives the money. The *holder* of commercial paper is the person in possession of it. The holder can be the payee, the drawee, or the drawer, but obviously only one of these parties can be the holder at one time.

Essentials of Commercial Paper

Under the Uniform Commercial Code, commercial paper, to be negotiable, must conform to the following requirements [UCC 3-104(1)].

It Must be in Writing and Signed by the Maker or Drawer

Commercial paper may be handwritten, typewritten, printed, or written by any other means that will make a mark. The signature may be

OBJECTIVE 3

List and explain the essentials and nonessentials of commercial paper.

Introduction to Commercial Paper   CHAPTER 23   363

written either at the bottom or in the body of the instrument, such as, "I, Fred Allan, promise to pay, . . . " [UCC 1-201(46)].

> **EXAMPLE 23.2**
>
> Forgue offered Aiello a $500 note in payment for merchandise she had purchased. Although the note specified payment within 30 days, Aiello refused to accept it because it was written in pencil.

The device used in writing a note does not affect its negotiability. Anything that will make a mark is satisfactory. Consequently, a note written in pencil is as enforceable as a note written by any other means.

Only the person who writes his or her name on a note as the maker or on a check or bill of exchange as the drawer is liable for it. The liability is the same even if the person signs a trade name or an assumed name. As a result, in a note bearing the signature, "Charles Lamb, Agent for Clark Insurance Company," Lamb is personally liable. The phrase "Agent for Clark Insurance Company" merely describes Lamb. If the note were signed, "Clark Insurance Company, by Charles Lamb, Agent," the company would be liable. Lamb would have clearly indicated that he had signed for his employer.

It Must Contain an Unconditional Promise or Order to Pay a Definite Sum in Money

The promise in a note or the order in a bill of exchange must be unconditional. Statements requiring that certain things be done or that specific events take place before payment make the instrument a simple contract rather than commercial paper. Contrary to popular opinion, an IOU is not a promise to pay: It is merely an acknowledgment of a debt.

> **EXAMPLE 23.3**
>
> Spiegelgras received a note from someone who owed him money. The note contained the statement, "payment to be made from my income tax refund check." It was held that this note was not negotiable because payment depended on the Internal Revenue Service finding that a refund was due. In case of a lawsuit, this instrument would be considered a simple contract. Suppose that, instead of the provision about the tax refund, the note contained the statement, "This note is in payment of purchases made in January." This statement would not affect the negotiability of the note because it does not in any way limit, restrict, or condition payment.

Commercial paper must be payable in money—any money that has a known or established value. An instrument payable in a foreign currency is nevertheless negotiable.

It Must be Payable on Demand or at a Definite Time

Commercial paper must be payable on demand or at some definite time. A note payable "on or before July 1, 20--," "one month after sight" or "on presentation" is negotiable because the time of payment is certain.

An instrument payable "within 60 days after death (of a named person)" is not payable at a definite time and is not negotiable. A promise to pay when a person marries or when he or she reaches a certain age is not a promise to pay at a definite time because the person might never marry or might die before reaching the specified age. In such instances, the instruments are nonnegotiable.

It Must be Payable to Order, to Bearer, or to Cash

Unless an instrument contains such words of negotiability as *payable to bearer*, *payable to the order of*, or *payable to cash*, it is not negotiable.

A Bill of Exchange Must Name or Indicate the Drawee with Reasonable Certainty

The person who is expected to pay a bill of exchange—the one to whom it is addressed—must be named or otherwise indicated in the instrument with reasonable certainty for the instrument to be considered negotiable.

NONESSENTIALS OF COMMERCIAL PAPER

Certain items may be omitted from a note without affecting its negotiability. Because consideration is presumed, the words *for value received* are not needed in a note. Also, the consideration or value given by the maker or the drawer need not be specified.

If the date of a note is not given, the holder may write in the date when the instrument was issued without affecting its negotiability. If this date is not known, the date when the paper was received is considered the date of issue. Commercial paper may be *antedated* (dated previously) or *postdated* (dated ahead).

The place of business or home of a maker of a note is presumed to be where the instrument was drawn or where it is payable if this information is not given on the paper.

In a note, if the amount payable expressed in figures differs from the sum stated in words, the amount expressed in words is considered the true amount. If the sum stated in words is not also expressed in figures, this omission does not affect the negotiability of a note.

The numbering of (or the failure to number) commercial paper does not affect its negotiability.

Checks

The check is used more than any other instrument of credit as a means of making payment, both to settle debts and to pay for purchases.

Checks need not be made out on the printed forms supplied by banks. Any writing that includes the essential elements of negotiability is considered a valid check when signed and delivered by the drawer. However, many banks today prefer that the encoded number assigned a depositor be shown on every check written by him or her. For proper processing through computers and other electronic machinery, these numbers are recommended, although they are not legally necessary.

Relationship Between Bank and Depositor

A check provides a safe means of transferring money and serves as a receipt when paid and canceled by the bank. It may circulate through several persons, banks, and organizations. The bank must honor a check when it is properly drawn against the money the drawer has on deposit, or the bank will be liable to the drawer for damages.

Payment of Checks

Checks are always payable on demand. The Uniform Commercial Code provides that, with respect to the liability of the drawer, a reasonable length of time for presentation for payment is 30 days after the date of the check or after issue, whichever is later. A bank may pay a check presented more than 30 days after its date, but it is not required to do so. A check presented more than six months after its date is known as a *stale check* [UCC 4-404].

There is no time limit for the presentation of a certified check (discussed later) for payment. The bank must honor it whenever the holder demands payment.

EXAMPLE 23.4

Shuster received a check from Cavanagh and presented it to her bank for payment. Cavanagh's bank, for reasons of its own, refused to honor the check, although Cavanagh had sufficient funds on deposit to cover it. Cavanagh can sue her bank for any damages that she may have suffered from injury to her reputation.

Certified Checks

A merchant who sells goods to a person whose credit standing is not known may request the customer to make payment by **certified check,** a check that the bank has promised to pay when it is presented for payment. If the drawer's funds on deposit are sufficient to cover the amount of the check, the teller or cashier will write or stamp across the face of the check the word "certified" and the date. The teller will then sign his or her name and title and make an entry in the depositor's account indicating that the depositor's balance has been reduced by the amount of the check. While actual cash is not set aside for the payment of the check, a notation of the transaction is made on the depositor's record. The bank assumes absolute liability for payment. It should be noted that under the UCC, unless otherwise agreed by contract, the bank has no legal obligation to certify a check [UCC 3-411(2)].

certified check A check that the bank has promised to pay when it is presented for payment.

Liability for Certified Checks

If a drawer of a check has the bank certify it, he or she remains conditionally liable for payment of the check until the holder can reasonably present it for payment. However, when a check is certified at the request of the payee or holder, the drawer and all prior indorsers are released from all liability. The reason is that the payee or holder could have requested payment instead of certification.

> **EXAMPLE 23.5**
> Sherwin asked her bank to *stop payment* (a service offered by banks whereby a depositor can have the bank refuse to pay a depositor's check when it is presented for payment) on a check that she had certified. The bank refused to stop payment, even though the check had not yet been presented for payment.

In Example 23.5, the bank was justified in refusing to honor Sherwin's request. By certifying the check, the bank had assumed absolute liability for its payment. Certification assures the payee or any subsequent holder that the check is genuine and that the bank will honor the check when it is presented for payment.

OBJECTIVE 4

Describe cashier's checks and traveler's checks.

cashier's check A check issued by a cashier or other designated officer of a bank and drawn against bank funds.

Cashier's Checks

A **cashier's check,** sometimes called an *official check* or a *bank check,* is issued by the cashier or other designated officer of a bank and drawn against bank funds. A depositor may request such a check when, for example, he or she intends to use it to pay for merchandise from an out-of-town dealer who will not accept a personal check.

A bank check is made payable either to the depositor who purchases it from the bank or to the person who is intended to cash it. If the check is made payable to the depositor, he or she indorses it to the person to whom it is being transferred.

Traveler's Checks

A *traveler's check* is a certified check issued in a denomination of $10 or more by certain banks, travel agencies, and financial services companies. The issuer usually charges the purchaser of traveler's checks a fixed rate (a fixed fee of perhaps one percent) to issue them.

For persons who are traveling, especially in foreign countries, traveler's checks are a safe form in which to carry money because anyone finding or stealing them would have difficulty using them. Only the purchaser who signed the checks when he or she bought them may negotiate them. They are convenient because they are accepted almost all over the world.

To cash a traveler's check, the purchaser countersigns it in the presence of the person who is converting it into cash or accepting it in payment of a purchase. However, with the growing availability of ATMs and the widespread acceptance of credit cards in foreign countries, the use of traveler's checks has declined somewhat in recent years.

Bad Checks

A *bad check* is one against a bank in which the drawer has insufficient funds on deposit to cover the check or no funds at all. Most states have a statute making a person who issues a check drawn on a bank in which he or she has no account guilty of the criminal offense of larceny. In some states, it is a criminal offense for a person to intentionally issue a check on a bank in which that person has an account, but has insufficient funds on deposit. The law in most states allows the drawer of a check a specified number of days, usually five or ten, in which to make it good.

Forged and Raised Checks

Forgery is the act of fraudulently making or altering a check, a note, a draft, or some other document, to the financial loss of another. A forged document is also termed a forgery. Both the intent to defraud and the creation of a liability must be proven for an act to constitute

---

traveler's check A certified check, useful when traveling in foreign countries, that is issued in denominations of $10 or more by certain banks, travel agencies, and financial services companies.

OBJECTIVE 5

Discuss the law and liability as applied to bad checks and to forged, raised, or altered checks.

bad check A check against a bank in which the drawer has insufficient funds on deposit to cover the check or no funds at all.

forgery. A person who commits a forgery is guilty of a crime. A *forged check* (one signed by a person other than the drawer) and a *raised check* (one on which the amount has been raised by the payee or bearer) are two of the most common types of forgery.

Liability for Forged and Raised Checks A depositor who opens a checking account with a bank must fill out a signature card and leave it on file with the bank. The bank is then assumed to know the depositor's signature and is liable if it pays any checks on which the drawer's signature has been forged. The depositor has the responsibility of notifying the bank of a forgery within a reasonable time, usually set by statute, after receiving his or her monthly statement and cancelled checks. Failure to do so will release the bank from its liability.

Because the bank alone has the opportunity to inspect a check at the time of payment, it is wholly liable if it pays any raised checks unless the drawer, through carelessness, wrote the check in such a way that it could easily be altered. Although the drawer was careless, if the bank could have readily detected the alteration, it may be held liable.

Courts have repeatedly held that when a check is drawn in such a careless and incomplete manner that a material alteration can easily be made without the check looking suspicious, the drawer has prepared the way for forgery and is liable if it is committed.

Postdated Checks

Sometimes the drawer of a check will postdate it. A person may write a *postdated check* when insufficient funds are in the bank at the time the check is drawn, but the person expects to deposit sufficient funds to cover it by the date on the check. A person may also postdate a check for self-protection when some act is to be completed by the payee before the date of the check. Such a check has the effect of a promissory note at the time it is drawn. It is a mere promise to pay, at a future date, the amount specified. A postdated check may not be cashed by the payee before the date shown on the check. By accepting a postdated check, the payee agrees to not cash it before the date indicated.

Stopping Payment on Checks

A *stop-payment order* is an instruction that a depositor gives to his or her bank not to pay a particular check. The notice can be given at any time before a check is presented for payment. If the bank does not do as requested by the drawer and cashes the check, it is liable to the depositor for the amount paid. A small charge is usually made by

---

forged check A check that is signed by a person other than the drawer.

raised check A check on which the amount has been raised by the payee or bearer.

postdated check A check drawn when a person has insufficient funds, but dated such that sufficient funds will be available when it is cashed.

OBJECTIVE 6

Explain the rules and procedures for stopping payment on a check.

the bank for the service of carrying out a stop-payment order [UCC 4-403(1)].

If the drawer of a check dies before the check is paid, the bank may nevertheless honor it. The Uniform Commercial Code provides that the death of the drawer of a check does not revoke the authority of the bank to accept, pay, or collect an item or to account for proceeds of its collection until the bank learns of the death and has a reasonable opportunity to act. Even with knowledge of the depositor's death, a bank may pay or certify checks drawn on it before the death and for ten days thereafter unless ordered to stop payment by a person claiming an interest in the account [UCC 4-405(1)].

Electronic Funds Transfer Systems

OBJECTIVE 7

Discuss electronic funds transfers, automatic teller machines, and point-of-sale systems.

electronic funds transfer (EFT) A variety of electronic applications for handling money.

In past years, it was said that the use of commercial paper would result in a "cashless" society. There is now speculation that the use of electronic fund transfers may result in a "checkless" society. ***Electronic funds transfer (EFT)*** refers to a variety of electronic applications for handling money.

Applications of Electronic Funds Transfer Systems

EFT systems offer a variety of convenient and useful applications, including ATMs, point-of-sale systems, and direct deposit and withdrawal, to name a few.

Automated Teller Machines
An *automated teller machine (ATM)* performs many functions that tellers in a bank had done previously. Typically, a depositor will activate the machine by inserting a plastic card encoded with information to be read by the machine, identify himself or herself by entering a personal identification number (PIN), and choose from a menu of bank transactions. The customer can make inquiries about the status of the account, withdraw cash, make deposits, and transfer funds from one account to another. The usefulness of the customer's identification card is further enhanced when banks are linked by networks that connect different banks into a local, national, or international system. A traveler in California can insert a plastic card into a Los Angeles bank's ATM and withdraw cash and have the withdrawal charged to his or her New York bank account.

Banks in foreign countries are similarly linked with U.S. banks, and it is now possible for a traveler in London, Paris, Barcelona, or

Hong Kong to use an ATM to withdraw local currencies and have the amount charged to a U.S. account at the prevailing rate of exchange.

Point-of-Sale Systems A *point-of-sale system* allows a consumer to transfer funds from a bank account to the merchant's bank account to pay for merchandise purchased. The terminal is located at the merchant's place of business.

Direct Deposits and Withdrawals The electronic movement of funds from one bank account to another has many useful applications, for example, when an employee authorizes an employer to deposit his or her wages to the employee's bank account electronically instead of paying him or her by paycheck.

Other Applications of EFT Some banks offer a service that gives customers who have personal computers access to information about their accounts, allows depositors to transfer funds from one account to another, and permits bank customers to authorize the bank to pay regular bills. Pay-by-phone systems have been introduced that allow depositors to telephone their bank's computer and authorize payment of certain bills and transfer funds to other accounts or to third parties.

The transfer of funds between banks is still another application of EFT. Although this service has some usefulness to individual customers, it has far-reaching effects on the worldwide banking system. Because of the speed with which it processes financial settlements, EFT facilitates international trade.

The Electronic Funds Transfer Act

The most comprehensive federal legislation in this area is the Electronic Funds Transfer Act (EFTA) of 1979, which went into full effect in 1980. The act establishes the rights, responsibilities, and liabilities of consumers in dealings with financial institutions. Because the purpose of the act is consumer protection, it does not govern transfers among financial institutions or among businesses.

The EFTA limits consumer liability to $50 if the consumer notifies the card issuer within two days of learning that a card has been lost or stolen. If the customer fails to notify the issuer within two days, the consumer's liability increases to $500.

The EFTA also requires the institution to provide written receipts each time an ATM is used and monthly statements on which electronic transactions are shown.

CHAPTER SUMMARY

1. Commercial paper consists of contracts, but differs from ordinary contracts in two ways: the presumption of consideration and assignability.

2. Promises to pay consist of a written note or letter in which one person promises to pay a certain amount of money to another at a definite time. Orders to pay typically use an expression such as *pay to the order of* and give commercial paper negotiability.

3. For commercial paper to be negotiable, it must be in writing and signed by the maker or drawer, contain an unconditional promise or order to pay a definite sum of money, be payable on demand or at a definite time, be payable to order or to bearer, and a bill of exchange must name or indicate the drawee with reasonable certainty. Nonessentials include the words *for value received* or specific mention of the consideration or its value (because consideration is assumed). Dates, specifying the place of business or home of the maker of the note, and numbering the commercial paper, are all nonessential to negotiability.

4. A cashier's check is issued by the cashier or other designated officer of a bank and drawn against bank funds. A traveler's check is a certified check issued in a denomination of $10 or more by certain banks, travel agencies, and financial services companies.

5. Most states have laws making a person who issues a bad check guilty of larceny; however, many states allow a person some time to make good on the check. A bank is liable for forged checks, but the depositor is responsible for informing the bank of forgeries in a reasonable time. A bank is responsible for paying a raised check if an alteration is readily detectable.

6. A depositor at a bank can place a stop-payment order by giving the bank an instruction not to pay a particular check.

7. Electronic funds transfer systems offer convenient and useful electronic money-handling applications, including automatic teller machines, point-of-sale systems, and direct deposit and withdrawals, among others.

Chapter 23 Assessment

MATCHING LEGAL TERMS

Match each of the following definitions with the correct term in the list below. Write the letter of your choice in the answer column.

- **a.** bad check
- **b.** draft, or bill of exchange
- **c.** cashier's check
- **d.** certified check
- **e.** check
- **f.** drawee
- **g.** drawer
- **h.** holder
- **i.** maker
- **j.** negotiability
- **k.** payee
- **l.** postdated check
- **m.** promissory note
- **n.** raised check
- **o.** stop-payment order

1. A person who is in possession of commercial paper.
2. An instrument that is essentially a depositor's order to his or her bank to pay money to a party named on the instrument.
3. A characteristic of a credit instrument that allows its transfer from one party to another.
4. A type of commercial paper that is essentially a written promise to pay money to a designated party.
5. The party to commercial paper who makes a promise.
6. The party to commercial paper who is designated as the one to receive payment.
7. The party to a bill of exchange against whom it is drawn.
8. The party who draws a bill of exchange against another.
9. A check drawn against an account with insufficient funds or against a bank in which the drawer has no funds.
10. A check that bears a date later than the date on which the check was written.
11. A check for which the bank assures that the drawer has sufficient funds to make payment.
12. A notice to a bank requesting that a certain check not be paid.
13. A check drawn against a bank's own funds.
14. An unconditional written order from one party to another directing him or her to pay a sum certain to a third party.
15. A check on which the amount has been altered to increase it.

Introduction to Commercial Paper   CHAPTER 23

Chapter 23 Assessment

TRUE/FALSE QUIZ

Indicate whether each of the following statements is true or false by writing *T* or *F* in the answer column.

16. The law presumes that commercial paper was issued for value. 16. _____

17. A subsequent holder of commercial paper can have no greater rights than the original holder. 17. _____

18. The words *pay to the order of* are required for an instrument to have negotiability. 18. _____

19. A "stale check" is one that is presented six months or more after it was written or issued. 19. _____

20. The main purpose of a certified check is to ensure that funds are on deposit to cover the check. 20. _____

21. A person who adds his or her name to a promissory note to strengthen it is known as a comaker. 21. _____

22. A bank can refuse to honor a depositor's check even if it is properly drawn and there are sufficient funds on deposit. 22. _____

23. A postdated check is one that is written subsequent to the date appearing on the instrument. 23. _____

24. The Uniform Commercial Code provides that a reasonable length of time for demand for payment of a check is one year. 24. _____

25. If a depositor requests in a timely manner his or her bank to stop payment on a check written by the depositor, the bank must bear responsibility if the check is cashed. 25. _____

DISCUSSION QUESTIONS

Answer the following questions and discuss them in class.

26. Explain the two ways in which commercial paper differs from ordinary contracts.

_____
_____
_____

27. Discuss the major differences between the two basic kinds of commercial paper—orders to pay (checks and drafts) and promises to pay (notes).

_____
_____
_____

Chapter 23 Assessment

28. If a checkbook is stolen and checks are written by the thief and cashed, who bears the loss?

29. Discuss the law and liability as applied to bad checks and to forged, raised, or materially altered checks.

30. Discuss circumstances that might require stopping payment on a check.

31. What are the benefits and drawbacks to the consumer of using electronic funds transfers, automatic teller machines, and point-of-sale systems?

THINKING CRITICALLY ABOUT THE LAW

Answer the following questions, which require you to think critically about the legal principles that you learned in this chapter.

32. Financial and Banking System The complexity of the financial and banking system is a bit staggering. What might be done to simplify the system for consumers?

33. Travelers Checks Issuers of traveler's checks encourage buyers to retain unused checks as a form of "emergency fund." Who benefits from this practice and why?

Introduction to Commercial Paper   CHAPTER 23   375

Chapter 23 Assessment

34. Postdated Checks The payee of a postdated check has no right to demand payment if the account is closed or insufficient when the check is presented to the bank. Should the practice of writing postdated checks be illegal?

_____
_____

35. A Question of Ethics The practice of "check kiting" provides an opportunity to "borrow" interest-free by cashing a check for which there are inadequate funds on deposit. If the check writer makes a deposit to cover the check in time to avoid a "bounced check" charge, is this practice ethical?

_____
_____
_____

CASE QUESTIONS

Study each case below and answer the questions that follow by writing *Yes* or *No* in the answer column.

36. Safety of Funds Bolena sold some valuable jewelry to McGovern, whom she had never met before. She was concerned about whether McGovern's check was good and whether there were sufficient funds on deposit in McGovern's account to cover it.

a. Would a certified check relieve Bolena's concern? a. _____

b. Would a cashier's check relieve Bolena's concern? b. _____

c. Would McGovern's promissory note give greater security? c. _____

37. Parties to a Check Wiggins had a checking account at her local bank. She wrote out a check to Shin, a handyman, in payment for services he had provided.

a. Is Wiggins the drawee? a. _____

b. Is Shin the drawee? b. _____

c. Is her bank the drawee? c. _____

38. Safety of Travelers Funds Hausen was planning an extensive trip to Europe and wanted to avoid carrying large sums of cash.

a. Would you advise Hausen to carry certified checks? a. _____

b. Would you advise Hausen to carry traveler's checks? b. _____

c. Would you advise Hausen to charge all his purchases on credit cards? c. _____

Chapter 23 Assessment

39. Postdated Checks Tandy wanted to issue a check in payment of her rent, due June 1, before leaving on a vacation trip on May 15, but she did not have sufficient funds on deposit in her checking account. Her employer automatically deposits her paycheck to her bank on the last day of each month.

a. Should Tandy issue an antedated check? a. _____

b. Should Tandy issue a postdated check? b. _____

c. Should Tandy borrow money from the bank to pay the rent? c. _____

CASE ANALYSIS

Study each of the following cases carefully and then briefly state the principle of law and your decision.

40. Negotiability of Note Grove Hotel hired Fortas, an electrical contractor, and paid him with a promissory note for $3,400. The note stated that it was "with interest at bank rates." *Did the stipulation about interest rate affect the negotiability of the note?*

Principle of law:

_____

_____

Decision:

_____

_____

41. Postdated Check Graver gave Srau a postdated check for $2,000 as a deposit on a sailboat as acceptance of Srau's offer to sell the boat. Later, after Srau sold the boat to someone else, he claimed that the check was not really part of a binding contract because it was postdated and therefore created a qualified acceptance. *Did postdating the check affect its negotiability?*

Principle of law:

_____

_____

Decision:

_____

_____

42. Refusal to Pay Draft Higgins was a used-car dealer. He purchased a Corvette, giving the seller a draft drawn by him on the First State Bank of Albertville in the amount of $8,115. This draft was later presented by the seller to the bank for payment. Meanwhile, Higgins sold the car to Holsonback, who paid with a draft on the Albertville National Bank in the amount of $8,225. When the Albertville National Bank requested Holsonback to pay the draft, he refused, claiming that there was a problem with the certificate of title. The issue was raised as to whether, under the Uniform Commercial Code, negotiable instruments can be issued conditionally. *Did Holsonback have the right to withhold payment on the draft because of the problem with the certificate of title?* [*Holsonback v. First State Bank,* 394 So.2d 381 (Alabama).]

Chapter 23 Assessment

Principle of law:

Decision:

43. **Negotiable Instruments** After Balkus died intestate, his sister claimed that she was entitled to certain money because among Balkus' possessions there were bank deposit slips for a savings account maintained by Balkus. On each deposit slip was a handwritten notation, "Payable to Ann Balkus Vesley on P.O.D. the full amount and other deposits." Each slip was dated and signed by Balkus. Both parties treated "P.O.D." as meaning "payable on death." Vesley claims that the deposits are negotiable instruments, and that she was a holder in due course. *Are the deposit slips negotiable instruments under the Uniform Commercial Code?* [*Estate of Balkus*, 381 N.W.2d 593 (Wisconsin).]

Principle of law:

Decision:

LEGAL RESEARCH

Complete the following activities. Then share your findings with the class.

44. **Working in Teams** Working in teams of three or four, interview personnel at your local bank to check liability for lost or stolen bank-issued ATM, credit, and debit cards.

45. **Using Technology** Using the Internet, investigate legal safeguards to protect electronic transfer of funds.

PART 5   Commercial Paper

CHAPTER 24

Transfer and Discharge of Commercial Paper

PERFORMANCE OBJECTIVES

After studying this chapter and completing the assessments, you will be able to:

1. Identify the purpose of indorsing checks.
2. Describe the four kinds of indorsements.
3. Describe the four requirements that qualify a person as a holder in due course.
4. Distinguish between personal and real defenses against payment of commercial paper, and list the types of defenses in each case.
5. Explain presentment and dishonor of commercial paper.

LEGAL TERMS

indorsement
indorser
indorsee
blank indorsement
special indorsement
restrictive indorsement
qualified indorsement
holder in due course
personal defense
real defense
counterclaim
material alteration
presentment
dishonored

The Ease of Transfer and Discharge

One of the valuable characteristics of commercial paper in our personal and business lives is the ease with which it can be transferred from one person to another and the ease with which final settlements can be made. This chapter considers the various legal principles and procedures that are used to transfer and discharge commercial paper.

Indorsing Commercial Paper

OBJECTIVE 1

Identify the purpose of indorsing checks.

indorsement When the holder of commercial paper signs his or her name, with or without words, on the back of an instrument to transfer ownership to another.

When the holder of commercial paper signs his or her name, with or without other words, on the back of the instrument, this writing is referred to as an *indorsement.* The effect of an indorsement is to transfer ownership of a paper to another. When the transferee (the person to whom the instrument is transferred) receives the indorsed instrument, that person becomes the new holder, or owner, of it. This result is what is meant when we say that a paper has been negotiated. In this way, commercial paper takes the place of money for the payment of debts and purchases of goods and services.

> **EXAMPLE 24.1**
>
> Hatfield received a check from a customer that read in part, "Pay to the order of Harriet Hatfield." Hatfield signed her name on the back of the check and gave it to Tai. By so doing, she transferred (negotiated) the check to Tai, who then became the holder, or owner, of the check.

indorser The person who signs his or her name to a negotiable instrument.

indorsee The person to whom a negotiable instrument is transferred.

The *indorser* of an instrument is the person who signs his or her name on it; the *indorsee* is the person to whom the instrument is transferred.

Commercial paper is usually indorsed on the back. The indorsement may be printed or written by hand, typewritten, or even stamped. To be valid, the indorsement must be written for the entire amount stated in the instrument. Attempting to transfer only part of the face value of the negotiable instrument by indorsement invalidates the negotiation.

Kinds of Indorsements

OBJECTIVE 2

Describe the four kinds of indorsements.

Any of the following indorsements may be used in transferring commercial paper. The choice of indorsement will depend on the purpose of the transfer.

380 PART 5 Commercial Paper

Blank Indorsement

A ***blank indorsement*** is an indorsement in which the name of the payee is written by the payee on the back of a negotiable instrument. According to the Uniform Commercial Code, an instrument indorsed in blank is payable to anyone who is in possession of it; it is called a bearer instrument [UCC 3-111].

Technically, an instrument made payable to bearer is negotiable by delivery only; that is, the bearer is not required to indorse it. As a practical matter, however, banks require the bearer of such an instrument to sign it on the reverse side for purposes of identification.

The Uniform Commercial Code also provides that "where an instrument is made payable to a person under a misspelled name or one other than his own, he may indorse in that name or his own or both; but signature in both names may be required by a person paying or giving value for the instrument" [UCC 3-204].

> **EXAMPLE 24.2**
>
> Newson received from a customer a check indorsed in blank. Because of the blank indorsement, the check is a bearer instrument. Newson can negotiate it merely by delivery. In all probability, anyone accepting the check from Newson would insist that she indorse it. The transferee would require this indorsement so that if the check proved to be bad and the bank refused to honor it, Newson would have to pay.

Special Indorsement

A ***special indorsement,*** or *full indorsement,* is one in which the payee specifies the person to whom, or to whose order, it is to be paid. The instrument can be further negotiated only when it has been indorsed by the specified person.

> **EXAMPLE 24.3**
>
> Porenta requested that a friend, Hartley, cash a dividend check for her. Hartley gave Porenta the money and accepted her check, which she had indorsed in blank. Hartley had just moved to another city and decided to use the check to open a new account at a local bank. To protect himself in case he lost the check before he could open the account, he wrote over Porenta's signature indorsement, "Pay to the order of Thomas Hartley." He had the right to do so and it was probably prudent.

The Uniform Commercial Code specifically provides that the holder of an instrument may convert a blank indorsement into a full

---

blank indorsement An indorsement in which the name of the payee is written by the payee on the back of a negotiable instrument.

special indorsement An indorsement in which the payee specifies the person to whom, or to whose order, it is to be paid.

indorsement by writing "Pay to the order of (transferee's or holder's name)" over the indorser's signature [UCC 3-204]. In Example 24.4, Hartley is the transferee and Porenta is the indorser.

Restrictive Indorsement

restrictive indorsement An indorsement with a signature to which words have been added restricting further indorsement of the instrument.

A *restrictive indorsement* is a signature to which words have been added restricting the further indorsement of the instrument. According to the Uniform Commercial Code, however, a restrictive indorsement does not prevent further transfer or negotiation of the instrument. The holder has the rights of any purchaser of commercial paper except that he or she must do with the instrument as the indorsement directs [UCC 3-206].

The phrases "For deposit only" and "Pay to [indorser's bank] for deposit only" are restrictive indorsements that are often used when deposits are sent to a bank by messenger or by mail. "Pay [Herbert Fredericks] only" and "Pay [Herbert Fredericks], for collection" are other examples of restrictive indorsements.

> **EXAMPLE 24.4**
>
> While on vacation, Egan received a check in payment of a debt. Because it would be several weeks before she could deposit it personally in her bank, she indorsed it "For deposit only—Patricia Egan," and mailed it to the bank. If the check should be lost in the mail or stolen, it could not be cashed by the holder.

Qualified Indorsement

qualified indorsement An indorsement in which the indorser avoids liability for payment even if the maker or drawer defaults on the instrument.

In the case of a *qualified indorsement*, the indorser avoids liability for payment even if the maker or drawer defaults on the instrument. A qualified indorsement, using a phrase such as "without recourse," can be used together with a blank indorsement or special indorsement. The use of a qualified indorsement does not affect the negotiability of an instrument.

OBLIGATIONS, WARRANTIES, AND DISCHARGE OF INDORSERS

The indorser of a promissory note or the drawer or indorser of a bill of exchange is liable for the payment of the instrument if the following conditions are met:

- It has been properly presented for payment to the maker of the note or to the acceptor, if any, of the bill of exchange.

- Payment has been refused by the maker or acceptor.
- Notice of the refusal has been given to the drawer or indorser.

To ensure the negotiability of commercial paper, the Uniform Commercial Code assumes the following warranties in every indorsement [UCC 3-417]:

1. The instrument is genuine. If the maker's or acceptor's signature is forged, the indorser is liable to a subsequent holder for payment of the paper.
2. All prior parties were qualified to enter into a legally binding contract. If the maker or a prior indorser refuses to pay because he or she is a minor or otherwise incompetent, any indorser whose name follows that of the incompetent party is liable for payment of the instrument.
3. The instrument is a valid and existing obligation. If the maker refuses to pay because the paper has been materially altered or was given for a gambling debt or for any other illegal reason, the holder can recover against the indorser.
4. The indorser will pay what is due on the paper to the holder or to any subsequent indorser who had to pay on the instrument if it was not paid when presented for payment. Only an indorser who wrote "without recourse" above his or her name is exempt from this warranty.
5. The indorser is the true owner of the paper (has good title to it). If he or she found or stole the paper and transferred it to another by indorsement, the indorser is liable for any loss suffered by the indorsee. An indorser of an instrument is released from liability by (1) any act that completes the negotiation of the instrument, such as payment; (2) the release of a prior party's obligation or the release of the debtor; (3) the intentional cancellation of the indorser's signature by the holder; (4) a valid tender of payment by a prior party; or (5) an agreement binding on the holder to extend the due date of the instrument.

Holder in Due Course

A *holder in due course* of commercial paper, according to the Uniform Commercial Code [UCC 3-302], has taken the paper in good faith and for value, before maturity, and without actual or constructive notice (notice inferred from circumstances) of any defects in the instrument. He or she is sometimes called a *bona fide* holder

holder in due course
A holder who has taken a negotiable instrument in good faith and for value, before maturity, and without actual or constructive notice of any defects in the instrument.

OBJECTIVE 3

Describe the four requirements that qualify a person as a holder in due course.

for value without notice. (*Bona fide* is a Latin phrase meaning "in good faith.")

For a person to be a holder in due course of a negotiable instrument, the following must be true:

- The paper must be complete and regular on its face. If it is apparent from the appearance of the instrument that it has been altered, the holder is not considered a holder in due course.
- The paper must have been acquired on or before the due date. The fact that commercial paper is past due is considered notice that something might be wrong with it. Under the Uniform Commercial Code, if the buyer of overdue negotiable paper did not have notice or knowledge that it was overdue, he or she could be a holder in due course. However, a person who accepted a demand instrument (a promissory note payable upon demand) later than a reasonable length of time after it was issued is considered to have been aware that it was overdue (in the case of a check, 30 days is deemed to be a reasonable time).
- The paper must have been acquired for a valuable consideration. The consideration may have been the reasonable value of the instrument itself, or it may have been any detriment, injury, or loss suffered by the holder in taking the instrument.
- The paper must have been taken in good faith and for value. A person who has acquired a commercial paper for a sum much smaller than the face value of the instrument appears to have acted in bad faith unless the person can show that he or she acted prudently by checking into the reasons for the low value before accepting it.

Any holder of an instrument, other than the payee, who might know of a fraud or learn of it before negotiating the instrument to a holder in due course, cannot later become a similar holder even if title to the instrument is transferred to him or her from the holder in due course.

EXAMPLE 24.5

Svensson had a $500 note that had been made out to him by Pappas. He offered the note to Manchester at a 60-percent discount. Simple prudence suggests that Manchester should have tried to find out why Svensson was willing to sell the note at such a low price—or large discount. In short, she should have looked for a defect in the instrument. Without such a search, she would not be considered a holder in due course. If Manchester transferred the instrument before maturity to Cho, who paid value for it, not knowing that Manchester had purchased the note at a 60-percent discount, then Cho would be considered a holder in due course. However, if Manchester later reacquired the note from Cho, Manchester would not be considered a holder in due course because one cannot benefit from one's own wrongdoing.

DEFENSES AGAINST PAYMENT OF COMMERCIAL PAPER

A defense against payment of commercial paper that may be used against any party except a holder in due course is called a ***personal defense.*** A defense against payment of commercial paper that claims the instrument was void from the beginning is known as a ***real defense,*** or *absolute defense.* Real defenses may be used by the maker or acceptor against any party to a paper, including a holder in due course.

Personal Defenses

Personal defenses against payment of commercial paper relate to the acts or circumstances leading to the issue of the paper rather than to the paper itself. These defenses include lack of consideration, fraud, duress, undue influence, nondelivery of an incomplete instrument, nondelivery of a completed instrument, payment before maturity, and counterclaim.

Lack of Consideration Although consideration is presumed to have been given for a promissory note, proof by the maker that consideration was in fact lacking can be used as a defense against paying the instrument.

> **EXAMPLE 24.6**
> Moser gave his brother a 90-day promissory note as a gift. Before the maturity date, he changed his mind; when the note came due, Moser refused to pay it. If sued on the note by his brother, Moser could avoid paying it by proving lack of consideration.

Fraud, Duress, or Undue Influence If fraud, duress (threat of harm to person or property), or undue influence were used to induce a person to sign a negotiable instrument, the injured person may use any of these facts as defense against any person who is not a holder in due course.

The Uniform Commercial Code provides that, unless a person who takes an instrument has the rights of a holder in due course, his or her claim for payment is subject to "all defenses of a party which would be available in an action on a simple contract" [UCC 3-306].

OBJECTIVE 4

Distinguish between personal and real defenses against payment of commercial paper, and list the types of defenses in each case.

personal defense A defense against payment of commercial paper that may be used against any party except a holder in due course.

real defense A defense against payment of commercial paper that claims the instrument was void from the beginning.

Nondelivery of a Completed Instrument Sometimes a completed negotiable instrument comes into the possession of an immediate party (the payee indicated on the instrument) before the maker or drawer has delivered it. In such a case, the payee cannot collect on the instrument. If the payee, however, negotiates the instrument to a holder in due course, the new holder can enforce payment by the maker. As a result, the defense of nondelivery is not valid against a holder in due course.

> **EXAMPLE 24.7**
>
> Tomar, a wholesaler, agreed to accept Brinner's note in payment for goods. When Tomar went to Brinner's office to collect the note, no one was there, but on Brinner's desk he found the completed note made out to him. If Tomar took the note without waiting for delivery by Brinner, he could not enforce payment if Brinner refused to pay it. But if Tomar sold the note to Sund, who becomes a holder in due course, Sund could collect on the instrument.

Nondelivery of an Incomplete Instrument Under the Uniform Commercial Code, no distinction is made between lack of delivery of a completed and an incomplete instrument. In either case, it is treated as a personal defense, not effective against a holder in due course [UCC 3-306].

Payment Before Maturity Suppose the maker of an instrument paid it before maturity but failed to get the paper itself back. In this case, he or she would be discharged from further liability to immediate parties (the payees), but will remain liable on the note if it should come into possession of a holder in due course.

Counterclaim The maker of a note or the drawer or acceptor of a bill of exchange may deduct from the amount demanded by an immediate party any amounts owed him or her by the payee. This type of claim is called a ***counterclaim.***

counterclaim When the maker of a note or other drawer or acceptor of a bill of exchange may deduct from the amount demanded by an immediate party any amounts owed him or her by the payee.

Real Defenses

Real, or absolute, defenses to payment of commercial paper, good against anyone, include forgery, material alteration, lack of intent to execute commercial paper, incapacity of the parties to contract, and illegality created by law.

Forgery Commercial paper on which the signature of the maker has been forged is void. Even a holder in due course cannot collect on an instrument if he or she obtained title after a forgery. Indorsers of a forged instrument who negotiate the paper are liable. The reason is that there are implied warranties of indorsers that an instrument is genuine, that the indorser has good title to it, and that all prior parties had the capacity to contract.

> **EXAMPLE 24.8**
>
> Misuki found a blank check that belonged to Pierce, a neighbor. Misuki filled out the check for $500, made it payable to himself, and signed Pierce's name—a forgery. He then indorsed the check and transferred it to Bader with a special indorsement in payment of a debt. Bader indorsed the check and cashed the check at Pierce's bank. When the forgery is discovered—as it will be when the cancelled check is returned to Pierce—the bank must return the money to Pierce's account because it cashed a forged check. It will, however, look to the indorsers, Misuki and Bader, to recover the loss.

Material Alteration A change made to an instrument that affects the rights of the parties is called a *material alteration,* and it releases the maker from liability for payment to the party responsible for the changes. No one may enforce the altered instrument. The maker, however, must pay the paper according to its original terms. Changing the place or date of a paper and adding or changing an interest rate are examples of material alteration.

The Uniform Commercial Code provides that the loss falls upon the party whose conduct in signing a blank instrument made the fraud possible, that is, whose negligence or recklessness invited alterations by subsequent holders [UCC 3-406].

material alteration A change made to an instrument that affects the rights of the parties.

> **EXAMPLE 24.9**
>
> Stirks used a check to pay Moore, a merchant, $100 for a purchase. Moore raised the amount of the check to $1,000, indorsed it, and cashed it at a bank other than the one on which it was drawn. When the check was returned to Stirks' bank for collection, the bank noted the alteration and refused to pay it. The bank that cashed the check can hold Stirks liable only for the amount for which the check was originally drawn.

Lack of Intent to Execute Commercial Paper A person cannot be held liable, even by a holder in due course, if he or she signs an instrument that is apparently not negotiable and the paper is later fraudulently converted into a negotiable instrument. Fraud in executing an instrument is an absolute defense, but fraud related to the circumstances surrounding the issuing of a paper and not to the paper itself is a personal defense.

> **EXAMPLE 24.10**
>
> Jackson believed she was signing a receipt for the delivery of an appliance when, in fact, she was signing a note. If she can prove that she had not been negligent and that she was tricked into signing the paper, she may present this fraud in the execution of the instrument as a defense against payment, good against any holder.

If Jackson had paid for merchandise with a note and later found that the goods were not of the quality contracted for, her defense against payment would be fraud in the making of the contract. This defense is a personal defense valid against anyone except a holder in due course.

Incapacity of Parties to Contract An incompetent person who makes, signs, and delivers a negotiable instrument cannot be held liable for its payment. The defense of incompetence is valid against anyone, even a holder in due course.

Illegality Created by Statute Often state statutes expressly declare that commercial paper given for gambling transactions or at usurious rates of interest is void. Paper issued under such circumstances is unenforceable, no matter who holds it.

PRESENTMENT OF COMMERCIAL PAPER

To establish the liability of the indorsers of commercial paper, the holder must engage in what is known as *presentment,* that is, tender a note to the maker and demand its payment, or show a draft to the drawer and request its acceptance or payment, on or after the maturity date at the place stated in the instrument.

The Uniform Commercial Code states that presentment may be made by mail or at the place of acceptance or payment specified in the instrument. If no place is specified, presentment may be made at the place of business or residence of the party who is to accept or pay. Because the liability of the maker of commercial paper is absolute, presentment and demand are not necessary to bind him or her.

Commercial paper must be presented for payment during business hours on the date given in the instrument. A demand instrument such as a check or note must be presented for payment within a reasonable time after issue.

OBJECTIVE 5

Explain presentment and dishonor of commercial paper.

presentment When the holder of a note tenders it to the maker and demands payment, or shows a draft to the drawer and requests its acceptance or payment, on or after the maturity date at the place stated in the instrument.

EXAMPLE 24.11

Chilton bought merchandise from Ramos and paid with a 60-day note. Ramos negotiated the note to Brill for value. Brill presented the note to Chilton for payment several weeks after the maturity date. When Chilton refused to pay, Brill attempted to collect from Ramos. She could not do so. Ramos, as an indorser, was released from liability when the holder, Brill, failed to present the note for payment when it became due.

DISHONOR OF COMMERCIAL PAPER

A negotiable instrument is considered **dishonored** if it is not accepted when presented for acceptance, if it is not paid when presented for payment at maturity, or if presentment is excused or waived and the instrument is past due and unpaid.

The holder of dishonored commercial paper must give notice of the dishonor immediately—a bank by midnight, and by any other person by midnight of the third business day after dishonor—to the drawer and to all indorsers, to hold them liable on the instrument. Any drawer or indorser to whom such notice is not given is relieved from liability [UCC 3-508].

If notice is given that paper has been properly presented for acceptance or payment and that acceptance or payment has been refused, then notice of nonpayment is unnecessary.

dishonored When a negotiable instrument is not accepted when presented for acceptance, not paid when presented for payment at maturity, presentment is excused or waived, or the instrument is past due and unpaid.

EXAMPLE 24.12

Verdigo, holder of a note, indorsed it to Zikmond in payment for a boat he purchased. When Verdigo discovered some major defects in the boat, he refused to pay the note. As a holder of the note, Zikmond immediately gave notice of the dishonor to the previous indorsers. In so doing, he is protected from loss if he has to go to the other indorsers, in addition to Verdigo, to obtain payment.

CHAPTER SUMMARY

1. The purpose of indorsing a check can vary, but generally it is to transfer commercial paper from one party to another.

2. A blank indorsement is one in which the name of the payee is written by the payee on the back of a negotiable instrument. A special indorsement is one in which the payee specifies the person

to whom, or to whose order, it is to be paid. A restrictive indorsement is a signature to which words have been added restricting further indorsement of the instrument. A qualified indorsement is one in which the indorser avoids liability for payment even if the maker or drawer defaults on the instrument.

3 The four requirements for being a holder in due course are: **(a)** the paper must be complete and regular on its face; **(b)** the paper must have been acquired on or before the due date; **(c)** the paper must have been acquired for a valuable consideration; and **(d)** the paper must have been taken in good faith and for value.

4 Personal defenses against payment of commercial paper can be used against anyone except a holder in due course; real defenses can be used against any party, including a holder in due course. Personal defenses include lack of consideration; fraud, duress, or undue influence; nondelivery of a completed instrument; nondelivery of an incomplete instrument; payment before maturity; and counterclaim. Real defenses include forgery; material alteration; lack of intent to execute commercial paper; incapacity of the parties to contract; and illegality created by statute.

5 Presentment occurs when a holder tenders a note to the maker and demands its payment, or shows a draft to the drawer and requests its acceptance or payment, on or after the maturity date at the place stated in the instrument. A negotiable instrument is deemed dishonored if it is not accepted when presented for acceptance, not paid when presented for payment at maturity, or if presentment is excused or waived and the instrument is past due and unpaid.

Chapter 24 Assessment

MATCHING LEGAL TERMS

Match each of the following definitions with the correct term in the list below. Write the letter of your choice in the answer column.

- **a.** *bona fide*
- **b.** blank indorsement
- **c.** counterclaim
- **d.** dishonorment
- **e.** holder in due course
- **f.** indorse
- **g.** indorsement
- **h.** indorser
- **i.** material alteration
- **j.** personal defense
- **k.** qualified indorsement
- **l.** presentment
- **m.** real defense
- **n.** restrictive indorsement
- **o.** special indorsement

1. An indorsement by which the payee of an instrument transfers it to the order of another person.

2. The person who writes his or her name on the back of an instrument.

3. The person to whom an instrument is transferred.

4. The practice of the holder of commercial paper writing his or her name on the back of an instrument.

5. An indorsement that transfers an instrument but limits the liability of the indorser.

6. An indorsement that transfers an instrument to whoever has possession of it.

7. An indorsement that limits the transfer of an instrument to a particular person or for a particular purpose.

8. A person who has accepted commercial paper in good faith, for value, before maturity, and without notice of any defects in the instrument.

9. A claim for not paying commercial paper that relates to the circumstances leading to the issuing of the paper rather than to the paper itself.

10. A claim that states that the instrument was void from the beginning.

11. The deduction of amounts owed claimed by the maker of a note or the drawer of a draft from the amount demanded by an immediate party.

12. Important changes in an instrument that affect the rights of the parties.

13. Exhibiting a note to its maker and demanding payment.

14. Refusal to pay a commercial paper.

15. A Latin term meaning "in good faith."

Chapter 24 Assessment

TRUE/FALSE QUIZ

Indicate whether each of the following statements is true or false by writing *T* or *F* in the answer column.

16. The writing that a holder puts on the back of a negotiable instrument is known as a negotiation.   16. _____

17. An indorsement of an instrument must be for the entire amount.   17. _____

18. The Uniform Commercial Code attributes an implied warranty to an indorsed instrument that the signature is genuine.   18. _____

19. An indorser of an instrument is released from liability by any act that discharges the instrument, such as payment.   19. _____

20. If it is apparent that an instrument has been altered, the holder is not a holder in due course.   20. _____

21. A blank indorsement of an instrument in his or her possession.   21. _____

22. An instrument with a special, or full, indorsement is payable only to the person named in the indorsement.   22. _____

23. A restrictive indorsement prevents further negotiation of an instrument.   23. _____

24. If an instrument indorsed in blank is lost, the finder may not legally negotiate it.   24. _____

25. The words "for deposit only" signify a blank indorsement.   25. _____

DISCUSSION QUESTIONS

Answer the following questions and discuss them in class.

26. Why would a person who receives a check want to limit its negotiability and how would this be done?

27. Under what circumstances are a minor's checks valid?

Chapter 24 Assessment

28. What kind of an indorsement allows an indorser to avoid liability for payment even if the maker or drawer defaults on the instrument?

29. Describe the defenses against payment of commercial paper that are concerned with the acts or circumstances leading to the issue of the paper rather than to the paper itself.

30. What is the difference between a contract and a negotiable instrument as it concerns consideration?

31. State statutes usually declare that commercial paper given for gambling transactions or at usurious rates of interest is void. Can a person pay off an illegal gambling debt by check?

THINKING CRITICALLY ABOUT THE LAW

Answer the following questions, which require you to think critically about the legal principles that you learned in this chapter.

32. Delivery of Negotiable Instrument If all other requirements of a negotiable instrument have been met except delivery, should payment depend on delivery, and if so, why?

33. Liability of Indorser The innocent indorser of a forged instrument who negotiates the paper is liable. Is this fair? Explain your answer.

Chapter 24 Assessment

34. Indorsements Should an indorsement written in pencil be legally acceptable? Why or why not?

35. Material Alteration How do significant changes made in an instrument affect the rights of the parties to it?

36. A Question of Ethics Is it ethical for direct mail marketers to include a document that resembles a check made payable to the addressee, when closer examination reveals certain conditions such as, "good only toward the purchase of . . ."?

CASE QUESTIONS

Study each case below and answer the questions that follow by writing *Yes* or *No* in the answer column.

37. Raised Check Sikonen gave his check for $5 to Rivera, but in so doing he neglected to fill in the customary wavy line following the amount in the words. Rivera indorsed the check to Montana, who easily increased the amount to $500 and then presented the check to Sikonen's bank for payment.

   a. Will Sikonen be required to bear the loss because of his negligence in writing the check? a. _____

   b. Will Rivera have to bear the loss because of his negligence in indorsing a check that could be so easily altered? b. _____

   c. Will the bank be required to bear the $495 loss for cashing an altered check? c. _____

38. Defenses Laredo found a checkbook belonging to Waldron, drew a check, signed Waldron's name to it, and gave it to Kelly. The payee, Kelly, indorsed the check to a holder in due course, who presented it to the bank for payment. The bank refused to pay the check.

   a. Will Waldron's account be charged for the check, since he lost the checkbook? a. _____

   b. Is forgery a real defense, and may it be used against the claims of a holder in due course? b. _____

   c. Is a holder in due course protected against all types of defenses? c. _____

394   PART 5   Commercial Paper

Chapter 24 Assessment

39. Stale Check Church accepted a three-year-old check that Field indorsed to her. When Church presented the check for payment, the bank refused to honor it and informed Church that the account had been closed for a year.

   a. Is a person who accepts a demand instrument, such as a check, more than a reasonable time after issue considered to have been given notice that the instrument is overdue?

   a. _____

   b. Is the drawer of a check responsible to all holders in due course for a period of seven years?

   b. _____

   c. Can Church sue the drawer to collect the check?

   c. _____

CASE ANALYSIS

Study each of the following cases carefully and then briefly state the principle of law and your decision.

40. Bearer Instrument McCutchon wrote a check payable to "cash" while he was in a supermarket. Before he got to the cashier, he realized that he had lost the check. *Is this a bearer instrument, payable to any holder?*

Principle of law:

_____
_____

Decision:

_____
_____

41. Personal Defense Poulakis sold a word-processing machine using fraudulent means to Welson, who paid for the machine with a promissory note for $1,200. When Welson discovered the fraud, she refused to honor the note when a subsequent holder presented it for payment. Welson claimed fraud as a defense. *Will Welson succeed in avoiding payment to a holder in due course?*

Principle of law:

_____
_____

Decision:

_____
_____

42. Negotiability Locke gave two promissory notes to Consumer Food, Inc. in payment for merchandise he purchased. The notes said, "Buyer agreed to pay to seller." Consumer Food, Inc. assigned the notes to Aetna Acceptance Corporation. *Were these notes negotiable instruments?* [*Locke v. Aetna Acceptance Corporation*, 309 So.2d 43 (Florida).]

Chapter 24 Assessment

Principle of law:

Decision:

43. **Postdated Check** Gentilotti, father of an illegitimate son, drew a check for $20,000 in 1969 payable to the son's order. The check was dated July 1, 1985, but provided on the face of the check that, should Gentilotti die before that date, "this check shall be payable immediately." Gentilotti issued the check to the son's mother, the legal guardian. Gentilotti died on July 4, 1980. Despite the available funds, the bank, acting on orders of Gentilotti's executor, refused payment when the check was presented. The drawer's executor refused payment on the grounds that the obligation was not due. *Was the postdated check valid?* [*Smith v. Gentilotti*, 359 N.E.2d 953 (Massachusetts).]

Principle of law:

Decision:

LEGAL RESEARCH

Complete the following activities. Then share your findings with the class.

44. **Working in Teams** Working in teams of three or four, interview personnel at your local bank to describe the circumstances under which the bank might refuse to cash a check drawn on an account held at the bank.

45. **Using Technology** Using the Internet and search engines, investigate cases involving both testamentary and *inter vivos* trusts.

PART VI

BUSINESS AND TECHNOLOGY

CHAPTER 25 Computer Privacy and Speech

CHAPTER 26 Conducting Business in Cyberspace

CHAPTER 25

COMPUTER PRIVACY AND SPEECH

PERFORMANCE OBJECTIVES

After studying this chapter and completing the assessments, you will be able to:

1. Explain why and how cookies and e-mail can threaten a person's right to privacy.
2. Identify and explain the major provisions of the Electronic Communications Privacy Act, the Computer Fraud and Abuse Act, the Electronic Funds Transfer Act, and other federal and state statutes that govern cyberspace.
3. Discuss the major policy implications relating to online gambling.
4. Distinguish between forms of speech that are constitutionally protected and those that are not so protected.
5. Discuss the potential liability of an Internet Service Provider in the area of defamation.
6. Explain how computer users are protected against unwanted computer speech, such as obscenity and spam.

LEGAL TERMS

cookie
password
hacker
virus
defamation
slander
libel
public figure
spam

Technology and Individual Liberty

The majority of people in the United States either own or have access to a computer and to the Internet. As a result, there is a new and increasingly significant threat to individual privacy. Most experts agree that the rapid advances in technology being experienced today make it difficult for most people to maintain online anonymity or distance between themselves and powerful interests. Online marketers of products and services have quickly recognized that learning about consumers online behavior presents a real opportunity to increase sales. Similarly, there are those in our society, who for thrill or personal gain, would seek to discover personal information about you. Many federal and state statutes have been passed to address these issues; but it must be remembered that laws are developed slowly and methodically, while technology continues to advance at a rapid rate.

Computer Privacy

There are two distinct rights of privacy that are generally recognized in the United States. The first is a constitutional right to privacy, which has been upheld by the U.S. Supreme Court. However, there is a second kind of privacy that, prior to the prominence of computer use, did not need much protection. This privacy protects information about individuals from widespread distribution. Where people shop, what videos they rent, how much life insurance they have, and what kind of pet they own are all bits of personal information that people may or may not wish to share with others. In the past, when such information was stored in the home, individuals were protected by the laws against trespassing. No one could enter a home without permission and gather this information. However, now that this information is stored on computers and across networks, the law has had a difficult time providing as much protection.

There are also times when people may make statements on the Web pertaining to their views on certain issues. These views may be expressed in chat rooms, on listservs, or in e-mail messages. In most cases, a person's privacy is not protected when they make such statements by using these technologies.

EXAMPLE 26.1

Pietro, who works for Howard Sportswear, received an employee evaluation that was not especially laudatory. Angry that he did not get the raise to which he believed he was entitled, Pietro wrote a series of

Photo 25.1

Storing Private Information

Traditionally, people have stored private information at home or in office files. *How have technologies and the Internet changed the way our private information is kept?*

OBJECTIVE 1

Explain why and how cookies and e-mail can threaten a person's right to privacy.

cookie A file that is imbedded on the hard drive of a computer, often without a person's knowledge, that collects and stores information about the user and his or her online behavior, including Web sites that he or she has visited.

statements on USENET, complaining that his employer treated their employees poorly. The President of Howard Sportswear learned of the postings, and Pietro was fired. In this case, there is little that Pietro can do to get his job back.

Cookies

A *cookie* is a file that is imbedded on the hard drive of a computer, often without a person's knowledge, that collects and stores information about the user and his or her online behavior, including the Web sites that he or she has visited. Cookies can be used as important marketing tools because they let companies that sell or advertise on the Web know which products and services interest a person.

While there are currently no laws prohibiting the use of cookies to gather information regarding adults, the Children's Online Privacy Protection Act prohibits this practice when minors are involved, unless there is parental consent.

Consumers who believe that their right to privacy is being violated by the imbedding of cookies can complain to the Federal Trade Commission, a federal regulatory agency that is responsible for ensuring that companies do not use unfair trade practices.

Electronic Mail

Frequently, federal and state courts will determine a person's right to privacy according to what an individual might reasonably expect under the circumstances. For example, if you mail a letter to a friend, you could reasonably expect that no one other than the recipient will read the letter. Similarly, persons who provide information via electronic mail (e-mail) from their homes can reasonably expect their statements to be private; hence the content of e-mail messages is considered protected. The Electronic Communications Privacy Act (ECPA) makes it a federal crime to monitor e-mail during real time; i.e., when it is being sent or received. It should be pointed out, however, that law enforcement officials may monitor e-mail when they are granted such right by a court.

The law relating to e-mail is applied differently when a person is at work. Employees have no reasonable expectation of privacy while they are on the job, and in fact an employer may read an employee's e-mail at any time, even without first obtaining the employee's consent. The ECPA specifically provides that employers may view e-mail. Despite the fact that the law expressly grants this right to employers, it should be noted that most employers nonetheless have policies to the effect that e-mail messages sent or received while on the employer's premises, or while using the employer's computer equipment, may be read by the employer. These policies may also state that an employee is forbidden to encrypt messages, or install passwords unknown to the employer or without the employer's permission.

Even if an employer promises not to read an employee's e-mail messages, courts in some states have still ruled that the promise does not create a reasonable expectation of privacy; an employer may change his or her mind later, without letting the employee know.

> **EXAMPLE 26.2**
>
> Jackson, an employee of Chang Manufacturing Co., regularly placed orders for raw materials with Kleinman Glass Corporation. Jackson spoke frequently on the telephone with Ruiz, and developed a friendly relationship with her. Jackson sent Ruiz an e-mail message asking her to go out to dinner with him. Jackson's immediate supervisor at Chang read the e-mail, wrote a memorandum disciplining Jackson for violating company policy, and placed a copy of the memorandum in Jackson's personnel file. Jackson's discipline would be upheld by a court, and if Jackson applied for another position at a different company, the contents of the e-mail message could be disclosed to the prospective employer.

The ECPA also grants an *Internet Service Provider (ISP)* the right to monitor e-mail messages without a subscriber's consent. Despite possessing this legal right, most ISPs have their subscribers electronically sign a Service Agreement, in which the subscriber acknowledges that the ISP may examine the contents of both sent and received e-mail messages, and that there is no expectation of privacy.

COMPUTER CRIME

Many computer crimes, particularly those in which the computer is used as a means of engaging in criminal activity, are simply technologically advanced versions of standard crimes. A bank employee, for example, who programs the bank's computer to make deductions from one or several accounts and to deposit the funds into an account set up and controlled by the employee, could be prosecuted for embezzlement even though he or she had not touched actual currency.

Another type of computer crime concerns unauthorized access to computer data. Computers are often connected to other computers by telephone, modems, cable lines, or satellite, so that funds or data can be transferred from one to another. While a ***password*** is needed to gain access to computers, often simple, obvious passwords are unwisely chosen. As a result, unauthorized individuals can easily guess what they are and gain access. Lack of security relating to confidential passwords also results when these keys fall into the wrong hands.

Unauthorized access to computers can result in several different kinds of violations, including the following:

- invasion of privacy
- unauthorized use of the computer itself (using another person's property without permission)
- manipulation of financial, medical, or other records
- unauthorized access to databases

password A secret series of characters that allows a user to access a file, computer, or program.

> **EXAMPLE 26.3**
> City Central College had facilities for students to use computers and access the Internet. Students had special passwords that enabled them to access an information database through the City Central College Library. Elkin learned Wilbur's password and used it to access the database to gather information for a term paper. The charges incurred by Elkin's unauthorized use of the password appeared on Wilbur's credit card. This use is not very different from Elkin using Wilbur's credit card to purchase merchandise at the local department store.

Unauthorized use of computers have been used to transfer funds from one bank account to another, to change students' grades in college computer files, and to credit accounts for purchases made.

A person who gains unauthorized access to computers more for mischief than for criminal intent is called a ***hacker.*** Such people enjoy the challenge of gaining access and creating mischief without necessarily profiting from their activities. Another serious and equally senseless problem affects computers users: a ***virus.*** The term *virus* in this context refers to instructions hidden in software; it has come into use because of the many similarities between these hidden software messages and a biological virus. Like a biological virus, a computer virus can lie dormant in a computer for long periods and spring into action at a predetermined date and time, or when a certain event happens. Because software provides instruction to a computer, certain instructions can direct the computer to do any number of things, including erase data, generate data that takes up valuable storage space, and conceal the virus. Some viruses are little more than a hacker's prank, consisting of instructions that tell the computer to display "Gotcha," or some other harmless message, on the user's screen on a certain date and time. Not all viruses are pranks, however, and some cause major disruptions in computer operations. Frequently, viruses are spread by attaching themselves to the user's e-mail list, located in the computer's address book on the hard disk.

hacker A person who gains unauthorized access to computer systems more for mischief than for criminal intent.

virus A program or selection of code that is loaded onto your computer system without your knowledge and runs against your wishes.

Computer Crime Legislation

Specific computer crime statutes have been enacted by both federal and state legislatures. These statutes include the Electronic Communications Privacy Act, Computer Abuse and Fraud Act, Electronic Funds Transfer Act, and other laws that govern in cyberspace.

The Electronic Communications Privacy Act

The Electronic Communications Privacy Act (ECPA) is a statute that addresses hacking and other forms of illegal conduct by making it a federal crime to gain unauthorized access to any communication that is stored on a computer system. This law states that individuals may not gain access without permission to an electronic communication system, or to exceed the authorization they have been granted. It is important to note that according to the ECPA, an individual must act intentionally to commit a crime. Accidentally intruding on another person's computer files is not a crime under the ECPA.

OBJECTIVE 2

Identify and explain the major provisions of the Electronic Communications Privacy Act, the Computer Fraud and Abuse Act, Electronic Funds Transfer Act, and other federal and state statutes that govern cyberspace.

It is also a crime under the ECPA to disclose to a third party the contents of stored computer information that has been obtained without permission. This is simply common sense; for if a person does not have permission to retrieve the information, he or she certainly does not have permission to disclose it to someone else.

The Computer Fraud and Abuse Act

Enacted in 1984, the Computer Fraud and Abuse Act (CFAA) became the first federal computer crime statute in the United States. This legislation covers the following areas:

- *National Defense.* It is an unlawful use of a computer to gain access to secret information that could affect national security.
- *Financial Institutions.* It is unlawful to use without authorization a computer to gain access to the financial records of a financial institution—including information held in any file required by a consumer reporting agency.
- *Government Computers.* It is unlawful to access without authorization any department or agency computer used for federal government business.

In addition to these areas, the CFAA at times expands upon the ECPA, discussed earlier. While under the ECPA there must be an intent to exceed authorization for a crime to be committed, the CFAA does not require such intent if the intrusion onto another person's stored information causes damage. In other words, even if a person's intent is good, but his or her conduct accidentally causes damage, he or she may be prosecuted for a federal crime under the CFAA.

> **EXAMPLE 26.4**
>
> Witkowski released a *worm* (a type of virus that replicates itself and uses memory, but that cannot attach itself to other programs) to demonstrate vulnerabilities in the Maslow Company's computer system. Witkowski created the worm in such a way that its presence could be detected by experts, but that would not create any problems. Unfortunately for both Witkowski and the Maslow Company, the worm attached itself to the company's mainframe and spread to all the personal computers and terminals in the company, creating millions of dollars in damage due to lost and corrupted files. Witkowski is guilty of violating the CFAA, despite his good intent.

The Electronic Funds Transfer Act

The Electronic Funds Transfer Act (EFTA) makes it a federal offense to use any device that is part of an electronic transfer mechanism to steal money, goods, or services or to alter data, interrupt wire transmissions, or use stolen codes or passwords, when the purpose of such activity is to obtain something of value unlawfully.

General Criminal Law

Various federal criminal statutes, not originally concerned with computers, are still frequently used to prosecute those who commit computer crimes. The most widely used of these statutes are those that prohibit fraudulent activity using the U.S. mail, known as mail fraud. Also used to prosecute computer crime are the statutes that prohibit using the telephone and other electronic communication equipment (e.g., a fax machine) for fraudulent activity, known as wire fraud.

Computer Gambling

Closely related to the issue of computer crime is that of computer gambling. Federal and state laws make most forms of gambling illegal. However, there are numerous exceptions to these types of regulations (e.g., state lotteries and horse racing) and some locations where legal gambling takes place (e.g., Las Vegas and Atlantic City).

Online gambling is not illegal at this time, although most states have pending regulations that would severely restrict how and when such gambling may take place. For example, many would argue that even if gambling were to remain legal, it should be restricted to those over eighteen years of age. It is important to note that the rules relating to legal purpose and competent parties in contract law apply to agreements made in the form of wagers placed online.

Pending federal legislation would disallow most, but not all, online gambling. For example, state lotteries, American Indian casinos, and racetracks could continue their operations as before, and venture into online forms of gambling as well. It is unclear, however, whether online gambling would be allowed in "real time" in places like Las Vegas and Atlantic City.

More problematic is the issue of how to regulate offshore gambling, where consumer protection laws do not apply. Because obtaining jurisdiction over the companies that operate online gambling operations is difficult, special legislation would need to be enacted to allow federal officials to take action when necessary. It also remains to be seen whether federal regulations will address the way in which the bets are placed—for example, prohibiting the use of credit cards and electronic transfers for the purpose of gambling. This issue is not trivial. It is estimated that there will soon be $6 billion wagered in online gambling.

OBJECTIVE 3

Discuss the major policy implications relating to online gambling.

COMPUTER SPEECH

Many of the laws that protect our right to free speech in traditional contexts, such as in public or in print, also apply to the expression of ideas using computers or network technologies such as the Internet.

Harmful Speech

The United States has always had a deep commitment toward maintaining an individual's right to *freedom of speech.* Protection afforded to freedom of speech is embodied in the First Amendment to the U.S. Constitution. A person's right to make statements that are unpopular, and at times even offensive or annoying, must be zealously guarded.

However, the freedom of speech is not absolute. Laws that prohibit speech, but that would be constitutionally acceptable, include the following:

- *Obscene Statements.* What constitutes obscenity is the cause of much disagreement. In general, obscenity is that which is judged as such by local community standards.
- *Defamatory Statements.* Speech that harms a person's reputation is referred to as **defamation.** This speech includes **slander,** which is spoken, and **libel,** which is written or published.
- *Certain One-to-One Communications.* Several statutes require that telemarketers, for example, cease telephoning when specifically requested.
- *Verbal or Written Threats to Person or Property.*
- *Intentional Infliction of Emotional Distress.* When the objective is to cause another person to sustain severe anxiety, the injured party may sue the offending party.

It is important to note that the rules of defamation vary depending upon whether one is a **public figure.** By becoming a public figure, such as a mayor, a baseball star, a rapper, or a rock musician, one implicitly allows others to write about him or her in newspapers and magazines, and to discuss his or her conduct on television and radio. These same principles hold true in cyberspace. Private figures, but not public figures, would be able to recover damages in the event statements were made about them in chat rooms, and listservs. Of course, truth is an absolute defense to a charge of defamation, even in cyberspace.

OBJECTIVE 4

Distinguish between forms of speech that are constitutionally protected and those that are not so protected.

defamation The intentional tort that occurs when a false statement is communicated to others that harms a person's good name or reputation.

slander Any false statement that harms a person's good name or reputation made in a temporary form, such as speech, and communicated to others.

libel Any false statement that harms another person's good name or reputation made in a permanent form, such as movies, writing, and videotape, and communicated to others.

public figure A person who has voluntarily chosen an lifestyle that in a free society naturally exposes them to close scrutiny by the media. To prevail for defamation, these figures must prove that false statements were made with actual malice.

It is also important to note that the rules of libel vary depending upon where the libelous statements are printed. In the case of newspapers, the defamed individual may not recover damages unless he or she can show that the newspaper acted with actual malice, a kind of reckless disregard for the truth, or knowledge by the newspaper that what they had printed was false. Recently, court cases have held that these same rules apply in cyberspace because numerous news and wire services distribute information online.

Liability of an Internet Service Provider

When a person is defamed in cyberspace, often he or she is not able to determine the identity of the individual who made the defamatory statements. People in chat rooms, and in mass e-mail exchanges, frequently do not disclose their identities, but use fictitious names instead.

When individuals learn that someone has posted an untruth about them, especially when such untruth harms them professionally, they often attempt to hold their ISP liable. Courts have consistently held, however, that ISPs are not liable for defamatory statements made while using their service, unless they had prior knowledge of such use.

OBJECTIVE 5

Discuss the potential liability of an Internet Service Provider in the area of defamation.

> **EXAMPLE 26.5**
>
> Cardone was a well-respected attorney in the practice of divorce law. He represented Mr. Hakim when he was sued by Mrs. Hakim for high alimony payments. Cardone accurately portrayed Mrs. Hakim as guilty of spousal abuse, and no alimony was awarded. Mrs. Hakim, while concealing her identity, posted several notices on a computer bulletin board that stated that Cardone had never passed the bar examination. While Cardone strongly suspected that it was Mrs. Hakim who was the author of the untruths, he could not prove it because the ISP refused to disclose Mrs. Hakim's online identity. Cardone then sued the ISP, but he was unable to recover.

However, suppose we add some additional facts to Example 26.5: One month after Cardone complained to the ISP, Mrs. Hakim struck again, this time depicting Cardone as having a criminal record. Cardone would most likely recover this time against the ISP because they had prior knowledge of the defamation, and as a result, would now have an obligation to protect Cardone from additional defamatory statements.

OBJECTIVE 6

Explain efforts to protect computer users against unwanted computer speech, such as obscenity and spam.

Obscenity

Sometimes pictures or words that are contained on Web sites are alleged to be obscene. These pictures and words—both considered speech—are deemed legally obscene if they depict sexual conduct in a manner that is patently offensive under contemporary community standards, appeal to the prurient interest, and, taken as a whole, lack serious literary, scientific, artistic, or political value.

Many experts argue that the problem with this legal definition of obscenity is that it is too vague and ambiguous. As a result, a federal statute passed to regulate Web sites that contain obscene material or child pornography has been ruled by the courts to violate due process of law; that is, to be unconstitutional. The dilemma facing many ISPs and search engines is that they are uncertain about whether specific Web pages, postings, and e-mail messages are obscene when they match such content against the above definition.

Spam

spam Unsolicited e-mail messages sent primarily for commercial purposes.

Not all e-mail messages are welcomed, requested, or expected. Unsolicited e-mail messages sent primarily for commercial purposes are popularly referred to as *spam.* Spam is undesirable because it can drain an ISP's resources, strain network bandwidth, and clog a user's e-mail folders. Spam should be distinguished from e-mail messages that are sent at the recipient's request; for example, when a person purchases an item from a brick and mortar company, and provides his or her e-mail address to the seller, it is with the expectation that he or she may receive e-mail.

Spam is desirable from the originator's point of view because it is inexpensive. It has been estimated that several thousand recipients can be reached with spam for less than $100, while it would cost many thousands of dollars to reach the same number of individuals with a postal service mailing. Suppliers are therefore induced to collect e-mail addresses, often culling these from newsgroups and Web pages. It is technologically possible to stop spammers (for example, by blocking e-mail from unwanted senders), but doing so is not commonplace.

From the legal standpoint, it is perfectly allowable for a seller to solicit via e-mail. While there are many federal and state laws that restrict the sending of faxes and regular mailings, only a couple of states (as of this publication, only California and Washington) have laws on the books addressing the issue of spam.

CHAPTER SUMMARY

1 Cookies can be used to invade a person's privacy because they contain information about an Internet user's behavior, including the sites he or she visits on the Web. E-mail can also be used to violate someone's privacy because it can sometimes be intercepted and read by unintended recipients.

2 The ECPA is a federal statute that makes it a crime to gain unauthorized access to any communication stored on a computer system. The CFAA protects the electronic communication systems involved in government, finance, and national defense. The EFTA makes it a federal offense to use a device that is part of an electronic transfer mechanism to steal money, goods, or services, or to alter transmissions, steal passwords, etc., for the purpose of obtaining something of value illegally. Other statutes, many not originally intended to cover computers, are now applied to computers and networks.

3 Online gambling has major policy implications because many legislatures would want to regulate the enterprise, impose age and other restrictions, and control offshore gambling, where U.S. consumer protection laws often do not apply.

4 While the U.S. Constitution guarantees the First Amendment right to free speech, this right is not absolute. Regulated or prohibited speech includes obscenity, defamation, certain one-to-one communications, threats to persons or property, and the intentional infliction of emotional distress, to name a few.

5 Generally, ISPs are not liable for defamatory statements made by using their service unless the ISP had prior knowledge of defamatory conduct on the part of the accused user.

6 Laws to protect computer users from obscenity and spam are currently developing. Obscene material can be illegal if it is deemed patently offensive by community standards, appeals to prurient interests, and lacks any serious value. Spam is legal, but states are beginning to pass laws that address the issue.

Chapter 25 Assessment

MATCHING LEGAL TERMS

Match each of the following definitions with the correct term in the list below. Write the letter of your choice in the answer column.

- **a.** defamation
- **b.** worm
- **c.** hacker
- **d.** cookie
- **e.** spam

1. A file that is imbedded on the hard drive of a computer, often without a person's knowledge, that collects and stores information about the user.   1. _____

2. A person who gains unauthorized access to a computer more for mischief than for criminal intent.   2. _____

3. A small, self-contained program that invades all computers in a network.   3. _____

4. An unsolicited e-mail sent for commercial purposes.   4. _____

5. Speech that harms a person's reputation.   5. _____

TRUE/FALSE QUIZ

Indicate whether each of the following statements is true or false by writing *T* or *F* in the answer column.

6. Individuals making statements in chat rooms have an absolute right to privacy.   6. _____

7. There are currently no laws prohibiting the use of cookies in the case of adult computer users.   7. _____

8. Employees have no reasonable expectation of privacy while they are at work; hence employers may read their e-mail without first receiving the employee's consent.   8. _____

9. Internet Service Providers have the legal right to monitor e-mail without the subscriber's consent.   9. _____

10. Employees who transfer money from their employer's account into their own account without authorization can be prosecuted for the crime of embezzlement.   10. _____

11. There are numerous state, but no federal, regulations covering the misuse of computers and data.   11. _____

12. In order to violate the Computer Fraud and Abuse Act, the individual must act with intent to create damage.   12. _____

13. Since most forms of gambling are illegal, most forms of online gambling are also illegal.   13. _____

14. Off-shore gambling refers to foreign citizens placing bets in casinos located within the United States.   14. _____

PART 6   Business and Technology

Chapter 25 Assessment

15. Slander is a spoken form and libel is a written form of defamation. **15.** _____

16. A newspaper that prints a story about a public figure, with knowledge that the story is untrue, could be held liable for defamation. **16.** _____

17. The law mandates that all Internet Service Providers require subscribers to use their true names when entering cyberspace. **17.** _____

18. Pictures and words are legally obscene if they depict sexual conduct in a manner that is patently offensive under contemporary community standards, appeal to the prurient interest, and, taken as a whole, lack serious literary, scientific, artistic, or political value. **18.** _____

19. When an individual purchases an item from a brick and mortar company, and provides his or her e-mail address to the seller, the individual is implicitly consenting to the receipt of spam. **19.** _____

20. Spam is illegal in the vast majority of states. **20.** _____

DISCUSSION QUESTIONS

Answer the following questions and discuss them in class.

21. Explain how the law protecting the privacy of e-mail differs depending upon whether the e-mail is sent from home or from work.

22. Identify at least three typical company policies that restrict e-mail sent or received by employees while on the employer's premises.

23. Name four rights that may be violated when individuals gain access to computers without proper authorization.

24. Give three examples of unauthorized uses of computers that can result in criminal prosecution.

Computer Privacy and Speech   CHAPTER 25   411

Chapter 25 Assessment

25. Distinguish the Electronic Communications Privacy Act from the Computer Fraud and Abuse Act in terms of intent to commit a crime.

26. Identify five types of laws that restrict speech, but would nonetheless be constitutionally permissible.

THINKING CRITICALLY ABOUT THE LAW

Answer the following questions, which require you to think critically about the legal principles that you learned in this chapter.

27. Computer Privacy Explain how the advent of computer usage created the need for new laws to protect privacy in the United States.

28. Cookies How does the presence of cookies on the hard drive of a user's computer impact negatively on an individual's right to privacy?

29. E-mail What justification might there be for an employer to be legally entitled to view an employee's e-mail without the employee's permission?

30. Spam What are some advantages and disadvantages of legally restricting spam in cyberspace?

Chapter 25 Assessment

31. A Question of Ethics Do you believe that it is fair to hold public figures to a different standard of privacy and defamation than private individuals?

_____
_____
_____

CASE QUESTIONS

Study each of the cases below. Then answer the questions that follow by writing *Yes* or *No* in the answer column.

32. Cookies Comfy Shoes, Inc. maintained a Web site for the online sale of its products. Comfy carried a complete line of men's, women's, and children's shoes. Included among its many shoe products were children's sneakers. Without obtaining authorization, Comfy placed cookies on the hard drives of all persons visiting their site.

   a. Does Comfy have a legal right to place cookies on the computer hard drives of men and women visiting its Web site? **a.** _____

   b. Does Comfy have a legal right to place cookies on the computer hard drives of children visiting its Web site? **b.** _____

   c. Could users complain to the Federal Trade Commission if they thought their privacy was being violated by Comfy? **c.** _____

33. Computer Crime Schroeder, a student at Plymouth College, entered a computer lab on campus, overrode the password system, entered the College's computer without authorization, and changed her grade in a Business Law course from a "D" to a "B+."

   a. Can Schroeder be charged with the crime of embezzlement? **a.** _____

   b. Can Schroeder be charged with hacking? **b.** _____

   c. Can Schroeder be charged with unauthorized access to databases? **c.** _____

34. Spam WeAreTravel Corp., a retail travel agency doing business in Pennsylvania, regularly sent computer messages to all persons who signed onto the firm's mailing list. In addition, the company sent e-mail to all persons residing in the same town as the agency.

   a. Does WeAreTravel Corp. have a legal right to send spam to the persons who signed onto the mailing list? **a.** _____

   b. Does WeAreTravel Corp. have a legal right to send spam to the persons who are residents of the town in which the company is located? **b.** _____

   c. Does WeAreTravel Corp. have a legal right to send 200 e-mails per day to these individuals? **c.** _____

Computer Privacy and Speech **CHAPTER 25**

Chapter 25 Assessment

CASE ANALYSIS

Study each of the following cases carefully. Then briefly state the principle of law and your decision.

35. **Computer Privacy** Timothy R. McVeigh (no relation to the Oklahoma City bomber) was a highly decorated seventeen-year veteran of the U.S. Navy. McVeigh was a gay male who, while using an alias, sent an e-mail message to a civilian navy volunteer through AOL. The volunteer searched through the AOL's member profile directory, learned some information about the sender, and eventually this information and McVeigh's identity found its way to senior officials in the navy. McVeigh was then found to be in violation of the military's policy of "Don't ask, don't tell," an offense which warrants discharge for homosexuality. McVeigh brought suit, attempting to prevent the military from ordering his discharge. *Will McVeigh be allowed to offer as an argument that his e-mail to the volunteer cannot be used against him due to his right to privacy?* [*McVeigh v. Cohen,* 983 Supp. 215 (Washington, D.C.).]

Principle of law:

Decision:

36. **E-mail** Michael A. Smith was a regional operations manager for the Pillsbury Company. In his capacity, he regularly used the company's e-mail server. The company regularly assured its employees that all e-mail communications would remain confidential and privileged. While at home, Smith then exchanged e-mail messages with his supervisor. Pillsbury read these e-mail messages, claimed that they were inappropriate and unprofessional, and terminated Smith's employment. Smith brought a lawsuit for wrongful termination, and Pillsbury requested that it be dismissed. *Will the court allow Smith's lawsuit to proceed, or will the case be dismissed?* [*Smith v. Pillsbury,* C.A. NO. 95-5712 (Pennsylvania).]

Principle of law:

Decision:

37. **Computer Crime Legislation** Robert Tappan Morris released into the Internet a worm that spread and multiplied. The worm found its way into computers at several educational and military sites, causing these computers to crash. Morris was charged with violating Section 2(d) of the Computer Fraud and Abuse Act of 1986. Morris was able to prove during a jury trial that, while in fact he had released the worm, he did not do so intentionally. Nonetheless, Morris was found guilty of violating the law. He appealed his conviction on the grounds that his access to these educational and military computers was not without authorization, since Morris did not intend to access them. *Will Morris be successful in his appeal of the guilty verdict?* [*United States v. Morris,* 928 F.2d 504 (Washington, D.C.).]

Chapter 25 Assessment

Principle of law:

Decision:

38. Liability of an Internet Service Provider "Rumorville," a daily online newspaper, was part of a journalism forum on the Internet published by Fitzpatrick. Subscribers to Compuserve, an Internet Service Provider, had access to Rumorville. "Skuttlebut" was a service that distributed news and gossip about journalism. Rumorville published items about Skuttlebut that were alleged to be defamatory and untrue. Skuttlebut sued Compuserve, arguing that this Internet Service Provider was liable for the defamatory statements carried by the service. *Will Skuttlebut be successful in a suit against Compuserve?* [*Cubby v. Compuserve*, 776 F.Supp.135 (New York).]

Principle of law:

Decision:

LEGAL RESEARCH

Complete the following activities. Then share your findings with the class.

39. Working in Teams In teams of three or four, draft a federal statute that might be enacted to address the issue of online gambling. Be certain to include who is covered and what forms of gambling are being regulated.

40. Using Technology Using the Internet, visit the Web site www.cookiecentral.com. Then view the contents of your cookie files, and describe your reaction to this information.

Computer Privacy and Speech   CHAPTER 25   415

CHAPTER 26

Conducting Business in Cyberspace

PERFORMANCE OBJECTIVES

After studying this chapter and completing the assessments, you will be able to:

1. Discuss the role of the Securities and Exchange Commission in the sale and trading of securities online.
2. Explain how the Federal Trade Commission protects consumers from deceptive online advertising.
3. Identify the copyright issues associated with selling music and other forms of entertainment online.
4. Explain how contracts formed online are offered, accepted, and signed.
5. Name the advantages of using Alternative Dispute Resolution to resolve legal disputes.
6. Discuss the current rules pertaining to states levying sales taxes for purchases made online.

LEGAL TERMS

- Securities Act of 1933
- primary market
- Securities Exchange Act of 1934
- secondary market
- Securities and Exchange Commission (SEC)
- Federal Trade Commission (FTC)
- deceptive advertisement
- Digital Millennium Copyright Act of 1998 (DMCA)
- Electronic Signatures in Global and International Commerce Act
- Alternative Dispute Resolution (ADR)
- nexus
- use tax
- Internet Tax Freedom Act

BUSINESS AND THE INTERNET

The 1990s ushered in an entirely new way of doing business. Words like *e-business, e-tailing, e-marketing,* and *e-contracts* found their way into the English vocabulary, and companies started taking the Internet seriously as an important new means of doing business. Firms that conduct business over the Internet, however, are subject to the same legal restrictions as traditional brick-and-mortar firms. This chapter examines the ways in which the law applies to conducting business on the Web.

SELLING SECURITIES ON THE WEB

There are two main federal statutes that cover the sale and distribution of securities in the United States:

Securities Act of 1933 The **Securities Act of 1933** covers the sale of securities (stocks, bonds, and other forms of investments) in the ***primary market,*** which is where an issuer (a corporation) sells its securities to the public. This act requires that issuers of securities that are selling them publicly must make certain necessary disclosures at the time that the securities are issued. The act includes the following important provisions:

- Issuers of securities must register the securities with the Securities and Exchange Commission.
- A registration statement must be filed that includes information on the securities offered, historical and current data about the issuing company, and how the company plans to use the proceeds from the offer.
- The issuing company must provide prospective investors with a prospectus, which is a document that provides relevant and important information about the company, its businesses, and its prospects.

In 1992, the SEC created a computerized system, known as the Electronic Data Gathering, Analysis, and Retrieval (EDGAR) system that allows companies to download required information directly into the government's computers. This system is also useful to the public, which can now access company information electronically.

Securities Exchange Act of 1934 The **Securities Exchange Act of 1934** covers the trading of these same securities in the ***secondary***

Securities Act of 1933 The federal law that covers the sale of securities in the primary market.

primary market The market in which an issuer (a corporation) sells its securities to the public.

Securities Exchange Act of 1934 The federal law that covers the sale of securities in the secondary market.

secondary market The market where one member of the public sells securities to another member of the public.

market, defined as the *place* where one member of the public sells securities to another member of the public. This act requires that companies periodically release important business information to the public and to investors. Among other things, it requires that insiders, or officers of the corporation, file a statement disclosing any equity securities they may hold in the company.

It is important to note that when we use the term *place* in the previous definition, we are not necessarily referring to a physical location. The Web, or cyberspace, is also considered a place, and securities are regularly bought and sold electronically.

> **EXAMPLE 26.1**
>
> The Washington Company sold common stock to O'Brien, who held the stock for several years and then resold it for a profit to Gupta. The Washington Company, the issuer, is governed by the 1933 Act when it sold the stock to O'Brien, and by the 1934 Act because O'Brien is legally entitled to resell the stock to Gupta.

The federal agency responsible for administering these two federal statutes, as well as several others, is the **Securities and Exchange Commission (SEC).** The SEC attempts to ensure that prospective investors have access to full and correct information about the companies whose securities they are interested in purchasing. Accordingly, the SEC requires that companies prepare forms and documentation containing financial and other information so that prospective investors can, if they so desire, review this information prior to investing money.

Since 1995, the SEC has addressed the issue of selling securities electronically by publishing a series of guidelines relating to such sales. The rules relating to online sales of securities can be summarized as follows:

- Information that is distributed electronically will satisfy the transmission requirements of the federal securities laws provided that the distribution results in delivery of information substantially equivalent to what the prospective investors would have received in paper form.
- There must be timely and adequate notice to prospective investors of the availability of this information.
- The electronic delivery must afford access to the information that is comparable to that afforded by paper copies.
- There must be evidence to demonstrate that delivery of the information to prospective investors was successful.

OBJECTIVE 1

Discuss the role of the Securities and Exchange Commission in the sale and trading of securities online.

Securities and Exchange Commission (SEC) The federal agency responsible for administrating various federal statutes aimed at ensuring that prospective investors have access to full and correct information about the companies whose securities they are interested in purchasing.

The SEC also acts to make certain that investors do not violate the SEC's antitouting rules. *Touting* occurs when an investor who owns shares of a company's stock posts notices online in chat rooms, on Web pages, and elsewhere, that indicate the value of the stock will increase. If enough individuals who read these postings believe that the touter is a disinterested expert, the demand for the shares will increase, the stock price will go up, and the touter has the opportunity to earn large amounts of money by selling the shares at the inflated price.

EXAMPLE 26.2

Felmuth, a 15-year-old computer maven, entered chat rooms and placed postings on Internet services on numerous occasions, pretending to be a financial analyst with an MBA from a respected university. Felmuth falsely implied that she had inside information that the Daya Corporation, a drug manufacturer, was on the verge of a major breakthrough in discovering a cure for a deadly disease. The Daya Corporation's stock rose five-fold in less than a week, and Felmuth made several hundred thousand dollars when she sold the stock for a huge profit. Felmuth is guilty of violating federal securities laws, will be required to repay all profits, and could spend some time in a juvenile detention center.

ADVERTISING ON THE WEB

The federal agency responsible for ensuring that advertising in the United States is truthful is the **Federal Trade Commission (FTC).** In addition, there are numerous state and local consumer protection agencies, as well as private, not-for-profit companies, that can assist in the event that a consumer is misled by a deceptive ad. A ***deceptive advertisement*** is defined as one that contains a material (important) misrepresentation, omission, or practice likely to mislead a consumer who acts reasonably under the circumstances.

Ads placed on Web pages are required to meet the same standards as ads placed in other media, such as print, billboards, television, and radio. If the FTC determines that a Web-based ad is deceptive, it has several options:

- The FTC can issue a cease and desist order, compelling the publisher to eliminate the Internet reference.
- The FTC can order an affirmative disclosure, requiring the publisher to revise the advertisement to include additional, truthful information.
- The FTC can require corrective advertising, informing future visitors to the Web page that previous information was deceptive.

OBJECTIVE 2

Explain how the Federal Trade Commission protects consumers from deceptive online advertising.

Federal Trade Commission (FTC) The federal agency responsible for ensuring that advertising in the United States is truthful.

deceptive advertisement An advertisement that contains a material (important) misrepresentation, omission, or practice likely to mislead a consumer who acts reasonably under the circumstances.

- The FTC can seek fines and other forms of civil remedies.
- In extreme cases involving fraud, the FTC can ask the federal Justice Department to file criminal charges, which can lead to imprisonment.

EXAMPLE 26.3

> Utopia Stationery sells silver-plated pen and pencil sets for $19.99. On its Web site, it advertised silver-plated pens for $19.99, and added that there would be a "free" silver-plated pencil provided with the purchase of a pen. Because the pencil is not really free at all, Utopia Stationery is guilty of creating a deceptive ad on its Web site and can be required to pay a fine.

SELLING ENTERTAINMENT ON THE WEB

OBJECTIVE 3

Identify the copyright issues associated with selling music and other forms of entertainment online.

In recent years, it has become popular for people to download music from the Web onto compact discs and other digital storage devices. Because the rightful owners of the music often have not granted permission and do not receive royalties from the pirated music, they have made efforts to stop companies from profiting from the distribution of online music. Court cases have made it clear that copyright infringement takes place even if the company provides a forum for music to be "shared" among subscribers.

EXAMPLE 26.4

> Napster, Inc. created one of the most frequently downloaded software applications in the history of the Internet. The company's software allowed users to share music and other entertainment files directly, person-to-person, and often at no cost. Several entertainment firms brought suit against Napster for copyright infringement. The court ordered the company to shut down its music file-sharing service until it could ensure that copyrighted works were protected and could not be shared using Napster's service.

The Digital Millennium Copyright Act of 1998

Digital Millennium Copyright Act of 1998 (DMCA) The federal act that provides that ISPs are not liable for copyright infringements by their subscribers or for information residing on their networks provided they accept certain specified policies.

Among numerous provisions, the federal **Digital Millennium Copyright Act of 1998 (DMCA)** provides that ISPs are not liable for copyright infringements by their subscribers, provided that they:

- adopt and reasonably implement a policy of terminating, in appropriate circumstances, the accounts of subscribers who are repeat infringers
- accommodate, and do not interfere with, the identification or protection of copyrighted works

The DMCA further protects ISPs from liability for copyright infringement even for information residing on their users' systems or networks, provided that:

- the ISP did not have knowledge of the infringing activity
- the ISP did not receive financial benefit directly attributable to the infringing activity
- upon receiving proper notification of claimed infringement, the ISP expeditiously blocked access to the infringed material

ENTERING INTO CONTRACTS ON THE WEB

The ability of parties to enter into agreements in cyberspace raises numerous questions. Offers are readily available on the Web, and the questions that arise are:

- How are offers in cyberspace accepted?
- Aren't agreements entered into on the Web contracts of adhesion?
- How does a computer user sign a contract made on the Web, especially a contract that must be in writing pursuant to the Statute of Frauds?

Accepting Offers on the Web

Remember that it is the offeror who determines how offers may be accepted. But also recall that silence on the part of the offeree generally does not constitute acceptance of an offer. These same rules are applicable in cyberspace.

Frequently, offers on Web sites include a button to be clicked by the user with his or her mouse that indicates acceptance. Most courts will acknowledge that by clicking the acceptance button, the offer has been accepted. It should be pointed out that the button need not explicitly read "I accept." It could, for example, use terms such as "I agree," "Yes," "I consent," or any other expression indicating that the offeree has read the offer and accepts the terms. Computer users who frequent Web sites should, therefore, be especially careful to click their mouse only after they have read the entire agreement and accept all of the terms.

Similarly, simply because a user visits a Web site will not constitute acceptance on the part of the user of an offer that is contained on that Web site. In other words, silence (not clicking the "I accept" button) does not constitute acceptance.

But what happens when the user has accepted the offer by clicking his or her mouse, but has not read all of the terms of the agreement?

OBJECTIVE 4

Explain how contracts formed online are offered, accepted, and signed.

Contracts of Adhesion on the Web

We have already seen that there are many instances in which contracts are formed without there being any real negotiating or bargaining by the parties. We have also learned that these agreements, termed "contracts of adhesion," are nonetheless valid unless they contain terms that are unreasonable. The same rules apply in cyberspace. If the Web site visitor has had an ample opportunity to read the terms, and if those terms are not unreasonable, a valid contract exists. Of course, all of the other elements of a contract must be met as well; for example, if the individual accepting the offer is a minor, the contract is voidable, and so on.

> **EXAMPLE 26.5**
>
> Motomba visited a Web page about her favorite pop group that indicated that she could subscribe to a monthly newsletter by clicking the "I subscribe" button. Motomba did not read the lengthy offer but simply clicked the button with her mouse. Later, Motomba learned that the terms of agreement stated in small print that, in addition to the newsletter, she would receive the latest CDs performed by the pop group. Motomba will be required to pay the reasonable price for the monthly newsletter, but will not be required to purchase the CDs.

Electronic Signatures

We have already seen that the Statute of Frauds requires that certain types of contracts must be in writing and signed by the party to be charged to be enforceable. In addition, even if the Statute of Frauds is not applicable, many parties to contracts prefer them to be in writing so that the terms are clearly spelled out.

Contracts made on the Web can easily be reduced to writing by simply printing the portion of the Web site containing the offer and the important terms of the contract. But how are these written contracts signed?

On October 1, 2000, the ***Electronic Signatures in Global and International Commerce Act*** took effect. This federal statute specifically states that electronic contracts containing electronic signatures are as enforceable as those that are printed on paper. Clicking the computer mouse on the "I agree" button, therefore, constitutes an electronic signature that will satisfy the writing requirement of the Statute of Frauds.

Of course, many new technologies are now needed to ensure that the person who is supposedly accepting the contract is the same

Electronic Signatures in Global and International Commerce Act The federal statute that specifies that electronic contracts containing electronic signatures are as enforceable as those that are printed on paper.

person as the person who is clicking the button. Some of these new, emerging technologies include:

- allowing a computer user to register acceptance by entering a Personal Identification Number (PIN)
- providing the computer user with hardware that can read the user's fingerprint or scan the user's iris
- providing the computer user with hardware that can electronically read the user's handwriting, and thus electronically register the user's signature

Finally, it must be pointed out that the Electronic Signatures in Global and International Commerce Act of 2000 does not apply to electronic signatures that appear on any of the following:

- wills, codicils, and related testamentary documents
- adoption or divorce papers
- court papers, such as orders, pleadings, and motions
- notices of cancellation or interruption in utility services
- notices of defaults, repossessions, foreclosures, and evictions
- notices of cancellation or termination of life or health insurance benefits
- certain notices relating to recalls of defective products
- documents relating to the transportation of hazardous materials

Settling Disputes in Cyberspace

Because it is expensive to proceed against a defendant in a court case, a person who is the victim of a breach of contract will frequently seek to have the dispute resolved by using alternative means. *Alternative Dispute Resolution (ADR)* is a system in which contract disputes and other disagreements are resolved by using means other than a lawsuit. Means of ADR include *mediation,* in which a neutral third party meets with the disputants to have them come to some form of settlement agreement; and *arbitration,* in which a neutral third party actually decides a case as if he or she were a judge and jury. (Many of the "court" shows on television are actually depicting arbitration proceedings.)

The advantages to ADR include:

- *Speed.* The matter is resolved quickly.
- *Finality.* Unless there is some type of misconduct, ADR results may not be appealed.

OBJECTIVE 5

Name the advantages of using Alternative Dispute Resolution to resolve legal disputes.

Alternative Dispute Resolution (ADR) A system in which contract disputes and other disagreements are resolved by using means other than a lawsuit.

- *Informality.* ADR does not use the same, strict rules of evidence used by a court.
- *Privacy.* ADR proceedings, unlike civil trials, are not generally open to the public.
- *Financial savings.* Because ADR proceedings are faster, with fewer legal motions, witnesses, etc., they are much less expensive for the disputants than court trials.

In cyberspace, numerous Web sites have been established for the purpose of providing forums for both mediation and arbitration of contract disputes. Simply proceeding to any Internet search engine will allow two parties to a contract, who each believe the other has breached the contract, to identify organizations that can provide a means of ADR.

Paying Taxes on Internet Sales

OBJECTIVE 6

Discuss the current rules pertaining to states levying sales taxes for purchases made online.

nexus A link or tie of a sale to a location so that a sales tax can be collected on the sales transaction.

In 1992, the U.S. Supreme Court ruled that a location must have a link or tie to a sale for the location to collect sales tax (*Quill v. North Dakota,* 504 U.S. 298). This link or tie is referred to as a **nexus.** It must also be pointed out that it is the buyer, and not the seller, who pays the sales tax, although it is typically the seller who collects the tax from the buyer and then turns the proceeds over to the state. In other words, a state that wants to collect a sales tax must levy the tax on a buyer who resides within the state and require a seller within the state to collect the tax.

When a consumer shops online, the state in which the consumer resides cannot legally collect the tax unless the online buyer happens to be purchasing the goods from an online seller who resides within the state.

EXAMPLE 26.6

Lebeda is a soap crafter who requires lye for her soap making. Because Lebeda resides in a rural area of Pennsylvania, she purchases the lye in quantity online from a manufacturer in California. Lebeda will not be required to pay Pennsylvania sales tax on the lye she purchases.

Many retailers that operate traditional brick-and-mortar enterprises also do business on the Web. Because cyberspace is not geographically based in any of the 50 states, these retailers typically establish separate legal entities for their Web-based businesses to avoid entirely collecting sales tax. To compensate for lost sales tax revenue, most states require that consumers who purchase goods out of state must pay a *use tax,* which is a tax to a consumer who uses goods within a state, as opposed to buying them within the state. However, use taxes are difficult to collect on small items sold on the Web, and most states do not make efforts to collect use taxes.

The result is that, as of now, states are losing great amounts of potential tax revenue as a result of Web-based sales. Over the next several years, the tax laws are certain to be modified to address this issue.

use tax A tax to a consumer who uses goods within a state, as opposed to buying them within the state.

Taxing Internet Access Services

In 1998, Congress passed the ***Internet Tax Freedom Act,*** which established a moratorium on taxing ISPs on the services they provide to computer users. The moratorium, which is a period of time during which no state may levy sales taxes on these ISPs, is currently in effect. Again, many states and localities are seeking changes to the law so that they may begin to tax the monthly fees that people pay to have access to the Internet.

Internet Tax Freedom Act A federal act that established a moratorium on taxing ISPs on the services they provide to computer users.

CHAPTER SUMMARY

1. In securities sales online, the SEC requires that information distributed electronically to potential investors is substantially equivalent to what would have been provided in paper form, that access to information is comparable to that afforded by paper copies, that there must be adequate notice to prospective investors of the availability of this information, and that there must be evidence demonstrating that delivery of information to prospective investors was successful.

2. The FTC protects consumers from deceptive online advertising by ensuring that advertising is truthful and by taking a variety of measures against online advertising that is false or misleading. If the FTC finds that Web-based advertising is deceptive, it has several options: It can issue a cease and desist order; require an affirmative disclosure; order corrective advertising; seek fines and other civil remedies; and in severe cases involving fraud, ask the Justice Department to file criminal charges.

3. The copyright issues associated with selling music and other forms of entertainment online involve the problem that the rightful owners often do not grant permission for its availability online and do not receive royalties when it is pirated.

4 Offers can be made online in much the same way they are made by other means, and the rules of acceptance are also similar. For example, by clicking a button that reads "I accept" or something similar, a user can accept and be bound by the terms of an agreement. Silence, or not clicking such a button, cannot be used as grounds for accepting an offer.

5 Advantages of using ADR include speed, finality, informality, privacy, and financial savings. Means of ADR include mediation and arbitration. These methods are also available on numerous Web sites that have been established on the Internet to provide forums for parties to resolve their problems. The many advantages of ADR have made it an increasingly popular means of resolving disputes.

6 Currently, states are losing a great deal of potential tax revenue because they are not collecting taxes on sales made over the Internet. The reasons include the difficulty of establishing a nexus for the transaction and of collecting use taxes in Internet-based transactions. The Internet Tax Freedom Act established a moratorium on taxing the services that ISPs provide to computer users. However, many states and localities are seeking to change the law so that people can be taxed on the monthly fees they pay to have access to the Internet.

Chapter 26 Assessment

MATCHING LEGAL TERMS

Match each of the following definitions with the correct term in the list below. Write the letter of your choice in the answer column.

- **a.** mediation
- **b.** primary market
- **c.** nexus
- **d.** secondary market
- **e.** arbitration

1. The place where a corporation sells its securities to the public.   1. _____
2. The place where one member of the public sells securities to another member of the public.   2. _____
3. A process in which a neutral third party meets with disputants to have them come to some form of settlement agreement.   3. _____
4. A process in which a neutral third party decides a case as if he or she were a judge and jury.   4. _____
5. A location's link or tie to a sale required in order for the location to collect sales tax.   5. _____

TRUE/FALSE QUIZ

Indicate whether each of the following statements is true or false by writing *T* or *F* in the answer column.

6. The Securities and Exchange Commission requires that prospective investors review all of a firm's financial information prior to purchasing any stock in the company.   6. _____
7. Touting occurs when an investor who owns shares of a company's stock posts notices online indicating that the value of the company's stock will increase.   7. _____
8. The Federal Trade Commission is responsible for ensuring that advertising in the United States is truthful.   8. _____
9. A deceptive advertisement is one that contains a material misrepresentation, omission, or practice likely to mislead a consumer who acts reasonably under the circumstances.   9. _____
10. The Federal Trade Commission does not have jurisdiction over advertisements that appear on Web pages.   10. _____
11. Companies that provide Web sites that are forums for music to be shared without permission of the owners are guilty of copyright infringement.   11. _____
12. Most courts will acknowledge that by clicking the "I accept" button, the user has accepted the offer contained on the Web page.   12. _____
13. Simply visiting a Web site can sometimes indicate an acceptance by the user of the terms contained on the site.   13. _____

Conducting Business in Cyberspace   CHAPTER 26

Chapter 26 Assessment

14. Contracts of adhesion in cyberspace are valid unless they contain terms that are unreasonable.

    14. _____

15. An electronic signature will not satisfy the Statute of Frauds.

    15. _____

16. The Electronic Signatures in Global and International Commerce Act pertains only to cases in which the offeror and the offeree are from different countries.

    16. _____

17. Mediation is a form of alternative dispute resolution in which a neutral party decides a case as if he or she were a judge and jury.

    17. _____

18. A disadvantage to alternative dispute resolution is that it is far more time consuming than litigation.

    18. _____

19. A state wishing to collect a sales tax levies the tax on the buyer of goods, but usually requires the seller to collect the tax.

    19. _____

20. A use tax is a tax to a consumer who uses goods within a state, as opposed to buying them within the state.

    20. _____

DISCUSSION QUESTIONS

Answer the following questions and discuss them in class.

21. Compare and contrast the two main statutes that cover the sale and distribution of securities in the United States.

22. State the four rules relating to online sales of securities, and explain their importance.

23. Evaluate the options that the Federal Trade Commission has in dealing with a firm that has placed a deceptive advertisement online.

24. How can Internet Service Providers protect themselves against a charge of copyright infringement?

Chapter 26 Assessment

25. Identify types of legal documents for which electronic signatures are not valid, and explain why the law excludes these.

26. Name five advantages for individuals who select alternative dispute resolution over litigation, and give an example of each.

THINKING CRITICALLY ABOUT THE LAW

Answer the following questions, which require you to think critically about the legal principles that you learned in this chapter.

27. Selling Securities on the Web How can the law better protect individuals who are considering making investments on the Web?

28. Advertising on the Web With the enormous amount of advertising placed on the Web, what can the Federal Trade Commission do to be certain that all Web-based advertising is truthful?

29. Entering into Contracts on the Web Why and how are contracts of adhesion especially problematic for offers made on the Web?

30. E-Signatures Describe some ways in which technology might be used to ensure that computer users signing contracts with e-signature are in fact the persons they are representing themselves to be.

Conducting Business in Cyberspace   CHAPTER 26   429

Chapter 26 Assessment

31. A Question of Ethics Several representatives of the entertainment media have suggested that a federal statute be enacted that would require all computers sold in the United States to incorporate software that would prevent making digital copies of music and video. Is it fair that consumers would lose the right to use their computers to make additional digital copies, for their own use, of songs and movies that they had purchased legally?

_____

_____

_____

CASE QUESTIONS

Study each of the cases below. Then answer the questions that follow by writing *Yes* or *No* in the answer column.

32. Selling Securities on the Web Mikai developed an exercise device that she sold on a Web site. Sales were brisk, and she soon discovered that she would need additional funds in order to purchase materials. She included on the Web site an invitation to the public to invest in her company by purchasing shares of stock.

    a. Must Mikai register these securities with the Federal Trade Commission?   **a.** _____

    b. If Mikai does not register the securities, can she be charged with violating the Securities Act of 1933?   **b.** _____

    c. Must Mikai provide financial information to investors prior to selling securities online?   **c.** _____

33. Advertising on the Web Dragos was interested in obtaining memorabilia relating to her favorite heavy metal band, Deaf Panther. Through a search engine, Dragos found a company called Web Pix, which offered autographed photographs of various celebrities, including Deaf Panther. Dragos ordered the photographs and charged the cost of these to her credit card. The signatures on the pictures turned out to be forgeries.

    a. Can Dragos complain to the Federal Trade Commission?   **a.** _____

    b. Can Dragos sue Web Pix for breach of contract?   **b.** _____

    c. Can Dragos sue Web Pix for a violation of securities law?   **c.** _____

34. Settling Disputes in Cyberspace Stavropolos purchased an antique doll for $700 from Elliott through a Web site known as e-Auctioneer. The description of the doll provided by Elliott stated that it was in "good condition," but when Stavropolos received the doll, she noted that it had a damaged leg. Both Stavropolos and Elliott agreed to be bound by the decision of a representative of e-Auctioneer, who inspected the doll.

    a. Is the contract between Stavropolos and Elliott valid, despite the fact that it was entered into in cyberspace?   **a.** _____

    b. Is the representative from e-Auctioneer an arbitrator?   **b.** _____

    c. If Stavropolos wishes to resolve the dispute as quickly as possible, would she be better off by filing a lawsuit against Elliott?   **c.** _____

Chapter 26 Assessment

CASE ANALYSIS

Study each of the following cases carefully. Then briefly state the principle of law and your decision.

35. Selling Securities on the Web Jonathan G. Lebed was a 15-year-old Internet maven who, over about a six month period, on eleven separate occasions, "engaged in a scheme in which he purchased large blocks of thinly traded stocks and, within hours of making such purchases, sent numerous false and misleading messages over the Internet touting the stocks that he had just purchased." Lebed sold these shares, usually by the next day. From these activities he realized a total profit during the period of $272,826. *Is Lebed guilty of violating the securities laws?* [In the Matter of Jonathan G. Lebed, a Minor, through his Guardian, Administrative Proceeding, File No. 3-10291 (Washington, D.C.).]

Principle of law:

Decision:

36. Advertising on the Web Kenneth Lipsitz sold magazine subscriptions through a friendly and congenial staff located in New York City. Numerous affidavits and complaints alleged that the magazines either never arrived, or they stopped coming long before the subscription was due to expire. Lipsitz was charged with deceptive advertising in New York. *Can Lipsitz be found in violation of the New York laws against deceptive advertising even though he sold subscriptions via e-mail and the Web?* [People v. Lipsitz, 663 N.Y.S.2d 468 (New York).]

Principle of law:

Decision:

37. Selling Entertainment on the Web Napster, Inc. provided a free service for visitors to its Web site that allowed users to share music digitally. Napster did not receive permission from the owners of the music. Several large recording studios that owned much of the music that was being shared filed a lawsuit against Napster, requesting that a federal court order Napster to cease its free online file swapping service. *Will the recording studios be successful in convincing the court to order Napster to cease these operations?* [A&M Records Inc. v. Napster, 239 F3d 1004 (California).]

Principle of law:

Chapter 26 Assessment

Decision:
_____
_____

38. **Entering into Contracts on the Web** Netscape offered all visitors to its Web site free "SmartLoad" software provided the visitor clicked his or her mouse on a designated box labeled "Download." A reference to a license agreement appeared on the screen in which the "Download" box was located, but the license agreement itself appeared on the next screen. The license agreement contained a clause requiring that any dispute between the parties proceed to arbitration, rather than to court. When six plaintiffs later filed suit against Netscape relating to the software, Netscape demanded that the suit be dismissed and that the plaintiffs all be compelled to have their claims arbitrated instead. *Will the plaintiffs be required to have their disputes resolved by an arbitrator, or will the court rule that the license agreement was not a part of the contract?* [*Specht et al. v. Netscape et al.,* 150 F.Supp.2d 585 (New York).]

Principle of law:
_____
_____

Decision:
_____
_____

LEGAL RESEARCH

Complete the following activities. Then share your findings with the class.

39. **Working in Teams** In teams of three or four, contact several retail stores in your city or town. Ask them if they maintain Web sites for consumers. Visit these Web sites, compare and contrast them, and present to the class your conclusions as to which of these are most effective in encouraging consumers to purchase the retailers' products and services.
_____
_____
_____

40. **Using Technology** Using the Internet and search engines, find several Web sites that offer products and services for sale. In addition to clicking an "I accept" button, how are computer users requested to accept offers? List several means.
_____
_____
_____
_____

PART 6   Business and Technology

PART VII

INTERNATIONAL BUSINESS AND THE ENVIRONMENT

CHAPTER 27 International Business Law

CHAPTER 28 Business and the Environment

CHAPTER 27

INTERNATIONAL BUSINESS LAW

LEGAL TERMS

comity
transnational institutions
General Agreement on Tariffs and Trade (GATT)
World Trade Organization (WTO)
International Monetary Fund (IMF)
World Bank
North American Free Trade Agreement (NAFTA)
trade sanction
tariff
expropriation
confiscation
domestication
boycott
Foreign Corrupt Practices Act (FCPA)

PERFORMANCE OBJECTIVES

After studying this chapter and completing the assessments, you will be able to:

1. Cite reasons for the increased need for international law.
2. Define international law.
3. Identify major sources of international law.
4. Discuss the doctrine of comity.
5. Discuss the importance of international law as it relates to trade between nations.
6. Explain the purposes of the World Trade Organization, the International Monetary Fund, the World Bank, the North American Free Trade Agreement, and the European Union.
7. State how trade sanctions and embargoes, export and import controls, and boycotts are used by governments to achieve economic and political ends.
8. Describe the major provisions of the Foreign Corrupt Practices Act of 1977.

Global Business

The increasing volume of international trade and tourism, the globalization of the marketplace, the growing incidence of multinational business organizations, and cultural exchanges have given rise to the need for international law. Although the use of English as the language of business is increasing, cultural differences, disparate legal systems, and fluctuating exchange rates remain major problem areas.

What Is International Law?

International law is the broad study of the legal systems of major countries, treaties, practices, tariffs and nontariff trade barriers, and import and export quotas. Also included in the study of international law are organizations—local and international—that regulate personal and commercial activity and facilitate international trade.

Sources of International Law

To appreciate the complex legal relationships that exist among nations, it is important to recognize that international law often develops to address the many issues that emerge in international trade.

International laws resulting from the trading relationships among nations have a rich history. In ancient times, the Romans ruled the western world; however, contrary to popular belief, their reign was based primarily on economic, rather than on military, might. Exercising control over trade through the Roman legal system (the international law of the day) allowed the Roman government to rule the world by maintaining order and peace. The philosophy of Roman international law controlling trade and commerce in a peaceful way came to be known as *Pax Romana* (meaning in Latin, "Roman peace"), and the phrase itself appeared on their minted coins.

While signing peace treaties is as old as war, efforts to negotiate peaceful solutions to international disputes culminated in the formation of the League of Nations following World War I. Unfortunately, the League failed to prevent war. Following World War II, the world's nations again organized a forum for peaceful negotiations and established the United Nations, an organization that now is involved in such diverse social and economic functions as the International Labour Organisation (ILO), the Food and Agriculture Organization (FAO), and the General Agreement on Tariffs and Trade (GATT).

OBJECTIVE 1
Cite reasons for the increased need for international law.

OBJECTIVE 2
Define international law.

OBJECTIVE 3
Identify major sources of international law.

In modern times, customary practices and treaties are the major sources of international law and are recognized in the Statute of the International Court of Justice (Article 38). Over 200 sovereign nations have the capacity to negotiate treaties and create legal obligations.

In the United States, Article II of the Constitution states that treaties are negotiated by the president and must be ratified by two-thirds of senators present. However, in practice, other methods are sometimes used.

Applying Other Country's Laws: The Doctrine of Comity

OBJECTIVE 4
Discuss the doctrine of comity.

comity A major legal principle involved in international law that holds the courts of one country should refrain from deciding cases involving the acts of persons from another country.

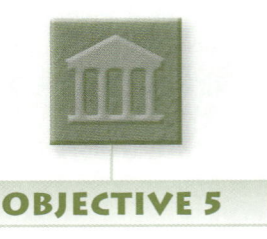

A major legal principle involved in international law is the doctrine of *comity*, which holds that the courts of one country should refrain from deciding cases involving the acts of persons from another country. The doctrine is discretionary and courts of individual countries decide whether to apply it based on the facts of each case.

International Trade Institutions

OBJECTIVE 5
Discuss the importance of international law as it relates to trade between nations.

transnational institutions Institutions established by several countries that agree to be legally bound by the rules of the organization.

General Agreement on Tariffs and Trade (GATT) An international agreement that provides a set of rules to ensure that there be no discrimination in trade by its signatories, and also spells out a process for resolving international trade dispute.

Trade among nations remains a vital ingredient to the economic health of the world's population. While countries are sovereign, and create and interpret their own sets of laws, the goal is that trade be governed by *transnational institutions*, whose purpose is to maintain legal and economic order in trade. These transnational institutions are established contractually by several countries that agree to be legally bound by the rules of the organization. A discussion of some of these transnational institutions follows.

The World Trade Organization

In 1947, an international agreement called the ***General Agreement on Tariffs and Trade (GATT)*** was entered into by a multitude of nations. Among its many provisions, GATT provided a set of rules to ensure that there be no discrimination in trade by its signatories, and also spelled out a process for resolving international trade disputes. Pursuant to GATT, countries can be granted Normal Trade Relations status by its neighbors, the purpose of which is to maintain an efficient and effective means of managing imports (goods from another country coming into the nation) and exports (goods being sold to other countries by companies from within the nation).

By 1995, tariffs became far less commonplace and most nations came to recognize that GATT was no longer sufficient. Accordingly, the new **World Trade Organization (WTO)** was formed. The WTO is responsible for overseeing the implementation of all multinational trade agreements negotiated now or in the future.

In addition to GATT (previously described), the WTO has authority for:

- GATS—the General Agreement on Trade in Services
- TRIPS—agreements on trade-related aspects of intellectual property rights
- TRIMS—Trade-Related Investment Measures

The International Monetary Fund

In 1944, several nations formed the **International Monetary Fund (IMF).** The purpose of this organization is to maintain a stable environment for the economies and the currencies of its members by providing protection against large fluctuations in the value of one currency versus another.

Most international experts agree that the IMF has performed its job admirably to date, but the IMF has also come under great pressure due to various economic downturns in several nations. The IMF is also criticized for failing to respond adequately to the economic challenges created in the early 1990s, subsequent to the dissolution of the Soviet Union, and the heavy borrowing by developing countries during the mid-1990s.

The World Bank

In 1944, the International Bank for Reconstruction and Development was created to provide relief to the countries suffering from the ravages of World War II. Now popularly referred to simply as the **World Bank,** this organization works closely with the IMF to ensure that developing countries have access to funds to stimulate their economies.

The World Bank has also come under a great deal of criticism for the following reasons:

- It has often provided funds to countries with arguably corrupt regimes that have squandered the funds rather than provide real relief to their economies.
- It has provided funds to developing countries, but despite the large inflow of money, major improvements in these economies have not been realized.

OBJECTIVE 6

Explain the purpose of the World Trade Organization, the International Monetary Fund, the World Bank, the North American Free Trade Agreement, and the European Union.

World Trade Organization (WTO) An international organization responsible for overseeing the implementation of all multinational trade agreements negotiated now or in the future.

International Monetary Fund (IMF) An international organization with the purpose of maintaining a stable environment for the economies and the currencies of its members by providing protection against large fluctuations in the value of one currency versus another.

World Bank An international organization that works closely with the IMF to ensure that developing countries have access to funds to stimulate their economies.

Regional Trade Organizations and Agreements

In addition to the above worldwide organizations, there exist numerous regional agreements and entities, whose purpose it is to provide legal, political, and economic processes to maintain an orderly relationship among the members.

For example, to promote trade, the United States, Canada, and Mexico have agreed to follow the rules of the ***North American Free Trade Agreement (NAFTA).*** Unlike many other regional agreements, the focus of NAFTA is strictly on economic trade, rather than on the political interrelationships among the three countries. The agreement provides that:

- The NAFTA countries will ensure that none of their national or local laws discriminate against the goods of the other countries.
- Each country will have greater market access within the borders of the other two.
- Some tariffs and import and export restrictions will be eliminated.

In 1994, twelve countries in Europe formed what is expected to eventually become "Euroland," an economic and political integration of the members into one entity. As a step in this direction, the *European Union (EU)* establishes a legal and political relationship among its members that promotes economic growth, as well as social and cultural affiliations. An example of the kind of interconnection among the members is the inauguration of the *euro*, the monetary currency of the EU.

THE INTERNATIONAL LEGAL ENVIRONMENT

Companies that conduct business in several countries face the challenge of having to comply with a variety of legal systems that sometimes conflict with one another.

The United States, for example, requires that foreign firms that conduct business here comply with all of the regulations that govern American companies. Many companies doing business internationally face the challenge of adapting to local customs and practices. In some countries, it is perfectly acceptable and indeed expected that there will be payments made to individuals to secure their business. In the United States, however, this type of activity amounts to bribery, which is both illegal and ethically unacceptable.

North American Free Trade Agreement (NAFTA) A strictly economic agreement between the United States, Canada, and Mexico aimed at promoting and facilitating trade among these nations.

In addition, companies that conduct business in other countries are frequently required to follow the laws of the country in which their headquarters are located.

Trade Sanctions

Many governments use legal restrictions on trade to achieve desired political results. Countries that enact a law prohibiting trade with specific countries are said to be using a *trade sanction,* also referred to as an *embargo.* These activities by nations are acceptable under international law, and are indeed incorporated in the charter of the United Nations. The charter also expressly allows trade sanctions and embargoes by regional organizations, such as the Organization of American States, the Organization for African Unity, and the Arab League.

Export and Import Controls

In addition to trade sanctions and embargoes, some countries may impose a *tariff,* a form of tax, or other restriction on exports or imports to attain economic results, such as protecting domestic industries or facilitating the production of certain crops.

Export licenses can be used as an adjunct of national security. The United States, for example, requires that exporters obtain a license prior to shipping certain goods to purchasers in other countries. If the product being sold is considered a threat to national security, for example, the export license will be denied, and the exporter will not be allowed to fulfill the contract.

In addition, many countries, to maintain a positive balance of trade (i.e., ensuring that the number of dollars of exports exceeds that of imports), place restrictions on the numbers and kinds of products that may enter into their nation. A set of restrictions of this kind is known as a *quota system.*

Governmental Actions

Many governments attempt to maintain control over the actions of foreign businesses operating within the host country by controlling the ownership of the foreign company's assets. These attempts can take three forms:

1. *Expropriation* is the act of the host country's taking title to all of the assets of the foreign company. In this case, the host country compensates the owners of the foreign firm.

OBJECTIVE 7

State how trade sanctions and embargos, export and import controls, and boycotts are used by governments to achieve economic and political ends.

trade sanction Also known as an embargo, a law enacted by a nation that prohibits trade with specific countries for the purpose of achieving political results.

tariff A form of tax on goods from a foreign country used for the purpose of attaining economic results.

expropriation The act of a host country taking title to all of the assets of a foreign company and providing compensation to the owners of the foreign firm.

International Business Law CHAPTER 27

confiscation The act of a host country taking title to all of the assets of the foreign company and not providing compensation to the owners of the foreign firm.

domestication When a host country mandates that at least partial ownership of a foreign company be sold to local citizens or companies prior to the foreign company conducting business within the host country's borders.

boycott When people refuse to purchase goods made by particular businesses. In some cases, citizens of a particular country refuse to purchase goods made by businesses located in other countries, regardless of whether their action is supported by the government.

OBJECTIVE 8

Describe the major provisions of the Foreign Corrupt Practices Act of 1977.

Foreign Corrupt Practices Act (FCPA) A federal statute designed to provide executives of American companies with rules and restrictions relating to paying persons in foreign countries to expedite business in these foreign nations.

2. ***Confiscation,*** as is the case with expropriation, this act involves the host country taking title to all of the assets of the foreign company. However, in the case of confiscation, there is no compensation given to the owners of the foreign company.
3. ***Domestication*** occurs when the host country mandates that at least partial ownership of the foreign company be sold to local citizens or companies prior to the foreign company conducting business within the host country's borders.

Boycotts

At times, citizens of a particular country refuse to purchase goods made by businesses located in other countries. This action, whether supported by the government or not, is referred to as a ***boycott.***

> **EXAMPLE 27.1**
>
> Morandim Corporation, a Canadian company, manufactures chemicals and regularly sells these to companies in the Middle East. Several of its customers, who are Arabic, require that Morandim provide written documentation demonstrating that it does not conduct business with firms in Israel.

The Foreign Corrupt Practices Act

In the 1970s, the Securities and Exchange Commission performed a study that indicated that over 400 United States companies were making in excess of $300 million in questionable and illegal payments to foreign officials. Accordingly, in 1977, the United States passed the ***Foreign Corrupt Practices Act (FCPA),*** a federal statute designed to provide executives of American companies with rules and restrictions relating to paying persons in foreign countries to expedite business in these foreign nations. Because customs and practices vary so greatly between countries, the law has helped numerous executives recognize what is and what is not acceptable conduct for U.S. firms, irrespective of acceptable ethical standards in the foreign country.

The FCPA makes it unlawful to bribe foreign government officials to obtain or retain business. Illegal activities include direct bribes paid by U.S. companies, as well as bribes paid through intermediaries. Bribes include money, gifts, or anything of value paid to a foreign government official, or to a foreign political party.

The FCPA makes it clear that to violate the law, the payment must be made "corruptly." The statute defines "corruptly" as "connoting an evil motive or purpose, an intent to wrongly influence the recipient."

While many executives have complained that they are unfairly restrained when doing business in foreign countries, most experts maintain that by reducing bribery, the quality of goods and services produced abroad increases, while international prices are kept at optimal levels. Most would agree that U.S. companies are simply being held to ethical standards generally accepted by the American people.

In 1988, the FCPA was amended so that corporations and their executives were less likely to be prosecuted for making payments to foreign officials. This amendment was intended to offset what was viewed as an unfair advantage enjoyed by firms from other countries that had no such restraints.

The Individual and International Law

Individuals, as well as companies, have rights and duties in foreign countries. These rights and obligations are increasingly important in the context of the international laws governing intellectual property.

Intellectual Property

Intellectual property includes both artistic as well as industrial property rights. Copyrights, patents, and trademarks are the principle areas involved. Related to these rights is industrial "know-how" or technology—particularly in developing countries in which technology is transferred between firms in different countries that have joint venture agreements. Nations and businesses have long had an interest in maintaining an orderly process in which intellectual property rights are protected.

The World Intellectual Property Organization (WIPO), a specialized agency of the United Nations, is an international organization that administers some 23 treaties concerning protection of intellectual property rights. In 1994, WIPO announced the formation of a center for the arbitration of disputes involving intellectual property rights.

Copyrights An author's or creator's literary, artistic, or musical work, and in some countries a creator's computer program (that can be fixed in a medium that would make it possible to communicate creative works), is protected by a *copyright*. These laws prohibit the reproduction or alteration of an author's work without his or her permission with the result that copyrighted materials are given at least minimal protection in most countries.

Patents A statutory privilege granted by a nation to inventors for a fixed period of years to exclude all others from manufacturing, using, or selling a patented product without permission from the inventor is called a *patent*. A U.S. firm can take advantage of world markets by either licensing foreign firms to manufacture a patented product or use an innovative manufacturing process in the manufacture of a product. A firm might seek a *parallel patent* in each of the countries that maintain a patent system.

Trademarks Trademarks, trade names, service marks, and certification marks are valuable tools used by businesses to identify their products and services. In most cases, the treatment of these valuable properties in international commerce does not greatly differ from domestic treatment. In the United States, the right to the trademark is granted by the mere use of it. Trademarks are viewed as property and as a result can be transferred or licensed to others. However, it is important to note that in most countries registration is a prerequisite for ownership and protection of the mark. Often, a foreign licensee must meet certain product quality requirements so that the use of the mark does not deceive the consumer or lessen the value of the mark to the owner.

CHAPTER SUMMARY

1. Giving rise to the need for international law is the increasing volume of international trade and tourism, the globalization of the marketplace, the growing incidence of multinational business organizations, and cultural exchanges.

2. International law may be defined as the broad study of the legal systems of major countries, treaties, practices, tariffs and non-tariff trade barriers, and import and export quotas. Also included in the study of international law are organizations—local and international—that regulate personal and commercial activity and facilitate international trade.

3. The sources of international law in modern times are customary practices and treaties, which are recognized in the Statute of the International Court of Justice. Over 200 sovereign nations have the capacity to negotiate treaties and create legal obligations.

4 The doctrine of comity holds that the courts of one country should refrain from deciding cases involving the acts of persons from other countries. The doctrine is discretionary and courts of individual countries decide whether to apply it based on the facts of each case.

5 Trade among nations is a vital ingredient to the economic health of the world's population. While countries are sovereign, and create and interpret their own sets of laws, the goal is that trade be regulated by transnational institutions, whose purpose is to maintain legal and economic order in trade.

6 The World Trade Organization is responsible for overseeing the implementation of all multinational trade agreements negotiated now or in the future. The International Monetary Fund maintains a stable environment for the economies and the currencies of its members by providing protection against large fluctuations in the value of one currency versus another. The World Bank ensures that developing countries have access to funds in order to stimulate their economies. The North American Free Trade Agreement governs economic trade among the United States, Canada, and Mexico. The European Union represents a legal and political relationship among its members that promotes economic growth, as well as social and cultural affiliations.

7 Trade sanctions and embargoes, export and import controls, and boycotts are all measures used by governments and citizens of one country to restrict the economic activities of businesses from other countries, by not allowing these foreign firms free access to markets.

8 The Foreign Corrupt Practices Act is a federal statute designed to provide executives of American companies with rules and restrictions relating to paying persons in foreign countries to expedite business in these foreign nations.

Chapter 27 Assessment

MATCHING LEGAL TERMS

Match each of the following definitions with the correct term in the list below. Write the letter of your choice in the answer column.

a. comity
b. transnational institutions
c. General Agreement on Tariffs and Trade
d. World Trade Organization
e. International Monetary Fund
f. North American Free Trade Agreement
g. European Union
h. trade sanctions and embargoes
i. import and export controls
j. tariffs
k. quota systems
l. Foreign Corrupt Practices Act

1. Restrictions on the numbers and kinds of products that may enter into a nation. 1.____

2. An organization that provides protection against large fluctuations in the value of one currency versus another. 2.____

3. A doctrine that holds that the courts of one country should refrain from deciding cases involving the acts of persons from another country. 3.____

4. Organizations established contractually by several countries that agree to be legally bound by the rules of the organization. 4.____

5. Government use of legal restrictions on trade in order to achieve desired political results. 5.____

6. Agreement that provides a set of rules to ensure that there be no discrimination in trade by its signatories. 6.____

7. An entity established to achieve economic and political integration of member countries. 7.____

8. A form of tax, or other restrictions on exports or imports in order to attain economic results, such as protecting domestic industries or facilitating the production of certain crops. 8.____

9. An organization responsible for overseeing the implementation of all multi-national trade agreements negotiated now or in the future. 9.____

10. A broad category that includes various activities, including licensing the sale of some goods to foreign buyers, intended to affect the inflow and outflow of goods and services. 10.____

11. An agreement among the United States, Canada, and Mexico that focuses strictly on economic trade. 11.____

12. A U.S. law that makes it unlawful to bribe foreign government officials to obtain or retain business. 12.____

Chapter 27 Assessment

TRUE/FALSE QUIZ

Indicate whether each of the following statements is true or false by writing *T* or *F* in the answer column.

13. International law is the broad study of the legal systems of major countries, treaties, practices, tariffs and nontariff trade barriers, and import and export quotas.   13. _____

14. There is little or no relationship between international law and international trade.   14. _____

15. The activities of the United Nations are limited to international law.   15. _____

16. The doctrine of comity holds that the courts of one country should refrain from deciding cases involving the acts of persons from another country.   16. _____

17. The purpose of transnational institutions is to maintain legal and economic order in trade.   17. _____

18. The purpose of the International Monetary Fund is to provide a clearinghouse for checks drawn on foreign banks.   18. _____

19. The European Union established a legal and political relationship among its members that promotes economic growth, as well as social and cultural affiliations.   19. _____

20. In some countries, it is common that there will be payments made to individuals to secure their business.   20. _____

21. In addition to trade sanctions and embargoes, some countries impose tariffs, a form of taxes, or other restrictions on exports or imports to attain economic results.   21. _____

22. Most countries recognize U.S. patents but not copyrights.   22. _____

DISCUSSION QUESTIONS

Answer the following questions and discuss them in class.

23. Cite reasons for the increased need for international law in recent years.

24. Discuss some of the ways international trade is regulated by international laws and treaties.

Chapter 27 Assessment

25. What are some reasons for embargoes and sanctions?

26. How do tariffs protect domestic industries and how do they hinder world trade?

27. Discuss the goals of NAFTA and the means it uses to achieve these goals?

28. How do governments attempt to control foreign businesses operating within their borders?

THINKING CRITICALLY ABOUT THE LAW

Answer the following questions, which require you to think critically about the legal principles that you learned in this chapter.

29. Laws and Culture Assuming that the law of a country reflects its customs, identify and discuss selected laws in foreign countries and how the customs influenced the enactment of these laws.

30. International Financial Institutions Discuss the goals and criticisms of the IMF and the World Bank.

31. Trade Sanctions Since trade sanctions often affect the people of a country more severely than their government, are sanctions a good way of achieving political goals?

446   PART 7   International Business and the Environment

Chapter 27 Assessment

32. GATT Under GATT, countries could be designated Normal Trade Relations status on economic criteria. Later this designation was awarded to countries that had achieved specific human rights objectives. Should economic criteria be used to foster moral goals?

_____
_____
_____

33. A Question of Ethics Should the FCPA impose U.S. ethical standards on the activities of U.S. businesses in international trade, even though the law puts these businesses at a competitive disadvantage with their foreign counterparts?

_____
_____
_____

CASE QUESTIONS

Study each of the cases below. Then answer the questions that follow by writing *Yes* or *No* in the answer column.

34. International Court Katsoulas, a U.S. car dealer, had a contract with a Korean automobile manufacturer for the delivery of several cars. When the manufacturer failed to deliver the cars as promised, Katsoulas threatened to bring the case to the International Court of Justice for a determination.

   a. Does Katsoulas have a course of action against the car manufacturer?　　　　　　　　　　　　　　　　　　**a.** _____

   b. Can Katsoulas successfully pursue his threat to take his complaint to the International Court of Justice?　　　　　　　　　　　　　　　　　　　　　　　　　　　　　　　　　　　　　**b.** _____

   c. If Katsoulis is unsuccessful in his threat to take his case to the International Court of Justice, does he have other avenues of redress?　　　　　　　　　　　　　　　　　　**c.** _____

35. Foreign Government Control Straley Corporation, a manufacturer of hand tools, had been exporting its products to several countries in Europe for 10 years and decided to establish a manufacturing operation there. The directors of the company met to select a country in which to begin operations. After much discussion, the board selected the country of Alvinia as the site. Following the selection, additional research revealed that the government of Alvinia had a record of taking over foreign businesses. Even if the government took over the firm, would any of the following types of appropriation be acceptable?

   a. Expropriation　　**a.** _____

   b. Confiscation　　**b.** _____

   c. Domestication　　**c.** _____

36. Foreign Corrupt Practices Act Bryerly, a U.S. sales representative for the U. S. firm, Zoom Airplane Company, was trying to close a deal with a foreign government for the purchase of 14 jet reconnaissance planes. He knew that competitors from two other countries were also bidding for the contract. Eager for the business, he offered a bribe to the government official who would be instrumental in making the decision.

Chapter 27 Assessment

a. Can Bryerly be prosecuted under the Foreign Corrupt Practices Act? a. _____

b. If sales persons from other countries can bribe officials and those from the United States cannot, are the U.S.-based personnel at a competitive disadvantage? b. _____

c. Are there other inducements Bryerly could legally offer the official? c. _____

CASE ANALYSIS

Study each of the following cases carefully. Then briefly state the principle of law and your decision.

37. Assault, False Imprisonment Before boarding an El Al Israel Airlines flight from New York to Tel Aviv, a passenger, Tseng, was subjected to an intrusive security search. Although not injured bodily, Tseng sued El Al for damages in a New York State court, asserting a state law personal injury claim for, among other charges, assault and false imprisonment. El Al removed the case to the Federal District Court, which dismissed the case on the basis of the Warsaw Convention. Articles of the Convention preclude a passenger from maintaining an action for personal injury damages under local law when her claim does not satisfy the conditions for liability. The Convention does not "permit recovery for psychic or psychosomatic injury." *Will Tseng be successful in her suit?* [El Al Israel Airlines, Ltd. v. Tsui Yuan Tseng (97-475) 122 F.3d 99, reversed.]

Principle of law:

_____
_____

Decision:

_____
_____

38. Trademarks Jerry Johnson, a passionate bicyclist, wanted to go into the business of manufacturing high quality bicycles. He found that both labor and component parts were quite inexpensive in Taiwan. Even adding the shipping charges to the United States, it was economically advantageous to assemble the bicycles in Taiwan. He chose the name "Winner's Choice," and a logo which he registered with the Taiwan government. Business boomed but his success was his downfall when his bicycles caught the attention of an American corporation that manufactured motorcycles and had previously registered the same trademark in the United States. The American firm brought suit against Johnson contending that he violated the Lanham Act, which regulates trademarks. Johnson maintained that he was a foreign company, and therefore not subject to U.S. trademark laws. *Is Johnson correct in his defense?*

Principle of law:

_____
_____

Decision:

_____
_____

Chapter 27 Assessment

39. **Boycott/Defamation** Yikes, a U.S.-based manufacturer of shoes, had manufacturing plants in several countries in Southeast Asia and enjoyed considerable success in world markets as a result of a number of factors, including its excellent products, low prices, efficient production, low labor costs, and widespread consumer product acceptance. In the midst of its success, a grass roots group took exception to the corporation's policies, particularly the firm's labor policies, which the grass roots group referred to as sweat shop conditions. The grass roots group set up a Web site on which numerous disparaging criticisms and a call for a worldwide boycott of Yikes' products were disseminated. In the opinion of Yikes management, the disparaging criticisms were without merit, yet the unfavorable publicity that would surely result from a defamation suit against the grass roots organization, didn't seem to offer much encouragement either. The mass media joined the fray and the position of Yikes increasingly assumed a defensive stance. They mounted a public relations campaign to defend their practices. *What would be a recommended course of action?*

Principle of law:

_____

_____

Decision:

_____

_____

LEGAL RESEARCH

Complete the following activities. Then share your findings with the class.

40. **Working in Teams** In teams of three or four, interview local small and medium businesses to learn of the experiences of the interviewees in dealing with various aspects of international law.

_____

_____

_____

_____

41. **Using Technology** Using the Internet and search engines, investigate the terms and organizations discussed in this chapter.

_____

_____

_____

_____

International Business Law **CHAPTER 27**

CHAPTER 28

BUSINESS AND THE ENVIRONMENT

PERFORMANCE OBJECTIVES

After studying this chapter and completing the assessments, you will be able to:

1. Explain how the federal government regulates itself in the area of environmental protection.
2. Identify the role of the Environmental Protection Agency.
3. Discuss how the Clean Air Act and Clean Water Act reduce pollution.
4. Cite provisions in Superfund that protect against illegally dumping waste.
5. Describe the theories of law under which private citizens may sue persons and businesses that harm the environment.
6. Identify several types of pollution that environmental laws regulate.

LEGAL TERMS

National Environmental Policy Act (NEPA)
Environmental Impact Statement (EIS)
Environmental Protection Agency (EPA)
Clean Air Act
Clean Water Act
Superfund
public nuisance
private nuisance
particle trespass
acid rain
greenhouse effect

The Development of Environmental Protection

The United States has been blessed with an abundance of natural resources, including waterways, wetlands, precious minerals, arable land, wildlife, coal, and forests. It was recognized early in the country's history that laws needed to be enacted that might afford some protection to our physical environment.

Early federal statutes dealing with environmental issues concerned themselves primarily with conservation of forests and wildlife. Because manufacturing had not yet reached a stage at which there was significant harm to the environment, there were few laws that regulated business activities with respect to the environment.

In the 1960s, this view changed. Citizens of the United States began to insist that strict environmental laws be enacted to maintain purity of air and water. Earth Day in 1970 became a symbol of the political activism of the time. It was realized that the operations of business firms impacted significantly upon the environment. As businesses manufacture goods for use by consumers, pollution is an unfortunate by-product. What is problematic for policymakers is balancing the importance of allowing businesses to produce at optimal levels, while at the same time, maintaining a watchful eye over the environment.

Photo 28.1

Environmental Protection

Over time, legislation has been developed to help protect the environment and our natural resources. *Why is environmental protection important, and how should business interests be weighed against our interest in a clean and healthy environment?*

Business and the Environment · CHAPTER 28

Today, environmental regulation is a distinct area of the law, and firms strive to comply with the myriad of statutes, regulations, and ordinances that cover the relationship between businesses and the environment.

Government's Regulation over Itself

In an effort to ensure that the federal government itself does not contribute to the destruction of the environment, Congress passed the ***National Environmental Policy Act (NEPA)*** in 1970. This law requires that any project (such as a dam, an arena, a canal, a highway, etc.) with significant federal involvement (such as federal financing) must have an approved ***Environmental Impact Statement (EIS)*** prior to the commencement of any work on the project. The Council on Environmental Quality issues guidelines for EISs. To be approved, an EIS must provide responses to several questions, including the following:

- What is the environmental impact of the proposed project?
- What negative environmental effects will result from the proposed project?
- What are the alternatives to the proposed project (including taking no action)?
- What short-term and long-term destruction of environmental resources will result from the proposed project?
- What irreversible and irretrievable commitments of resources will be consumed by the proposed project?

EXAMPLE 28.1

> Several groups in New York proposed that a new highway be constructed in New York City, to be called Westway. Plans for the highway included destruction of some old, wooden piers located in the Hudson River. Destroying the piers could adversely impact the number of striped bass whose habitat was in the river. It was alleged that the EIS failed to adequately address the striped bass issue, and Westway was never built.

Government Regulation of Business

In 1970, Congress created the ***Environmental Protection Agency (EPA),*** which has the responsibility of regulating business activities as they relate to the environment. The EPA:

OBJECTIVE 1

Explain how the federal government regulates itself in the area of environmental protection.

National Environmental Policy Act (NEPA) A federal law that requires any project with significant federal involvement to have an approved Environmental Impact Statement prior to commencement of any work on the project.

Environmental Impact Statement (EIS) An assessment of the environmental consequences of a planned project. An EIS is required for all projects with significant federal involvement and must be approved before work on the project can begin.

OBJECTIVE 2

Identify the role of the Environmental Protection Agency.

Environmental Protection Agency (EPA) A federal agency responsible for regulating business activities as they relate to the environment.

- Conducts environmental research.
- Assists states and municipalities with grants and technical advice.
- Administers the federal pollution laws that cover businesses.

MAJOR FEDERAL LEGISLATION PROTECTING THE ENVIRONMENT

Important federal legislation aimed at protecting the environment includes the Clean Air Act, Clean Water Act, and Comprehensive Environmental Response, Compensation and Liability Act (more popularly known as Superfund).

The Clean Air Act

The **Clean Air Act** of 1970 was created in recognition of the fact that pollution sometimes crosses the boundary lines of local jurisdictions and extends into two or more states. In effect, this law emphasized that when it comes to protecting the environment, state regulation is insufficient, and federal law is needed. At the international level, environmental protection is attained by treaties among countries. (See Chapter 28.)

Pursuant to the Clean Air Act, all states are required to develop air quality standards that are at least as rigorous as the federal standards. Such standards include:

- *Primary standards,* which serve to protect human life and health.
- *Secondary standards,* which serve to protect property, vegetation, climate, and aesthetic values.

In addition, the Clean Air Act covers two forms of pollution:

- *Stationary pollution,* which is caused by factories and other production facilities. This form of pollution is sometimes corrected by using scrubbers on smokestacks.
- *Mobile pollution,* which is caused by automobiles, trains, airplanes, etc. This form of pollution is addressed by the EPA's monitoring automobile manufacturers to ensure that they meet standards for minimum gasoline mileage requirements.

In 1990, the Clean Air Act was amended with a law exceeding 1,100 pages. These amendments require that emissions from automobiles contain fewer pollutants, that gasoline sold in the United States be cleaner, and that factories install new technologies to reduce the discharge of pollutants into the air.

OBJECTIVE 3

Discuss how the Clean Air Act and Clean Water Act reduce pollution.

Clean Air Act Federal legislation that requires all states to develop air quality standards that are at least as rigorous as the federal standards. This act sets primary and secondary standards, and regulates both stationary and mobile pollution.

Clean Water Act Federal legislation that sets minimum standards for water purity.

The Clean Water Act

In 1972, Congress enacted the **Clean Water Act,** which sets minimum standards for water purity in a manner similar to the Clean Air Act described previously. Included in such standards is "fishable and swimmable," an intermediate standard of water quality that allows the navigable waterways to be used for the propagation of fish and wildlife, and also allows such waterways to be used for recreational purposes.

Superfund

In 1980, Congress passed the Comprehensive Environmental Response, Compensation, and Liability Act (CERCLA). More popularly referred to as **Superfund,** this law regulates the dumping of waste onto land. If business firms illegally dump waste material, they can be held responsible for three times the actual cost of the clean up.

In addition, Superfund designates specific sites, mandating that these locations be cleaned up by their owners. The law also created a Hazardous Substance Trust Fund to help allay costs in addressing environmentally scarred land. Despite the national attention paid to this problem, however, applying the provisions of Superfund has not been an easy process, nor has it met with uniform success.

OBJECTIVE 4

Cite provisions in Superfund that protect against illegally dumping waste.

Superfund Federal legislation, otherwise known as the Environmental Response, Compensation, and Liability Act (CERLA), that regulates the dumping of waste onto land.

> **EXAMPLE 28.2**
>
> The Black Rock Coal Company went bankrupt in 1977. Black Rock owned 20,000 acres of environmentally damaged land and had numerous creditors who had never been paid. The land was designated as a Superfund site. A not-for-profit company called Earth Saviors received a federal grant to purchase the land, but will need to engage in a massive clean up before reclaiming the land for use as a park and wildlife preserve.

LAWSUITS BY PRIVATE CITIZENS

In the event that a business firm creates pollution or damages the environment in some fashion, in addition to being required to pay a fine, it may be held liable to private persons as well. There are several theories of law under which a private individual may bring a lawsuit against a business for creating pollution.

Negligence

Negligence is a tort that allows a plaintiff to bring a lawsuit against a defendant under state law for causing personal injury or property damage. Businesses that create pollution frequently cause injury to

OBJECTIVE 5

Describe the theories of law under which private citizens may sue persons and businesses that harm the environment.

people or damage to their property, and these businesses may be found liable by a court for the tort of negligence.

Nuisance

Most states have laws prohibiting the creation of a nuisance, a condition that affects a person's health, causes property damage, or interferes with a person's well being. (See Chapter 4.)

Businesses that cause pollutants to enter the air or water are creating a nuisance. There are two categories of nuisances:

- A *public nuisance* is created when the nuisance impacts public property, such as a navigable river or a state park. If a business causes pollution that then enters such river or park, any member of the public could file a lawsuit.
- A *private nuisance* is created when the nuisance impacts private property, such as a residence. If a business causes pollution that enters the person's residence, the affected individual could bring a lawsuit. Generally, state laws mandate that the affected individual notify the business in writing of the pollution's impact. If the business does not correct the problem, the affected individual may abate the nuisance (reduce the negative impact) on his or her own, and charge the business for the work.

> **EXAMPLE 28.3**
>
> Festa owned a home adjacent to a small manufacturing company owned by Hedberg, which placed numerous bags of unprotected trash near the property line. Festa observed the presence of vermin on her property and wrote Hedberg a letter requesting the removal of the trash, i.e., the abatement of the private nuisance. When Hedberg refused to attend to the problem, Festa hired a company to remove the trash and sent Hedberg the bill.

Trespass

Trespass is the unauthorized entry onto another person's property. Businesses that cause pollution are in effect sending pollutants onto another person's land or water. Most states recognize a cause of action for *"particle trespass,"* accepting the theory that businesses are trespassing on another person's property with their pollution particles.

TYPES OF POLLUTION

The most widely discussed forms of pollution are those that affect land, air, and water, discussed in some detail earlier in this chapter.

public nuisance A nuisance that impacts public property.

private nuisance A nuisance that impacts private property.

particle trespass The unauthorized entry of pollutant particles onto another person's property.

OBJECTIVE 6

Identify several types of pollution that environmental laws regulate.

However, there are numerous other types of pollution and environmental issues of great concern to society that are the subject of federal statutes.

Noise Pollution

Excess noise (as measured in decibels) can affect the health and well being of persons. Exposure to loud noise for extended periods of time can affect an individual's ability to hear, cause mood swings, and is even alleged to cause injury to fetuses. Noise pollution may also result in lower real estate values, as homeowners who live in close proximity to airports can frequently attest.

Pesticide Control

There are currently over 600 chemicals used in the preparation of over 50,000 pesticides. The continued use of a pesticide often causes insects to become immune to the chemical compounds, and as a result, the pesticide becomes ineffective. Stronger pesticides must then be created. In addition, many individuals are not comfortable with having their food grown in environments wherein pesticides are used.

Solid Waste Disposal

Most products are packaged in containers and wrappers that require disposal. The sheer volume of this waste material makes it extremely difficult to manage its disposal. Accordingly, numerous municipalities require that businesses and homeowners recycle paper and plastic products. Of course, the time and money necessary to manage efficiently and effectively a recycling program to some extent offsets the value of the program itself. Accordingly, it is well accepted that longer-term solutions must be found. Many companies have learned that by going "green," they are making products and packaging them in environmentally friendly ways. These companies have quickly discerned the positive public relations value of their regard for the environment.

Toxic Substance Disposal

Of great concern is the quantity of waste materials that can cause great harm to humans who are exposed to them. These toxic substances include medical waste and chemicals. Pursuant to the Toxic Substance Control Act of 1976, manufacturers are required to test chemicals thoroughly prior to introducing them into commerce. These tests must be conducted to determine the chemicals' effect on human health and on the environment.

Natural Resource Conservation

The United States has extraordinary forests and wetlands that have great aesthetic and economic value. Often, policymakers struggle with designing laws and regulations that can protect these resources without disturbing the natural ecological order. An example is the policy providing that forest fires started by an act of nature (e.g., a lightning strike) are allowed to continue to burn so long as the fire does not threaten human life and personal property. However, there is much debate about the propriety of allowing a fire to burn, sometimes out of control, so as not to disturb the ecosystem.

Acid Rain

Sulfur emissions, created primarily in the Midwest portion of the United States, cause pollutants to be discharged into the atmosphere and result in so-called ***acid rain.*** Because the jet stream flows from west to east, hit hardest by acid rain are the populated areas in the Northeast portions of the United States and Canada. Acid rain creates problems for forests and crops, kills fish, and destroys the paint finishes on automobiles.

acid rain Polluted rain that is caused by the discharge of sulfur emissions into the atmosphere.

A CHANGING GLOBAL ENVIRONMENT

There are several factors that influence the changing global climate, including the release of carbon dioxide into the atmosphere, the destruction of the rain forest, and the destruction of the ozone layer.

The Greenhouse Effect

There has been a concern that global temperatures are increasing over time. Increasing amounts of carbon dioxide (CO_2) released into the atmosphere create a condition known as the ***"greenhouse effect."*** The resulting rising temperatures can melt the polar icecaps, causing rising sea levels throughout the world. The result will be damage to coastal areas, as well as a host of ecological changes to the environment.

It must be pointed out that not all scientists are convinced that the data show clearly that temperatures are in fact increasing worldwide. The greenhouse effect is the subject of much scientific debate.

greenhouse effect The rising of temperatures due to the increasing amount of carbon dioxide that is released into the atmosphere.

Destruction of the Rain Forests

In recent years, there has been a growing recognition that economic interests are causing the gradual destruction of the world's rain forests found in tropical climates. This deforestation alters the distribution and circulation of water, which in turn can lead to drought, flooding, soil erosion, change in wind and ocean currents, and rainfall distribution. Another serious result of deforestation is that the absorption of carbon dioxide from the atmosphere is substantially reduced.

Destruction of the Ozone Layer

It is now generally recognized that the release of chlorofluorocarbons into the air has created damage to the ozone layer in the atmosphere. A hole in the ozone layer is most manifest over the South Pole, and is causing concern over its potential impact on human health. Chlorofluorocarbons are present primarily in aerosol cans and in freon, a cooling substance historically found in refrigerators and air conditioners (including automobile air conditioning systems).

Because the ozone layer protects the environment from the ultraviolet rays of the sun, damaging this protective shield could lead to major problems for agricultural products, forests, and wildlife. Most importantly, holes in the ozone layer can affect human health by causing skin and other forms of cancer and disease.

OTHER ENVIRONMENTAL ISSUES

As our knowledge of the universe increases, so does our recognition of environmental problems. There is growing concern about biodiversity and ocean and space pollution.

Biodiversity

Of concern to environmentalists is the notion that thousands of species are becoming extinct at an alarming rate. Numerous federal statutes have been passed protecting some of these endangered species, but many individuals argue that not enough is being done, and that not all species are being protected adequately.

Ocean Pollution

A developing environmental problem is that of ocean dumping, in which waste material is illegally deposited into the waters far off coastal areas. Currently, ocean dumping is allowed under limited circumstances. The EPA is charged with the responsibility of selecting appropriate sites and types of waste that may be discarded into the oceans by U.S. organizations.

Space Pollution

Environmentalists have recently turned their attention to the increased amount of "space junk" that is orbiting the planet. Satellites, no longer in use or in disrepair, continue to circle the earth. It is now estimated that there are 10,000 of these satellites in orbit.

CHAPTER SUMMARY

1 Government regulates itself in the area of environmental protection through the National Environmental Policy Act, which requires that any project with significant federal involvement must have an approved Environmental Impact Statement prior to the commencement of any work on the project.

2 The EPA regulates business activities as they relate to the environment. The agency conducts environmental research, assists states and municipalities with grants and technical advice, and administers to the federal pollution laws that cover businesses.

3 Pursuant to the Clean Air Act, all states are required to develop air quality standards that are at least as rigorous as the federal standards. The Clean Water Act set minimum standards for water purity in a manner similar to the Clean Air Act.

4 Superfund states that business firms that illegally dump waste material can be held responsible for three times the actual cost of the clean up. In addition, Superfund designates specific sites, mandating that these locations be cleaned up by their owners.

5 Theories of law under which a private individual may bring a lawsuit against a business for creating pollution include negligence, public nuisance, private nuisance, and trespass.

6 Types of pollution that environmental laws regulate include air pollution, water pollution, noise pollution, pesticide control, solid waste disposal, toxic substance disposal, natural resource conservation, acid rain, the greenhouse effect, destruction of the rain forests, destruction of the ozone layer, biodiversity, ocean pollution, and space pollution.

Chapter 28 Assessment

MATCHING LEGAL TERMS

Match each of the following definitions with the correct term in the list below. Write the letter of your choice in the answer column.

- **a.** National Environmental Policy Act
- **b.** Environmental Impact Statement
- **c.** Environmental Protection Agency
- **d.** Clean Air Act
- **e.** Clean Water Act
- **f.** Superfund
- **g.** public and private nuisance
- **h.** particle trespass
- **i.** acid rain
- **j.** greenhouse effect

1. A law that requires, prior to the commencement of any work, a declaration of the impact any major project will have on the environment.

2. Increasing global temperatures resulting from increasing amounts of carbon dioxide (CO_2) released into the atmosphere.

3. A law that sets minimum standards for water purity.

4. A federal agency with responsibility for regulating business activities as they relate to the environment.

5. Activities that negatively impact public or private property.

6. A cause of action that accepts the theory that a business can trespass on another person's property with its pollution.

7. A condition resulting from the discharge of pollutants into the atmosphere that creates problems for forests and crops, kills fish, and destroys the paint finishes on automobiles.

8. A declaration required, before beginning construction of a major project, that describes the impact of the project on the environment.

9. A law that regulates the dumping of waste onto land and designates specific sites, mandating that these locations be cleaned up by their owners.

10. A law that sets minimum standards for air purity.

TRUE/FALSE QUIZ

Indicate whether each of the following statements is true or false by writing *T* or *F* in the answer column.

11. The United States lacks the abundance of natural resources that other countries have.

12. Environmental regulation is not yet a distinct area of the law.

Chapter 28 Assessment

13. The Clean Air Act of 1970 deals only with pollution within the boundaries of each state.

    13. _____

14. Included in the Clean Water Act are standards for water quality that allow the navigable waterways to be used for the propagation of wildlife and for recreational purposes.

    14. _____

15. Applying the provisions of Superfund has been an easy process, and it has it met with uniform success.

    15. _____

16. Businesses that create pollution frequently cause injury to people or damage to their property. A court could find these businesses liable for the tort of negligence.

    16. _____

17. A public nuisance is created when a nuisance impacts public property, such as a navigable river, or a state park.

    17. _____

18. Many states recognize a cause of action for "particle trespass," accepting the theory that businesses are trespassing on another person's property with their pollution particles.

    18. _____

19. Excess noise (as measured in decibels) cannot affect the health and well-being of persons.

    19. _____

20. Pursuant to the Toxic Substance Control Act of 1976, manufacturers are required to test chemicals thoroughly prior to introducing them into commerce.

    20. _____

DISCUSSION QUESTIONS

Answer the following questions and discuss them in class.

21. Explain how the federal government regulates itself in the area of environmental protection.

22. Identify several types of pollution which environmental laws regulate. Which ones do you consider most important?

23. How is the Superfund intended to defray costs of cleaning polluted sites?

Chapter 28 Assessment

24. Discuss tort remedies that individuals can use against polluters.

25. The release of carbon dioxide into the atmosphere, the destruction of the rain forests, and the destruction of the ozone layer adversely affect the atmosphere. Can additional domestic regulations or international treaties halt the continuing damage more effectively?

26. Despite the warnings on containers of toxic substances, injuries and accidents still occur. Should there be additional regulations, or are there other ways to protect an individual?

THINKING CRITICALLY ABOUT THE LAW

Answer the following questions, which require you to think critically about the legal principles that you learned in this chapter.

27. EPA Discuss the EPA guidelines for preparing an environmental impact statement before a project can be approved. Are they adequate?

28. Environmental Legislation What are some of the specific rules imposed by the Clean Air Act and Clean Water Act—should these be more stringent?

29. Hazardous Substances Some substances offer both benefits and hazards. How should responsible individuals, corporations, scientists, and regulators weigh the gains and risks of these products?

Chapter 28 Assessment

30. Recycling Separating and recycling of plastic, glass, paper, and metal is costly for municipalities. Should these recycling collections be continued or should the monies be spent on other environmental objectives?

31. A Question of Ethics Most people agree that protection of the environment is an ethical issue. Society is frequently confronted with the conflict between achieving environmental goals and the economic impact on corporations, consumers, and taxpayers. How should this dilemma be addressed?

CASE QUESTIONS

Study each case below and answer the questions that follow by writing *Yes* or *No* in the answer column.

32. Environmental Protection Agency (EPA) The American Electric Power Company is contesting the accusation made two years ago by the EPA of violating the Clean Air Act. The company claims that it has solved the pollution problem. Meanwhile, in an unprecedented move, the company has bought the entire town of Cheshire, Ohio, the town they are accused of polluting. By this move they avoid the potential of lawsuits. The company, however, maintains they need the land to expand their plant.

    a. Does buying the homes of residents and the entire town mitigate the pollution problem?   a. _____

    b. Does the agreement of the residents of Cheshire to sell their homes solve the potential pollution problems for those who live downwind?   b. _____

    c. Does this seem like a good idea for the company?   c. _____

33. Private Nuisance LeatherLux Corporation, a manufacturer of upscale handbags, had been in business for twenty years and was considered a model corporate citizen of Cologne, Minnesota. Expanding, the company developed new tanning processes that resulted in noxious fumes and odors. The once-welcome company became *"corporatus non gratis."* A number of nearby residents of Cologne lodged a written complaint with LeatherLux detailing the impact of the pollution, as required by state law. LeatherLux ignored their plea. When the fumes and odors continued unabated, the residents sought tort relief.

    a. Do the residents have just cause for their lawsuit?   a. _____

    b. Are noxious odors measurable?   b. _____

    c. It is likely that the court would rule in favor of the residents?   c. _____

Chapter 28 Assessment

34. Toxic Substances ChemPlus Corp manufactured DeCorr, a widely used industrial chemical used to treat various metals to retard corrosion. Weston was working in a small shop immersing certain metal parts in a container of DeCorr, when a quantity of the chemical spilled on him. After washing off the chemical, Weston developed a painful rash and blisters. A supervisor contacted ChemPlus and was told that the company had no liability for Weston's injuries since there were adequate warnings on the containers. Calls to the Environmental Protection Agency were equally unavailing, since the manufacture of DeCorr was in compliance with the Toxic Substance Control Act of 1976.

   a. Is it likely that further pursuit of ChemPlus would result in a financial award to Weston?   a. _____

   b. Does the Toxic Substance Control Act require that all chemicals be entirely safe?   b. _____

   c. If the injuries were entirely the result of Weston's carelessness, is it likely that the state agency, which enforces workplace safety standards, would provide any additional help?   c. _____

CASE ANALYSIS

Study each of the following cases carefully and then briefly state the principle of law and your decision.

35. Environment/Wildlife Bronx Reptiles, Inc. has been importing live animals, including reptiles, into the country approximately twice a week since 1993. Mr. Edelman, the owner, testified that he knew of the International Air Transport Association (IATA) guidelines for importing wildlife—how specific species should be shipped and of the container requirements. Yet over the years, his company has been cited, and civil fines paid for many violations. In a shipment of iguanas and boa constrictors from Colombia, many were found dead due to improper ventilation. Small mammals shipped from Egypt were also found dead. Finally in 1995, when frogs imported from the Solomon Islands died due to improper packing and dehydration, Bronx Reptiles, Inc. was convicted of that portion of the Lacy Act that makes it a misdemeanor to "knowingly cause any wild animal . . . to be transported to the U.S. . . . under inhumane or unhealthful conditions." Mr. Edelman countered that because frogs were reptiles, they were not covered by the statute. The judge ruled that frogs are, in fact, amphibians and, in any event, fall within the statutory proscription. *Is it possible to prove that Edelman "knowingly" caused the inhumane conditions?* [*United States of America v. Bronx Reptiles, Inc.* 949 F. Supp.2d 481 (E.D. N.Y. 1998).]

Principle of law:

_____

_____

Decision:

_____

_____

Chapter 28 Assessment

36. **Environmental Conservation** A coalition of conservation organizations and environmentalists brought an action to determine (1) whether the Forest Service has met the procedural requirements of the National Environmental Policy Act (NEPA), and (2) whether this proposed action is consistent with the Green Mountain National Forest Land and Resource Management Act. The coalition challenged the Forest Service's decision not to prepare an Environmental Impact Statement (EIS) before embarking on its proposed timber-cutting action in a part of the Green Mountain National Forest. The coalition felt that the action would have "potential negative impact on black bears" whose habitat would be disturbed and "endanger the neo-tropical bird population." The district court found that the Forest Service failed to consider all relevant factors when determining the environmental significance of its proposed action and was directed to prepare a site-specific EIS and enjoined from further timber harvesting and road building until completion of the EIS. *Is it likely that the court will rule in favor of the coalitions?* [*National Audubon v. Hoffman,* 917 F. supp. 280 (D. Vt. 1995).]

Principle of law:

Decision:

LEGAL RESEARCH

Complete the following activities. Then share your findings with the class.

37. **Working in Teams** In teams of three or four, check labels on various products such as chemicals, cleansers, insecticides, and herbicides. Look for warnings and EPA information. Discuss your findings.

38. **Using Technology** Using the Internet and search engines, investigate the Environmental Protection Agency. In what types of activities is this federal agency involved?

GLOSSARY

A

abandonment In contract law, the condition that exists when a minor has left home and given up all rights to parental support.

acceptance An indication made by the offeree that he or she agrees to be bound by the terms of the offer.

accession The right of an owner of property to any increase in the property.

acid rain Polluted rain that is caused by the discharge of sulfur emissions into the atmosphere.

administrative agency A governmental body responsible for the control and supervision of a particular activity or area of public interest.

administrative hearing A trial-like judicial proceeding, without a jury, in which an administrative agency rules on matters of the law that the agency is charged with enforcing.

administrative law The body of rules, regulations, and decisions created by administrative agencies.

administrator A personal representative named by the court to perform as the executor would in instances in which the deceased person has not left a will, or if the executor named in the will is deceased or lacks capacity.

adverse possession When title to land is acquired by a person's exclusive, continuous, open, known, and hostile use of the property over a period of time.

age of majority The age at which a person is legally recognized as an adult and bound by the terms of their contracts.

agent A person authorized to act on behalf of another and subject to the other's control in dealing with third parties.

alternative dispute resolution (ADR) A system in which contract disputes and other disagreements are resolved by using means other than a lawsuit.

antenuptial agreement A promise made by a person planning to marry that is enforceable only if it is put in writing before the marriage takes place.

anticipatory breach When a party to a contract announces his or her intention to break the contract in the future.

apparent authority An accountability doctrine whereby a principal, by virtue of words or actions, leads a third party to believe that an agent has authority, but no such authority was intended.

arson The willful or malicious act of causing the burning of another's property.

assignee The third party to whom rights are transferred in an assignment.

assignment The transfer of a contract right to a third party who can receive the benefits of the contract. In the context of a lease, when a tenant transfers his or her entire interest in the entire premises for the remaining length of term of the lease.

assignor The person who transfers his or her rights in an assignment.

attorney in fact The person appointed as agent when the power of attorney is exercised.

auction sale A sale in which goods are sold to the highest bidder. The buyer is the party making the offer, or bid.

GLOSSARY

B

bad check A check against a bank in which the drawer has insufficient funds on deposit to cover the check or no funds at all.

bailment A transaction in which the owner of tangible personal property transfers it (not as a gift) to another party while still retaining ownership.

bailment for the sole benefit of the bailee A bailment relationship in which only the bailee receives any benefit from the relationship.

bailment for the sole benefit of the bailor A bailment that exists when the bailor entrusts an article to the bailee for storage or safekeeping without charge, as a favor.

bailee The party in a bailment who receives the goods.

bailee's lien The right of the bailee in a bailment for work and services to hold, and if necessary, to sell the property if the bailor does not pay for the services or work done.

bailor The party in a bailment who retains ownership and transfers possession of the goods.

bargain and sale deed A deed that simply grants the property to another. No particular warranties are given, but state statutes assume that certain implied warranties are present.

barren promise A promise to pay an existing debt, to obey the law, or a similar promise of something already owed.

beneficiary An individual who receives gifts of personal or real property by will.

bequest A gift of personal property by will.

bill of lading A document prepared by the carrier or the shipper for goods to be shipped by land or water; if shipped by air, an air bill is prepared.

bill of sale A written statement that the seller is passing ownership to the buyer.

blank indorsement An indorsement in which the name of the payee is written by the payee on the back of a negotiable instrument.

boycott When people refuse to purchase goods made by particular businesses. In some cases, citizens of a particular country refuse to purchase goods made by businesses located in other countries, regardless of whether their action is supported by the government.

breach of contract When a party to a contract refuses to perform as required by the contract or performs in an unsatisfactory manner.

bribery The act of offering, giving, receiving, or soliciting something of value to influence official action or the discharge of a public duty.

C

carrier's lien A carrier's legal right to hold a shipment until payment is made.

case law A body of court decisions that involves the same or similar facts.

cashier's check A check issued by a cashier or other designated officer of a bank and drawn against bank funds.

certified check A check that the bank has promised to pay when it is presented for payment.

champerty An agreement to encourage a lawsuit in which one or more of the parties has no legitimate interest.

check A written order drawn on a bank by a depositor that requests the bank to pay, on demand and unconditionally, a definite sum of money to the bearer of the check or to the order of a specified person.

GLOSSARY

churning The unreasonable buying or selling of securities to generate commissions.

Clean Air Act Federal legislation that requires all states to develop air quality standards that are at least as rigorous as the federal standards. This act sets primary and secondary standards, and regulates both stationary and mobile pollution.

Clean Water Act Federal legislation that sets minimum standards for water purity.

code of ethics A set of rules that a company or other group adopts to express principles of ethical behavior that are expected of its personnel.

codicil A document, separate from the will, in which a person can make legal changes to his or her will.

comity A major legal principle involved in international law that holds the courts of one country should refrain from deciding cases involving the acts of persons from another country.

commercial paper A number of legally binding and commercially acceptable documents that are used to transfer money from one person to another.

common carrier An individual or firm in the business of transporting goods between certain points as allowed by the various state commissions that regulate carriers.

common law The body of recorded decisions that courts refer to and rely upon when making later legal decisions.

community property Property that is acquired during a marriage.

comparative negligence A form of negligence that requires the court to assign damages according to the degree of fault of each party.

competence The state of being mentally capable of understanding the terms of a contract.

competent party A person of legal age and at least normal mentality who is considered by law to be capable of understanding the meaning of a contract and is permitted to enter into a valid contract.

conditional sale A sale with contract provisions that specify conditions that must be met by one of the parties.

conditional sales contract A sales contract that includes conditions that must be met either before or after the sale is completed.

conditions In the context of a lease, restrictions that limit the use of the property.

conditions precedent Conditions in a sales contract that must be met before title passes.

conditions subsequent Conditions in a sales contract that must be met after title has passed.

confiscation The act of a host country taking title to all of the assets of the foreign company and not providing compensation to the owners of the foreign firm.

consideration The promise to give up something of value that a party to a contract has a legal right to keep, or to do something that the party is not otherwise legally required to do.

consignee The person or party receiving goods in a bailment relationship.

consignor The person or party shipping goods in a bailment relationship.

constructive bailment A bailment in which goods are thrust upon a bailee who does not have any choice about whether he or she wishes to serve as bailee.

consortium Companionship, usually of a spouse.

contract A legally enforceable agreement that is created when two or more competent parties agree to perform, or to avoid performing, certain acts that they have a legal right to do and that meet certain legal requirements.

GLOSSARY

contract for labor and materials A sales contract for goods of special design, construction, or manufacture.

contract for sale A legally enforceable agreement intended for the immediate transfer of title to personal property in return for consideration.

contract for sale with the right of return A contract for the sale of goods that gives the buyer both title to the goods and the opportunity to return them to the seller at a later time.

contract of adhesion A contract drawn by one party that must be accepted as is on a take-it-or-leave-it basis.

contract of agency An agreement between a principal and an agent by which the agent is vested with authority to represent the principal.

contract to sell An agreement to sell future goods.

contributory negligence A legal defense that involves the failure of an injured party to be careful enough to ensure personal safety.

conversion The wrongful exercise of dominion and control over another's personal property.

cookie A file that is imbedded on the hard drive of a computer, often without a person's knowledge, that collects and stores information about the user and his or her online behavior, including Web sites that he or she has visited.

counterclaim When the maker of a note or other drawer or acceptor of a bill of exchange may deduct from the amount demanded by an immediate party any amounts owed him or her by the payee.

counteroffer A response to an offer in which the terms and conditions of the original offer are changed.

covenants Agreements made by either a landlord or a tenant to do certain things.

cover When the seller fails to deliver the goods, the right of a buyer to buy similar goods elsewhere to substitute for those not delivered by the seller.

crime An offense against the public at large punishable by the official governing body of a nation or state.

culture The set of shared attitudes, values, goals, and practices that characterize a social, racial, religious, or corporate group.

custom of the marketplace What a warranty usually means in similar transactions.

D

decedent A deceased person.

deceptive advertisement An advertisement that contains a material (important) misrepresentation, omission, or practice likely to mislead a consumer who acts reasonably under the circumstances.

deed The instrument, or document, that conveys an interest in real property between parties.

defamation The intentional tort that occurs when a false statement is communicated to others that harms a person's good name or reputation.

defendant The party against whom a lawsuit is brought and from whom recovery is sought.

delegation The appointment of a third party by a party to an existing contract to perform contractual duties that do not involve unique skills or abilities.

Digital Millennium Copyright Act of 1998 (DMCA) The federal act that provides that ISPs are not liable for copyright infringements by their subscribers or for information residing on their networks provided they accept certain specified policies.

GLOSSARY

disaffirmance In contract law, to indicate by a statement or act an intent not to live up to the terms of a contract.

disclaimer A denial or repudiation in an express warranty that places specific limitations in the warranty.

dishonored When a negotiable instrument is not accepted when presented for acceptance, not paid when presented for payment at maturity, presentment is excused or waived, or the instrument is past due and unpaid.

domestication When a host country mandates that at least partial ownership of a foreign company be sold to local citizens or companies prior to the foreign company conducting business within the host country's borders.

draft An unconditional written order to a person or bank instructing him or her to pay money to another, third person.

drawee The person who received the order to draw or to pay.

drawer The person who draws or creates a draft or bill of exchange.

duress The act of applying unlawful or improper pressure or influence to a person to gain his or her agreement to a contract.

E

easement A right or interest in land granted to a party to make beneficial use of the land owned by another.

electronic funds transfer (EFT) A variety of electronic applications for handling money.

Electronic Signatures in Global and International Commerce Act The federal statute that specifies that electronic contracts containing electronic signatures are as enforceable as those that are printed on paper.

emancipation In contract law, the condition that exists when minors are no longer under the control of their parents and are responsible for their contracts.

embezzlement The wrongful taking of money or other property that has been entrusted to a person as a part of his or her job.

eminent domain When ownership of real property is taken by the government and the previous owner is compensated at the fair market value of the property.

environmental impact statement (EIS) An assessment of the environmental consequences of a planned project. An EIS is required for all projects with significant federal involvement and must be approved before work on the project can begin.

Environmental Protection Agency (EPA) A federal agency responsible for regulating business activities as they relate to the environment.

estoppel A bar to using contradictory words or acts in asserting a claim against another.

ethics The philosophical study of what is right and wrong, good and bad.

European Union (EU) A union of twelve European countries formed to establish economic, legal, political, and cultural ties between the member nations.

eviction An action that denies the tenant the use of the premises.

executive branch The branch of a government body that consists of an elected executive, including his or her appointed staff.

executor A personal representative named in a will to handle matters involving the estate of a deceased person.

existing goods Goods that physically exist and are owned by the seller at the time of sale.

GLOSSARY

express authority An agent's authority that the principal voluntarily and specifically sets forth as oral or written instructions in an agency agreement.

express contract A contract that explicitly states the agreement of the parties, either orally or in writing.

express powers Powers that are explicitly stated; for example, in the U.S. Constitution.

express warranty An explicit, specifically stated promise.

expropriation The act of a host country taking title to all of the assets of a foreign company and providing compensation to the owners of the foreign firm.

extortion The act of taking or demanding money or other property from someone by using force, threats of force, or economic harm.

F

Federal Trade Commission (FTC) The federal agency responsible for ensuring that advertising in the United States is truthful.

f.o.b. destination When title passes from the seller to the buyer when the goods are delivered to the buyer.

f.o.b. shipping point When title to goods passes from the seller to the buyer when the carrier receives the shipment and it is understood that the buyer will pay the transportation charges.

false pretenses A broad category of crimes that involves activities intended to deceive others or to obtain goods by making false claims.

fee simple When an owner of a freehold estate holds it absolutely, meaning he or she can sell it, give it way, or leave it to his or her heirs.

felony A crime punishable by death or by imprisonment in a federal or state prison for a term exceeding one year.

forbearance The promise to refrain from doing something that a party has a legal right to do.

Foreign Corrupt Practices Act (FCPA) A federal statute design to provide executives of American companies with rules and restrictions relating to paying persons in foreign countries to expedite business in these foreign nations.

forged check A check that is signed by a person other than the drawer.

forgery The false making or alteration of a writing with the intent to defraud.

formal contract A contract that is written and under seal; also known as a specialty contract.

franchisee The independent company in a franchise agreement.

franchisor The parent firm in a franchise agreement.

fraud The intentional misstatement, or nondisclosure of a material (essential) fact made by one party with the hope of influencing the other party.

freehold estate An estate in which a person owns the land for life and forever.

full warranty The promise that a defective product will be repaired without charge and within a reasonable time after a complaint has been made.

fungible goods Goods that are generally sold by weight or measure.

future goods Goods that do not exist at the time of the sales transaction, but are expected to come into the possession of the seller.

GLOSSARY

G

gambling agreement An agreement in which performance by one party depends on the occurrence of an uncertain event.

General Agreement on Tariffs and Trade (GATT) An international agreement that provides a set of rules to ensure that there be no discrimination in trade by its signatories, and also spells out a process for resolving international trade disputes.

general release A written agreement in which an aggrieved party can discharge in whole or in part a claim resulting from an alleged breach of contract.

gift The voluntary transfer of property by one party to another without consideration or payment of any kind.

government-granted franchise A legal monopoly in which a state or federal government grants a person or firm a license to conduct a specific business, usually an essential service.

gratuitous promise A promise that does not require some benefit in return.

greenhouse effect The rising of temperatures due to the increasing amount of carbon dioxide that is released into the atmosphere.

guarantor The party who guarantees the promises assigned.

guaranty A promise to pay the debts or settle the wrongdoings of another if he or she does not make settlement personally.

H

hacker A person who gains unauthorized access to computer systems more for mischief than for criminal intent.

holder The person in possession of the commercial paper.

holder in due course A holder who has taken a negotiable instrument in good faith and for value, before maturity, and without actual or constructive notice of any defects in the instrument.

hotelkeeper A person or firm in the business of offering lodgings or temporary shelter to guests and transients.

I

implied authority The authority of an agent to perform acts that are necessary or customary to carry out expressly authorized duties.

implied contract A contract that does not explicitly state the agreement of the parties, but in which the terms of the agreement can be inferred from the actions or conduct of the parties, the customs of the trade, or from the conditions or circumstances.

implied powers Powers that arise as a result of an interpretation of the express powers by the courts.

implied warranty A guarantee suggested or inferred from known facts and circumstances.

implied warranty of fitness of purpose The law's assumption that goods are fit for their intended purpose.

implied warranty of merchantability The law's assumption that goods sold by a merchant-seller are fit to be sold and are adequate for the ordinary purposes for which such goods are sold.

impossibility of performance When unforeseen circumstances make it impossible to fulfill the terms of a contract. In these cases, the contract is considered void.

incidental beneficiary Someone who will benefit as an indirect consequence of a contract, although that was not the intent of the contracting parties.

GLOSSARY

incompetent Being unable to make binding contracts due to having an unsound mind and being unable to safeguard one's own interests and affairs.

independent contractor One who contracts to do a job and who retains complete control over the methods employed to obtain completion.

indorsement When the holder of commercial paper signs his or her name, with or without words, on the back of an instrument to transfer ownership to another.

indorsee The person to whom a negotiable instrument is transferred.

indorser The person who signs his or her name to a negotiable instrument.

injunction A restraining order that in some states is permanent.

intentional concealment Deliberately hiding material facts.

interest The charge for using borrowed money, generally expressed as an annual percentage of the amount of the loan (principal).

International Monetary Fund (IMF) An international organization with the purpose of maintaining a stable environment for the economies and the currencies of its members by providing protection against large fluctuations in the value of one currency versus another.

Internet Tax Freedom Act A federal act that established a moratorium on taxing ISPs on the services they provide to computer users.

intestate Having died without leaving a valid will.

invitation to trade An announcement published for the purpose of creating interest and attracting a response by many people. It is not considered a valid offer because it does not contain sufficient words of commitment to sell.

irrevocable agency An agency contract that cannot be terminated by a principal in which the agent has an interest in the subject matter of the agency in addition to the remuneration that he or she receives for services.

J

joint tenancy When two or more persons own equal shares of personal property.

judicial branch The branch of a government body that determines if there have been violations of the law and interprets the law if there are questions about what the law means in particular situations.

judicial review The process by which a court determines the constitutionality of various legislative statutes, administrative regulations, and executive actions.

jurisdiction The authority of a court, as granted by a constitution or legislative act, to hear and decide cases.

L

landlord The owner of real property who gives up his or her right of possession.

larceny The act of taking and carrying away the personal property of another without the right to do so.

lease The document in which the terms of a rental agreement are written.

leasehold estate An estate in which a person has an interest in real property that comes from a lease.

legacy A gift of money by will.

legality of purpose The requirement that the intent of a contract be legal for the contract to be enforceable.

GLOSSARY

legislative branch The branch of a government body that consists of elected representatives who have the responsibility for passing laws that represent the will of the people.

lessee In the context of a lease, the party who contracts to lease the property from the property owner, or lessor.

lessor In the context of a lease, the property owner who contracts to lease the property is the tenant, or lessee.

liable Being judged legally responsible.

libel Any false statement that harms another person's good name or reputation made in a permanent form, such as movies, writing, and videotape, and communicated to others.

life estate A freehold estate in which a person has an ownership interest only for his or her lifetime.

limited warranty A written warranty that does not meet the minimum requirements of a full warranty.

living will A document in which a person directs his or her physician or health proxy to forgo certain extraordinary medical procedures in especially dire circumstances.

M

maker The party to a promissory note that makes the promise.

malpractice A subdivision of negligence that refers to a professional's improper or immoral conduct in the performance of his or her duties through carelessness or ignorance.

material alteration A deliberate change or alteration of an important element in a written contract that affects the rights or obligations of the parties.

memorandum A written contract or agreement.

minor A person who has not yet reached the age of majority.

misdemeanor A less serious crime that is generally punishable by a prison sentence of not more than one year.

misrepresentation A misstatement of material fact that results in inducing another to enter into an agreement to his or her injury.

mistake A belief that is not in accord with the facts.

mitigate The obligation of the injured party to protect the other party from any unnecessary damages.

monopoly power A situation in which one or more people or firms control the market in a particular area or for a particular product.

moral consideration Something that a person is not legally bound to do, but that he or she may feel bound to do because of love, friendship, honor, sympathy, conscience, or other reason.

morals Beliefs that govern society's attitude about what constitutes good and bad behavior.

mutual agreement The state of mind that exists between an offeror and an offeree when a valid offer has been accepted, and the parties know what the terms are and have agreed to be bound by them. Mutual agreement is also known as "a meeting of the minds."

mutual-benefit bailment A bailment in which both the bailee and the bailor derive some benefit, and as a result, each has rights and duties.

N

National Environmental Policy Act (NEPA) A federal law that requires any project with significant federal involvement to have an approved Environmental Impact Statement prior to commencement of any work on the project.

GLOSSARY

necessaries Goods and services that are essential to a minor's health and welfare.

negligence The failure to exercise necessary care to protect others from unreasonable risk of harm.

negotiability The ability to be transferred freely from one person to another and be accepted as readily as cash.

nexus A link or tie of a sale to a location so that a sales tax can be collected on the sales transaction.

North American Free Trade Agreement (NAFTA) A strictly economic agreement between the United States, Canada, and Mexico aimed at promoting and facilitating trade among these nations.

novation When all parties to a contract agree to a significant change to a contract.

nuisance An unlawful interference with the enjoyment of life or property.

O

offer A proposal made by one party (the offeror) to another person (the offeree) that indicates a willingness to enter into a contract.

order bill of lading A receipt similar to a straight bill of lading, only negotiable and proof of title that can be used to transfer title from one person to another.

order instrument An item of commercial paper that contains the key words of negotiability, *pay to the order of*, or their equivalent.

ordinance A law that is passed by a local government, such as a city council.

P

parol evidence rule The rule that any spoken or written words in conflict with what the written contract states cannot be introduced as evidence in a court of law.

particle trespass The unauthorized entry of pollutant particles onto another person's property.

password A secret series of characters that allows a user to access a file, computer, or program.

past consideration A promise to repay someone for a benefit after it has been received.

payee The party to a promissory note to whom the promise is made.

periodic tenancy A possession interest in which a lease continues for successive periods for the same length of time.

perjury The crime of intentionally giving false oral or written statements under oath in a judicial proceeding after having sworn to tell the truth.

personal defense A defense against payment of commercial paper that may be used against any party except a holder in due course.

personal property All kinds of property other than real property, such as an automobile, clothing, a computer, and so on. It can be tangible or intangible.

personal representative The person responsible for settling the affairs of the decedent.

personal-service contract A contract in which a party hires a specific person to perform certain duties and who has a substantial interest in having only the hired person perform.

plaintiff The party who begins a lawsuit by filing a complaint in the appropriate court.

pledge A promise to donate money to a church, hospital, charity, or other organization.

postdated check A check drawn when a person has insufficient funds, but dated such that sufficient funds will be available when it is cashed.

power of attorney An instrument in writing by which one person, as principal, appoints another person as agent and confers the authority to perform certain specified acts on behalf of the principal.

GLOSSARY

precedent A model case that a court can follow when facing a similar situation.

preexisting duty An obligation that a party is already bound to by law or by some other agreement. The party may not use this as consideration in a new contract.

presentment When the holder of a note tenders it to the maker and demands payment, or shows a draft to the drawer and requests its acceptance or payment, on or after the maturity date at the place stated in the instrument.

primary market The market in which an issuer (a corporation) sells its securities to the public.

principal A person who authorizes an agent to act on her or his behalf and subject to her or his control.

private nuisance A nuisance that impacts private property.

product liability The liability of a manufacturer or seller for injury to users and third parties.

professional A person who does highly specialized work that depends on special abilities, education, experience, and knowledge.

promisee In the making of a contract, the party to whom a promise is made.

promisor In the making of a contract, the party who makes a promise.

promissory note A written note or letter in which one person promises to pay a certain amount of money to another at a definite time.

proper form The requirement that the form of a contract be correct for the terms of the contract to be enforceable.

property Tangible and intangible possessions of which one can have ownership.

public figure A person who has voluntarily chosen a lifestyle that in a free society naturally exposes them to close scrutiny by the media. To prevail for defamation, these figures must prove that false statements were made with actual malice.

public nuisance A nuisance that impacts public property.

puffery A general expression of opinion, typically in a sales context, that is used to persuade a prospective purchaser to buy. It does not constitute a misrepresentation of material fact or create a warranty.

Q

qualified indorsement An indorsement in which the indorser avoids liability for payment even if the maker or drawer defaults on the instrument.

quiet enjoyment The right to use the leased premises without unreasonable interferences from the landlord or third parties.

quota system A set of restrictions that a country may implement to maintain a positive balance of trade by placing restrictions on the numbers and kinds of products that may enter into the nation.

R

raised check A check on which the amount has been raised by the payee or bearer.

ratified An approval of a contract made by a minor after reaching maturity.

real defense A defense against payment of commercial paper that claims the instrument was void from the beginning.

GLOSSARY

real property The ground and everything permanently attached to it, including land, buildings, trees and shrubs; the air space above the land, and ground below are also included.

rejection The express or implied refusal by an offeree to accept an offer.

remote party Someone with the right to make legitimate sales as a representative of the owner of the goods, although they themselves are not titleholders.

replevin An action to recover possession of specific goods wrongfully taken or detained by another.

restraining order A court order prohibiting the performance of a certain act. In some states, a restraining order is temporary.

restraint of trade A limitation on the full exercise of doing business with others.

restrictive indorsement An indorsement with a signature to which words have been added restricting further indorsement of the instrument.

revocation The calling back of an offer by the offeror before an offer has been accepted or rejected.

S

sale of approval A contract for the sale of goods subject to the buyer's approval.

sale or return An agreement whereby the seller will accept the return of goods at the request of the buyer to maintain goodwill, rather than because the seller is legally obliged to accept the returned goods.

secondary market The market where one member of the public sells securities to another member of the public.

Securities Act of 1933 The federal law that covers the sale of securities in the primary market.

Securities and Exchange Commission (SEC) The federal agency responsible for administrating various federal statutes aimed at ensuring that prospective investors have access to full and correct information about the companies whose securities they are interested in purchasing.

Securities Exchange Act of 1934 The federal law that covers the sale of securities in the secondary market.

slander Any false statement that harms a person's good name or reputation made in a temporary form, such as speech, and communicated to others.

spam Unsolicited e-mail messages sent primarily for commercial purposes.

special indorsement An indorsement in which the payee specifies the person to whom, or to whose order, it is to be paid.

specific performance A court order directing a person to perform—or not perform—as he or she agreed to do in a contract.

stare decisis The practice of relying on previous decisions in which similar disputes arose.

Statute of Frauds A law requiring certain contracts to be in writing to be enforceable.

statutory law The field of law involving statutes, which are laws passed by Congress or by state legislatures.

stop-payment order An instruction that a depositor gives to his or her bank not to pay a particular check.

stoppage in transit When the buyer is insolvent, the right of an unpaid seller to stop goods in transit and order the carrier to hold them for the seller.

GLOSSARY

straight bill of lading A receipt for the goods to be shipped and an acknowledgement that the goods have been received and will be transported to the destination indicated.

strict liability The doctrine under which people may be liable for injuries to others whether or not they have been negligent or committed an intentional tort. That is, it is not necessary to prove fault to establish strict liability.

subculture An ethnic, economic, regional, religious, or social group with attitudes or behavior that distinguish it from others within a larger culture.

sublease A transfer of the tenant's interest in part of the term of the lease and/or part of the premises.

substantial performance When a party to a contract, in good faith, executes all of the promised terms and conditions of the contract with the exception of minor details that do not affect the real intent of their agreement.

Sunday agreement A contract made on a Sunday. In a small number of jurisdictions, such contracts are invalid unless they are ratified on a weekday.

Superfund Federal legislation, otherwise known as the Environmental Response, Compensation, and Liability Act (CERLA), that regulates the dumping of waste onto land.

T

tariff A form of tax on goods from a foreign country used for the purpose of attaining economic results.

tenancy at sufferance A tenancy that exists only when a tenant wrongfully extends his or her tenancy beyond the term agreed upon.

tenancy at will A possession interest in which no specific time of lease is agreed upon.

tenancy by the entirety A form of joint ownership of property by husband and wife in which both have the right to the entire property, and upon the death of one, the other has title.

tenancy for years The most common type of possession interest in which the lease is for a specific period of time.

tenancy in common A form of joint ownership of property by two or more persons in which any owner's interest can be sold, transferred, or inherited.

tenant The person who agrees to pay for the use of real property.

tender of payment A money offer of payment of an obligation.

tender of performance An offer to perform that is considered evidence of a party's willingness to fulfill the terms of a contract.

term insurance A form of pure life insurance that does not include a savings feature.

termination by lapse of time When an opportunity to form a contract ends because the offeree fails to accept an offer within the time specified.

testator A person who makes a will.

testamentary capacity The requirement that a testator be of sound mind and legal age.

third-party beneficiary Someone who is not a party to a contract but is intended by the contracting parties to benefit as a consequence of a contract.

title Ownership and the right to possess something, unless the right to possess property has been given up by renting it to someone else.

title insurance A form of insurance that assures the buyer that there are no other claims to title.

tort A private wrong that injures another person's physical well-being, property, or reputation.

GLOSSARY

touting When an investor who owns shares of a company's stock posts notices online that indicate that the value of the stock will increase.

trade sanction Also known as an embargo, a law enacted by a nation that prohibits trade with specific countries for the purpose of achieving political results.

transient A guest whose stay is relatively uncertain.

transnational institutions Institutions established by several countries that agree to be legally bound by the rules of the organization.

traveler's check A certified check, useful when traveling in foreign countries, that is issued in denominations of $10 or more by certain banks, travel agencies, and financial services companies.

treason The levying of war against the United States, or the giving of aid and comfort to the nation's enemies.

trust A device or mechanism that permits personal or real property to be held by one party, the trustee, for the benefit of another, the beneficiary.

trustee A person who is entrusted with the management and control of another's property or the rights associated with that property.

U

unconscionable contract A contract that is so one-sided that it is oppressive and gives unfair advantage to one of the parties.

undue influence The improper use of excessive pressure by the dominant member of a confidential relationship to convince the weaker party to enter a contract that greatly benefits the dominant party.

Uniform Commercial Code (UCC) A set of laws that govern various commercial transactions that is designed to bring uniformity to the laws of the states.

unlicensed transaction An agreement with a person who does not have a required license.

use tax A tax to a consumer who uses goods within a state, as opposed to buying them within the state.

usury Charging interest higher than the law permits.

V

valid contract An agreement resulting in an obligation that is legally enforceable.

values Beliefs or standards considered worthwhile, and from which a society derives its moral rules.

vicarious liability The concept of laying responsibility or blame upon one person for the actions of another.

vicarious negligence Charging a negligent act of one person to another.

virus A program or selection of code that is loaded onto your computer system without your knowledge and runs against your wishes.

void contract A contract that is not enforceable from the beginning because it lacks one of the requirements of a valid contract.

voidable contract An agreement that can be rejected by one of the parties for a legally acceptable reason.

GLOSSARY

W

warehouse receipt Much like a bill of lading except that the goods are not being shipped but merely stored.

warehouser A person or firm that provides storage facilities.

warranty A guarantee or promise made by the manufacturer or seller that the goods or services offered really are what they are claimed to be, or that goods or services are what a reasonable person has a right to expect.

warranty deed A deed in which the grantor claims that he or she has title, and that the property is free of the claims of others.

warranty of habitability An implied warranty in which the landlord guarantees that the premises are reasonably fit for occupancy and that there are no defects that would impair the health, safety, or well being of the occupants.

whistleblower An employee that discloses to the government, media, or upper-management that the company is involved in wrongful or illegal activities.

whole-life insurance A relatively costly form of insurance protection that includes a savings feature.

will A person's declaration of how he or she wishes property to be distributed upon his or her death.

workers' compensation Worker protection provided for by state statutes that compensate covered workers or their dependents for injury, disease, or death that occurs on the job or as a result of it.

World Bank An international organization that works closely with the IMF to ensure that developing countries have access to funds to stimulate their economies.

World Trade Organization (WTO) An international organization responsible for overseeing the implementation of all multinational trade agreements negotiated now or in the future.

wrongful possession When property, such as stolen goods, is transferred without permission of the owner.

INDEX

A

Abandoned property, 299–300
Abandonment, 134, 334
    tenant's, 336
Absolute defenses, 385
    against payment of commercial paper, 386–388
Absolute liability, 272
Acceptance, 82
    characteristics of valid, 101–103
    as element of enforceable contract, 82
Accession, 301
Accident, unavoidable, 53
Accountants, liability of, 283–284
Acid rain, 457
Actual eviction, 335
Adhesion
    contracts of, 109–110
    on the Web, 422
Administrative agencies, 7, 65–66
    comparison of, with government, 69–71
    criticism of, 71–72
    examples, 65–66
    formation of, 67–69
    functions of, 67
Administrative hearing, 69
Administrative law, 7, 8
Administrator, 162, 345
Adverse possession, 307
Advertising, 100–101
    on the Web, 419–420
Agency
    by agreement, 246
    creation of, 245–247
    by necessity, 246
    by operation of law, 246–247
    by ratification, 246
    termination of, 251–252
Agent, 244
    authority of, 247–248
    classes of, 245
    duties of, 247–248
    duties of, to third parties, 250–251
    duties of principal to, 249–250
    duties to principal, 248–249
    right of appointment, 244–245
    torts and crimes, 248
Age of majority, 132
Agreements
    to answer for debts of another, 162
    antenuptial, 163
    on debt payment of deceased, 161–162
    defective, 105–110
    to defraud creditors and others, 148–149
    gambling, 146
    illegal, 145
    lacking consideration, 122–124
    made in comtemplation of marriage, 163
    made on Sundays or holidays, 145–146
    against public policy, 147–149
    to sell personal property, 163–164
    to sell real property, 163
    supported by moral consideration, 123
    supported by past consideration, 123–124
    termination by, 188
    that interfere with public service, 148
    that obstruct or pervert justice, 147–148
    that restrain marriage, 148
    that result in contracts, 81
    unable to be completed in less than one year, 162–163
    usurious, 146–147
    in violation of statutes, 145–147
Air bill, 208
Air rights, 303
Alteration, termination, 191–192
Alternative dispute resolution (ADR), 423–424
Antedated, 365
Antenuptial agreements, 163
Anticipatory breach, 193
Apparent authority, 247–248
Appeal boards, 7
Appellate court, state, 10–11
Appellate jurisdiction, 9
Approval, sale on, 227–228
Arbitration, 423
Architects, liability of, 284–285
Arson, 36
Assignability vs. negotiability, 361
Assignee, 175, 361
Assignment, 175, 335–336
    and delegation by law, 178–179
    form of, 176
    notice of, 176
    prohibited by law or public policy, 177
    of rights, 175–176
        and assignor's guaranty, 176
        form of, 176
        notice of, 176
        and transfer of right, 176
Assignor, 175, 361
    guaranty of, 175
Attorney in fact, 246
Attorneys, liability of, 285–286
Auction
    with reserve, 229
    sales, 164, 229–230
    without reserve, 229
Automated teller machines (ATM), 370–371

B

Bad checks, 368
Bailee, 316
    intentions of, 317
    returning identical goods, 317
Bailee's lien, 320
Bailment, 316
    characteristics of, 316–317
    common-carrier, 321
    constructive, 318, 321
    creation of, 316–317
    hotel, 320–321
    kinds of, and care during custody, 317–321
    mutual-benefit, 318–321
    parking-lot, 319–320

INDEX

for sole benefit of bailee, 317, 318
for sole benefit of bailor, 317, 318
for storage, 319
for work and services, 320
Bailor, 316
   -bailee relationship, 320
   bailment for sole benefit of, 317, 318
Bank check, 367–368
Bankruptcy of contracting party, 179
Bargain and sale deed, 306
Barren promises, 122
Bearer, transfer of money or commercial paper made out to, 213
Beneficiary, 346
Bequest, 346
Bids or estimates, calling for, 99–100
Bill of exchange, 362
   and indications of drawee, 365
Bill of lading, 208–209
Bill of sale, 208
Biodiversity, 458
Blank indorsement, 381
Bona fide holder for value without notice, 383–384
Boycott, 440
Breach
   due to frustration of purpose, 195
   termination by, 336
Breach of contract, 192
   remedies for, 195–197, 231–235
   resulting from deliberate/negligent act, 193–194
   termination by, 192–195
Bribery, 36–37
Burglary, 36
Burning to defraud, 36
Business
   application of ethics to, 21–23
   applications of law, 4
   and government, integrating ethics into, 24–25

Buyer(s)
   insolvency, 232–233
   refusal of acceptance of goods by, 231–232
   refusal to pay purchase price, 232
   remedies of, for breach of contracts, 233–235

C

Carrier's lien, 321
Case law, 6
Cashier's checks, 367–368
Certificate of title, 207
Certified checks, 367
Champerty, 147
Checks, 362, 366
   bad, 368
   forged and raised, 368–369
   payment of, 366–367
   postdated, 369
   relationship between bank and depositor, 366
   stopping payment on, 369–370
   traveler's, 368
Churning, 284
Civil law, 8
Clean Air Act, 453–454
Clean Water Act, 454
Codes of ethics, 22
Codicil, 348
Comaker, 363
Comity, 436
Commercial paper, 361
   characteristics, 361
   defenses against payment of, 385–388
   dishonor of, 389
   essentials of, 363–365
   indorsing, 380
   kinds of, 362–363
   lack of intent to execute, as real defense against commercial paper, 361
   negotiability vs. assignability, 361
   nonessentials of, 365–366
   parties to, 363

presentment of, 388–389
presumption of consideration, 361
Common carrier, 230, 321
   bailments, 321
Common law, 5–6, 33
Community property, 302–303
Comparative negligence, 55
Competence, 82
Competent parties, 82, 132
   as element of enforceable contract, 82
Computer
   crime, 402–403
   crime legislation, 403–405
   gambling, 405
   privacy, 399–402
   speech, 406–408
   unauthorized access to, 402–403
Computer Fraud and Abuse Act (CFAA), 404
Conditional promises, 210–211
Conditional sales contract, 210, 230
Conditions, 331
   precedent, 210–211
   subsequent, 211
Confiscation, 440
Consideration, 82, 119
   agreements:
      adequacy of, 120
      lacking, 122–124
      legality of, 119
      possibility of performance, 120
   characteristics of valid, 119–120
   as element of enforceable contract, 82
   general release, 122
   kinds of valid, 120–121
   lack of, as personal defenses against payment of commercial paper, 385
   presumption of, 361
   and Uniform Commercial Code, 121–122
Consignee, 321
Consignor, 321

INDEX

Consortium, 283
Constitutional amendments, 5
Constitutional law, 5, 8
Constitutional powers, 5
Constructive bailment, 321
Constructive eviction, 335
Consumer, termination to protect, 195
Consumer Protection Agency, 68–69
Contracting party
    bankruptcy of, 178
    death of, 178–179
Contract(s), 81
    of adhesion, 109–110
    of adhesion on the Web, 422
    of agency, 244
    agreements that result in, 81
    elements of enforceable, 82–83
    enforceability of, 88–89
    entire and divisible sales, 226
    form of, 165
    of intoxicated persons, 136–137
    kinds of, 83–87
    for labor and materials, 226–227
    of mentally impaired, 136
    minors', 132–136
    oral, written and implied, 225
    personal service, 191
    purposes of, 81
    remedies for breach of, 195–197, 231–235
    for sale, 224–225
    for sale with the right return, 227
    to sell, 225
    status of, 87
    that cannot be assigned, 177
    that include assignment restrictions, 177
    that require personal service, 177
    third parties to, 174–175
    unconscionable, 110
    on the Web, entering into, 421–423
    in writing, required, 160
    written, what to include, 164–165
Contractual capacity, 132
Contributory negligence, 55
Controls, export and import, 439
Conversion, 52
Cookies, 400
Copyrights, 441
Corporate responsibility, 21–22
Counterclaim, 386
Counteroffer, 102–103
Court system
    federal, 9–10
    jurisdiction, 9
    state, 10–11
Covenants, 331
Cover, 234–235
Credit card fraud, 38
Creditors, agreements to defraud, 148–149
Crime(s), 33
    of agent, 248
    in business world, 35–39
    classification of, 34–35
    and minors' torts, liability for, 135–136
Criminal law, 8
Crowell v. Benson, 71
Culture, 20
Custody, kinds of bailments and care during, 317–321
Custom of marketplace, 265
Cyberspace, settling disputes in, 423–424

D

Damages, landlord's duty to mitigate, 334–335
Death of a contracting party, 178–179
Debts, agreements to answer for another, 161–162
Deceased persons, debt payment of, 161–162
Decedent, 345
Deceptive advertisement, 419
Deed(s), 305
    delivery and recording of, 306
    types of, 306
Defamation, 47, 406
    defenses to, 51
Defective agreements, 105–110
Defendant, 3
Defenses against payment of commercial paper, 385–388
Delegation, 178
    of duties, 178
    by law and assignment, 178–179
Deliberate act, breach resulting from, 193–194
Delivery, 230–231
Design defect, 271
Digital Millennium Copyright Act of 1998 (DMCA), 420–421
Direct deposits and withdrawals, 371
Disaffirmance, 132
    of minors' contracts, 133–134
Discharge of indorsers, 382–383
Disclosed principal, 250
Dishonored of commercial paper, 389
Disputes in cyberspace, settling, 423–424
Divisible contracts, 86–87
    for sale, 226
Doctrine of comity, 436
Domestication, 440
Draft, 362
Drawee, 363
Drawer, 363–364
Duress, 109
    as personal defense against payment of commercial paper, 385

E

Easements, 304
Effect of tender, 190

INDEX

Electronic Communications Privacy Act (ECPA), 401–402, 403–404
Electronic Funds Transfer Act (EFTA), 371, 404–405
Electronic funds transfer (EFT), 370
Electronic funds transfer systems, 371–372
Electronic mail, 401–402
Electronic signatures, 422–423
Electronic Signatures in Global and International Commerce Act, 422–423
Emancipation, 134
Embargo, 439
Embezzlement, 35, 38
Eminent domain, 306
Employer and employee duties of, to each other, 253–255
Employer-employee and principal-agents, relationship differences, 252–253
Engineers, liability of, 284–285
Entertainment on the Web, selling, 420–421
Entire contracts, 86
  for sale, 225
Environmental Impact Statement (EIS), 452
Environmental protection, development of, 451–452
Environmental Protection Agency (EPA), 452–453
Environmental regulations, 152
Estate in fee simple, 305
Estoppel, 212
  examples of, 213–214
  transfer of title by, 212–214
Ethical business behavior, possible results of lack of, 24–25
Ethics, 19–20, 20
  applications to business, 21–23
  in business and government, 24–25
  codes of, 22
  and values, 20

Evict, landlord's right to, 333–334
Eviction, 335
Executed contracts, 87
Executive branch of government, 66
Executive function of administrative agency, 69, 70
Executor, 161–162, 345
Executory contracts, 87
Existing goods, 225
Express authority, 247
Express contracts, 85
Express powers, 5
Express warranties, 264
  by description, sample, or model, 265–266
  disclaimers, 266–267
  by promise, 265
Expropriation, 439
Extortion, 38

F

Failure
  to perform obligation, 194
  to warn, 271
False pretenses, 37
Federal courts, 9–10
Federal Trade Commission (FTC), 419–420
Fee simple, 305
Felony, 34
Financial planners, liability of, 283–284
Finder, responsibility of, concerning lost property, 298
Fixtures, landlord's right to keep, 334
F.o.b. destination, 230–231
F.o.b. shipping point, 230
Forbearance, 119
  promises of, 121
Foreign Corrupt Practices Act (FCPA), 440–441
Forged check, 368–369

Forgery, 37, 368
  as defense against commercial paper, 386–387
Formal contracts, 85–86
Franchisee, 151
Franchise(s)
  government-granted, 150
  private, 151
Franchisor, 151
Fraud(s), 105–106
  and innocent misrepresentation, distinctions, 108
  as personal defense against payment of commercial paper, 385
  statute of, 161–164
Freehold estate, 304–305
Frustration of purpose, breach due to, 195
Full indorsement, 381–382
Full warranty, 270
Fungible goods, 215
  transfer of title to, 215
Future goods, 225

G

Gambling agreements, 146
General agent, 245
General Agreement on Tariffs and Trade (GATT), 436–437
General release, 122
Gifts, 300–301
  types of, 346
Governmental applications of law, 4
Government-granted franchise, 150
Government-granted monopolies, 150–151
Government(s)
  and business, integrating ethics into, 24–25
  organization of, 66
  regulation, 452–453
Grand larceny, 36

INDEX

Grantee, 305
Grantor, 305
Gratuitous promises, 123
Greenhouse effect, 457
Guarantor, 176
Guaranty, 162

H

Habitability, warranty of, 332–333
Hackers, 403
Harmful speech, 406–407
Healthcare providers, liability of, 282–283
Hearings, 7
Hijacking, 36
Holder, 363
Holder in due course, 383–385
Holidays, agreements made on, 145–146
Holographic will, 346
Hotel bailment, 320–321
Hotelkeeper, 320
Humor and slander, 50–51

I

Illegal
　agreements, 145
　restraints of trade, 149–150
Illegality
　created by statute, 388
　effect of, 145
Implied authority, 247
Implied contracts, 85
　for sale, 225–26
Implied powers, 5
Implied warranty, 264, 267
　disclaimers of, 269
　of quality, 267–269
　of title, 267
Implied warranty of fitness for particular purpose, 268–269
Implied warranty of merchantability, 268

Impossibility of performance, 190–191
Incapacity of parties to contract, 388
In Causa Mortis gifts, 300–301
Incidental beneficiaries, 174–175
Incompetent, 136
Independent contractors, 254–255
Indorsee, 380
Indorsement(s), 380
　kinds of, 380–382
Indorser, 380
　obligations, warranties, and discharge of, 382–383
Injunction, 196–197
Innkeeper, 320
Innocent misrepresentation, 107
　and fraud, distinctions between, 108
Insider trading, 38–39
Insolvent, 232
Insurance agents/brokers, liability of, 286–287
Intellectual property, 441–442
Intent and passing of title, 210
Intentional concealment, 106
Intentional misrepresentation, 107
Interest, 146
International law, 435
　sources of, 435–436
International law, 8
International legal environment, 438–441
International Monetary Fund (IMF), 437
International trade institutions, 436–438
Internet access services, taxing, 425
Internet sales, paying taxes on, 424–425
Internet service provider, liability of, 407
Internet Tax Freedom Act, 425
Inter Vivos gifts, 300

Inter Vivos trust, 350
Intestacy, 349
Intestate, 162, 346
Intoxicated persons, contracts of, 136–137
Invitation to trade, 100
IOU, 364
Irrevocable agency, 252

J

Joint tenancy, 302
Judicial branch of government, 66
Judicial function of administrative agency, 70, 71
Judicial review, 5
Justice, agreements that obstruct or pervert, 147–148

L

Labor and materials, contract, 226–227
Landlord, 330
　duty to mitigate damages, 334–335
　right to keep fixtures and permanent improvements, 334
　right to rent, possession, and to evict, 333–334
　warranty of habitability, 332–333
Landlord-tenant relationship
　essential elements of, 330
　lease as basis of relationship, 331
Larceny, 36
Law
　business applications of, 4
　classification of, 8
　delegation by, assignment and, 178–179
　and ethics, relationships between, 20–21
　government applications of, 4
　impressions of, 3
　international, 435–436

INDEX

moral, 8–9
operation of system, 9
origins of, 4–7
personal applications of, 4
of real property, 208
of sales, 224
system of courts, 9–11
uniform commercial code, 7–8
Leasehold estates, 304, 305
Lease(s), 330
  comparison of, with license, 330
  law relating to, 331
  termination of, 336
Legacy, 346
Legality of purpose as element of enforceable contract, 82
Legislative branch of government, 66
Legislative function of administrative agency, 69, 70–71
Lessee, 330
Lessor, 330
Liability, 55
  of accountants/financial planners, 283–284
  of architects and engineers, 284–285
  of attorneys, 285–286
  of healthcare providers, 282–283
  of insurance agents and brokers, 286–287
  of internet service provider, 407
  for malpractice and negligence, 281
  for minors' torts and crimes, 135–136
  product, 270–272
  strict, 56–57, 272
  tort, 336–337
  vicarious, 56
Libel, 47, 406
  characteristics of, 48–49
  trade, 50
License, 304
  difference between lease and, 330
Lien, 320
  bailee's, 320
  carrier's, 321

Life estate, 305
Limited warranty, 270
Living trust, 350
Living wills, 348
Lost and mislaid property, distinction between, and mislaid property, 298–299
Lost goods, 211–212

M

Magistrate courts, 10
Magnuson-Moss Warranty Act (1975), 269
  full and limited warranty, distinctions between, 270
  provisions of, 269–270
Maker, 363–364
Malpractice, 281
Marriage
  agreements
    made in contemplation, 163
    that restrain, 148
Material alteration, 191, 387
  as real defense against payment of commercial paper, 387
Mediation, 423
Memorandum, 164–165
Memorandum of agreement, 84
Mentally impaired, contracts of, 136
Milkovich v. News-Herald, 6
Minor, 132
Minors' contracts
  avoidance of, 132–133
  enforceability of, 134–135
  ratification and disaffirmation, 133–134
  torts and crimes of, liability for, 135–136
Misdemeanor, 34–35
Mislaid-lost property, distinction between, 298–299
Misrepresentation, 106, 107, 108
Mistake, 108
Mitigate, 193

Money
  performance by payment of, 189
  transfer of, 213
Monopoly power, 149
Moral consideration, agreements supported by, 123
Moral law, 8
Morals, 20
Multiple ownership, 301–303
Municipal courts, 10
Mutual agreement as element of enforceable contract, 82
Mutual-benefit bailments, 318–321

N

National Conference of Commissioners on Uniform State Laws, 8
National Environmental Policy Act (NEPA), 452
Natural Resource Conservation, 457
Necessaries, 132
Negligence, 52–53, 454–455
  essentials of, 282
  kinds of, 54–55
  legal action, avoiding, 53
  liability for, 281
  persons who can be charged with, 281–282
  reasonable person, 54
  unavoidable accident, 53
Negligent act, breach resulting from, 193–194
Negotiability, 363
  vs. assignability, 361
Negotiable instruments, 361
Negotiable warehouse receipt, 209
Nexus, 424
Noise pollution, 456
Nondelivery as personal defense against payment of commercial paper, 386
Nonnegotiable warehouse receipts, 209

INDEX

North American Free Trade Agreement (NAFTA), 438
Novation, 179
   and assignment, differences, 179
Nuisance, 51–52, 455
Nuncupative will, 346

O

Obligation(s)
   failure to perform, 194
   of indorsers, 382–383
Obscenity, 408
Ocean pollution, 458
Offer(s), 82
   and acceptance, 82
   as element of enforceable contract, 82
   public, 101
   termination of, 103–104
   valid, 98–99
   on the Web, accepting, 421
Official check, 367–368
Operation of law, termination by, 192
Oral contracts, 83
Order bill of lading, 208–209
Order instrument, 363
Ordinance, 7
Original jurisdiction, 10
Owner, transfer of property to seller permitted to appear as real, 213–214
Ownership
   interests in real property, 304–305
   of property, 301–303
   right of, 207
Ozone layer, destruction of, 458

P

Parol evidence rule, 160–161
Partially disclosed principal, 251
Particle trespass, 455
Password, 402
Past consideration, 123
   agreements supported by, 123–124
Patents, 442
Payee, 363
Payment, before maturity, as personal defense against payment of commercial paper, 386
Pay to the order of, 363
Performance
   by payment of money, 189
   possibility of, and valid consideration, 120
   specific, 196
   tender of, 189–190
   termination by, 188–190
   termination by impossibility, 190–191
Periodic tenancy, 331
Perjury, 37–38
Permanent improvements, landlord's to keep, 334
Personal applications of law, 4
Personal defenses, 385
   against payment of commercial paper, 385–386
Personal property, 207–208, 297
   acquiring title to, 298–301
   agreements to sell, for $500 or more, 163–164
   distinguishing between, and real property, 297–298
   finding lost, 298–299
   individual and multiple ownership of, 301–303
Personal representative, 345
Personal-service contract, 177, 191
Pesticide control, 456
Petty larceny, 36
Plaintiff, 3
Pledge, 121
Point-of-sale systems, 371
Pollution, 455–457
Possession
   landlord's right to, 333–334
   sales
      by persons having rightful, 214
      by persons having wrongful, 214–215
   tenant's right to acquire and retain, 335
Postdated, 365
   checks, 369
Power of attorney, 246
Precedent, 6
Preexisting duty, 122–123
Presentment, 388
   of commercial paper, 388–389
Primary market, 417
Principal, 244
   duties of, to agent, 249–250
   duties of, to third parties, 250
   duties of agent to, 248–249
Principal-agent relationship, comparison of, with employer-employee relationship, 252–253
Private franchises, 151
Private nuisance, 51, 455
Probate court, 345
Product flaw, 271
Product liability, 270
   injury claims, reasons for, 271
   tort law, 270–271
Product-related injuries, liabilities for, 271–272
Professional, 281
Professional liability, 281
   of accountants/financial planners, 283–284
   of architects and engineers, 284–285
   of attorneys, 285–286
   of healthcare providers, 282–283
   of insurance agents/brokers, 286–287
   risk, reducing, 287
Promisee, 119
Promise(s)
   barren, 122–123
   of forbearance, 121
   gratuitous, 123
   for a promise, 120
Promisor, 119

INDEX

Promissory note, 193, 362
Proof of ownership, transfer of, to unauthorized seller, 214
Proper form as element of enforceable contract, 83
Property, 297
   abandoned, 299–300
   found in public vs. private places, 299
   kinds of, 207–208
   ownership, 301
   real and personal, distinguishing between, 297–298
   transfer of
      to seller dealing in same type goods, 213
      to seller permitted to appear as real owner, 213–214
Public figure, 406
Public nuisance, 51, 455
Public offers, 101
Public policy, agreements against, 147–149
Public service, agreements that interfere with, 148
Puffery, 106
Purchase price, refusal of buyer to pay, 232

Q

Qualified indorsement, 382
Quality, implied warranty of, 267–268
Quiet enjoyment, tenant's right of, 335
Quitclaim, 306

R

Rain forest, destruction of, 457–458
Raised check, 368–369
Ratification of minors' contracts, 133
Ratified, 133

Real defenses, 385
   against payment of commercial paper, 386–388
Real estate, 207
Real property, 163, 207, 297
   agreements to sell any interest in, 163
   buildings and fixtures, 303
   distinguishing between, and personal property, 297–298
   land, 303
   ownership interests in, 304–305
   rights in land other than ownership, 303–304
   tenant interests in, 331–332
   transfers of, 305–307
Reasonable person, 54
Regulations
   environmental and safety, 152
   zoning, 151
Rejection, termination of offer by, 104–105
Remainder estate, 305
Remedies
   for breach of contract, 195–197
   for breach of sales contracts, 231–235
Remote party, 214
Rent, landlord's right to, 333–334
Replevin, 234
Request for proposal (RFP), 100
Residuary, 346
Restraining order, 196–197
Restraints of trade, 149
   illegal, 149–150
   legal, 150–152
Restrictive indorsement, 382
Reversion estate, 305
Revest, 211
Revisions to wills, 348
Revocation, 104
   to wills, 348–349
Rights
   assignment of, 175–177
   in land other than ownership, 303–304

Robbery, 36
Robinson-Patman Act, 150

S

Safety regulations, 152
Sale(s)
   on approval, 227–228
   auction, 229–230
   conditional, 230
   contract, remedies for breach of, 224, 231–235
   contract for, 224–225
   law of, 224
   or return, 228–229
   by persons with rightful possession, 214
   by persons with wrongful possession, 214–215
   with right of return, 227–229
Seal on formal contract, 85–86
Secondary market, 417–418
Securities Act of 1933, 417
Securities and Exchange Commission (SEC), 418–419
Securities Exchange Act of 1934, 417–419
Seller
   failure to deliver goods, 234–235
   remedies of, for breach of contracts, 231–233
   transfer of proof of ownership to unauthorized, 214
   transfer of property to dealing in same type of goods, 213
   permitted to appear as real owner, 213–214
Settlor, 350
Severalty ownership, 301
Sherman Antitrust Act, 149–150
Shoplifting, 36
Simple contracts, 86
Slander, 47–48, 406
   characteristics of, 49–50
   humor and, 50–51

INDEX

Small claims court, 11
Solid waste disposal, 456
Space pollution, 459
Spam, 408
Special agent, 245
Special indorsement, 381–382
Special jurisdiction, 9
Specific performance, 196
Specific time, 210
Stale check, 366
Stare decisis, 6
State courts, 10–11
Statute of Frauds, 161, 422
 and written contracts, 161–164
Statute of limitations, 231
Statute(s), 6, 33
 agreements in violation of, 145–147
Statutory law, 6–7
Statutory remedies, for lost or mislaid property, 299
Stolen goods, 211–212
Stoppage in transit, 232–233
Stop-payment order, 369–370
Straight bill of lading, 208
Strict liability, 56–57, 272
Subculture, 20
Sublease, 335–336
Subscription, 121
Substantial performance, 188–189
Subterranean rights, 303
Sufferance, tenancy at, 332
Sunday agreements, 145–146
Superfund, 454
Survivorship, 302

T

Tariff, 439
Taxes on internet sales, paying, 424–425
Taxing internet access services, 425
Tenancy
 in common, 302
 by the entirety, 302
 at sufferance, 332
 at will, 332
 for years, 332
Tenant, 330
 abandonment, 336
 interests in real property, 331–332
 right to acquire and retain possession, 335
 right to assign or sublease, 335–336
 right to quiet enjoyment, 335
Tender
 effect of, 190
 of payment, 190
 of performance, 189–190
 valid, 190
Termination
 of agency, 251–252
 by agreement, 188
 by alteration, 191–192
 by breach, 336
 by breach of contract, 192–195
 by impossibility of performance, 190–191
 of leases, 336
 of offer, 103–104
 by operation of law, 192
 by performance, 188–190
 to protect consumer, 195
Term insurance, 287
Testamentary capacity, 347
Testamentary intent, 345
Testamentary trust, 350
Testator, 345
Testatrix, 346
Third party(ies)
 beneficiaries, 174
 contracts involving, 174
 duties of agent to, 250–251
 duties of principal to, 250
 rights of, 174–175
Time
 specific, and passage of title, 210
 termination of offer by lapse of, 104
Title, 207
 acquiring, to personal property, 298–301
 to fungible goods, transfer of, 215
 implied warranty of, 267
 passage of, 208–210
Tort, 33, 47
 of agent, 248
 law of, 47
 liability, 336–337
Touting, 419
Toxic substance disposal, 456
Trade
 illegal and legal restraints of, 149–152
 libel, 50
 sanction, 439
Trademarks, 442
Transactions, unlicensed, 147
Transfer
 and discharge, ease of, 380
 of real property, 305–307
 of title
  by estoppel, 212–214
  to fungible goods, 215
Transient, 321
Transnational institutions, 436
Traveler's checks, 368
Treason, 34
Trespass, 455
Trial courts, 10
Trust, 350
Trustee, 350
 accountability of, 351
 duties of, 351
 powers of, 351
Trusts, 350–351

U

Unconscionable contracts, 110
Undisclosed principal, 251

INDEX

Undivided interest, 302
Undue influence, 108–109, 347
  as personal defense against payment of commercial paper, 385
Uniform Commercial Code, 7–8
  and auction sales, 229
  on checks, 366–367, 370
  on commercial paper, 363–364, 385–389
  and concept of title, 207, 212–213
  and consideration, 121–122
  and contracts, 81, 86–87
  on contracts for labor and materials, 226–227
  on failure to perform, 191
  f.o.b. shipping point, 230
  and general release, 122
  on holder in due course, 383–385
  on indorsements, 381–382, 383
  on leases, 331
  on sale, 224–225
  and sale of approval, 227–228
  seller fails to deliver goods, 234–235
  and statute of limitations, 231
  stoppage in transit, 232–233
  on termination of offer by revocation, 104
  on unconscionable contracts, 110
  on valid acceptance, 101–103
  on valid offers, 98
  on warranties, 264–269
Unlicensed transaction, 147
U.S. Circuit Courts of Appeals, 10
U.S. Claims Court, 10
U.S. Supreme Court, 10
U.S. Tax Court, 10
Use tax, 425
Usurious agreements, 146–147
Usury, 146

V

Valid contracts, 88–89
Valid tender, 190
Values, 20
Vicarious liability, 56
Vicarious negligence, 54
Virus, 403
Voidable contracts, 89
Void contracts, 89

W

Wagering agreements, 146
Warehouser, 319
Warehouse receipt, 209
Warranty, 264
  of habitability, 332–333
  of indorsers, 382–383
Warranty deed, 306
Web
  advertising on, 419–420
  entering intro contracts on, 421–423
  selling entertainment on, 420–421
  selling securities on, 417–419
Whistleblower, 24
White-collar crime, 35
Whole life insurance, 286–287
Will(s), 345
  language of, 345–346
  purpose of, 345
  requirements of valid, 346–348
  revoking and revising, 348–349
  tenancy at, 332
  types of gifts and bequests, 346
Workers' compensation, 253
World Bank, 437
World Intellectual Property Organization (WIPO), 441
World Trade Organization (WTO), 436–437
Written contracts, 84–85
  for sale, 225–226
Wrongful possession, 214
  sales by persons having, 214–215

Y

Years, tenancy for, 332

Z

Zoning regulations, 151